A GUIDE TO FRENCH LITERATURE

D0096133

A Guide to French Literature
From Early Modern to Postmodern

Jennifer Birkett and James Kearns

St. Martin's Press
New York

A GUIDE TO FRENCH LITERATURE
Copyright © 1997 by Jennifer Birkett and James Kearns
All rights reserved. No part of this book may be used or reproduced in any manner whatsoever without written permission except in the case of brief quotations embodied in critical articles or reviews. For information, address:

St. Martin's Press, Scholarly and Reference Division,
175 Fifth Avenue, New York, N.Y. 10010

First published in the United States of America in 1997

This book is printed on paper suitable for recycling and made from fully managed and sustained forest sources.

Printed in Hong Kong

ISBN 0–312–17475–6 cloth
ISBN 0–312–17476–4 paperback

Library of Congress Cataloging-in-Publication Data
Birkett, Jennifer.
A guide to French literature : early modern to postmodern /
Jennifer Birkett and James Kearns.
p.   cm.
Includes bibliographical references and index.
ISBN 0–312–17475–6 (cloth). — ISBN 0–312–17476–4 (pbk.)
1. French literature—20th century—History and criticism.
I. Kearns, James, 1947–   . II. Title.
PQ305.B524 1997
840.9—dc21   97–1766
                                                           CIP

For Mollie Gerard Davis, MA DPhil (Oxon)
Fellow Emeritus, St Hilda's College, Oxford
Formerly Fellow and Tutor in French and Senior Tutor

With affection and gratitude
Jennifer Birkett

For Donald Charlton (1925–95)
Formerly Professor of French, University of Warwick

In fond memory of a true teacher
James Kearns

Contents

PART II   THE BOURGEOIS CENTURY, 1815–1914

Acknowledgements

Jennifer Birkett would like to thank Christine Jimack, Nicholas Hammond, Alec Hargreaves and Alex Hughes for their generous advice on various sections of the text, and Rachel Ashton, Les Brook, John Dunkley, Cedric May and Emma Tyler for answers to bibliographical questions. Mollie Gerard Davis kindly read the manuscript and offered incisive and helpful criticisms. The University of Birmingham provided support in the form of study leave to further the various research projects on which this text has drawn, and an excellent research library. Stan Smith's interest and encouragement made it possible to persevere to the end; to him, gratitude and love.

James Kearns would like to thank Keith Cameron, Malcolm Cook, John Flower, Martin Sorrell, Derek Watts and Elizabeth Woodrough, who read the manuscript at various stages and who gave generously of their time and constructive advice; the University of Exeter, which, like Birmingham, provided invaluable study leave support; and his wife Jane, who helped.

Both of us wish to thank the staff of the Bibliothèque Nationale, the British Library and the Senate House Library (University of London), who maintain the research resources which were indispensable for this work, and the editors of Macmillan Press, especially Margaret Bartley, without whose infinite patience and support this text could not have been completed.

Some minor changes have been made to spelling for quotations from sixteenth-century French texts, to assist modern readers. Unless otherwise indicated, translations from the French are our own.

James Kearns researched and wrote Part II (except for the section on 'Women's Stories' in Chapter 4) and the Novel and Poetry sections of Chapter 8; the rest of the text was researched and written by Jennifer Birkett.

Introduction

The Games of Literature: Subject/Language/History

Watt could not accept [events] for what they perhaps were, the simple games that time plays with space, now with these toys and now with those, but was obliged, because of his peculiar character, to enquire into what they meant: oh not into what they really meant, his character was not so peculiar as all that, but into what they might be induced to mean, with the help of a little patience, a little ingenuity.

(Samuel Beckett, *Watt*, 1953)[1]

Writing a narrative analysis of French literature is a risky enterprise these days. Turning history to critical account, negotiating with the canon, working to chronological structures, focusing on authors and texts, are activities still out of fashion in some critical circles. But as syllabuses in schools and universities focus more narrowly, on fewer writers, or are more broadly defined, under headings spanning disciplines and centuries, new readers are increasingly confronted with books with, apparently, no place in a continuum of cultural discourses: texts with no connections, whose life-history starts and ends in the moment of their first publication or of their latest recuperation by a modern reader. As literary research becomes more sophisticated and more technical, and as the expanding volumes of other-disciplinary knowledge are added to the baggage all critics must carry, finding a place of your own, to start reading for yourself, is a daunting business. A broad-brush chronological narrative is an indispensable instrument in that process of general orientation that accompanies particular readings of particular authors and texts.

The present Guide has been written to provide a map of some key points in the development of 'literature' in France from the early modern period to the present day, and to help readers of that literature recognise what the critical mapping process involves. It

1

points towards the range of contexts that have to be taken into account when interpretations are made, including the reader's own.[2] It introduces some of the new concepts and stances which are changing the critical terrain. Suggestions for further reading, given in the notes, are intended to be used by readers to discover other perspectives which might well take them down different paths.

The most interesting maps are those that give a sense of terrain with places still to explore and directions yet to be invented. It was with this point in mind that this Introduction opened on a quotation from that most influential maker of intellectual maps, Samuel Beckett (1906–89), the dramatist and prosewriter who has, arguably, most effectively understood, absorbed and transformed the landscape of Western culture – and, in the process, provoked its inhabitants into seeing quite differently, and with more freedom, their own place in it. As reader and writer, working both in England and in French, Beckett was shaped by the same historical and textual discourses as the writers and readers of the present Guide (two hot World Wars, one Cold one, colonialism and its oppressions, nationalism and internationalism, and that whole cultural tradition moulded by religion and rationalism that Lucky, the unhappy jester, exploded in the public's face in 1953, in the first Act of *En attendant Godot*).[3] As much as any of his contemporaries, and more than most, Beckett acknowledged the impossibility of conjuring 'a' 'real' meaning out of such – or, indeed, any other – experience, and worked out not so much a method as a stance, or a tone, to take in treating of it. Among his many brilliantly comic inventions, *Watt*, the last novel he wrote in English, with its account of the distortions of sense by the relentless drive of rationalising intellect, is a cautionary tale for all would-be inquirers into events (literary, historical or whatever).

A Guide to Literature does well to limit its pretensions. It can offer readers a few modest proposals about what might be going on behind that delusively simple sign 'French Literature'. With, the authors hope, a little less 'ingenuity' than Watt, it can gently nudge its matter into some clear shape and sense, but it must always be aware of the distortions of meaning that the quest for clear sense can bring.

But for all his refusal to give credence to absolute answers, and the ridicule he heaps on those who would claim to have found them, Beckett is committed to raising the questions which for writers, thinkers and critics at this latter end of the twentieth century have become the ones of greatest importance. These have to do with the shapes that creative imagination makes, in the working discourses it inherits, and the nature of the shaping process. Beckett's work explores and models how the subject finds itself in history, within discursive forms. This, for the present writers, is one of the most productive ways to orientate reading. Studying literature involves studying the kinds and shapes of the stories that the members of a culture tell themselves about themselves, and which they act out as subjects: that is, as beings who are simultaneously makers of and made by language, in history.

The tissue of history is made of multitudes of narratives and narrators. The central storyline picked out here is that of the changing subject – or rather subjects – of the French State. It starts with the aristocratic subject who came to consciousness in the small closed spaces of Renaissance high culture, along with the institutions of monarchy, finance and law on which that State was founded. It moves on to the more diversified subjects who came from the margins in the eighteenth and nineteenth centuries to constitute that loose baggy monster, the bourgeois subject of the post-1789 republics, together with its repressed others, bearers of anarchist, socialist and feminist alternatives. The narrative ends in the present, with the movement of feminist and post-colonial subjects towards the centre of the cultural and political stage.

Within this schema, the aim has been to chart how subjects come to speak themselves in terms of inherited culture and language and, in speaking, themselves constitute new authoritative centres. The material has been divided into three chronological sections (Renaissance to Revolution, the nineteenth century, and the twentieth). Sometimes observing but more often than not overrunning these boundaries, literary genres are developed, transformed, pushed aside or revived, as different interest groups work out what can or cannot be said in inherited forms. Comment has been centred on the language of texts. Within the limits of the space available, every possible opportunity has been taken to give critical comment on the detail of an author's writing, characterising the individual voice that writing produces and its relation to the voices of others.

Giving space to comment on language means cutting back elsewhere. Some writers, groups, or areas of interest which other critics might have chosen to emphasise have been marginalised or left out altogether. The kinds of factors involved in making such decisions are not always foregrounded, but they set up the matrix in which 'literature' is defined. They set the shape and limits of the map and the ways in which it can be used. Before giving an account of what the present Guide has put in or taken out, it will be helpful to review the rules of that favourite critical game: loading the canon.

* * *

One of the most important of contemporary academic debates is the argument on the canon: which books an educated person should have read, studied, or simply heard of. What matters is what criteria are used for including or excluding texts from the list. Modern scholarship has pointed out how many factors, interests and prejudices are involved in the debate.

One is the institutional factor. Canons grow out of decisions taken by the influential critics and scholars in a discipline, and whether other academics decide to challenge or ratify these can often (though not always) relate to what they see as advantageous for their own careers. These decisions are taken within the wider political scene of the countr(ies) involved, and they will often (though not always) depend on what role the institution where the academic is working thinks it plays in that wider scene. Gayatri Spivak has formulated the position trenchantly:

> [I]n one way or another academics are in the business of ideo-
> logical production; even academics in the pure science are
> involved in that process. This possibility leads to the notion of
> disciplinary as well as institutional situation, and then to the
> subtler question of precise though often much mediated func-
> tions within the institution of a nation state. . . . Our institutional
> responsibility is of course to offer a responsible critique of the
> structure of production of the knowledge we teach even as we
> teach it.[4]

A major critique of the role of canonical literature in France and the social institutions which disseminate it has been made by the sociologist Pierre Bourdieu (b. 1930) in his *Ce que parler veut dire: l'économie des échanges linguistiques* (1982).[5] Bourdieu argued that literary language is the place where the idea of 'correct' language is made and reproduced, and as such it is instrumental in manufacturing the order and hierarchies of modern society. Not everyone has equal access to and power within language and literature, though it is ideologically important for the State that everyone believes they have. In this way, the illusion of social unity is maintained. People's share of the linguistic inheritance (what he called their 'capital culturel' ['cultural capital']) is different, depending on their social and economic conditions. For some people, writing and getting work published and accepted as part of the literary mainstream is easier than for others. Bourdieu's lively polemic has been an invaluable support to, for example, feminist authors and critics or writers from the former French colonies, struggling to get onto the bookshelves or into the academies.

The political dimension of literary canons is an important subject for Britain in the 1990s, as higher education is being opened to wider access. (The expansion began much earlier in France and, indeed, most other Western countries.) In the process, rough justice risks being done to syllabuses caught by economic pressures which reduce the range of options available, and by ideological pressures to favour writers and readings who encourage the reproduction of mainstream ways of thinking and seeing, rather than informed criticism of them. In France, it is interesting to note the limited and traditional range of texts selected in recent years for the *agrégation* (the qualifying examination for teachers in advanced secondary education and above), as well as the lengthy justificatory reports the members of *agrégation* juries have taken to writing about the conformist values they are applying in their assessments. Much livelier texts, and a less straitjacketed approach, have been in evidence in the *baccalauréat* syllabus, presumably on the assumption that most of the students concerned will not proceed to influential posts as teachers.[6]

Surrounding and, increasingly, interwoven with the world of academic institutions is the world of the marketplace. Publishers have always shared a substantial part of the responsibility for the making of canons, and the present volume has made regular reference to the changing state of printing and publishing in the course of French literary history.[7] Régis Debray's *Le Pouvoir intellectuel en France* (1979)[8] argued that the university intellectuals who from the 1880s dominated the cultural world in France lost their power to the publishers in the 1930s, when the great literary prizes were founded. He went on to describe how since May 1968 both have been swept up into the ambit of the electronic media. Book programmes on radio and, especially, television now set the standards and define the important writers of the contemporary moment.

How publishers help establish the canon retrospectively, for earlier periods, is a different question. Publishers choose texts for publication drawing on a mixture of academic advice and their own market instincts and information. This mostly means a pull to conservatism. Few publishers are willing to risk texts or studies of texts which do not already have a visible presence on school or university syllabuses. Even with the appearance of the large publishing conglomerates such as MATRA and hypermarket-sized outlets such as FNAC, few members of the general reading public in France come across texts they have not been formally introduced to in the course of their education. The 'classics' now appearing on French supermarket shelves contain no surprises, and reinforce rather than expand known frontiers. A survey undertaken by the review *Lire* in 1982[9] to establish a list of the ten greatest French writers of all time invited readers to choose from a list of forty which included sixteen from the nineteenth century and only nine from the twentieth – none of them likely to rock the boat of contemporary culture or politics (Giono, Colette, France, Montherlant, Pagnol, Saint-Exupéry, Claudel, Genevoix, Proust). *Lire*'s own readers elected Molière, Hugo, Balzac, Voltaire, Zola, Baudelaire, Proust, Montaigne, La Fontaine and Flaubert. An independent opinion poll commissioned by the magazine at the same time, of a representative sample of the French population, produced agreement on Hugo, Molière, Balzac, La Fontaine, Zola and Voltaire, but in place of the others preferred Jules Verne, Lamartine, Alexandre Dumas and Racine.

Establishing a canon across the boundaries of national languages has traditionally been academics' business. Increasingly, however, translations have begun to make texts available to a wider public. In the process of choosing by what texts national literatures are to be represented to each other – that is, which texts will be translated – a wide range of interests can demand to come into play. In *Rethinking Translation* (1992), Lawrence Venuti wrote of the opportunities translation presents for political intervention in the canons:

> A text . . . is . . . constrained by the social institutions in which it is produced and consumed, and its constitutive materials,

including the other texts that it assimilates and transforms, link it to a particular historical moment. It is these social and historical affiliations that permit translation to function as a cultural political practice, constructing or critiquing ideology-stamped identities for foreign culture, contributing to the formation or subversion of literary canons, affirming or transgressing institutional limits.[10]

As a result, the texts available in translation in different countries at different moments can give very different ideas of what 'French literature' is. Richard Jacquemond's essay in Venuti's collection, 'Translation and Cultural Hegemony', described the special interest of the Nasser regime in the 1950s and 1960s in directing the Egyptian public towards a particular kind of post-war French writing: 'The diffusion, from Egypt, of the first Arabic translations of Jean-Paul Sartre, Albert Camus, and later of Beckett and Ionesco almost coincided with the diffusion of these works in other languages, and their reception was all the more remarkable since these works were more alien to the values of an Islamic society, as we would expect them to be, than most of the previous translations' (p. 144). The regime's purposes, Jacquemond explained, were both pedagogical (to 'educate the people') and political (to provide support for the 'revolutionary mobilization of the masses'). Later in his essay, Jacquemond noted the growing reciprocal interest of mainland France, since decolonisation, in Arab francophone production, which during the 1980s represented something between 200 and 300 titles a year in both fiction and non-fiction. Two authors have recently reached the best-seller lists: the Moroccan Tahar Ben Jelloun, whose novel *La Nuit sacrée* won the 1987 Prix Goncourt, sold more than 1.5 million copies, while the Lebanese Amin Maalouf has since 1987 sold nearly 0.5 million copies of his historical novels *Léon l'Africain* and *Samarcande*. Such writers are beginning now to make an appearance in academic syllabuses in both France and the UK.

Finally, a separate point must be made of the contributions to the debate on the French canon that came at the end of the eighties from feminist academia in a volume of essays on *The Politics of Tradition: Placing Women in French Literature*.[11] These essays discussed the work of the canon-formers – Boileau, La Harpe, Sainte-Beuve – in relegating women writers to margins and footnotes or burying them in minor categories, and explored the reasons why this happened. Naomi Schor, for example, argued that:

> [George] Sand deserves a place in the new, revised French canon of nineteenth-century literature. More precisely, Sand deserves to recover the eminent place she occupied in the old, unrevised French canon established by the Sorbonne between 1871 and 1914, during a period of intense national affirmation following the humiliating defeat of 1871.
>
> ('Idealism in the Novel: Recanonizing Sand', p. 57)

Though Sand should not now, Schor added, take her place as the author of the rustic idylls beloved by the turn-of-century public, but as 'the exemplary feminist author of such novels as *Indiana, Valentine* and *Lélia*' (p. 58). The essays go beyond single-issue gender politics. Anne-Marie Thiesse and Hélène Mathieu challenged the way literature has been studied in France for the *agrégation* by means of manuals and anthologies of excerpts, and traced the political and ideological exclusions from the anthologised canon over the past century, which have swept out women writers and radicals ('The Decline of the Classical Age and the Birth of the Classics'). Lucienne Frappier-Mazur, in 'Marginal Canons: Rewriting the Erotic', traced changes in the canonical status of the erotic and pornographic and showed how these categories have been revalorised by contemporary women's writing on the body. Frappier-Mazur argued that excluding erotic and pornographic texts from the canon of what is allowed to be known makes for less than perfect understanding of 'mainstream' texts. Without knowing Sade, readers will make only partial sense of Flaubert, Baudelaire and the Goncourts.

* * *

The present volume has its main focus in the traditional canon of the academic syllabus as it has developed in France and Britain since the 1970s. This focus was chosen in the knowledge that most readers who come to the Guide will do so from the academic context, whether as French specialists or as exponents of Comparative

Literature, European Studies or Cultural Studies. That canon is under review for a variety of reasons, both good and bad.

Some of the canon in this present version is angled differently, in the light of the new thematic and disciplinary perspectives by which French Studies now operates. A number of less familiar figures are included, or given more space, at the expense of others who have by now had at least their fair share of attention and perhaps a little more. Space constraints ruled out starting with medieval literature. This was regrettable, given its formative importance and the regular return to the medieval inheritance which is a feature of French culture, and given too the fresh perspectives being brought to medieval studies by a new generation of critics.[12] However, some cut-off point had to be established. An academic argument can be presented for starting an account of the modern subject in the sixteenth century, with reference to Renaissance and Reform, and the first chapter of the Guide does this. Otherwise, re-angling has not brought with it any drastic reduction in the space given to writing before 1870. The relation between past and present, and how that relation is revised and assessed, is an important issue for every generation, not least our own.

Women's writing and francophone literature have been given increased importance commensurate with the changes they are making to the cultural landscape in general and the fresh impetus they are giving to academic research. They are not yet visible enough on most teaching programmes, but the movement is there. Contemporary novel, poetry and especially theatre are also under-taught; as is also the case for the earlier periods, specialists are few and not enough new researchers are being funded for training. The new novels, poems and plays are included here for their own sake, and also to help break a vicious circle.

This, then, is one account of the history of French literature, for readers to re-produce – though not, it is hoped, in the negative sense Bourdieu gave to cultural reproduction. The text that follows offers one part, and one version, of the material that constitutes the subject: what readers will go on to make of it is matter for themselves.

Part I
The Making of the Modern Subject

1

Renaissance and Reform, 1515–1600

I   STATING THE SUBJECT

Between the Christian feudalism still flourishing in France at the end of the thirteenth century, and the secular politics and economy of the modern French State, lie whole worlds of difference. Cultural history since the nineteenth century has presented the period of the Renaissance as a watershed in the move to the modern – a radical and conclusive break with the medieval past, in which the classical narrative of bourgeois enterprise begins. Recent historians, in contrast, have preferred to emphasise the continuum of change, marked by uneven development, in which no one moment conclusively marks the start of the new. Combining the two perspectives, it is possible to see the sixteenth century in France as a distinctive moment of historical and, most of all, ideological significance: one where the process of change is at its most visible, caught in the light of the two major movements of literary Renaissance and religious Reform, and where identifying change, and laying claim to it, was the defining business of the day.

The period is marked by metaphors of change. Its own preferred 'rebirth' and 'reformation' emphasise the claim to spiritual and moral transformations, with their primary reference to the cultural sphere. Linking culture and economy, with hindsight, another might be added: 'reinvestment', to evoke a process in which economic, social and cultural capital, invested in areas of diminishing return, was being cashed up and placed in areas with a better promise of growth. Reassessment of the dominant institutions, language and hierarchy of the Christian heritage was a key dynamic of this modernising world. The return to the classical inheritance – the culture, ethics and politics of the ancient city-states and the Roman Imperium – was another, helping create an idea of a confident, energetic France, in a competitive Europe rapidly being transformed by the growth of mercantilism, the influx of New World silver, and most of all, the invention of the printing press.

Writers of the period committed to accelerating change, excited by the freshness of their own vision, had neither incentive nor time to seek out and credit signs of change in existing systems and previous generations. The satire of François Rabelais (1494–1553), raging at the deadweight of medieval scholasticism, has fixed in the Western cultural imagination an image of a people engaged in an epic process, forging themselves anew, creating a race of giants. The most celebrated emblem of French Renaissance is Rabelais's Gargantua, born with an insatiable thirst for life and knowledge, gulping down the heady wines of the new humanist learning, with its refreshing faith in the human capacity for the good and the better, and the new creed of Evangelical Reform, with its New Testament message of Truth and Love. And after Gargantua come his children, Pantagruel and his friends, fired by love of life and Pauline charity, setting out from Touraine on a quest for under-standing that holds up to deadly ridicule the unwanted ideas and institutions of the old medieval world.

What they claimed to find on the way was humanity. The giant infant of Rabelais's Renaissance played a major part in formulating the concept of the individual subject in which modern Western culture is founded. This was a humanity which was (and remains) subject in two senses. In literary and philosophical history, it is the self-conscious subject, seeing itself as if for the first time, with pleasurable surprise, in the mirror of its own works and words. Louise Labé wrote in the Preface to her *Poésies* (1555):

[Q]uand il advient que nous mettons par écrit nos conceptions . . . nous redouble notre aise: car nous retrouvons le plaisir passé qu'avons eu, ou en la matière dont écrivions, ou en l'intelligence des sciences où lors étions adonnés. Et outre ce, le jugement que font nos secondes conceptions des premières nous rend un singulier contentement.

[When we put our thoughts into writing . . . our delight is doubled, because we rediscover the pleasure we took in the past either in the matter we were writing about or in the under-standing of the objects of knowledge with which we were then engaged. And on top of that, the judgement our present thoughts make of those past ones brings us a very particular satisfaction.]

In the history of politics and society, that personal subject comes to self-realisation at the moment of the person's subjection to the State – that soon-to-be-Absolute State whose constitution emerged with and through the turmoil of the sixteenth century.[1]

In this period, French society first established the constitutional limits of the power of its monarchy, in relation to those competing groups who carried society's different energies (aristocrats, Churchmen, merchants, populace), and saw the start of processes which would end with all the competitors turned into instruments of a centralised power.[2] What was important in all this was not so much who the King was, as what particular interests he could be made to represent. This was the issue the sixteenth century fought over, on the battlefield and in the cultural arena, in its broadsheets, chronicles and books. The end product was a notion of kingship which consolidated the place of the aristocracy at the top of the political hierarchy, enabling it to complete the passage from feudal society to modern State with its wealth and political power intact, and to hang on to them right through to the Revolution. Jean Bodin (1530–96), the first theorist of sovereignty (*Les Six Livres de la République*, 1576), attributed to the King a new absolute power to create and enforce his own laws, but he also defined limits to that power in the interests of individual wealth and property, denying the king the right to levy taxes at will on his people, or seize goods arbitrarily. For 'people', in this case, read the nobility.

In the sixteenth century, society's categories remained relatively stable. At the top was the landed nobility. Most important throughout both sixteenth and seventeenth centuries was the *noblesse d'éprée*, the warrior caste who secured France's expansion, protecting and extending the boundaries of a nascent nation against challenges from England, Italy and Germany. The fighting that began in 1494, with the invasion of Italy by Charles VIII, continued up to the end of the reign of Louis XVI. (The unsuccessful Italian enterprise concluded in 1559 with the Treaty of Cateau-Cambrésis, its lowest point the taking of François Ier as hostage in February 1525.) In increasing competition with the warriors were the *noblesse de robe*, members of the old-established Parlements, whose legal and financial administrative powers and talents ran the system that both sustained the authority of the King and could raise major challenges to it. Their powers were strengthened by the sale of legal and fiscal offices which the monarchy undertook in the sixteenth century to pay for its wars. They were confirmed by the *paulette*, introduced in 1604, which enabled the purchasers of offices to hand them down to their heirs. Hard on their heels came the *bourgeoisie*, engaged in administration, trade and finance (less successful in the two last than their Italian and German counterparts, who preferred solid investment in trade and, later, manufacturing to the buying of places). Finally, the general populace, there to be worked and taxed, supplied raw material for the King's armies and labour for the great estates.

Political shifts of power between these groups related to economic imperatives. The medieval monarchy had built an apparatus to deal with the administration of justice. The need now was for the King to organise finance: to protect trade and to establish the administration of national tax levies. In the first third of the century, France shared with the rest of Europe a period of economic expansion, helped by population increase, improvements in agricultural production, and technological innovations (in 1535, both France and England saw the introduction of the blast furnace). Improving land and sea communications fostered trade. France's colonial expeditions, such as Jacques Cartier's Canadian enterprise (1534–42), brought a widening of intellectual horizons but no financial rewards. Other countries, however, prospered from colonial enterprise, and France felt secondary effects. The influx of Spanish silver after 1560 stimulated production (and inflation). The increasing organisation of the money supply throughout the century is a marker of the successful consolidation of the State. Mints established at Paris, Bayonne and Rennes operated under State licence and were organised by a Monetary Tribunal (*Cour des Monnaies*). In 1756, the Estates General established a monetary commission, of which Jean Bodin was the leading light.

In the last third of the century, the French economy fell behind the rest of Europe as the King's short-term political needs took precedence over wealth creation. Merchants, whose interest was in the growth of international trade, wanted the European market to fix the exchange value of money and the level of prices. Instead, mercantilism was the order of the day: that is, the State set exchange rates and prices at levels advantageous to itself, to finance expanding bureaucracy, sustain Court consumption, and, most of all, pay military expenses. The weak Valois dynasty triggered France's mid-century financial crisis by over-commitment to foreign wars, compounded by the costs of internal religious conflict.

Within the jockeying for position by the nascent nation-states of Europe, and the power struggles in France itself, culture, and especially literature, had its own role to play. Learning and writing, formerly the province of the Church, began to slip into the hands of secular powers. In the first half of the century, the centre of cultural patronage was the Court of Marguerite de Navarre (1492–1549) in Béarn, South-West France. Sister of François Ier, Marguerite became Queen of Navarre in 1527. She helped set up and expand foundations of learning such as the Universities at Nîmes and Bourges. Bourges especially became a centre of Evangelical Reform and welcomed as teachers Jean Calvin (1509–64) and his second-in-command, Théodore de Bèze (1519–1605). A supporter of moderate Catholic Reform, Marguerite encouraged and protected the theologians and scholars of the evangelical *groupe de Meaux* and the creative writers of the Reform – the poet Clément Marot (1496–1544), Bonaventure des Périers (*c*.1510–*c*.1543, author of the *Cymbalum Mundi*, 1537, banned as a satire on Catholic faith) and Rabelais himself, who dedicated to her the third volume of the adventures of his dynasty of giants. In the second half of the century, the centre shifted to Bourges and the Court of Marguerite de France, sister of Henri II, and then, in the reign of Charles IX, to Paris. Poetry like that of the Pléiade was tied explicitly to the enhancement of the prestige of the ruling monarch, marking the daily round of Court life with masquerades, eclogues, wedding songs, epitaphs and elegies. Ronsard's unfinished epic *La Franciade* (1572) aimed to perform for the monarchical France of Charles IX the same function as Virgil's *Aeneid* for Augustus's Rome, celebrating the new birth with historical 'proofs' of legitimacy on which the ink was still wet.

Writers of this period helped invent an ideology of King and nation, and most of all, of the subjects without whom neither could exist. Most particularly, they built into the cultural unconscious through their forms and language those values, often contradictory, which constituted the enterprising individual subject and served the purposes of the developing State. On the one hand, they proclaimed their confidence in humanity's competence to organise the elements of its world, celebrating the open mind and the expanding intellectual and geographical frontier. On the other, they harnessed enthusiasm and enterprise to a hierarchical sense of order.

II FORGING A LANGUAGE

The first step in the making of the nation and the national subject was the making of its language. The humanist learning that invigorated the national tongues of Europe began with the revival of scholarly interest in the ancient languages that were the foundations of Christian culture. The rereading of the Greek and Latin philosophers and poets and of the sacred texts of Christianity (Gospels and Epistles in Greek, and Old Testament in Hebrew) generated the desire to publicise and debate ideas, values and interpretations that often differed sharply from received moral and religious truths. At the same time, familiarity with the rich semantic, syntactic and stylistic resources of the ancient tongues threw into relief the relative poverty of the vernacular (the common tongue: French) and its inadequacy as a vehicle for exposition and debate. French needed fresh invention, both as the language of evangelical Catholic and Protestant Reform and as the instrument of a new poetry of self and material world.

The need to think, write and speak change in a language accessible to the whole of the nation was not uncontested. Latin remained important as the language of European diplomatic negotiation and scholarship. Significant scholarly and creative writing in Latin was still produced in the first half of the century. Jean Dorat (1508–88), who introduced the Pindaric ode to France, wrote his own poems in the Pindaric mode. The Latin dramas of George Buchanan (1506–82) and Marc-Antoine Muret (1526–85) helped contemporaries rediscover the form of classical tragedy. But there were limits now to what could be said in Latin in and about modern France.

Official recognition of the importance of French to the national identity came with the Edict of Villers-Cotterêts (1539), by which François Ier required judgements in the law courts to be delivered solely in French. Étienne Dolet (1509–46), scholar and printer, who had already written a learned commentary on Latin (1536–8), published in 1540 a treatise on translation and punctuation in French. Robert Estienne (1503–59), printer to François Ier and later to Calvin in Geneva, offered in his *Dictionaire françois-latin* (1539) the first codification of the vocabulary of French. Somewhat later, attempts to establish and codify spelling were made by scholars such as Jacques Peletier du Mans (1517–82) in his *Dialogue de l'ortografe e prononciation françoese* (1550) and Louis Meigret (*c*.1510–60), in his *Tretté de la grammère francoèze*. In 1562, Ramus (Pierre de la Ramée, 1515–72) produced his *Gramere*. Key texts of ancient and Italian scholarship and creative writing were translated into French, addressing and creating a wider audience for the new learning, in the new language. In 1537, Jacques Colin made available his version of Baldessare Castiglione's *Il libro del cortegiano* (1528), the key guide to Renaissance ethics and manners and one of the vehicles through which the sensibility of Italian Neoplatonism (see below) reached the wider cultured public. Clément Marot (1496–1544), one of the best-known poets associated with Protestant Reform, translated Virgil and Ovid; his translations of the Psalms (1541 and 1546) constituted both an important political gesture and a significant experiment in metrical innovation. (Jacques Lefèvre d'Étaples had already translated the Epistles and Gospels in 1523. In 1530, he produced the first complete translation of the Bible into French.) Jacques Peletier du Mans translated Horace's *Ars poetica* in 1541 and Jacques Amyot, Plutarch's *Lives* in 1559, possibly the most influential text of the century after Castiglione's *Courtier*, and the one in which Montaigne grounded his *Essais*. Translation, as du Bellay agreed in his *Défense et illustration de la langue française* (1549), was a primary step in the making of a new language – though not, he thought, a mode in which good poets stayed for long.

The theologians of the Sorbonne lost their monopoly on knowledge. The Library of the reformed Abbey of Saint-Victor, with its well-catalogued holdings in philosophy, mysticism and science, was open to the public. With the encouragement of François Ier, scholars such as Guillaume Budé (1468–1540) laid the foundations of the future Collège de France and the Bibliothèque Nationale. In the 1540s, the reputation of Jean Dorat at the Collège de Coqueret drew the young scholars and future poets of the Pléiade: Pierre Ronsard, Joachim du Bellay, Jean-Antoine de Baïf, Rémy Belleau, Étienne Jodelle and Pontus de Tyard. From here grew the Academies of the second half of the century, such as de Baïf's Académie de poésie et de musique, established in 1570 by Charles IX, or the Palace Academy, established by Henri III. Their model was the mid-fifteenth-century Platonic Academy of Florence and they continued the work of its associates, Marsilio Ficino (1433–99) and Pico della Mirandola (1463–94), exploring the connections of philosophy, science and religion. From Dorat's Platonist teaching, the Pléiade acquired their understanding of the explanatory mission of poetry, transmitting truths to the uneducated by means of fables and symbols (see, for example, Pierre Ronsard, *Abrégé de l'art poétique français*, 1565).[3]

As important as all these were the independent printers' shops. In Paris, Étienne Dolet and Robert Estienne, humanist scholars in their own right, provided the conditions for the newly-fortified vernacular to spread throughout the nation. Printers employed teams of translators to make scholarly works available in French; they helped select and propagate the key texts; they helped determine how the texts were read. Printers were responsible for developments in cataloguing and indexing which made it possible for individual scholars to get a grip on the multitude of texts. Printing turned scholarship from the medieval condition to the modern. From a simple exercise in individual memory, preserving and glossing the single text, it became a collaborative conjunction of texts and minds across ages and frontiers, in which an author could assess, synthesise and transform collective wisdom. The products of scholarship, through printing, left the convent for the public domain. From poetry and philosophy to politics was now one short step.[4]

In his great study of Rabelais, Mikhail Bakhtin has drawn together the threads that connect learning and language:

> We see at what a complex intersection of languages, dialects, idioms and jargons the literary and linguistic consciousness of the Renaissance was formed. The primitive and naive coexistence of languages and dialects had come to an end; the new consciousness was born not in a perfected and fixed linguistic system but at the intersection of many languages and at the point of their most intense interorientation and struggle. Languages are philosophies – not abstract but concrete, social philosophies, penetrated by a system of values inseparable from living practice and class struggle. This is why every object, every concept, every point of view, as well as every intonation found their place at this intersection of linguistic philosophies and was drawn into an intense ideological struggle.[5]

In the first half of the century, the prose of François Rabelais offers a brilliant representation of the ideological struggle for language. Disciple of Erasmus, monk, secular priest, student of law and medicine, practising doctor, Rabelais built his burlesque allegory-cum-satire, charting the growth and spread of Renaissance values, on first-hand experience of the politics of knowledge. The five-book epic negotiates joyfully the minefield of sixteenth-century discourses, letting all speakers have their say. *Pantagruel* (1532) begins with the language of education. Pantagruel's whirl-wind tour of the universities of France leaves him competent to trade jargon and absurdities with the best of the professions (Bk II, chs 10–13) and horrified at the useless knowledge, agreed and superstition which constitute medieval scholarship, bawdily paro-died in the narrator's version of the catalogue of the Bibliothèque de Saint-Victor (Bk II, ch. 7). *Gargantua* (1534), narrating the birth and childhood of Pantagruel's father, links education and religion, lampooning the jargon and superstitions of theologians and monks. Against the medieval cult of pilgrimages and indulgences, Rabelais sets the reformed discourse of individual prayer and virtuous living. Individualism and the rule of order are brought together in the Abbey of Thélème, a community built on the direct negation of every monastic precept except that of charity, and regulated only by responsible individual choice, which always, in this Utopia, chooses the common good.

The *Tiers Livre* (1546) turns the investigation of the new learning into that of sound living, hanging onto Panurge's comic dilemma of how to get married without getting cuckolded the serious question of how, with no clear authority to guide them, individuals can stay afloat in life's stormy seas. The quest for the answer continues into the *Quart Livre* (1548–52), which seeks to accommodate increasingly bitter debates over religious differences. Shiploads of monks sail by on their way to the Council of Trent (ch. 18), most, deservedly, shipwrecked; on their islands, the Papefigues and the Papimanes dispute the authority of the Pope and the divinity of his edicts, the Decretals which, says Rabelais, siphon off French wealth to Rome (chs 45–54). The quest ends in the posthumous *Quint Livre* (1562–4; uncertainly attributed to Rabelais) with the oracular utterance of the Divine Bottle, urging the seekers to drink before they speak and let their speech be inspired by the good cool wine of true scholar-ship. This is the same wine offered in the Prologue to the *Tiers Livre* by the philosopher-fool Diogenes, shouting his wares in the marketplace. The Cynic's barrel, the bottomless tub of everything good, Christian and pagan, is offered freely to all-comers, dispensing laughter and abuse in equal measure. On the voyage, Pantagruel holds the vessel steady, sails it away from dangerous reefs of heresy, keeps his disputatious crew together and, most important, helps them keep up their disputes. What matters is not so much *what* the joyful fellowship meet as *how* they meet it – not the theological differences that beset their journey, so much as the conversations, anecdotes, and joke-swapping to which they give rise. Whatever self-seeking end Panurge has in mind, Pantagruel travels in the hope of finding true language.

The carnival of Rabelais's language, brimming over with delight in the abundance of the Renaissance inheritance, refused to align itself with factions and found a place for any and every competing tongue. The language of the marketplace, street cries, oaths, public and private celebration, foreign languages, regional dialect, the jargons of law, medicine, religion were all satirised, parodied, pastiched but, most important, included. From the middle of the century, making language involved the drawing of battle lines – and fewer, more bitter jokes.

Joachim du Bellay (*c*.1522–60) modelled his great manifesto of Pléiade theory, the *Défense et illustration de la langue française* (1549), on the work of the Italian Sperone Speroni.[6] But it was also a point-by-point refutation of the *Art poétique* (1548) of Thomas Sébillet, theoretician of the school of Marot. At the root of the argument was the difference of Catholic and Protestant allegiance, a politico-religious division which became embodied in opposing aesthetic options. The Protestant Marot, an early convert to humanist Reform, translator of Virgil, Ovid and Petrarch and writer of the first Pindaric ode in French, also remained attached to the forms of French medieval tradition (ballads, *chansons, blasons*) and his work, for all its humanist allegiance and innovation, became associated with popular, democratic, and Biblical forms. Du Bellay, concerned to effect a change of cultural direction in line with the centralising ambitions of the Valois Court, conceived of poetry as an elitist project, requiring special training and knowledge. The poetic forms prescribed in his *Défense* excluded the medieval, designated ignorant, domestic and trivial, and preferred those classical and Italian models which enabled the poet to show his erudition and technical expertise: epigrams, elegies, odes (after Horace, Pindar) and sonnets (Petrarch), comedies, tragedies and the long poem (after Homer, Virgil, Ariosto).

Du Bellay's treatise advocated ransacking the classical past and the Italian present to reconstruct medieval French for fresh uses. Some elements might be completely original – for new objects, new words must be coined. But chiefly, inventing the language should proceed by imitation. This should not be servile copying, mere translation, but the kind of imitation – du Bellay describes it variously as 'digestion' and 'grafting' – which enabled the Romans to take over and transform the culture of the Greeks. His two metaphors caught that twinning of nature and artifice which is particular to the game the Pléiade played with language, using the devices of art to create a new 'nature'. The genius of their poetry was to give the appearance of naturalness to the objects it created. In the particular instance of the *Défense*, it was his own public and the King's people that du Bellay called into being. These were the future generations who would gather round those French poets who obeyed the concluding call to 'remember' the glories of classical Gaul:

Vous souvienne de votre ancienne Marseille, seconde Athènes, et de votre Hercule gallique, tirant les peuples après lui par leurs oreilles, avec une chaîne attachée à sa langue.

[Remember ancient Marseilles, the second Athens, and Gallic Hercules, dragging nations behind him by the ears, with a chain attached to his tongue.]

Theory turned into practice in the sonnets of *Les Antiquités de Rome* (1558), dedicated to Henri II with the wish that the Gods grant the King the delight of rebuilding in France a greatness that the poet would paint in the King's own tongue. The collection celebrated simultaneously the grandeur of ancient Rome and nascent France, and the decadence of modern Rome, the political rival, and the Papal Court, the arch-enemy. In the satirical sonnet sequence *Les Regrets* (1558), du Bellay wrote as a self-styled 'prisoner' in the Roman Court, in the diplomatic entourage of his uncle, the Cardinal. On the one hand, the poet offered an acerbic satire of the hypocrisy and arrogance of the Papal Court. Sonnet LXXX sets the clashing sounds and colours of Papal ceremony, and the venal machinations of Florentine bankers and Roman whores, against the ruins of old Rome, their crumbling symbol. On the other, du Bellay evoked his yearning for his home country, his own royal Court and the opportunities available there to luckier friends. Thwarted ambition is the other side of homesickness, expressed in an artful lyricism that harnesses nostalgia to political ends. The much-anthologised sonnet XXXI, that celebrates 'la douceur angevine' ['the sweetness of Anjou'], swiftly brushes in the austere detail of a simple rustic landscape, to stand as symbol of an energetic, uncorrupt young nation in implicit contrast to the decadence of Rome.

The same linking of poetic and political authority and ambition appears in the work of that greatest of Pléiade poets, Pierre de Ronsard (1524–85).[7] Ronsard explained to the reader in the preliminary Address to *Les Quatre Premiers Livres des Odes* (1550) that 'je me travaille faire entendre aux étrangers que notre langue (ainsi que nous les surpassons en prouesses, en foi et religion) de bien loin devancerait la leur, si ces fameuses Sciamaches d'aujourd'hui voulaient bien prendre les armes pour la défendre, et victorieusement la pousser dans les pays étrangers'. ['I am striving so that foreigners shall understand that just as we are far above them in martial deeds, and in religion and faith, so would our language be far above theirs, if the hatchet-wielding critics of our own day would but take up arms in its defence, and carry it victorious into foreign lands.'] His advice in the 1578 edition of his *Œuvres* to the apprentice poet reading his *Franciade* used politically- and economically-conscious metaphors, drawn from the relation of courtier to King and merchant to Prince, to encourage poets to build the language by exploiting all the resources of the body politic:

> Je te conseille d'user indifféremment de tous dialectes . . . entre lesquels le courtisan est toujours le plus beau, à cause de la Majesté du Prince: mais il ne peut être parfait sans l'aide des autres, car chacun jardin a sa particulière fleur, et toutes nations ont affaire les unes des autres: comme, en nos havres et ports, la marchandise bien loin cherchée en l'Amérique se débite partout. Toutes provinces, tant soient-elles maigres, servent aux plus fertiles de quelque chose comme les plus faibles membres et les plus petits de l'homme servent aux plus nobles du corps.

> [I advise you to use all dialects indiscriminately . . . the courtly dialect is always the finest, because of the King's Majesty, but it cannot be perfect without the help of the others. Every garden has its special flower, and each nation must deal with every other, just as in our ports and harbours goods fetched from far-away America are sold everywhere. Every province, however mean, is of some use to the richer ones, just as man's smallest, weakest limbs serve the noblest parts of his body.]

Ronsard's odes (Bks 1–4, 1550; Bk 5, 1552), the first full imple-
mentation of the Pléiade programme of linguistic renewal, boasted
of their debt to Horace, Pindar, Hesiod and Anacreon. Ronsard
used the Pindaric ode, with which its inventors celebrated the great
athletic triumphs, to celebrate the greatness of power at the Court
of Henri II: the patrons of the new learning (the King, his family
and his ministers) and the exponents of learning, fellow-members
of the Pléiade. Politician, poetry and poet must work together to
create a just, tolerant and moderate nation. His poem for Michel de
l'Hôpital (placed in charge of national finances in 1554 and Chancellor of France in 1560) opened in the Pindaric tradition with an
invocation to the Muses for the 'docte fureur' ['learned frenzy'] of
Apollonian inspiration: the kind of inspiration that the Pléiade,
taught by Dorat, made their own, a cool energy, channelled and
ordered by carefully learned technique and scholarship. (The term
is used in contrast to 'Dionysian' inspiration, the intoxicated frenzy
that can descend on learned and ignorant alike.) Poetic frenzy, duly
harnessed, would enable the power of the King's Chancellor to grip
the imagination of the nation. The Horatian odes, simpler in expression, focused on more apparently personal themes: the fleeting
nature of time, the brevity of life, and the correspondingly intense
pleasure of the sensuous moment. The ode to the *Fontaine Bellerie*
builds an alliterative effect and rhythmic variations to evoke the
exquisitely sharp contrasts of crystal splashing water, burning
summer heat, and thick, torpid shade. Like du Bellay's Angevin
'home', this pastoral idyll was also part of the Valois invention of
'France', the dream of a nation established in its own rich resources.
Sensuous pleasure reaches its peak in the Anacreontic odes, in, for
example, 'Louanges de la Rose', with its swirling invocation of the
delights of wine and roses. The image of the rose, hallmark of
Ronsard's poetry, carried its resonances into both private and public spheres. Ronsard's rose emblematised the dream of perfect
living, in all its variety and fullness, which fired the poet's imagination and which he offered, in turn, to his contemporaries. From the
fragile purity of the dawn rosebud, to its midday blooming into
heavy perfumed sensuality, it offers rich material satisfactions,
there for the plucking. These roses are no innocents. Bejewelled,
gowned, in Royal crimson, seducing the beholder with the scent of
the Gods, they naturalise a particular political ideal: they stylise the
dream of the Valois State.

Ronsard's two books of *Hymnes* (1555 and 1556) disseminated in poetic form the vision of the cosmic order that constituted the Renaissance world view. What interested Ronsard were the wider horizons that for him marked out the limits within which humans resolved their own destinies. The harmonies of his poetry embody the harmony of the spheres, the orderly, grandiose sweep of the planets that shape the future of men and nations. In his hymns to Eternity, Heaven, and the Stars, these divine harmonies are linked to the harmonies that divinely-ordained rulers work to maintain on earth. This scientific and philosophical poetry, an important new mode (see also, for example, Maurice Scève's *Microcosme*, 1562), was also in Ronsard's hands political poetry, writing into the natural constitution of the universe respect for a particular order and values.

III   TOWARDS A NEW SENSIBILITY

The mirror that French writing of the sixteenth century held up to the private lives of the writers and their contemporaries was shaped in forms clearly different from the mirror of tradition. Some – Clément Marot,[8] Mellin de Saint-Gelais (1491–1558) – continued to write in the light of courtly or *gaulois* (bawdy) national traditions. Other writers, influenced by Petrarch and by Italian Neoplatonism, inscribed sensual desire into more serious formations, which brought it into relationship with new forms of Christian idealism.

Petrarchan style, modelled on the Italian poet's representation of his forbidden and unfulfilled love for the married Laura, was not too far removed from the medieval tradition of courtly love. It linked carnal desire with aspiration to heavenly loves, but without abandoning any of the sensuality of its initial impulse. It produced strongly personal, emotional poetry, in which the love of abstract Beauty pales beside the images of intense physical desire for the body of the woman. More ascetic was the Neoplatonist mode, linked to the philosophy of Marsilio Ficino.[9] In 1484, Ficino published his Latin commentary on Plato's *Symposium* (*Banquet*), later known as his *De Amore*, which synthesised Platonist and Christian doctrine. Ficino envisaged a pattern of ascent to the understanding of Goodness, Truth and Harmony through Love, inspired by the vision of Beauty. The beauty of human women was the mirror of divine Beauty, and the lover of human women was set on a mystic way, by which initial physical attraction was transcended and replaced by the attraction of moral and spiritual Beauty. Dante's love for Beatrice, glimpsed only once, in passing, was the model. Ficino's doctrine set down three principal beauties, of soul, body, and voice, which were known through understanding, sight, voice and hearing. In his account, physicality was refined, as far as possible, to abstract notations. Neoplatonist formulations are heavily stylised. The lover, pierced by the arrow of the loved one's glance, lies bleeding and dying, is racked by love's poison, is pursued by the pagan gods of hunting or battle. Pain is the lover's keenest pleasure. He lives torn between earthly and heavenly desire – antithesis is the mark of the style, expressing the tension and permanent dissatisfaction which is the lover's preferred condition. Many of the symbols and allusions used in this language are obscure and inaccessible to non-initiate readers. Neoplatonist writing (and the visual representations with which it was linked, and frequently published, in the form of emblem books, poem linked to picture) implied and created an elite community of readers.

Both modes of writing sexual experience orientated the individual subject towards the material and secular world of the present. Whether they said physical pleasure was to be enjoyed or denied, sought for itself or transmuted into suffering, they gave it a new dignity as the centre of human concerns. They offered patterns and symbols for individuals to represent themselves and their place in a society that had broken with its medieval past. Subjects now defined themselves in the language and relationships of human community, not by the figures and laws of Christian theocracy. Ficino's Neoplatonism smoothed the passage across the ideological break, maintaining the language of Christian mysticism at the same time as it shifted its centre: no longer Christ and his Redemption, but individual human subjects, regulating their own struggle with desire.

Poetry, with its strict rhymes and rhythms, formal patterns of procedure, and the central role it gave to symbol and image, was the preferred Renaissance mode for the representation of individual desire. In the poetic forms the period evolved, emotional intensity and strict order went hand in hand. In the period 1535–45, Neoplatonist sensibility found the ideal conditions for its first flowering in Lyons, the point of entry for Italian trade to Northern Europe, home to a flourishing Italian merchant and banking colony and since 1473 France's major printing and publishing centre. The most celebrated canonically of the representatives of the École

Lyonnaise, Maurice Scève (*c*.1501–60), published in 1544 his Petrarchan *Délie, objet de plus haute vertu*, a sequence of *dizains* larded with
abstruse Neoplatonist references.[10] The Délie in question, Scève's
mistress Pernette du Guillet (*c*.1520–45), returned the compliment
in her posthumously published *Rymes* (1545).

Pernette's work is slight in comparison with that of her contemporary Louise Labé (1522–66).[11] Daughter of a rope manufacturer
with advanced ideas on women's education, an assiduous student
of the Italians, Labé focused the poetic mirror to produce, within an
essentially masculine erotic discourse, a clear image of feminine
difference. The single volume of her works which she herself
published in 1555, bringing together a prose *Débat de Folie et
d'Amour* and the elegies and sonnets of *Poésies*, reversed the Neoplatonist hierarchy by turning woman, object and vehicle of poetic
desire and speech, into its author. The Preface called for more
women to experience the pleasure of learning and writing, and to
aspire to independent poetic fame rather than mere housekeeping.
The poetic text itself was less ambitious: there, thirst for fame
(always the subtext of male contemporaries' poetry) disappeared,
to be replaced by the simple, plangent expression of the pain of
women's desire. Caught in the restrictions which contemporary
society placed on both women's speech and women's sensuality,
Labé's antitheses are nevertheless as sharp as those of her male
counterparts. Sonnet XIV is conceived in negatives, using the trope
of death to convey the pleasure of setting eyes, voice, and hand to
praise the beloved. In contrast, the voice of Sonnet XVIII abandons
itself to 'madness', throws aside discretion, and asserts its determination to 'sally forth' into love's battle.

Ronsard's love poetry is an unproblematic celebration of the hunt
and the winning of the trophy – or rather, the series of trophies
inscribed in his odes and sonnet sequences: *Les Amours* (1552),
Amours de Marie (*Continuation des Amours*, 1555; *Nouvelle Continuation des Amours*, 1556), and the sonnet cycle for Hélène (1578, 1584,
1587). The odes and sonnets inspired by Cassandra Salviati, a
Florentine banker's daughter, are more obviously stylised, invoking
Petrarchan clichés to figure not so much a woman as an icon of
desire, and casting in precisely-controlled antithetical abstractions
the conflicts aroused in the poet by the lady's – or rather, Love's –
indifference. The pleasure of representing sensual experience, not
sensuality itself, is the centre of this poetry: the thrill is in the
writing of the erotic experience. The poems addressed to 'Marie

Dupin' (probably an invented figure) strike a lighter note, with a change of model from Petrarch to Theocritus and the Neolatinist Marullus and the use of simpler vocabulary and less formal rhythms. But 'Marie' too is only another point in the chain of symbols, 'Heaven's miracle, Nature's mirror', the point where the two realms, Heaven and Earth, meet. The 'Sonnet sur la mort de Marie', mourning Henri III's Marie de Clèves, deeply moving in its personal tone, is a demonstration of the poet's ability to transcend loss through language. Nature passes; culture remains. The ephemeral 'Marie' disappears into abstractions and allusions. The poet buries her silent ashes with his own tears and symbols – the antique jar of milk and basket of flowers which summon the (poetic) powers who will turn her body into the emblematic ideal roses of imagination: 'Afin que vif et mort ton corps ne soit que roses' ['So that in life and in death, your body is all roses'].

The sonnets for Hélène de Surgères, maid of honour to Catherine de Médicis, renew the theme. The poetry foregrounds itself and the poet's capacity to eternalise transient beauty. The loved woman, like nature, the rose, and time itself, is for the poet a means to an end: Hélène is his Parnassus, and with such a mistress, 'Le Laurier est à moi, je ne saurais faillir' ['The laurel is mine, I cannot fail'] (Bk II, Sonnet 57). In Ronsard's poetry, public and private concerns and ambitions intermingle, and give each other substance. The lyrical thirst for love is tied to the epic craving for glory.

Creative prose, in its infancy, was not on the whole much marked by the new sensibility. The short story form, influenced by the Italian novella – the long short story – and the oral popular tale, drew the roles and relations of men and women in the old *gaulois* tradition. A typical collection might be the *Nouvelles Récréations et joyeux devis* (1558) of Bonaventure des Périers or the scabrous anecdotes of the abbé de Brantôme, Pierre de Bourdeille (1540–1614), published posthumously in his *Mémoires . . . contenant les vies des dames galantes de son temps* (1666). Chivalrous romance remained popular, especially with the first translation by Herberay des Essarts in 1540 of *Amadis de Gaule*, from the Spanish original. These narratives of courtly love were still marked by the misogyny of Jean de Meun's version of the *Roman de la Rose*, denounced by Christine de Pisan (c.1364–c.1431) in the previous century. Rabelais's discussion in the *Tiers Livre* of marriage and cuckoldry indicated no interest in the changing definitions of male and female sensuality.

The private faces drawn by male writers of prose register little change. It was left to the very few women writers of the period to highlight the brutal reality behind Gallic romp and explore the possibilities of the new sensibility. Hélisenne de Crenne (*c*.1520–*c*.1550), for example, in the novel *Les Angoisses douloureuses qui procèdent d'amours* (1538), shows the unromanticised side of adultery, in the suffering of a wife imprisoned by her husband because she loves another. The first extended enquiry into the changing relationships of men and women in love and marriage, surveying the manners and morals of the Court, began in the 1530s with the *Heptaméron* of Marguerite de Navarre.[12] In contrast to Marguerite's Neoplatonist religious poetry, which is all about renunciation of the world (*Le Miroir de l'âme pécheresse*, 1531; *Les Prisons*, written 1547), the tales invite their reader into a debate on the best way to live in a society engaged in self-transformation. Published posthumously in 1558, the text adapts the form of Boccaccio's *Decameron* to produce the beginnings of the modern realist novel, with its complex conscious interplay of word and world.

The *Heptaméron* presents a framed version – or rather, versions – of reality which opens up the gap between the truth of the narrator's perspective and that of the tale that is told. Cut off by flood from the unreflective round of everyday life, eight narrators exchange and debate stories, as a way of passing the time. Out of the flood of words comes a realisation of the conflicting worlds the speakers inhabit. The stories cover the gamut of contemporary styles and themes, from ribald accounts of the pleasures of the sexual chase, narrated with gusto by men and women alike, to the torment of women at the hands of fathers and husbands and instances of heroic suffering by lovers who die for unrequited love. Between narration and discussion, perceptions and attitudes sharpen and change, and a novel awareness is reached of the rights and desires of both sexes. The exchange concludes in praise of marriage, as the place where desire can find fulfilment and security. For the first time, human feeling – individual subjectivity – is acknowledged not as simply part of nature but as something that is also *made*, shaped by the institutions of Church and State, and open to question and change.

IV   SUBJECT TO REFORM: THE RELIGIOUS FACTOR

In the first part of the century, the discourses of Reform and Counter-Reformation played a key part in the making of individual and nation. General questions of the nature of authority and the status of individual judgement and responsibility were focused in such specific issues as the relationship between faith and works, the nature of the sacraments, and the place of laymen within the Church. Subjects learned the hard way that personal salvation and politics went hand in hand.

Evangelical Reform began as a movement within the Catholic Church, critical of contemporary abuses and preaching three main doctrines: return to the Scriptures (stripped of the glosses of their medieval commentators) and the simple morality of the Gospels; justification by faith rather than works (that is, an end to pilgrimages and the buying of indulgences); and the importance of direct communion with God through prayer, without the need for priestly mediation.[13] The centre of Reform in France was the *groupe de Meaux*, led by Bishop Guillaume de Briçonnet, which welcomed the teachings of Erasmus (1468–1536) and Martin Luther (1483–1546), even after the condemnation of Luther's 'errors' by the Sorbonne in 1521. The Reformers within the Church were tolerated until the 'affaire des placards' of 17 October 1534, when, overnight, posters appeared in all the main cities and on François Ier's bedroom door, denouncing the 'superstitions' of the Catholic Mass. The same year saw the launch by the Catholic Church of its Counter-Reformation to tackle clerical corruption and superstitious practices. The Jesuit Order was founded to spearhead the movement. (Though by the time the Council of Trent reported in 1564, divisions were beyond repair and the only resource was the authoritarian declaration that the Pope was sovereign in matters of faith and doctrine.)

It was not Luther, however, but Jean Calvin, who established his Church in the new city-state of Geneva in 1536, who most influenced the progress of Protestant Reform in France. His *Christianae religionis institutio* (*The Institution of Christian Religion*), published in Latin in 1536, appeared in French in 1541. In clear and simple language, Calvin argued for stripping Christian doctrine of its non-Biblical medieval accretions, for the non-hierarchical organisation of the clergy, and, crucially, for a role for the laity.

In the second half of the century, religious debate cloaked the factional struggles of the great aristocratic families for the throne: the Catholic Guises, the Protestant Bourbons and the 'moderate' opportunist Catholic Valois. Between 1562 and 1598, France suffered eight religious wars. Protestants were massacred, at Wassy in 1562, in Paris on St Bartholomew's Day, 24 August 1572. Catholics were assassinated, often by other Catholics (in 1588, the leaders of the Guise, by the Valois King Henri III, and in 1589, Henri III, by an assassin of the extremist Catholic Ligue). The Edict of Nemours (1585) sent Protestants into mass exile. The closing years of the century saw the bloodiest fighting, between the Ligue and the forces of the Protestant Henri de Navarre, crowned Henri IV in 1589, inaugurating the Bourbon dynasty. The tide turned with the King's abjuration of Protestantism in 1593, rallying a 'moderate' Catholic establishment terrified by the growing number of peasant uprisings, not all religious, in the 1580s and 1590s. The Edict of Nantes (1598), restoring toleration of Protestantism, finally sealed the peace between Protestants and moderate Catholics. The Ligue and the Spanish troops supporting them were driven out of France.

Writing moved with and made explicit the tensions of religious politics. The early Reformers had seen no conflict between their Christian faith and the classical learning that had inspired that faith's renewal. Desiderius Erasmus, the greatest exponent of Renaissance syncretism (the fusion of pagan and Christian discourses), published in 1500 his *Adagiorum Collectanea* (*Adages*), a handbook of the best-known tags of classical literature, and in 1516 his edition of the Greek New Testament. His *Enchiridion militis christiani* (*The Manual of the Christian Soldier*), published in 1504, declared the importance of both prayer and humanist knowledge, and presented the ancient poets and philosophers as guides for Christian morality. Ronsard's 'Hercule chrétien', published in 1556 in the Second Book of his *Hymnes*, glorifying Christ with a list of prefigurations in classical myth, was in this tradition.

The Pléiade's concern to create an elitist culture for a Catholic court led them chiefly to classical subjects and form for their dramatic experiments (Étienne Jodelle, *Cléopâtre captive*, 1552/53; Jacques Grévin, *César*, 1561).[14] Protestant humanists had made a point of adapting Biblical material to disseminate doctrinal concepts. Théodore de Bèze, Calvin's deputy and Professor of Greek at Lausanne, wrote his *Abraham sacrifiant* (1550) to dramatise for his pupils the superiority of faith to reason. But divides were not absolute. In *De l'art de la tragédie* (1572), the Protestant Jacques de la Taille looked to classical dramatic models and in his *Saül le furieux*, published in the same year but written in 1562, he combined Senecan form with the Biblical theme of the fall of the elect from grace. The best of the tragedies of the Catholic Robert Garnier

(1545–90), *Les Juifves* (1583), dramatising Nebuchadnezzar's perse-cution of his Jewish subjects, evoked the pain and bewilderment of pious subjects caught up in a ruler's ambitions for absolute power.

Ronsard's poems against the Reformers (1560–3) charted the rising tide of 'moderate' Catholic anger in the early war years. The first versions of the *Discours à Guillaume des Autels* (1560) and the *Discours des misères de ce temps* and its *Continuation* (1562) acknowl-edged the need for Catholic reform, adding pious thanks for the efforts of his Guise patrons in the Catholic cause. The *Remonstrance au peuple de France* (1563), a bitter satire on the disorder caused by Lutheran doctrine, ended in a vigorous invocation to the warrior God of the Israelites. Ronsard's force was matched in the Protestant camp by the visionary lyricism, Biblical thunder and violent grief of the soldier-poet Théodore Agrippa d'Aubigné (1552–1630), whose epic *Les Tragiques*, written 1577–9, was not however published until 1616.[15] Towards the end of the century, the long-suffering populace was finally given a voice of its own. The *Satire Ménippée de la vertu du catholicon d'Espagne*, published in 1594 but circulating in manuscript form before 1588, composed by a group of moderate humanist Catholics, parodied the debates of the Estates General in 1593, when the Ligue tried to nominate a Catholic King. The self-interest of foreign Legate, parvenu noble, bigoted Sorbonne doctor is satirised, each in its own brilliantly-mimicked rhetoric. The dominant voice is that of the Third Estate, pronouncing the sufferings and exasperation of Paris.

V   MICHEL DE MONTAIGNE (1533–92): THE BODY IN HISTORY

By the closing years of the century, Gargantuan aspirations had come down to human size. This must, however, be considered no mean achievement, when the model of human performance – the new human subject – turns out to be Michel de Montaigne.[16]

Montaigne's father was a wealthy gentleman of recent nobility and the family money had been made in trade. Montaigne himself was persuaded to undertake a career of public service as a magis-trate in the Parlement of Bordeaux. A private man, he resigned his office in 1570 to devote himself to reading and writing, return-ing occasionally to the public world to answer calls of high diplomacy or local politics. Not, then, an exceptional history; but the ordinariness of his life contrasts with the richness with which he lived, meditated and, most important, wrote it.

The three editions of the *Essais*, which appeared in 1580, 1588 and posthumously in 1595, indicate a divided identity. The citizen, punctiliously fulfilling public duties as soldier or magistrate, often conflicted with the private individual, the scholar and the man. This split subjectivity was simultaneously set out and resolved in writing. More clearly than anyone else of his generation, Montaigne figures the paradox of the relationship of self and society in the originary moments of the French State. The flowering of his liberal, humane identity, and the vigorous curiosity of his enquiring intellect, cannot be separated from his acknowledgement of the limits that circumscribe them. Montaigne's ethic of moderation in all things, his refusal to take sides with factions and causes, steering a cautious centre way, always concedes the primacy of established order.

This celebration of the acknowledgement of limits as the condition of self-possession was part, perhaps, of the reason for the welcome given the posthumous edition of his *Essais* by contemporaries more than ready for an ethic of moderation after the tumult of civil war. Those successors who most admired him, such as the *philosophes* of the Enlightenment, Voltaire and Rousseau, who were to make similar negotiations between subject and State, appreciated his balancing act. His eclipse in the seventeenth century indicates how much the absolutism of the state of that day exceeded the ambitions of its forerunner. The modern reader finds it hard to recognise the demon who is Pascal's Montaigne: the arch-representative of the self-indulgent private self, the epitome of rebellious humanity, the idle sceptic who is the prime target of the *Entretien avec Monsieur de Saci* (1778) and of key sections of the *Pensées* (1670). In 1676, he was to be found on the Vatican's *Index* of forbidden books.

The scepticism (or Pyrrhonism) that so annoyed Pascal is indeed everywhere in Montaigne's work. Its nature and implications were set out in the *Apologie de Raimond Sebond* (*c*.1576), written under the influence of the Sceptic philosopher Sextus Empiricus. Montaigne began his study to defend the intellectual validity of Sebond's attempt to use reason to support the Christian faith. Rapidly, however, he turned to developing ideas suggested by the theme of scepticism itself. Christianity, he muses, is less a matter of revelation than an accident of birth and geography. We are Christians in the same way as we are Perigordians, or Germans. We cannot know God through our reason, because the rational evidence is not there. Religion is received on authority. What reason tells us about religion is that reason can tell us nothing. Our thinking, he continues, anticipating the eighteenth-century sensationalists, is limited by our material conditions. We can only conceive things that are within our scope. Our senses set limits to our ability to know, which is why (as Descartes would shortly repeat) we cannot tell reality from dream. Pyrrhonism is a way of thinking that alerts the mind to possible error, even if it cannot lead directly to truth. Scepticism is a state of mind that leads to the good life of moderation, tolerance, imperviousness to ambition and desire. Pyrrhonists aspire to the Stoic *ataraxia*, which Montaigne defines as the quiet contentment that comes to those who are free of the delusion that they understand everything. Uncertainty, which Pascal later confronted with fear and despair, holds no terrors for him. There is firm ground, he reassures the reader, in experience, especially experience of oneself. Openness to the world gives the courage to live with the recognition that both self and life are flux and process.

Writing about self is the substance of the *Essais*. The three editions present three different states of the text, enabling the reader to follow the development of Montaigne's personality and style. Early essays follow a format that is standard for the period, with brief discussions of moral topics, using anecdotes and comments taken from the Ancients. But very quickly, Montaigne enters into a discourse of his own. Influenced by Plutarch, whose *Lives* were his favourite reading, he turns to writing as a form of autobiography. This is best seen in the long pieces of his Third Book (1588). In language that would not be out of place in our own times, he offers a discourse conceived within the discourse of others. He places what he says within the hum of voices that surrounds him: the would-be authoritative men of science and letters, philosophers, politicians, kings and people, men and women, including and levelling them all, for all, in the last analysis, are simply human bodies. As the essay 'De l'expérience' (Bk III, ch. 13) declares: '[A]u plus élevé trône du monde si ne sommes assis que sus nostre cul' ['On the highest throne in the world, we still have to sit on our bums'].

What bodily discourse seeks is simple: nature, peace, life, freedom. These are the recurring themes of the essay on experience, written 1587–8, where what matters is not only what is said but the form of the saying. The essay takes the form of a conversational monologue, producing a *voice*. Confident, relaxed, the voice creates an impression of authority, offering the listener statements, facts and truths. Immediately, the impression is undercut as Montaigne apologises for writing so much about himself: 'j'écris de moi et de mes écrits comme de mes autres actions, . . . mon thème se renverse en soi' ['I write about myself and my writings like any other of my acts, . . . my theme turns in on itself']. Turning in on itself, this text moves not in a straight narrative line, dictating a simple message, but in layers, through anecdotes and digressions, all with depths of their own, creating a multi-dimensional world of words. Time too falls out of conventional linear order. The voice casts back into its own past, or that of others, forward to its own future, to the only full stop, death, Montaigne's great obsession. The present is that of the conversation the voice conducts with itself, and with the reader/listener, written into the text, because language works like that, with speech, says Montaigne, belonging half to the speaker, half to the listener, knocked to and fro, just like a game of tennis.

There is more order than at first sight appears in the apparently desultory structure of this essay. The investigation of what knowledge and reason might be in theory leads logically to an enquiry into practical living. Certain themes recur: freedom, tolerance, moderation, the relations of mind and body, what it is to be human, to be me. Knowing is presented as a process, a series of intuitive, self-transcending leaps of desire. The only accessible object of knowledge is oneself. Would-be knowers must go to Nature, where they will discover that they have faculties (judgement, memory, passions) and that these faculties are flawed. These discoveries will not lend themselves to coherent expression, only to utterance as flashes of disconnected insight, modelled, Montaigne points out, in the form of the very sentences Montaigne himself is writing.

The body in this philosophy is where knowing begins, by observation from life, and knowledge here means power. Montaigne has learned, Stoically, to use routine to keep the desires or pains of his body in check, and to use his intellectual faculties, especially his imagination, to change bodily pain by changing his attitude to it. Writing autobiography is an act of self-protection. If he feels pain in the present, his fear of its implications can be conjured away by reading notes which preserve his recollections of similar pain in the past, which passed without consequence: 'À faute de mémoire naturelle j'en forge de papier' ['Having no natural memory, I forge a paper one']. Montaigne's autobiography is a history of his body. He charts obsessively the state of his health, as child, soldier, old man. Body knowledge is the basis of his political understanding: a frugal upbringing among ordinary people, he says, led him naturally to take their side. Familiar knowledge of the body, in life, eases the passage to the unknowable; death, for the true scholar of the body, is simply one more of Nature's changes.

The conclusion of the essay draws together in a generality these separate elements of Montaigne's thoughts on experience. Experience is for having, and enjoying. Most of all, you must know you are enjoying it. As Montaigne himself used to make his servants wake him up so that he could understand the pleasures of sleep, so must his reader become self-conscious and self-reflective. Self-knowledge, he optimistically concludes, is the foundation for the good life, and in his view, the finest lives are those which conform 'au modèle commun et humain, avec ordre, mais sans miracle et sans extravagance' ['to the common human model, in orderly fashion, shunning extravagant, showy wonders']. The 'common human model' Montaigne constructed in words, on paper, out of the best a humanist century had put together, set succeeding generations a standard to which they have constantly returned.

2

Classicism: Writing in the Absolute State, 1600–80

I SUBJECT TO AUTHORITY

From the close of the Civil Wars to the 1630s and 1640s, beginning with the Duc de Sully's reforms of taxation, economic policy, overseas trade and agriculture (1599), France enjoyed a period of economic expansion. Commercial treaties were signed with England (1604) and Russia (1629). There was successful colonial settlement in the West Indies (1625) and Canada where, by 1680, the French colonial empire extended from Quebec to the mouth of the Mississippi.

These early years, however, were far from peaceful ones. The assassination of Henri IV in 1610, leaving the throne to his nine-year-old son Louis XIII, with Louis's mother, Marie de Médicis, as Regent till 1617, saw the resumption of struggles between aristocracy and King. Richelieu's steady accession to the power he held as first Minister of France (1624–42) began in 1616. His subjugation of noble conspiracies, including those mounted by the King's mother, was complicated by Huguenot rebellions which only ended with the final capitulation of La Rochelle in 1628. The late 1630s saw a period of major financial and military crisis, with taxation increased to record levels to finance the Thirty Years War (1618–48).

In 1642, as the English King Charles confronted his Parliamentary challengers on the battlefield, Richelieu's death conferred power on his deputy, Mazarin. The death of Louis XIII in 1643 produced another minor as King, the five-year-old Louis XIV. Mazarin successfully manoeuvred through the years of economic contraction and crisis that followed, and the last major noble rebellions (the Fronde of 1648–53). Noble and parliamentary claims to participate in government were still not resolved when Louis XIV began his personal reign in 1661, at Mazarin's death. In that same year, when Jean-Baptiste Colbert took up the post of Minister of Finance, which he held until his death in 1683, the French revenue showed a deficit of 22 million francs. The famine of 1661–2 was one of the three worst of the century. Not until the 1670s was the régime finally consolidated.

These are the struggles of which traces still remain in the canonical literature, heavily cloaked by the efforts of both the King's great ministers to set the national culture to propagating the absolute power of the monarch and the centralised State. The glamour of the *Grand Siècle* masked not only aristocratic resistance but popular tensions and disorder. Inflation, heavy taxation, chronic debt, epidemic, food crises, sparked regular peasant uprisings from the early 1620s to the mid-1670s, culminating in 1675 in the revolts in Brittany and Bordeaux. Later historians, it has been argued, perpetuated the myth of the Age of Splendour for reasons of their own. Voltaire, looking for examples of benevolent absolutism to oppose to the decaying but still repressive forms of his own day, set the reigns of Henri IV, Louis XIII, and Louis XIV against that of his own Louis XV to argue the case for conservative reforms. His *Le Siècle de Louis XIV* (1751) is in this respect a Utopian fiction of enlightened despotism.[1]

With the systematic incorporation by Richelieu and then Mazarin of the nation's resources into the apparatus of a centralised State, embodied in the King at Versailles, culture became even more overtly a matter of public interest. Richelieu's sharp understanding of the power of the press contributed to the consolidation and expansion of the printing industry, centred in Paris.[2] His policies fuelled a lucrative pamphlet war, in which he employed his own writers. Théophraste Renaudot, editor of the first Paris weekly, *La Gazette* (founded 1 April 1631), openly served the interests of Cardinal and King. Expansion of printing was accompanied by its closer regulation and the tightening of state censorship (four official royal censors were created in 1623), to the gradual exclusion of the interventions of the Church. In the period 1638–43, the guild undertook its own internal reorganisation, in its own market interest. The first explosion of Jansenist controversy (the debates on grace, 1643–7, renewed in 1649) produced another lucrative stream of unauthorised polemic, which led to a Government crackdown in 1657. The issue of printing privileges was tightened up from 1661 onwards, at the same time as the King began to increase the number of pensions awarded to preferred writers.

In 1634–5, Richelieu founded the Académie Française as a means of providing State encouragement for the arts and, as a by-product, a new form of artistic monitoring and self-censorship. Its first intervention, at Richelieu's express orders, was an examination of Corneille's innovative drama *Le Cid* (1637), which had raised a storm of controversy for the so-called irregularities and improprieties of its themes and form. The forty immortal men of letters (no women were deemed eligible or fit to join their number until the 1980s) undertook as their as their central task the standardisation of the French language. The first edition of their *Dictionnaire* was published in 1694. In the same spirit, Claude Favre de Vaugelas, an Academy member, produced in 1647 his *Remarques sur la langue française*, a code of polite usage based on the practice of the soundest authors and members of the Court – the women, he noted, as much as the men. Initially, the result was a fruitful consolidation of the sixteenth century's creative work on the language, continuing the pruning job on vocabulary and syntax begun by François de Malherbe (1555–1628) in the name of elegance and simplicity. But as the regulatory impetus spread, its usefulness became more questionable. The Jansenists Arnauld and Lancelot, no friends to Louis XIV, based their *Grammaire générale et raisonnée* (1660) on structural principles akin to those of his State, seeking to impose an ideal order on the flux of historical discourse. The Grammar abandoned the historically-sensitive criterion of usage for abstract principles of logic and Cartesian reason. The effects of the arbitrary authority it tried to exert over language lingered on long after the detail of its regulations stopped making sense, limiting the opportunities for fresh initiatives of creative imagination.

The self-policing of the intellectual community through the Academy was reinforced by the salon culture fostered by the distinguished women excluded from Academy membership. The gatherings presided over by the marquise de Rambouillet (1588–1665) and Madeleine de Scudéry (1607–1701) encouraged not only the expansion of cultural activity but also the dissemination of aesthetic, social and linguistic norms. Madeleine de Scudéry's *romans à clé* (*Artamène, ou le Grand Cyrus*, 1649–53; *Clélie, histoire romaine*, 1654–60, with its famous allegorical map of Love, the 'Carte de Tendre') staged the activities of salon contemporaries in thin historical disguise. Preciosity, developed in the salons, which aimed to produce a subtle metaphorical discourse for the analysis of the passions, at its best helped generate the innovatory work of the classical moralists and dramatists. At its worst, as Molière's parodies would indicate, it tortured language and stifled experience.[3]

II   DRAMATISING MATTERS

The Renaissance had brought into French high culture the forms and themes of the great Ancient dramatists: from the Greeks, Sophocles and Euripides (and the theory of tragedy Aristotle derived from their work); from the Romans, Plautus, for comedy, and for tragedy the dramatically incompetent but morally authoritative Seneca. A gap had developed between the new plays staged for the learned elite in colleges and private houses, and the popular homegrown theatre that remained attached to the medieval forms of mysteries, moralities and farces. The gap began to close in the early years of the seventeenth century as another generation of dramatists, who had grown up in the two cultures, introduced into the professional public theatre the highly successful modes of pastoral and tragi-comedy.[4]

The pastorals of Honorat de Racan (1589–1670) and Jean Mairet (1604–86) and the light tragedies of Théophile de Viau (1590–1626) contributed to the evolution in the theatre of a language of refined sentimental analysis matching the vogue in poetry and the novel launched by *L'Astrée* (1607–27), the best-selling pastoral romance by Honoré d'Urfé (1567–1625).[5] The more distinctively dramatic tragi-comedies of the prolific Alexandre Hardy (c.1572–1632) thrilled audiences with their sensational scenarios, twisting plots and spectacular action. The elements were there for a new kind of theatrical writing which could combine historical action and the study of human behaviour, allowing closer representation and debate of issues in contemporary public and private life. 'Life', of course, had a limited resonance. By the middle of the century, what had been relatively mixed audiences had narrowed to Vaugelas's elite of Court and Town, watching newly-formed professional troupes under royal and ministerial patronage.

Seventeenth-century historical tragedy was produced by practising dramatists, but its development was helped as well as hindered by the debates fostered by theorists such as Hippolyte-Jules de La Mesnardière (*Poétique*, 1639) and the abbé d'Aubignac (*La Pratique du théâtre*, 1657).[6] Its ultimate codification appeared in the *Art poétique* (1674) of Nicolas Boileau-Despréaux (1636–1711), where the watchwords of classical theatre were presented as propriety and truth to nature. The 'nature' in question was assumed to be universally and essentially unchanging. Nature is, however, as the Romantics would later point out, a concept whose meaning is transformed by each generation. In the classical generation, 'nature' was defined from a rationalist, hierarchical and authoritarian perspective, and its distinguishing features were declared to be simplicity, harmony and order. The 'truthful' representation of such a nature required specific techniques. Dramatists should observe the three unities of action, time and place, providing a single plot, with any sub-plots linked to the development of the main action, plot duration of, at most, twenty-four hours, and a single setting. 'Propriety' decreed an end to melodramatic actions in general and on-stage effects in particular, and to any behaviour or language that stepped outside polite convention. The faculty to be flattered was not imagination but reason, or rather, a common-sense version of rationalism which set a premium on simple, logical form, eliminating the gratuitous and the quirkily individual. Good order required the regulation of every detail. All entrances and exits, for example, had to be strictly motivated. No-one could get into the action without being accounted for.

Tragedy and comedy were defined as distinct genres, each with its own function. Tragedy took elevated subjects from ancient history and fable, tales of heroes and kings, to explore the great themes of the 'human condition' – in practice, what aristocratic society deemed the most significant subjects of the contemporary moment, conflicts of love, duty and loyalty, problems of the relative priority to be given to private desire and the desire of authorities (family, father, State or King). Comedy dealt with private everyday matters: affairs of marriage and property, conflicts between generations, the follies and small adventures of 'ordinary' people – the lesser aristocracy, wealthy bourgeoisie and their servants and hangers-on. The least of the effects of this arbitrary distinction between private and public spheres is that it reinforces the categorisation of individuals into social hierarchies. More important is that it establishes larger hierarchies of human activity, in which public life is more significant than the private sphere. Affairs of State are more important than private desires.

Classical drama represented a world where rules were the condition of existence. Deviations from the norm required justification – of the kind both Pierre Corneille (1606–84) and Jean Racine (1639–99) found themselves providing in the form of prefaces, dedications and studies appended to their published plays. The genius of the best exponents lay in large part in their ability to 'naturalise' the arbitrary rule. In an even larger part, it lay in their ability to replace by the imaginative quality of their language, and the acuteness of the intellectual and psychological perceptions it carried, the emotional force of the visual effects which both before and after the classical moment were the distinctive feature of dramatic form. Debarred from exploiting well-developed scenic resources, their only plastic tools the actor's face and voice, Corneille and Racine could still represent contemporary reality just as it was: a web of words binding individuals, a matrix of discourses that both generated and frustrated personal energies, constraining them into the production of a single, unified spectacle.

III THE TRAGIC PERSPECTIVE: NEGOTIATING WITH HISTORY

Seventeenth-century theoreticians of drama saw its function as moral rather than political: modelling appropriate modes of conduct for the audience. Discussion centred on Aristotle's identification of *catharsis* – the purging of the passions by the arousal of pity and fear – as the main dramatic effect. It was not clear however what Aristotle meant by catharsis, nor how the process might work. Corneille's three *Discours* on drama, written in reply to Chapelain's presentations of the Academy's criticism of *Le Cid* (*Sentiments de l'Académie sur le Cid*, 1637) and d'Aubignac's *La Pratique du théâtre* (1657), and published in the 1660 edition of his plays, engaged robustly with Aristotle's commentators. No audiences, Corneille thought, went to a theatre to see the staged misfortunes of human beings just like themselves. Nor did they leave the theatre with the resolve to damp down ardour and ambition in the interests of a quiet life. Audiences, in his view, wanted to wonder at extreme characters like his own, historical exceptions, whose vices and virtues were dazzlingly different. If Aristotle really did argue the doctrine attributed to him, it was only because he was writing in a political context in which art *had* to present itself as a bastion of public order. Racine's published formulations were more diplomatic, and limited to his prefaces (his private marginal comments on his own copy of Aristotle's *Poetics* were published in 1951 as *Principes de la tragédie*). The preface to *Phèdre*, for example, argued unctuously for the importance of using drama to reinforce moral lessons: here passion was presented only to show what disorder it generated, and vice painted in colours that showed its ugliness. But

Phèdre itself (1677) staged desire, crime, guilt and punishment in a collocation that was fascinating in its own right, and pushed prescriptive moralising into second place.

In practice, the morality of tragedy was for both Corneille and Racine not a question of prescription but of description. What was described, or rather, presented, was the tensions of private relationships evolving within particular political circumstances. In the first half of the century, Corneille's plays dramatised still-unresolved tensions between the individual subject and the institutions of State demanding the subject's allegiance. In the second, Racine's tragedies presented characters still apparently confronted with choices, but effectively bound by the consequences of choices made by a previous generation. Corneille's characters were still making history. Racine's characters inhabited a landscape built of historical necessity.

For audiences still fresh from the drama of the Fronde, Corneille's plays represented heroes seeking to reconcile their personal desire for love, power or glory with the demands of God and King.[7] Increasingly, the King himself became the focus of interest, and serving the King was the road to self-fulfilment. But in Corneille's vision of what constituted human greatness, for King and subject alike, it is always the choices of individuals, and more particularly, the spectacle of choosing, that are the centre, and produce the lyrical energy of his language.

Le Cid (1637) was designated a tragi-comedy by its author, already famous for the comedies he had staged in the early 1630s (*La Galerie du Palais, La Suivante, La Place royale*), but it already operates with all the power of the tragic mode. The rivalries of two aristocratic fathers sweep their children into the cycle of outdated vendettas. Rodrigue and Chimène make the self-denying choice of sacrificing their love as a mark of respect for family honour. But the demands of a State in crisis, defined by the King, overrule both love and tribal loyalty. Rodrigue must forget all other imperatives and take to the battlefield at his King's command to defend country and religion. Chimène's duty, as a woman, takes a more passive form: to submit in silence when the King declares her the prize for Rodrigue's success. Submission and sacrifice are the themes that generate the lyrical and dramatic pleasure of the play. The sacrifices of subjects are mirrored by the greater sacrifices of their rulers. The plangent monologues of the Infanta, the King's daughter, play a chorus role, quiet commentaries from the margin that double and intensify the bloody, clamorous drama between aristocratic subjects that occupies the centre of the stage. The Infanta's lyrical laments, ending in self-imposed silence, express a passion for Rodrigue that the princess's reason chooses to repress. Her unrewarded anguish puts into perspective the couple's self-interested struggles with honour, shame and love and points to the gulf between the monstrous heroism of royalty and that of lesser mortals.

Monstrous heroism, born of imperatives of State, is again the theme of *Horace* (first performed 1640), which dramatises the growing pains of a new empire. The tragic excitement here is in the unpicking of acts of choosing which are simultaneously right and wrong, voluntary and inevitable. Political and historical necessity requires that as Rome grows to greatness, Albi must be swallowed up. The sons of two great families, though linked by marriage and betrothal, must fight to the death as representatives of their two nations. Horace offers a chilling spectacle in the manner in which he assumes his duty to Rome, to the exclusion of all other feeling. When his brothers-in-law are slain, he turns his sword on his sister for cursing the Roman virtues that led to her lover's death. Only the Emperor has the authority to pass judgement on the hero's conduct in this crisis of conflicting values, and his reasoning proceeds with logical precision. Horace's murder of his sister was indeed a monstrous crime against humanity, nature and the gods. There was, however, no alternative. Servants like Horace are the necessary instruments of state power and the acts that cement that power are beyond the laws of commonplace humanity.

In *Cinna* (staged 1640), the royal hero, identified with the State, holds the spotlight throughout. To maintain the stability of his empire, Auguste must maintain empire over himself, inventing within himself the resources to control his anger and pain at his subjects' treachery. Cinna's motives for conspiring against him, in contrast, are purely selfish. Cinna wants Émilie, who demands he kill the Emperor to avenge her family. *Polyeucte* (1641–2) adds another dimension to the problem of conflicting imperatives, with the hero, freshly converted to Christianity, forced to choose between Christian God, Roman State and love for his wife. Here again, the Emperor plays the most magnanimous role, looking for reconciliation. The only ruler to fail the test of self-denying generosity is a woman, Cléopâtre, whose will directs the course of *Rodogune* (staged 1644), Corneille's favourite among his plays, which analyses the destructive effects of absolute power exercised for private ends.

In Corneille's plays, the twists and turns of plot were still important, representing situations still open to resolution by human decisions. In Racine's world of closed moral and political options, action is seized at a point just beyond the final crisis, where whatever happens can no longer make any difference. The drama is intensely ironic. Conflicts in principle still exist. There are still preferences to be expressed for one set of values over another, and much of the tragic force of the plays arises from the clarity with which the issues are recognised. But the outcome of choice is always a foregone conclusion. History, variously figured as Fate, the gods, politics or passion, leaves individuals no option but to pursue desires whose realisation is not in their hands.[8]

Racine's anti-humanist emphasis on the powerlessness of fallen human nature to act without the grace of God echoes the historical situation of his generation, subjects caught in the defining power of authority, Church or State, charged with responsibility but denied power. The paradox in which Racine's heroes are constructed, decreed guilty of crimes of which they are the instruments, not the agents, is famously characterised in the preface to his last pagan drama, *Phèdre*. Phèdre is the representative Racinian heroine, neither guilty nor innocent; committed by the force of destiny and the anger of the gods to an illicit passion for her stepson Hippolyte, which she is the first to condemn.

Personal choices, desire and imagination appear to dictate action in *Andromaque* (staged 1667). Andromaque, the widow of the Trojan prince Hector, struggles to reject marriage to her Greek captor Pyrrhus, King of Epirus, while still trying to negotiate the safety of her son Astyanax. The hot, bloody vision of the recent past blots out for Andromaque both present and future. In her mind's eye, her would-be suitor is forever fixed in a single landscape, conjured up in a few lines of compelling rhythms and vivid imagery: Troy in flames, the body of Hector dragged round its walls, her father slaughtered, while Pyrrhus, his entrance lit by Troy's burning palaces, carves his way towards her through the bodies of her brothers. The Greek princess Hermione, betrothed to Pyrrhus for reasons of State, is turned to an avenging Fury by love, jealousy and humiliation. Oreste, mad with love for Hermione, cuts the dramatic knot by assassinating Pyrrhus as he sets the wedding wreath on Andromaque's head. All four, at the end of the day, are instruments, not agents, of the historical drama. Throughout the play, the spectator's attention is fixed by the poetry on the anguish of individual passions, figured by the hissing serpents that writhe, in Oreste's hallucinations, on the head of a vengeful Medusa–Hermione. The poetic image, as so often in Racine's work, functions for most of the play to present individual desire as remorselessly directing the world to its destruction. But in the end, desire, it would seem, first destroys itself. The three Greeks die, victims of their own passion; Pyrrhus's soldiers acknowledge the Trojan captive Andromaque as their Queen; the world slips back into political order.

In *Andromaque*, as in many of Racine's plays, a pattern emerges in which the account of the disarray of passions (sexual desire, political ambition, thirst for vengeance) leads to a conclusion where passion is reformulated in a sequence of rites: marriage, coronation, sacrifice. Racine's is very much a ritual drama, in the sense in which Artaud uses the term in the 1930s, articulating at every level (plot, character relations, language) the passionate impulses of human nature in forms that hide none of their force. He differs from his twentieth-century counterparts in that his drama harnesses those energies to a drive for order. More particularly, and in contrast with Corneille's work, it represents the drive for order as something intrinsic to the way the world is made – a necessity in the state of things – that is independent of individual efforts and decisions.

Britannicus (staged 1669) offers a nightmare glimpse of a world where ritual sanctions have almost lost their power, and absolute authority is in the hands of a ruler, Néron, who observes no interest but his own. *Bérénice* (1670), in contrast, is the dream of the ideal order which emerges when every authority acknowledges a duty to a higher authority still. Bérénice, Queen of Palestine, agrees with Titus, King of Rome, that their love is a political impossibility. Roman law forbids rule by a foreign Queen; and the Roman people still remember the disastrous passion of Caesar for his Egyptian Queen. The play's famous adherence to the unities (a single dilemma resolved in two hours, in the space of a single ante-chamber) is not just a technical tour de force. It embodies a very particular vision of the demands of a political moment. The 'majestic sadness' which Racine's preface points to as the source of tragic pleasures in the play comes from the swiftness with which hero and heroine acknowledge the irrelevance of individual desires confronted with the limits set by history and the interests of the State: no happiness outside the law. The poetry is an elegiac celebration of self-denial, repression and renunciation. *Mithridate* (1673), though cast in a very different mode, dramatises similar themes. This reputedly most Cornelian of Racine's dramas, crammed with blood, battle, poison and death, father–son rivalries for possession of a mistress and a kingdom, ends with the tyrant Mithridate putting aside his own passions to ensure that the defence of his kingdom against Rome's imperial ambition continues in the next generation.

Arguably, Racine's two greatest dramatisations of the destructive power of individual desire, set against the orderly society of authoritarian rule, are *Phèdre* and *Athalie*, which close respectively his pagan and Biblical sequences. The strength of these plays derives from their complex invocations of myth, worked up in both instances into powerful image-systems which construct clear and forceful oppositions. In particular, Racine makes brilliant – and not dissimilar – use in both works of gender stereotypes. In Phèdre and Athalie, the two pagan Queens, Racine feminises the bloody, tumultuous energies of the past which gave birth, certainly, to the present, but which must now be repressed so that the present can come to maturity on its own terms. The repression is not a simple one. Cast into these powerfully seductive figures, the past oppresses, terrifies, but also exerts a monstrous, magnificent fascination.

In *Phèdre* (1677), the Queen herself denounces her desire for Hippolyte, son of the husband she believes to be dead. She knows what is wrong with that desire: the wish, against all natural order, to live life a second time. In Hippolyte she sees another, younger Thésée. But her self-loathing is combined with the proud awareness of the tradition of revolt and transgression which is her inheritance. She is the daughter of Minos and Pasiphae, the tyrant who sacrificed generations of young men and women in his labyrinth and the woman who coupled with Zeus in the form of the Bull. Thésée, and the young lovers Hippolyte and Aricie, are the latest in the line of victims of those black energies of nature which Phèdre incarnates, mirror image of the Bull from the sea who rises up to cause Hippolyte's bloody death. They will also, however, be the last, by Phèdre's own decision. Swallowing a poison brought to Athens by Médée, another witch-Queen, she makes a painful expiatory death, to restore light and purity to the world her presence had fouled. The last speech of the play goes to Thésée, embodiment of outraged reason and justice, who declares his intention to blot out all memory of his wife, and whose final act is to adopt into his family the dutiful daughter, Aricie. The gesture opens the old world of passion to a new rational future.

In *Athalie* (1691), the past refuses to go quietly. The play offers a spectacular confrontation of rival principles: Baal against Jehovah, matriarchy against patriarchy, austere spirituality against the mysteries of the flesh. This is the struggle of the Queen, daughter of Jezabel, against the Priest, grandson of Aaron and guardian of the Law. The play is not a tragedy in the same sense as those which precede it. Pity and fear are evoked, for the small band in the Temple guarding the child-King, Joas, from the devouring Mother-figure, but the atmosphere of hopeless doom is absent. History in this play is explicitly transformed from a past burden to a future promise, embedded prophetically in the drama in the lyrical chants of the choir and the triumphalist rants of the High Priest Joad. This is a play to satisfy the severe piety of its patron (it was written, like its predecessor *Esther*, for performance by the pupils of Madame de Maintenon's charitable foundation at Saint-Cyr) and of the Jansenists. The repression of the challenge to the Father's authority is brutal and absolute. Athalie's death, in a welter of blood, doubles the death of her mother, dashed to the pavement by the will of Jehovah and her blood, as the Bible says, licked up by the dogs.

Repression, and the relentless return of the repressed, is the motor of Racine's drama. On the one hand, there is the repression of the monstrous vitality of the past, to make the civilised order of the future. History, crowded into the stage present of the drama, the Racinian antechamber, revived in the memories and voices of its inhabitants, is purged, a necessary sacrifice to progress. On the other, there is the repression of the present, focused by the classical emphasis on the drama of words and the refusal of spectacle.

In Racine's theatre, the desiring, feeling body is brilliantly displaced into language-effects. His long periodic sentences recreate in their complexity, their precise detail and their rhythmical variation the contradictions and convolutions of his tormented characters. The techniques of preciosity are skilfully exploited to intensify the violence of feeling at the same time as they withhold it from the audience's immediate apprehension. Allusion and periphrasis, by hinting at the presence of taboo subject matter, make obscenity appear more obscene. Phèdre's confession to her nurse of her incestuous love for her stepson is a frenzied account of her struggles not to name a forbidden passion: 'ce Dieu que je n'osais nommer' ['the

God I dared not name'] (Act I, Sc. 3). The rhythm of the alexandrine foregrounds in the discourse symbolic figures of real and painful death. Néron licks his lips over Julie's tears, in a sinuous, liquid line whose last words point prophetically forward to a bloodier flow: 'J'aimais jusqu'à ses pleurs que je faisais couler' ['I loved even the tears I caused to flow'] (Act II, Sc. 2). Occasionally, images of a different kind, stark and concrete, stand out in shocking contrast to this precious discretion. Athalie's mother Jézabel, appearing to her daughter in a dream in all her regal splendour, is suddenly transformed into the bloody mess left by the dogs: 'un horrible mélange / D'os et de chair meurtris, et traînés dans la fange / Des lambeaux pleins de sang . . .' [a terrible mixture / Of mangled flesh and bones, trailed in the mud / Shreds soaked in blood'] (Act II, Sc. 5). The dead metaphors of precious cliché (the 'fire', 'flames' and 'chains' of love) are constructed into fresh contexts. In Phèdre's confession to her nurse, the fire of her passion ('ma flamme'), figured in the burning incense on Venus's altars, the smoking sacrifices to the goddess, is finally acknowledged to be the 'black flame' of incest ('une flamme si noire'), which can only be quenched and purged by death.

IV COMIC CONCLUSIONS

The high comedy of classicism, most notably represented by the work of Molière (pseudonym of Jean-Baptiste Poquelin, 1622–73), was as much the child of its historical moment as was tragedy.[9] Its relationship, his comic playwright Dorante declared, was in fact closer, and its commitment to the contemporary could make it significantly harder to write:

> [J]e trouve qu'il est bien plus aisé de se guinder sur de grands sentiments, de braver en vers la Fortune, accuser les Destins, et dire des injures aux Dieux, que d'entrer comme il faut dans le ridicule des hommes, et de rendre agréablement sur le théâtre des défauts de tout le monde. Lorsque vous peignez les hommes, il faut peindre d'après nature. On veut que ces portraits ressemblent; et vous n'avez rien fait si vous n'y faites reconnaître les gens de votre siècle.

> [I think it is much easier to get on your high horse with your fine feelings, fight Fate with poetry, rail against Destiny and abuse

Divinity, than to get into the skin of human silliness and represent on stage everybody's little failings without giving offense.
When you paint men, you must paint them according to nature.
The portraits have to be like; and if you have not produced a
recognisable image of the people of your own time, then you
have not produced anything.]

(*La Critique de l'École des femmes*, 1663, Sc. 6)

To do this, he continued, and at the same time make an audience
laugh, was no mean feat: 'c'est une étrange entreprise que celle de
faire rire les honnêtes gens' ['making good gentlefolk laugh is a
funny thing'].

In pursuit of funny things, Molière stood the tragic world view
on its head. His universe represented the same relationships as its
tragic counterparts and like them was peopled by devotees of self-
interest, monstrous egos in conflict. But a change of form turns
history into farce, as the audience of *Les Précieuses ridicules* (1659)
would have been forced to acknowledge, faced with Mascarille's
project to write up the whole of Roman history as a sequence of
madrigals (*Les Précieuses ridicules*, Sc. 9). Even more effective was
the change of setting, from the public spaces of the rulers of ancient
history to the domestic places of seventeenth-century aristocracy
and bourgeoisie. The heart-searchings of ancient Kings, confronting
battlefields, funeral pyres and avenging gods, are out of place in
the aristocratic salon or the bourgeois drawing-room. Modern life
simply isn't all that bad.

The recuperative powers of comic form are tested in two plays
in particular. *Dom Juan ou le Festin de pierre* (1665) presented the
diabolical egoist deliberately defying the strictest sanctions of
religion and society, corrupting and destroying the bodies and souls
of others, ending only in the flames of hell. *Le Misanthrope* (1666)
was a monster of another kind, forcing on his contemporaries his
own iron moral standards and ending in another hell, a cold loneliness of his own making. These are certainly not comic characters,
and the situations they create are not intrinsically funny. Dom Juan
exploits the ignorance of peasant girls, the powerlessness of peasant
youths, and the selflessness of his aristocratic victim, Elvire. Alceste
exploits society's codes of polite tolerance to exercise his own cruel
intolerance with impunity. But tragic potential is defused by the
reductive comic perspective in which their enterprises are placed.

No man is a hero to his valet: and Molière's world-vision always includes the view from where the valet stands. Dom Juan's adventures, seen through the shocked but complicitous eyes of his servant, Sganarelle, are reduced from catastrophe to carryings-on. When Sganarelle comments in the opening scene that a great lord given to evil is a dreadful thing, the rhetoric of condemnation turns in his mouth to clucking cliché. When the sinner is swept off to hell, Sganarelle's terror at the vision of retribution is swamped by the horror of losing his wages.

Molière's satire showed no mercy to the follies of the modern. Self-seeking, injustice and oppression, deceit and, most of all, hypocrisy were roundly condemned. *Les Précieuses ridicules*, like *Les Femmes savantes* (1672), targeted the social-climbing imitators of the worst excesses of Parisian salon life, for the damage done to language and morals by their self-important prudery and lack of brains and taste. Tyrannical heads of family were attacked for keeping their wives morally and intellectually imprisoned (*L'École des femmes*, 1662), marrying off their children for money, position or mere personal convenience (*L'Avare*, 1668; *Le Bourgeois Gentilhomme*, 1670; *Le Malade imaginaire*, 1673) or, simply, revelling in their patriarchal power. In *Le Tartuffe* (1664; first authorised representation 1669), Orgon is vulnerable to the religious confidence trickster because of his insistence on being absolute master in his own home and his declared pleasure in annoying his family (Act III, Sc. 7). The sharpest barbs were kept for the men of the professions – Churchmen, lawyers and, especially, doctors – who tried to mask ignorance and rapacity with costume and jargon (*L'Amour médecin*, 1665; *Le Médicin malgré lui* (1666); *Le Malade imaginaire*).

But the modern itself was enthusiastically embraced, and granted a future that it was denied in tragedy. In the comic tradition, young lovers triumph, servants collude successfully against unjust masters, the spiteful, grasping old are outwitted by the pretty, witty, decent young. King, Law and Reason come round in the end to secure a happy ending. However dismal the oppressions and repressions, Molière's carnival has its own machinery for turning them to laughter. The caricaturist's eye and ear mark every attempt to check and purge pleasure – every threat to the operations and relations of the natural human body. The precious project to save women's modesty by purging the language of unseemly syllables (*Les Femmes savantes*) and the hypochondriac's systematic purging of his system with enemas and laxatives (*Le Malade imaginaire*) are of a kind. The comic script employs all the linguistic and spectacular resources at its disposal – puns, parody, mime, farce, burlesque, song and dance – to send the forces ranged against human happiness spinning into confusion, confessing their own folly. The emblem of Molière's comedy is the Miser, Harpagon, staring the audience in the face with a shock of terror as he suddenly realises through his accelerating frenzy that the arm he has arrested is his own.

But at the end of the play, even Harpagon is saved. Molière's comedy is an act of affirmation of the society it represents, as the concluding exchange of comic playwright and his lady Muse in the *Critique de l'École des femmes* makes plain. There is always, says Dorante, a resounding argument and no-one will give in; then the valet comes to announce supper, and all the masters go in to eat round the same table. As Uranie concludes: 'La comédie ne peut pas mieux finir, et nous ferons bien d'en demeurer là' ['There's no better end to a play, so it's a good idea to stop there']. Its glimpses of frenzy safely enclosed inside the codes of polite conduct, a play argument tucked in before a good supper, classical comedy continued as a workable genre into the late eighteenth century, a safety-valve for Order – right up to the last moment, when the valets grew tired of waiting.

V   MAXIMISING MORALITY

Defining 'human nature' and prescribing norms and codes of behaviour had once been the prerogative of the pulpit. By the middle of the seventeenth century, it was taken for granted that such activities should also be a preoccupation of secular culture.[10] Literature, in the variety of its forms, offered a range of different ways for individual subjects to participate, actively and passively, in the elaboration and dissemination of common values. Drama, addressing a relatively wide range of social orders, was a collective and collectivising experience. The novel spoke to private subjects in the seclusion of an individual room or, reading together, as members of small closed groups. Essays, discourses, treatises, in poetry or prose, presented public matter for private consumption; letters and lyrical poems reversed the process. That particular product of the period, the maxim, led a double life as debating point in the salon and authoritative utterance on the printed page.

By such processes, society built its moral consensus. Salon

conversation points turned into Tables of the Law, a narrow band of prescriptions for appropriate ways of seeing, feeling and acting which were the glue for a social order founded on hierarchies of gender and rank. Women, certainly ran the salons.[11] Women contributed in increasing numbers to the literature of moralist prescription and description. Representations of changing aristo-cratic manners and morals were to be found in the letters of Marie de Rabutin-Chantal, marquise de Sévigné (1626–96), or in the trea-tises on women's rights and functions by Montaigne's editor, Marie le Jars de Gournay (1565–1645) (*Égalité des hommes et des femmes*, 1622; *Le Grief des dames*, 1626), as well as in the work of women novelists. But the groundrules of these representations were established in a masculine perspective; and the briefest con-sideration of authorities in philosophy and ethics indicates that it was male writers who produced the lapidary pronouncements and statements of universal principal which set the terms of debate.[12]

The chief architect of the break of secular thought from the authority of the Church was the mathematician and philosopher René Descartes (1596–1650).[13] Descartes's *Discours de la méthode pour bien conduire sa raison et chercher la vérité dans les sciences* (1637) was an attempt to find a way for human reason to work its way confidently to philosophical truths. It was responsible for a num-ber of concepts which inspired and conditioned the best thinking of the Enlightenment (the importance of banishing from one's mind all prejudices and assumptions derived from authority alone, and of proceeding by systematic critical analysis and methodical doubt) as well as others equally influential but consid-erably more flawed (the appeal to common sense, and the auto-matic credence given to clear and distinct ideas). The cornerstone of this project was the Cartesian *cogito*, from the Latin *cogito ergo sum*: 'I think, therefore I am', in which the thinking human subject replaced God as primary source of knowledge, the centre of the intellectual universe. God was still part of Descartes's universe but reduced to an after-thought, an ancillary who vouched for the soundness of the conclusions to which human reason came.

Descartes himself would not have accepted this account of his theses. Fully aware of political risks, he professed in his *Discours* total submission to the laws and religion of his country. Certainly, the formulations of his new philosophical discourse necessarily lay very close to that of the Christian theology which was the prevailing discourse of his day, especially in its ethical dimension. At first

sight, the Christian description of natural man as a warring compo-
sition of body and spirit is in harmony with Descartes's idealist
distinction between body and mind, as independently functioning
sources, respectively, of the instincts and the intellect, the passions
and reason. But one difference tips the scale. For the theologians,
the primary object of discussion would be the gift of divine grace
without which fallen humanity could not function. In Cartesian
discourse, the focus of study is human reason, and the mechanics of
its interaction with the passions that move the human machine (see
also *Les Passions de l'âme*, 1649).

Grace was still a crucial matter for another mathematician-
philosopher, Blaise Pascal (1623–62), who combined the driving logic
of Cartesian rationalism with a capacity for intuitive thinking (which
he expressed as a preference for 'heart' over 'reason').[14] In the realm
of mathematics, this led him to ground-breaking discoveries in the
calculus of infinity and the theory of probability. In philosophy and
ethics, his intuitive excursions, fuelled by the austere enthusiasms of
his conversion to Jansenism, produced a highly pessimistic account
of human reason and nature and their dependence on divine
authority. *Les Pensées*, the fragments of Pascal's apologia for the
Christian religion, published posthumously by Port-Royal in 1670,
argued that reason was incompetent when it came to major questions
of knowledge, especially knowledge of God. Pascal condemned
what he saw as the futility of speculative reason and the emptiness
of its claims, particularly as represented in the thought of Descartes
and Montaigne (though his own work takes theirs on board), and
argued the advantages of inductive reason: the *esprit de finesse*, which
he contrasted with the Cartesian *esprit géométrique*. At the end of the
day, faith in God and submission to divine law, he declared, leads
further than any reliance on human powers. The persuasive force of
the *Pensées* lay less in the intellectual strength of its arguments (where
logic and superstition sit side by side) than in its appeal to the
emotions through dramatic images of human fragility and divine
magnificence, or sentence-rhythms framed for lyrical seduction or
rhetorical intimidation. Satirical shafts, ironic cuts, outbursts of vehe-
ment indignation slip with unchristian ease from a pen which had
already practised its polemical skills on the Jesuits in the *Lettres
provinciales* (1656–7), a witty denunciation of Jesuitical morality. The
Pensées invoked all the tricks of the writer's trade to persuade
readers to abandon new-born philosophical confidence in humanity's potential to seize command of self and world.

Theoretical debates about the nature of human thought and feeling and the authorities by which it should be regulated were complemented by works which focused directly on the day-to-day exchanges of the writer's social world. The *Réflexions ou sentences et maximes morales* (1665; *Nouvelles Réflexions*, 1678) of François de la Rochefoucauld (1613–80) presented a view of human motivation and abilities as pessimistic as any of Pascal's analyses.[15] This ironic and misogynist analysis of the world of the salon aristocracy identified ambition and self-interest as the motive forces of society, expressed in jealousy, deceit and hypocrisy, practised principally by women, against men. Its sharp, authoritarian abstractions, proclaimed as the distillation of long experience and precise observation, sought to turn a partial perspective into universal truth. Virtues, for La Rochefoucauld, were only masks for vice, and honest affection and moral integrity were excluded from a passion-dominated world. The index to the 1678 edition, tabulating the areas of discussion, gave twenty references to the passions and a mere three to reason. Pascalian retreat, however, from worldliness into ascetic seclusion, was not to be contemplated. The salon moralist sought a means of survival within the social jungle, which he found in the aristocratic code of *honnêteté*. The code was elaborated by Nicolas Faret (*L'Honnête Homme, ou l'art de plaire à la cour*, 1630), the Chevalier de Méré in, for example, his posthumously-published *Discours de la vraie honnêteté* (1700), and the Epicurean philosopher, letter-writer and essayist Saint-Evrémond (1614–1703). In La Rochefoucauld's version, its fundamental precept was the willingness to be constantly present on the social stage conforming to society's conventions. Proper behaviour was less a matter of following conscience than of social performance: 'C'est être véritablement honnête homme que de vouloir être toujours exposé à la vue des honnêtes gens' ['The truly honourable man is one who is always eager to be exposed to the gaze of honourable men'] (Maxim 206).

The mirror of conduct held up by La Rochefoucauld to the salon world provided a satisfactory reflection well into the next century. The poetic skills of Jean de la Fontaine (1621–95) animated the same analysis in lighter, satirical vignettes which drew on the animal fables of Aesop (*Fables choisies mises en vers*, 1668–94).[16] In 1746, the marquis de Vauvenargues (1715–47) could still repeat it in his far duller *Introduction à la connaissance de l'esprit humain, suivie de réflexions et maximes*. But only twenty years after the publication of

La Rochefoucauld's book, social performance was already receiving a less favourable press from Jean de la Bruyère (1645–96), the son of administrators and peasants, who joined the nobility by office-purchase in 1673 and who held the post of tutor to the children of the Prince de Condé and subsequently secretary and librarian to the family. The very different rhetoric of his popular collection of maxims and portraits, *Les Caractères ou les mœurs de ce siècle* (1688), which went into eight revised editions during his lifetime, marked the beginnings of a realisation that the principles of individual behaviour and the organisation of social relationships were under-going major change.[17]

In La Bruyère's text, abstract pronouncements of universal principle sit alongside forms which aim to give an impression of the swift movement of the real world of social exchange. From a less privileged background, standing on the edges of the noble world, he charted the emergence of a morality dedicated to the cult of money and social status. The self-interest ('l'amour-propre', or 'l'intérêt') that La Rochefoucauld said ruled the world takes on a new gloss: *financial* interest (VI, 59) is now the prime mover, the ethic of the taxfarmers and speculators, *Honnêteté* is no longer a matter of noble birth, or even of the practice of a salon code. 'Honourable' has slipped to 'honest', and the appearance of honesty is enough: 'L'honnête homme est celui qui ne vole pas sur les grandes routes' ['An honest man is one who doesn't steal on the highway']. La Bruyère's observations deconstruct contemporary social practice and demythify contemporary ideologies. His tableaux show up the sham of a monarchical order that claims to derive its moral authority from God. In Church, the eyes of 'devout' courtiers turn to the King, not to the altar. Outside the Church, Biblical language cloaks regal exploitations; the King is not the shepherd, but the wolf of his flock. Hatred and violence are no longer shown simply in the relations between men and women in the salons. La Bruyère points to the widening gaps between categories and conditions of society, fostered by envy and exploita-tion. The rhetoric of the text re-enacts the disintegration of what was once (nostalgically) perceived as a coherent world.

The sixteen chapters over which the material is divided are crammed with vignettes, caricatures, tableaux of varied lengths, with no clear interlinking. The structure of the sentences, extended and chopped up by a plethora of commas and semi-colons, generates a sense of breathlessness, of a world racing beyond the grasp of its speakers. For La Bruyère, it is the writer-sage, the secular intellectual and 'homme de bien' (II, 30), to whom society now looks for order. The text opens with a section on 'Les Ouvrages de l'esprit', explaining the role of writing in maintaining moral vision. But the sage is soon forced to acknowledge the extent to which the moralist's project is circumscribed by political imperatives. Satire, he admits, dare not take on the biggest subjects: the sharp observer of imminent social catastrophe explicitly declines to comment on the corrupting conservatism of the Absolute State.

One text in this century stands out for the discretion and delicacy with which it approaches those questions of self-knowledge and moral responsibility on which others speak with such authoritative confidence. Madame de Lafayette (1634–93) was the author of the first novel to present a serious psychological analysis of human relationships rather than a simple telling of stories (in the manner of the medieval romance), a set of courtly love-games (*L'Astrée*), or the parodies of those forms which constituted the 'realist' novels of the early seventeenth century (Charles Sorel, *La Vraie Histoire comique de Francion*, 1623–33; *Le Berger extravagant*, 1627; Paul Scarron, *Le Roman comique*, 1651–7). *La Princesse de Clèves* (1678) was a ground-breaking representation of how the consciousness of the individual subject is shaped by the social and political structures in which it is situated and how, literally, the language the subject is given to speak marks out the possibilities and the limits of its being.[18]

The heroine of the title, a fairytale princess at the court of Henri II, enters the story in a condition of complete unselfconsciousness. She starts life possessed of all the attributes for happiness (wealth, position, beauty, intelligence and charm). She depends completely on the authority of her mother, who has instilled in her the values of filial and Christian submission. She believes in virtue, purity, fidelity and sincerity, but for her these are simply words, untested by experience. She accepts without question the marriage arranged by her mother and takes up her place at Court. For the first time, she is confronted with unfamiliar discourses, which she has to negotiate alone. This is a world ruled by La Rochefoucauldian codes of self-interest, licentiousness and deceit, where women exist primarily as bodies: partners in sexual intrigue, or contracted away in the marriages of political, diplomatic or financial convenience, which serve the interests of the State or the great noble families. Her own passions are awakened for the first time by the Court's most notorious seducer and she is forced to become an active player in the game. The text increasingly represents her listening with, presumably, growing understanding to anecdotes of other women's experience in situations similar to her own – with an increasing sense of her own incompetence.

The genius of Madame de Lafayette lies in her depiction of the impossibility, for such a subject, of achieving the level of self-awareness and the capacity for choice that mark the subjects represented by male moralists. A woman in the Princess's situation, written over by others' discourses, has no means of moving beyond the confusions of feeling and chaos of ideas that those discourses generate. Hers is a stunted and limited subjectivity, brilliantly evoked in her few short inner monologues, half-formed questions that trail off in a cloud of incomprehension, in the various representations of her as picture, image of speechless beauty framed by the gaze of the rake, Nemours, and finally in the inscription on the tombstone that closes, in conventional cliché and authorial irony, her stunted career: 'sa vie, qui fut assez courte, laissa des exemples de vertu inimitables' ['Her life was short but she left examples of inimitable virtue'].

3

Enlightenment and Revolution, 1680–1815

I A ROOM WITH A VIEW

In the scholarly library at the end of the sixteenth, seventeenth and eighteenth centuries, as represented by the private studies of Montaigne and La Bruyère and that great public enterprise entrusted by the Revolution to Chamfort, the Bibliothèque Nationale, the core remained the same collection of humanist classics, that bore witness to the intellectual and political empires of Greece and Rome. Writers in such a library might well feel that having a hold on the classical inheritance amounted to having a hold on the world, as texts continued to address one another across that continuum. But as Renaissance evolved towards Revolution, the context of the library changed radically, and with it, the nature of what one text could say to another. The classical originals were no longer alone on the shelf: they addressed the eighteenth-century reader from alongside those other very different texts they had already helped generate within the French context. In the landscape outside the study stood new readers with other preconceptions. When modern critics describe culture as *intertextual*, they mean that it is constantly woven and rewoven not only out of the inter-changes of ideas in books but also out of the social and historical discourses out of which books and ideas are generated. As the Enlightenment understood, texts are sites of material practices.[1]

The classics of antiquity that underpinned the Empire in Rome and the Absolute Monarchy in France now shared in the founding of the bourgeois State. Such processes are slow ones and literary history only marks the most conspicuous points where diplomatic negotiations between past and present turn to war. The *Querelle des Anciens et des Modernes*, which broke surface towards the end of the seventeenth century, debating the superiority of modern literature over its ancient models (see, for example, Bernard Le Bovier de

Fontenelle, 1657–1757, *Digression sur les anciens et les modernes*, 1688), was the prelude to the great battle of the Enlightenment over fundamental issues concerning the nature of authority and knowledge.

A shift of similar importance from the middle of the twentieth century has been marked first by attacks on the Enlightenment and what is seen as the repressive face of its rationalist epistemology and ethics, and secondly by attempts to recuperate some of the Enlightenment's most useful positions. Among the former might be cited the Marxist Theodor Adorno's critique of its categories of reason and nature, or the postmodernist rejection of the belief in history-as-progress that has been an important instrument of social change. In contrast, philosophers such as Habermas or the later Foucault have renewed the great debates of the Enlightenment texts: the relation between subject and society, the nature of free will and responsibility, and the relations between ideas and truth, words and meaning.[2]

In canonical language, the fifty years spanning the turn of the seventeenth century, roughly between 1680 and 1730, saw the shift from the age of authority to the age of critical reason.[3] Two texts throw the difference into relief: a sermon by Jacques-Bénigne Bossuet (1627–1704) and a book by Voltaire (pseudonym of François-Marie Arouet, 1694–1778). The first issued from the Cardinal's Parisian pulpit, at the centre of established cultural and political order. The second came to Paris from an English press, an illicit document from the pen of an exiled *philosophe*.

The *Oraison funèbre de Marie-Thérèse d'Autriche*, delivered in 1683, celebrated the absolute monarchy to which the Cardinal Bishop of Meaux devoted his life. The double authority of Church and State was codified in his *Politique tirée des propres paroles de l'Écriture Sainte*, which he began writing in 1677–9 and which was published posthumously in 1709, and reinforced in his historical studies: the *Discours sur l'histoire universelle* (1681) and the *Histoire des variations des églises protestantes* (1688), in which all deviations from Catholic tradition were marked down as signs of untruth. It was Bossuet who in 1682 helped draft the 'Gallican Charter' (*Déclaration des quatre articles*), that skilful negotiation of the demands of Papal and monarchical authority that contrived to define French Catholic independence of the Vatican without provoking an irrevocable split. His funeral oration for the Queen, a classical example of pulpit rhetoric, with its rolling, elegant, authoritative periods, praised the absolute power wielded by her husband, the focus, he declared, of the moral, political and intellectual life of the nation. The dead Queen became a model of edifying piety, submission, and self-denial, doubly obedient to God and King.

Voltaire's *Lettres philosophiques* (1734) was a short printed book, written in informal, witty prose, to provoke debate.[4] (The text first appeared in 1733 in London as *Letters Concerning the English Nation*, and in France as *Lettres sur les Anglais*, without the celebrated letter on Pascal which rounds off the edition of 1734 and sharpens the point of the attack.) Voltaire invited fellow-citizens to consider with him the effects on individuals and nations of an excess of authoritative utterance. The freedom and variety damned by Bossuet here inspired a flurry of letters detailing a range of innovatory ideas and ways of thinking. Kings and cardinals must stand aside for men of reason, science and commerce. Religion was at best an absurdity and at worst a monstrosity. The evidence spoke for itself. An Absolute State was oppressive and impoverished. Better to have free thought, free trade and a flourishing economy – as in England, where the floor of a bustling Stock Exchange saw the civil intercourse of men of all denominations.

Between these two texts, the centre and the margins of French culture and politics had been redefined. The process was not simply one of developing ideas: on the contrary. Bossuet spoke with a confidence unshaken by transformations already taking place in his own disciplinary field. The *Tractatus theologicopoliticus* (1670) of the Dutch philosopher Baruch Spinoza (1632–77) had already confronted the inadequacies of the Scriptures, especially the Gospels, with their tales of miracles and prophecies. Superstition, Spinoza argued, was not religion; it was a deformation encouraged by the rulers of the earth, to keep down the ruled. Religion should be a moral option, and 'God' a concept accessible to reason. Richard Simon's contribution had been less dramatic, but at least as devastating. In his *Histoire critique du Vieux Testament* (1678), this Hebrew scholar, attempting to use philology to demonstrate the authenticity of the Biblical text, ended up showing the opposite. Re-presented in the polemic form of the clandestine manuscripts shortly to enter circulation, or later in the eighteenth century in the published work of Voltaire or Diderot, such ideas would disclose their full revolutionary potential.[5] Voltaire's handy little *Dictionnaire philosophique portatif* (1764) made hay with the bizarre origins of the Old Testament canon, the theological, historical and intellectual inconsistencies within the texts and their bloodthirsty morality. At the same time, it pointed with scarcely-contained fury at the power wielded by those whose authority rested on such flimsy and irrational foundations.

What made the difference between 1683 and 1734 was the change of social and economic conditions. In the early years of Louis XIV's reign, the Treasury had benefited from Colbert's careful fiscal policies and measures to promote manufacturing and trade at home and colonial expansion overseas. The surplus from this activity funded the protectionist war against Holland in the 1670s, which ended in modest victory at the price of renewed financial problems at home. Successful maritime trade did not compensate for agricultural depression and famine in the countryside. The sale of more offices and the imposition of fresh taxes financed the War of the League of Augsburg (1689–97) and the War of the Spanish Succession (1701–13), which both saw the whole of Europe leagued against an over-ambitious France. Economic instability at home was compounded by competition from the rising powers of Holland and England. England in particular, as Voltaire never tired of pointing out, had a system that recognised the importance of enterprising merchants and kept idle aristocrats in their place.

Economic process was assisted by political incompetence. Three years before the English Revolution, in a masterstroke of folly, French Absolutism had produced the Revocation of the Edict of Nantes, withdrawing civil rights and privileges from Protestants. Thousands of Huguenots fled to England and Holland, taking with them the skills that helped found the English weaving industry. This error of triumphalism was later matched by the Papal Bull *Unigenitus* in 1713, marking the defeat of the Jansenist faction by their Jesuit rivals in a way that provoked the resurgence and revolutionary transformation in France of a movement that had been falling out of fashion. A mysticism which in the previous century had proclaimed human impotence in the face of a glorious divine will now encouraged individuals to revolt. By the end of the eighteenth century, one of the most thought-provoking images of resistance to authoritarian power is Suzanne, the recalcitrant nun of Denis Diderot's novel *La Religieuse* (written in 1760, circulated in 1780 and published in 1796), who begins her convent career in private prayer, independent Bible-reading and the near-sensual ecstasy of mystical communion with God and ends it denouncing the role of closed religious institutions in preserving the order of the Absolute State.

The death of the King in 1715 left France in the hands of a Regency with nowhere to go for new answers, even had the will existed for fresh questions. The sale of offices and the encouragement of speculation peaked in the débâcle of the economy in 1720 under the Scottish banker Law, who flooded the country with worthless banknotes. The episode was satirised in the *Lettres persanes* (1721) of Charles-Louis de Secondat, baron de Montesquieu (1689–1755), who saw in it the cause of the moral as well as the economic ruin of the nation (Lettre CXLVI).[6] The same text offered a differently-angled insight into the origins of current weakness with the political fable of the Troglodytes (Lettres XI–XIV). In his tale of the near-destruction of the cave-dwelling people, narrated in answer to the question whether human happiness lies in the satisfaction of individual desire or the practice of virtue, Montesquieu tested out the competing theories of the English philosophers Thomas Hobbes (1588–1679) and John Locke (1632–1704) on what human nature is and what form of civil society is most appropriate to it. A society composed of individuals committed to competitiveness and self-seeking cannot survive, even if it tries to compensate for the ferocity of self-interest by choosing to live under authoritarian rule. In contrast, a handful of virtuous Troglodytes prospers and flourishes in open and self-regulated communities, regulated by the pleasures of altruism. The fable concludes with the rejection of the need, in such a community, for any king. Morality, in the new ideology, is firmly lodged in the individual, not the monarch.

II SCIENTIFIC SUBJECTS

The Huguenots who had taken their industrial skills to England and Holland had also taken their tradition of independent thinking. This connected with the indigenous radicalism of their new countrymen to produce a flowering of critical literature, which became available in France through a number of illicit channels.

From Amsterdam, Pierre Bayle (1647–1706) issued a stream of books and pamphlets (*Pensées diverses sur la comète*, 1682–3) culminating in the magnificent broadside against authority which was his *Dictionnaire historique et critique* (1697). This was a catalogue of contemporary knowledge, which meant, effectively, a catalogue of errors, since what authority – the Ancients – had called truth could readily be shown to be nonsense. In footnotes filling most of the page, Bayle engaged in provocative refutations of blatant absurdities. Even more important were the methodological and moral principles underlying his arguments, which laid the foundation for the logic of the Enlightenment. Philosophy for him was not speculative, but practical. Ideas, he urged, had ethical and social consequences, which is why it mattered so much that ideas should aim to be true. The worthwhile in religion was not its magical but its ethical content. Religion should exhort its followers to be reasonable and benevolent – that is, to be social beings. Individual reason and conscience, not authority, should take responsibility for thought and action. Reason should always be sceptical, critical of all conclusions including its own.

No one person, or even one age, Bayle acknowledged, could possess truth in itself. Knowledge was a collective product, generated more often than not by learning from mistakes. For him, as for his Enlightenment successors, identifying and discrediting error was as important as establishing what was true. Last, but by no means least, knowledge was to be shared by all, not hoarded by an elite. The vulgarisation of knowledge, the dissemination of information and ideas in forms that could easily be understood and applied, was the hallmark of this new age. Bayle's counterpart, Fontenelle, writing in France, commented in his pioneering attack on superstition, the *Histoire des oracles* (1687), on the gullibility of peoples, which was one of the major reasons why error and exploitation flourished. It was to the eradication of ignorance and credulity that the Enlightenment turned its attention.

From England, the *Bibliothèque anglaise* (1717–28) and the *Bibliothèque britannique* (1733–77) disseminated the empiricism, humanism and scepticism of Shaftesbury, Locke and Hume and the physics and metaphysics of the mathematician-philosopher Isaac Newton (1642–1727). From its early stages, the French Enlightenment was marked by English models of thought. It was, as Voltaire said in his *Lettres philosophiques*, another world over the Channel. Theology was subordinate to philosophy, and philosophy itself was quite different. Cartesian metaphysics, with its distinction of body and spirit, its faith in innate ideas and its concept of God as prime mover of the universe had, in Voltaire's view, provided in France a last refuge for scoundrels such as the Christian apologist Malebranche. English philosophy was focused on man and the physical universe. Not speculation but scientific experiment and observed fact were its starting points.

The association of science and philosophy transformed individuals' concepts of themselves and their place in the world. The *Lettres philosophiques* established a roll of honour of men of science, beginning with the empiricist Francis Bacon (1561–1626), and placed an account of Newton's physics at the threshold of its account of new ways of thinking. Newton's work on optics could point to the relativity of perception and consequently of knowledge. The information received by the senses varied with contexts and conditions. 'Facts' were not as clear and simple as they might seem. Even more important, the Englishman's light and open universe, ordered by gravity, was a world of freedom, in direct contrast to the oppressive mechanistic, matter-crammed system posited by the Cartesian *plenum*, and one where there was, Voltaire indicated, room to move and make changes.

An abbreviated account of Newton's *Principia* had first appeared in France in 1715 in *Le Journal des savants*, set in explicit opposition to the Cartesian system. The *philosophes* reran his experiments. Emilie du Châtelet (1706–49) translated his *Principia Mathematica* and in 1740 published her own *Institutions de physique*, which tried to synthesise the theories of Newton and Leibniz (1646–1716). From the 1750s, Newtonian physics was generally accepted (see also the article 'Secte' in the 1765 edition of Voltaire's *Dictionnaire philosophique*).

Another Englishman, John Locke, had founded the science of experimental psychology. Locke's *Essay Concerning Human Understanding* (1690) disposed, Voltaire explained (*Lettres philosophiques*, Lettre XIII), of the Cartesian belief that ideas were innate. Ideas were not given by God. 'Mind' appeared, according to Locke's observations of his own thought processes and the ways in which children constructed ideas, to reach its complex abstractions by combining simple sensations.

The door was pushed open for the recognition of the secular and material nature of thought. The focus shifted from the soul (an even less tractable concept than the mind) to the interactions of the body and the world. In 1746, the abbé Étienne Bonnot de Condillac (1715–80) presented the doctrines and implications of sensationalist psychology in his *Essai sur l'origine des connaissances humaines*, to which he added in 1754 a *Traité des sensations*. If ideas came from the senses, it was difficult to see how individual subjects, at the mercy of their environment and physical constitution, could be held responsible for their feelings, thoughts and actions. The classical belief in universal reason, cherished by the first generation of the Enlightenment, might well prove just as shaky a foundation for morality as religion had done. Conduct could no longer be labelled 'good' or 'evil'. Rather, it was 'natural' or 'against nature' – and this, in its turn, raised the issue of what 'nature' might be.

The regulation of relations between individuals and the wider community needed rethinking. Logically, as the abbé Julien de La Mettrie (1709–51), author of an *Histoire naturelle de l'âme* (1745), argued in his *L'Homme machine* (1748), societies could not justify punishing individuals whose 'natural' desires went against what others said was the collective good. Claude-Adrien Helvétius (1715–71) presented in *De l'esprit* (1757) a completely materialist, determinist and atheist account of human nature and behaviour. Motivated only by passions, moved solely by pleasure or pain, with no independent reasoning faculty, individuals could not be held responsible for their actions; objective morality, in consequence, must be a chimera. *De l'homme* (1772) took an optimistic view of the consequences of such a condition, declaring with lyrical enthusiasm that individuals engaged in the quest for happiness, following the pure light of natural reason and virtue, without the fear and ignorance that came from religious prejudice, could also be good family members and good citizens. The Baron d'Holbach (1723–89) argued similarly in his blunderbuss of a treatise, *Système de la nature* (1770), which put the arguments within the grasp of a wider public. The marquis de Sade, who wrote from prison in Vincennes in 1783 asking his wife for a copy of d'Holbach's text, based his fictional libertines' diatribes on nature and crime on passages lifted wholesale from the sensationalists. The exhortations to virtue in the originals were ignored. Indeed, Sade complained bitterly in his *Histoire de Juliette* (1797) of the 'cowardice' of *philosophes* who would not pursue the logic of their arguments.

Of all contributors to the sensationalist debate, the boldest and also the most judicious was probably Denis Diderot (1713–84).[7] Preoccupied throughout his career with questions of individual happiness and morality and the just society, Diderot began his work with an *Essai sur le mérite et la vertu* (1745), a translation of Shaftesbury's defence of theism, to which he added approving footnotes. He rapidly abandoned Shaftesbury for a position based on the scepticism of Spinoza (*Pensées philosophiques*, 1746, and *La Promenade du sceptique*, 1747) and underpinned by his own interests in the more speculative aspects of sensationalist psychology and the fast-expanding sciences of biology and medicine. His *Lettre sur les aveugles à l'usage de ceux qui voient* (1749) considered the blind English mathematician Nicholas Saunderson, whose concept of space came entirely from touch, and whose criteria of moral value were similarly built on very different presumptions and priorities from those of sighted colleagues. Medical science and philosophical speculation, forced to the limits of dream, came together in the *Entretien entre d'Alembert et Diderot*, the *Rêve de d'Alembert* and the *Suite de l'entretien* (all written 1769, published 1830) in an enthusiastic assertion of consciousness as a material process.

In the dialogue form, Diderot could produce many-angled representations of the interactions of individual and society and open up the debate on the balance of interests between them without settling into a single simplistic position. *Le Neveu de Rameau* (written 1761–74), constructed as a chance encounter with an acquaintance in the buzz of the Paris streets, evoked the thrilling terror of negotiating a world crammed with unfamiliar subjects. In its kaleidoscope of themes, the recurrent motif is that goodness and criminality, like genius and mediocrity, are born, not made. Characters can be contained but not changed, so why not, perhaps, simply seek to contain them, as lightly as possible, and enjoy the social spectacle staged by human nature in all its forms. In the bosom of the family, philosophical detachment was demonstrably less easy. In the *Entretien d'un père avec ses enfants* (written 1771–83, published 1798), magistrate father and *philosophe* son discuss the tensions between individual judgement and the demands of the law. The young idealist is eager to change the world, while his father is committed to keeping order in the face of ever-threatening chaos, conscious of the complexity of situations, the partiality of knowledge, and the fallibility of judgement. A second son, a priest, has a smaller but respected voice in their debate. There are other voices, too, whose exchanges constitute the moving matter of society. Law, religion and philosophy are the three main agencies which regulate the interaction of private and public spheres, the exchanges of the family house and the streets outside. But there is also the doctor, passing through with quick, incisive comment, too busy curing disease to spend time on theory. Almost unnoticed, mother and daughters bustle in and out with slippers and support. Almost – but not quite – the last word goes to a young woman neighbour, with a radical contribution on the relations of men and women, an important area of social change.

Another dialogue, the *Supplément au Voyage de Bougainville* (written in 1772, published 1796), took a very long perspective – a Pacific island – to make a clear opposition of libertarian and authoritarian social values. The young French Catholic missionary, all desire repressed under his suit of black broadcloth, confronts the open sensuality of the naked Tahitian. Diderot unpicks the functional purposes and corresponding moral values attributed to sexual desire in Europe and in Tahiti. In both, the body is an instrument of wealth and power, regulated by a small self-interested elite. In Europe, the Church regulates sexual intercourse to further its own accumulation of wealth. In Tahiti, the fathers of the family-community encourage sexual activity in all men, and certain categories of women, for breeding purposes, to provide labour for the land. Preference goes to the relative freedoms and use-values of Tahiti, though yet again, Diderot raises the unresolved question of the equity of women's social role and place.

III DREAMS OF REASON: JEAN-JACQUES ROUSSEAU

The rationality of the Enlightenment was not all scepticism and logically consistent analysis. In the first place, the *philosophes* wanted to establish truths that were not just scientifically sound but morally useful. This set limits to the terms in which they were able to think and the conclusions they were prepared to draw. In the second place, innovative thinking proceeds as much by leaps of the desiring imagination as by methodical reasoning. The Enlightenment, for all its scorn of the 'imagination' and 'metaphysical speculations' of previous generations, found a place for imagination of a certain kind: a faculty that could dream up ways of seeing the present as a base for different futures, that could see new subjects appearing in all areas of society, and that could create languages that could draw those subjects into the making of new worlds. Diderot's *Paradoxe sur le comédien* (written 1773–6, published 1830) captured the complexity of the Enlightenment mind in its image of the creative genius, who brings both rational detachment and imaginative empathy to the analysis of others' experience and can find forms to represent it which will capture and move others' imaginations. Such an approach produced texts which in their day marshalled tremendous political energies and have continued to provide fuel for interventions in subsequent moments of French and European history.

Jean-Jacques Rousseau (1712–78), self-styled Citizen of Geneva, son of a watchmaker, was the first representative of the republican and democratic spirit to sulk and stumble his way through the salons of Paris and out onto the banners of world-wide revolution. Of all the *philosophes*, his was probably the intellect that used most effectively all the tools of rationalist and emotional rhetoric to argue what was always, as he confessed, an interested case. The effectiveness derived in equal parts from his discursive skills and the fact that what he was saying was what the public wanted to hear: that untrammelled freedom was the right of every man (though not of every woman – *Émile, ou de l'éducation*, 1762, sketched an emancipatory programme for boys, while Émile's sister Sophie was educated for a supporting role) and that societies should be organised with freedom as their foundation.

More than any other of the founding studies of political science offered in the eighteenth century (for example, Montesquieu's *De l'esprit des lois*, 1748), Rousseau's political writings were unrepentantly abstract and idealist. That in no way diminished their appeal to a whole range of interests, with varying discontents and aspirations but a single craving for change. Rousseau articulated the widespread unease at the beginnings of industrialisation and the economic and political changes it brought in its wake. He spoke for an equally widespread – and connected – desire for a new definition of what it is to be human, with an emphasis on spontaneity and emotion rather than calculating reason. Most significant, he gave voice to the aspirations of the Third Estate to share power in a society in which they were no more than marginal. The Italian Marxist Galvano Della Volpe, properly alert to the conservative implications of some parts of Rousseau's work, nevertheless distinguishes him from the bourgeois liberal tradition represented by Locke, Kant, Humboldt and Constant and links him with Marx and Engels as originators of democratic tradition.[8]

Rousseau's career began in 1750, with his prize-winning *Discours sur les sciences et les arts*, considering the question whether the revival of the arts and sciences had helped or hindered the progress of morality. Rejecting others' celebrations of the civilising power of reason, he offered a nostalgic image of primitive simplicity: an ideal natural place from which humanity was inexorably turning away. This figuration of a lost fullness of nature, stripped of religious connotations, was one of Rousseau's major contributions to the Enlightenment project, and also a founding image of Romanticism.[9] He turned nature into an emblem of a different mode of existence which could challenge artificial systems of social privilege. The blissful state of nature reappeared in his *Discours sur l'origine et les fondements de l'inégalité parmi les hommes* (1755), together with a speculative list of the human qualities that went with it. To the features generally posited by other philosophers (memory, imagination, reason, self-interest), Rousseau added compassion (the motor force of social co-operation) and, equally important, the capacity for change. In a speculative account of how humanity surrendered its 'natural' freedom for social enslavement, he blamed the introduction of industry and agriculture. These had led to the specialisation of labour, the hierarchy of employers and workers, the concept of property and the desire to accumulate property.

Whatever its weakness as an account of actual historical process, this narrative worked well as a critical model of the contemporary situation, identifying areas for reform. Rousseau isolated the contradiction needing resolution, between the rights of what has been called the 'possessive individual' (for whom the sense of selfhood is inseparably linked to the ownership of property) and the rights of society as a whole (which guarantees individuals' secure ownership of property, through its laws and policing). This 'possessive individual', a relatively revolutionary subject in Rousseau's own moment, was later to become the bedrock of the Western bourgeois State.[10]

Debate over the mutual duties of kings and subjects must give way to discussion of how the rights of citizens of a State could be regulated. This was the radical thrust of Rousseau's great idealist treatise *Du contrat social* (1762). Its incendiary opening, dealing with the usurped authority of monarchs, introduced an attempt to imagine a social formation whose main priority was to establish the greatest possible measure of individual freedom, using the instrument of law. The key was the revolutionary concept of popular sovereignty: a collective will for the general good to which all members of society agreed to subject themselves. In return, individuals were guaranteed by that sovereign collective will the security of their property and persons.

The *Contrat* is the most rationalist in structure of Rousseau's texts, with its progressive argument, clear categorisation of themes and apparently precise definition and distinction of terms. It is also absolutely dependent on a powerfully imaginative rhetoric, which drives home its assertions and glosses over the flaws in its often specious arguments. The *Contrat* is Rousseau's equivalent of Diderot's *Rêve de d'Alembert*: the dream of Reason, outstripping its present resources but, in its dreaming, helping make a new version of the real. Rousseau imagines what for his impoverished nation is the impossible: that society should be stable and fair and all individuals be able to follow their own desire. He cannot rely on society's members to provide their own regulatory mechanisms, but must import a charismatic Legislator, who will use religion to underpin his authority, and invoke the coercive force of public opinion to regulate private behaviour.

Similar manipulative strategies structure other areas of Rousseau's writing. *Émile, ou de l'éducation* devises a programme that will bring out a boy's 'natural' abilities. The key is the personal relationship that binds the boy's affections to the will of his master. (Book IV of *Émile* includes the *Profession de foi du vicaire savoyard*, another recuperation of religion for Rousseau's own purposes; in this case, to guarantee individual free will and moral responsibility.)

In Rousseau's third great text of 1762, his novel *La Nouvelle Héloïse* (1762), the sleights-of-hand are laid bare. A first half devoted to the representation of the energies liberated by the passionate affair between two dependent subjects, Julie, the aristocrat's daughter, and Saint-Preux, her tutor, is followed by a second movement in which the two are bound into separate places in a more benevolent but still authoritarian system. On the model estate at Clarens, which Julie governs on behalf of her *philosophe* husband, Wolmar, individual feeling is turned to serve social purpose. If Wolmar is the Legislator of the *Contrat social*, then Julie acts like the religious apparatus that mediates the Law, handing out smiles and incentives to the workers on the estate, holding together the little world with the illusions of satisfied desire. In the end, the system proves unviable, unable to satisfy the energies which it exploits. Julie drowns herself, ostensibly to save one of her children but, in the logic of the text, because nothing in the life she has been given to live matches the dreams glimpsed with Saint-Preux. Individual desire, as conceived in Rousseau's novel, cannot in the end, by any manipulation, be reconciled with the competing desires of others. Repressive violence – the death of the desiring subject – is a structural part of rationalist society.

The desiring subject was also the theme of Rousseau's autobiographical writing: *Les Confessions de J. J. Rousseau* (composed at the end of the 1760s, published 1782–9); the three *Dialogues* (composed 1772–6, published 1780–2); and *Les Rêveries du promeneur solitaire* (composed 1776–8, published 1782). These offered the first model of the Romantic subject, defining itself by its wants and pain and turning refusal into its way of relating to society. The subject retreats into an illusion of self-sufficiency, seeking to build itself an alternative world of words.

In these autobiographical narratives, arguably his most significant contribution to the discourses of French culture, Rousseau, representative of the middle-range middle-classes, invented a new form to articulate a subjectivity that came to self-consciousness as consciousness of limits and denial. His blend of fact and reverie presented ambition, with all its frustrations, evasions, and outbreaks of rebellion. He charted, necessarily, a frenzy which readers more securely positioned in society must categorise as madness. The literary achievement is to have written that 'madness' in a readable form. These narratives are not to be taken as chronicles. The chronicle is certainly there in the apparent subject matter, egocentric, trivial and obsessive: Rousseau's struggle to find a central place in contemporary society, his arguments with fellow *philosophes*, encounters with women, clashes with authorities and institutions. But this is only the scaffolding that contains the growth of a personality. The real content is the writhing emotion: shame, guilt, humiliation, gasping self-justification, exhausted craving for self-annihilation, all generated by the desire to make a mark.

The surface structure of *Les Rêveries du promeneur solitaire* is that of a notebook, a series of jottings on the apparently random train of thought that occupies Rousseau on his botanising rambles. In fact, this is a highly constructed work, whose paragraphs and sentences, as long and complex as any in their nearest model, Montaigne, are a calculated representation of an ego committed to inscribing self in writing, having been denied inscription in history. What emerges is the sense of a would-be imperialising subject who aspires to be everywhere but who finds himself in no place at all. Memory leads him into a labyrinth of unhappy places and emotions: frustration, as the pleasure of a lonely walk in the Alps is abruptly terminated by the sound and sight of a stocking factory in full production; humiliation at being caught out in lies or acts of selfishness; failure to act up successfully to the (double) standards of society; rejection by intellectual equals and social superiors. There is one moment of fantasised perfect happiness, entering into harmony with nature, rocking in a boat on the lake around his beloved Île de Saint-Pierre, dreaming himself to the edge of dissolution in the people-less landscape, skies, rippling water. Julie drowns; 'Rousseau', in his reveries, floats, in a sea of words.

IV   EXPANDING HORIZONS

The Rousseauist movement inwards had its counterpart, throughout the century, in a different set of gestures, which sought to expand the horizons of known geographical space. This led in its turn to equivalent extensions of self-understanding.

In the seventeenth century, the search for new sources of wealth had led to an increase in the activities of explorers and colonisers in Asia (China and Indonesia), South America, Africa and the West Indies, and North America. Jean Chardin's *Journal du voyage du chevalier Chardin en Perse et aux Indes orientales* appeared in 1686. The baron de La Hontan published his accounts of his travels in Canada from 1704–5 onwards; Tavernier's account of his travels in Turkey, Persia and the Indies (*Les Six Voyages de Jean-Baptiste Tavernier*) appeared around the same time. In 1771, the comte de Bougainville published his account of his epic *Voyage autour du monde*.

Travel books carried into the heart of the Absolute State visions of difference – other customs, laws, religions, moralities – and supplied some of the most transformative themes and images for the *philosophes'* criticism of the state of affairs at home. Montesquieu separated the rationalist and the superstitious elements in Islam, and used each in turn to attack the follies of Christian France (*Lettres persanes*). Voltaire's Chinese Sage fronted attacks on the Christian God, arguing for tolerance and commitment to the general social good; his Japanese ridiculed religious sectarianism; his Greek gardener and Turkish pasha politely debated the dividing line between personal freedom and the rights of the State (*Dictionnaire philosophique*: articles 'Catéchisme chinois', 'Catéchisme du japonais', 'Catéchisme du jardinier'). Less-developed societies in the Americas or the Pacific islands provided images of a 'state of nature' which not only fuelled the debate on the best form of social organisation for natural man, but encouraged the drawing of comic contrasts between the man of nature and the man of modern

France. Diderot's pale missionary and bronzed Tahitian (*Supplé-ment au Voyage de Bougainville*) are out of the same drawer as Voltaire's handsome young Huron, whose robustly comic sexual exploits are a vivid contrast to the pallid prudery of French counts (*L'Ingénu*, 1767).

Nearer the end of the century, a more complex set of projections in the marquis de Sade's novel *Aline et Valcour* (written 1786–9, published 1795) drew a contrast between the oppressive society of pre-Revolutionary France and the worlds in which the younger generation might find refuge. For the journey into unknown territory, which is the unknown of France's future, Sade offered two scenarios. At worst, there was the savage kingdom of Butua on the cannibal coast of Africa; at best, the happy community organised by Zamé, half-European, half-native, benevolent hereditary governor of the island of Tamoa in the latitudes of the Friendly Islands. In Sade's Utopia, the ideal was a protected enclave which allowed a maximum of personal freedom, with savage instincts held in check by a minimum of direction so that the pleasures and comforts of society could safely be enjoyed. Like Rousseau, Sade recognised that the threat to the ideal lay in the premises on which it was constructed. The individual right to the satisfaction of desire runs up against the equal rights of other desiring individuals. The greatest threat that can be envisaged by Zamé, son of the European officer who colonised the island, is the advent of another European coloniser, in search of gain. The possessive individual of Enlighten-ment stalks every page of Sade's texts, where the greatest monster that can be envisaged is the one with his own face.

Exploring other (people's) countries, expanding moral horizons, and filling the private and public purse, are related activities in which writers took considerable interest. In 1734, Voltaire's *Lettres philosophiques*, looking to England, drew a rosy picture of a world in which economic exchange could be the foundation of a humane society. Two years later, he sent his friends his poetic eulogy of luxury (*Le Mondain*, 1736). His mid-century *Candide* (1759), charting the naive hero's confrontations with the possessors of money and power, was less optimistic. The black slave lying by the Paraguayan roadside, arm and leg chopped off for trying to escape from the sugar plantations of the Jesuit colonisers, marks the point where the Enlightenment began to question its faith in the world it had helped create.

In the latter part of the century, as public energies began to be harnessed to a national goal – the making of a colonial Empire – the moral dilemma was starkly exposed. The *Histoire philosophique et politique du commerce et des établissements des Européens dans les deux Indes*, edited by the abbé Raynal (1713–96) with the primary aim of encouraging more and more successful colonisation, brought together the issues of the pre-Revolutionary moment: trade, politics and philosophy.[11] Raynal, who had made his money in the slave trade and subsequently rejected it, was connected with the salon of the baron d'Holbach and frequented the salon of the King's Finance Minister, Necker. Diderot collaborated on the first edition, dated 1770. A revised edition appeared in 1772; altogether, there were at least 17 editions between 1772 and 1780. A third, more scandalous version, in which Diderot took even more of a hand, went into 17 editions between 1781 and 1787 – having been condemned by the Parlement in 1781 for its attacks on Church and monarchy. Raynal's work attacked the wars of conquest conducted by States and by religious interests and argued that they were far less effective than the peaceful humanitarian penetration of countries by trade. The whole enterprise only fell from public sight when the post-Revolutionary State embarked on a second wave of territorial conquest.

The final horizon of all the writing of the Enlightenment is an economic one.[12] None of the *philosophes* is unaware of the economic imperatives which underlie the reconstruction of the French State and its subjects. Detailed debates are left to the emerging specialists, the Physiocrats, who began as individual contributors of economic articles in the *Encyclopédie* in the mid-1750s and later became a coherent group, developing a shared economic doctrine which presented agriculture as the primary source of wealth (François Quesnay, *Tableau économique*, 1758; Mirabeau *père*, *L'Ami des hommes*; Lemercier de la Rivière, *L'Ordre naturel et essentiel des sociétés politiques*, 1767; Pierre-Samuel Dupont de Nemours, *Physiocratie*, 1768, and *Abrégé des principes*, 1773). But the new parameters of discussion and the points of most intense debate are everywhere in evidence. In his *Dictionnaire philosophique*, Voltaire gave his own uncompromising account:

> Le genre humain, tel qu'il est, ne peut subsister, à moins qu'il n'y ait une infinité d'hommes utiles qui ne possèdent rien du tout; car, certainement, un homme à son aise ne quittera pas sa terre pour venir labourer la vôtre; et, si vous avez besoin d'une paire

de souliers, ce ne sera pas un maître de requêtes qui vous la fera.

[The human race, as it is, cannot continue unless there is an infinite number of useful men with no possessions of their own; a well-to-do man is not going to leave his own estate to come and plough yours; and if you need a pair of shoes, you won't get a lawyer to make you one.]

(article 'Egalité')

With the Enlightenment, writers and books moved out of the study into the open air of a changing social landscape, and writing was itself transformed by the wholesale commitment to participate in change. The fulcrum of that movement, the operative symbol of the great collective engagement, was the monumental multi-volume illustrated *Encyclopédie, ou Dictionnaire raisonné des sciences, des arts et des métiers* (Paris, 1751–72), edited by Diderot and d'Alembert with contributions from the whole philosophical community.[13] The text brought together and presented, for the instruction of the general public, the new knowledge in new fields that was needed to make the new world work.

Useful knowledge generated useful writing. In Diderot's Tree of Knowledge, drawn at the threshold of the text to illustrate the changed hierarchies and categories of knowledge, the highest place went to the study of the human world. History came first, in the form of the history of human work (the mechanical arts and sciences) and then civil history, setting up a new hierarchy of workers, scholars and kings. The imaginative arts followed, and then the rational sciences, especially philosophy. Men of letters were presented as agents of civilisation. Theology, revealed knowledge and ecclesiastical history slipped to the bottom of the tree. As important as the actual knowledge offered was the model the text gave of how and why knowledge is best acquired. The idea of progress – the permanently-expanding horizon of a world with less suffering and more justice – was to come through a working collaboration of creative, practical, open minds across the whole diversity of disciplines. The age of reason was also the age of dream.

V   A NOVEL SUBJECT

The books that shaped the reading publics of the Enlightenment and the future citizens of the Revolutionary State were more than still-life displays of ideas. They constructed novel worlds of discourse with which readers were beckoned to engage, beginning in their own private worlds a process of transformation which engaged with the transformations of the public sphere.

The theatre was still the most popular form of high culture in a society where illiteracy, though decreasing, remained around 50 per cent.[14] In comedy, Pierre Carlet de Chamblain de Marivaux (1688–1763) presented games of misunderstanding, subterfuge and caprice, whose strength lay in the elegance of their bantering exchanges (*La Surprise de l'amour*, 1722; *La Double Inconstance*, 1723; *Le Jeu de l'amour et du hasard*, 1730; *L'École des mères*, 1732). Nearer to the revolutionary moment, Pierre-Augustin Caron de Beaumarchais (1732–99) invoked the liberating possibilities of the comic mode. Neither *Le Barbier de Séville, ou la précaution inutile* (1775) nor its sequel, *Le Mariage de Figaro, ou la folle journée* (1784), were the revolutionary texts that a changed political context would later allow Beaumarchais to claim them. But there was certainly a sense of freedom in the games played by children and valets against fathers, guardians and masters, in the easy colloquial dialogues and in the introduction of sub-plots, tableaux and spectacle.

Voltaire introduced new themes into classical tragic form with plays attacking religious fanaticism, authoritarianism and intolerance, subjects taken from national history rather than ancient myth, and characters whose sensibility, intellect and ethics were resolutely modern (*Zaïre*, 1732; *Mahomet ou le fanatisme*, 1742; *Mérope*, 1743). But a form constructed to create intense psychological effects was less appropriate to convey the thrill of political and philosophical debate. After the mid-century, Diderot experimented with prose drama to stage the dilemmas of bourgeois family life, on the model of the English dramatist Lillo's *The London Merchant* (*Le Fils naturel, ou les Épreuves de la vertu*, published 1757; *Le Père de famille*, 1758). His theory was more interesting than his practice (see *Entretiens sur 'Le Fils naturel'*, composed 1757; *Discours sur la poésie dramatique*, 1758; and *Paradoxe sur le comédien*, written over the period 1769–73).

But as the century proceeded, prose fiction took over from theatre as the place where society found its preferred representations of itself. Despite censorship and copyright prohibitions, texts became more widely available for purchase or for loan from the *cabinets de lecture* which appeared from the 1740s, and by the eve of the Revolution were disseminated through Paris and the provinces.[15]

Narrative pleasure – the freedom and the fun of story-spinning – sped the progress of Enlightenment. Comic novels such as *Le Diable boiteux* (1707) by Alain-René Lesage (1668–1747) or Diderot's *Les Bijoux indiscrets* (1748) offered sheer entertainment. So did the short stories popular from the beginning of the century: the fairy-stories developed by Marie-Catherine d'Aulnoy, Charles Perrault, Jeanne Marie Le Prince de Beaumont, oriental tales and historical tales.[16] The number of collections and individual tales printed more than doubled from the middle of the century onwards, offering light, witty, often licentious fantasies (Crébillon fils, *Le Sopha*, 1742; Jacques Cazotte, *Le Diable amoureux*, 1772; Dominique Vivant Denon, *Point de lendemain*, 1777) as well as the moral tales published by writers such as Marmontel from the late 1760s to the end of the 1770s.

In the hands of Voltaire, the genre became both entertaining and enlightening. In Voltaire's fantastic landscapes, the enemy's ideas, stripped of mystificatory glosses, satirised to absurdity, confessed their lack of substance. The black comedy of *Candide ou l'Optimisme* (1759), that masterpiece of condensation, is a catalogue of the brutalities out of which human experience is woven, a tissue of anguish which gives the lie to philosophers and men of religion who chatter on of Optimism and Providence. In the very structure of his narrative, Voltaire rejected the prejudice of an ordered universe controlled by an omnipotent, reasonable author. The quest of Candide for his beloved, that most traditional of storylines, runs into sand. There is an expulsion from Eden, much crucifixion, but no Redemption. The action zigzags frenetically across the globe, punctuated by earthquakes, shipwrecks, volcanic eruptions, cannonshot. In *Le Taureau blanc* (1774), Voltaire's great Old Testament satire, linguistically the wittiest of his tales, kings, priests and prophets line up to confess their day is done. The enlightened proto-feminist Princess Amaside, tired of the deceptions practised by the father-narrators of her world, demands tales she can believe, true tales that might have some meaning for a young woman whose father is about to cut her lover's throat.

But arguably the most significant form of pleasure experienced by the eighteenth-century reader was the pleasure of self-discovery. The concept of the private subject gained ground with the growth of the fashion for private reading and the idea of a personal relationship between reader and book. Reading novels with his father, according to the opening pages of the *Confessions*, was for Rousseau the moment of first self-awareness. Rousseau tried to direct in his turn the way his readers were shaped as reading subjects, paternally pre-empting their responses in his prefaces, using forms such as the letter-novel to engage their sympathies, demanding they read in a new way, not as sophisticates but as seekers after virtue. The private libraries of ordinary citizens offer evidence of fan-like devotion in response.[17]

The Church fought hard to resist the shift of power from pulpit to publishing house.[18] The abbé Armand-Pierre Jacquin (*Entretiens sur les romans*, 1755) dismissed the novel as a trivial genre, pure entertainment. The feudal loyalties of epic narrative were a better lesson than private loves: epic elevated the soul, while novels softened the heart. But already in 1734, the abbé Nicolas Lenglet-Dufresnoy (*De l'usage des romans, où l'on fait voir leur utilité et leurs différents caractères*) had sold the pass, declaring that the aim of the novel was to represent in fictional images the ordinary course of human life and draw from them useful instruction. Novels analysed the passions, he argued, and helped bridge the gap between the tumultuous instincts of individuals and the State's concern with social order.

Novelists emphasised their efforts towards more realism. Important experiments in narrative voice were made in the 1730s by Crébillon fils (Claude-Prosper Jolyot de Crébillon, 1707–77), the abbé Antoine-François Prévost d'Exiles (1697–1763) and Marivaux. Novels written in first-person forms as memoirs or letters could be seen to carry in themselves the mark of truth. The effectiveness of the device might not be immediately apparent to a twentieth-century reader confronting such lurid narratives as Prévost's *Le Philosophe anglais ou Histoire de Monsieur Cleveland* (1731–9) or *Le Doyen de Killerine* (1735–40), spiced with cannibalism, rotting corpses and incestuous loves. But in other texts, it was clear that a different kind of writing was emerging. At issue was much more than claiming a story was 'true'. In their best applications, these forms were exploited to problematise the idea of narrative 'truth', to open up the notion of 'reality' as a configuration of different perspectives and to explore the way in which individual voice and the collective experience of history and society were related. Emergent individual voices were shown defining themselves in (or sometimes, against) a society increasingly regulated by codes and conventions. It is in this way that the novel of this period can first be defined as 'historical', in that its own narrative structures re-enacted the resistances of contemporary history:

> [T]he thematic evolution of the eighteenth-century French and English novel can be understood as a gradual coming to terms with the complexities of a genuine historical consciousness, one which conceives of the identity of individuals and societies, and the orders of authority that modulate their behaviour, in terms of a continual process of recounting and rearticulation that is regulated by, and derives its authority from, the accumulating context of its own past narratives. Within such a model . . . story and history, are but different faces/phases of the same equation . . . .[19]

Umberto Eco's praise of what he sees as the unique achievements of twentieth-century narrative does the past insufficient credit:

> In our century it has been recognised that novels can be forms of philosophical reflection on the world, a reliable vehicle for a form of truth, which is probably the influence of existentialism from Kierkegaard onwards. Our way to understand the world now is a narrative way; in psychology, perception, in artificial intelligence, in history, what we are doing is to wrap our experience in the form of a narrative. A novel is no longer a way of fictionally making variations on our experience but a way to exercise our fundamental cognitive ability.

> (*Guardian*, 14 August 1993)

Earliest of the memoir novels was Lesage's 12-volume *Histoire de Gil Blas de Santillane* (published in three stages, 1715, 1724, 1735). Set in an unconvincing Spain, the first-person picaresque narrative offered insights into the moral and political evolution of France from the death of Louis XIV in 1715. Gil Blas represented a new kind of hero, fit for an age of change: a determined survivor, talented, flexible, ready to serve any patron who chanced along.

Missing from Lesage's text was the differentiation of voices that Marivaux brought to novels such as *La Vie de Marianne* (1731–42) or *Le Paysan parvenu* (1734–5). Marianne constructed her narrative of herself in a double perspective, writing as an older woman of secure social position looking back on her unformed adolescence in the twilight land outside society's elite. Marivaux's reputation as the founder of the novel of psychological realism rests on his observation of the tensions and embarrassments generated from the different realities in which social groups live, and the skill with which he evoked how personality is constructed out of these scarring moments when boundaries are crossed.

In the more complex memoir-narrative frame invented by Prévost for the *Histoire du chevalier des Grieux et de Manon Lescaut* (1731), des Grieux poured his love-tale into the tolerant ear of the Man of Quality, who then included it in his own *Mémoires* (*Mémoires et aventures d'un homme de qualité qui s'est retiré du monde*, 1728–31). In the fantasy-frame, if nowhere else, an older generation could be shown making room for a younger generation's images of desire. *Les Égarements du cœur et de l'esprit, ou Mémoires de M. de Meilcour* (1736–8), by Crébillon *fils*, was a novel of seduction and education which took a different track, showing the young man made into the bearer of the corrupt values of his elders. The much later memoir of Diderot's nun (*La Religieuse*), a multi-functional narrative, played productively on the border between realistic fiction and historical fact. Diderot's brilliant construction of the perspective of the victim in a closed, repressive world was conceived originally as a practical joke on a *philosophe* friend. The friend, like the reader who shares his place as recipient of the text, was fired to real-life action by the 'authentic' note of 'Suzanne's' plea.

The narrative perspectives of the letter-novel offered equally varied opportunities to explore the situation of individuals in the world of the historical real. The text might take the form of a one-sided correspondence, with the imputed author often female. Where the real-life author was male, this can set up interesting tensions for the modern critical reader. In Crébillon *fils*'s *Lettres de Mme la marquise de M*** au comte de R**** (1732), the woman writing is presented as self-confessed victim of her own passions, pleading, self-recriminating, and utterly dependent on her lover. A more resilient female voice appeared in Françoise de Graffigny's *Lettres d'une Péruvienne* (1747), purportedly written by a woman taken into slavery and transported to Europe, initially illiterate and unable to speak French, to a betrothed (her brother) left behind in Peru. This writing is less a means of communication than a way to construct a way of surviving in an alien discourse. The writer of the letters that make up the novel by Marie-Jeanne Riccoboni (1713–92), *Lettres de mistriss Fanni Butlerd à Milord Charles Alfred Caitombridge* (1757), seems in contrast a more self-indulgent figure, holding up in her letters a mirror of her sensitive soul.

It has been a critical convention to describe novels of this sentimental cast, often considered the special province of women writers, as limited to the private sphere. This underplays the significance of the substantial increase in the numbers and output of women writing in the eighteenth century. Feminist criticism has pointed out that the eighteenth century was increasingly aware of the dependence of the public sphere on the private. When Marie-Jeanne Riccoboni or Isabelle de Charrière (1740–1805, author of *Lettres de Mistriss Henley publiées par son amie*, 1784; *Caliste, ou continuation des lettres écrites de Lausanne*, 1787) analysed the plight of women in love or caught in unhappy marriages, they were implicitly questioning the economic and legal order as well as the moral principles on which their world was founded. The legislative structures governing the transmission of property, which operates mainly through marriage and inheritance, assumed that women would accept unquestioningly a dependent and functional role within personal and family relationships. Feminist claims for equality, more eagerly canvassed towards the moment of Revolution, led to challenges to that role, especially with the realisation by Revolutionary politicians of the part that could be played by changes in marriage law in breaking up the great aristocratic family fortunes. The vicissitudes of the long-contested legislative proposals on separation and divorce throughout the Revolution, from the passing of the radical laws permitting separation and divorce (September 1792) to the inauguration in 1804 of Napoleon's highly-conservative *Code Civil*, which removed the right of divorce and returned women to the tutelage of fathers and husbands, are a story in themselves.[20]

It was, however, male authors who made most explicit how the politics of gender connected with other political configurations. Within a framework of two different but interconnected stories, written up by a number of correspondents, Montesquieu's *Lettres persanes* gave glimpses of the multiplicity of perspectives and interests which constitute a society in transition. Two Persians, travelling in Europe, write home of their confrontations with philosophical, religious, social and political habits far removed from their own. In the defamiliarising and liberating play of fresh perspectives, both the travellers and the Europe in which they travel are summoned into new positions. But as the journey runs on, its excitements are displaced by the tale of blacker developments back in Persia. Hints of rebellion in the harem – that private space of absolute power – filter into the Chief Eunuch's letters to his master, who answers with repression. The end of both journeys towards freedom comes with a denunciatory suicide note to the master from his favourite slave, Roxane, who has led the palace revolt. Rousseau's *La Nouvelle Héloïse* also identified the harem as the heart of the ordered society. Julie and Saint-Preux might think they have a right to the passion that flowers in the 'private' space marked out by their letters, Julie's boudoir and their own bodies. But that space is owned by Julie's father before her marriage and thereafter by her husband, and is the foundation of social structures in which fathers and husbands play the dominant part. Choderlos de Laclos (1741–1803), whose letter-novel *Les Liaisons dangereuses* (1782) was set in satirical relationship to Rousseau's love-story, rejected the possibility of maintaining social order on the presumption that intelligent women could be confined within traditional limits. The letter-intrigues fomented by the marquise de Merteuil, Laclos's equivalent of Montesquieu's Roxane, bring the world of the salons to near-destruction.

A unique exploration of the relations between history and story was offered in Diderot's *Jacques le fataliste* (written over a period, between the late 1760s and 1778, and first published in full in 1796), modelled on Lawrence Sterne's *Tristram Shandy* (1760–7). The text presents a disorderly universe held together only by repeated assertions of human will and determined (in every sense of the word) practical action. In this narrative of a journey with no beginning and no end, where digression is the rule of the game, the disembodied narrative voice tosses the reader to and fro in time and space. The narrative oscillates between third-person chronicle and the vivid direct speech of others who elbow their way in to tell their own tales. Jacques, the servant, is a demi-God, a mini-Diderot, who also dictates the tempo and direction of the journey, holding it suspended while he spins his tales to an enthralled master. Debates about predestination, determinism and freewill, good and evil, serve literally as pretexts to fill the time marked out by the journey. The real issue is how much human voices shape the world of time and space, and the answer is in the text. 'Reality' is an interplay of human voices, physical needs, sensations of pleasure and pain.

What most fascinates Jacques the servant, who is responsible for keeping the world going, is how communication works and, especially, how communication determines action. Effective communication, Diderot establishes, lies in words that are reinforced by body language and also in the way the patterns of narrative are spun. The clever spinner of the narrative thread can keep the rest of the world dangling.

Prose fiction, a genre still unformed, offered an open cultural space to explore the conflicts of established and emergent subject positions in eighteenth-century France, and their different sensibilities and moral priorities. Choosing whose story to tell, and inventing the discourse to bring the tale home to the reader, were processes which involved writers in both social and textual fabrication. Prévost, claiming in the Preface to *Manon Lescaut* to have written a moral guide, made it clear that 'morality' was in process of change. The conduct his books approved represented a shift from the severity of older generations to a gentler standard, founded not on Law but on heart, a cult of sensibility which appealed to and created a new readership. He described them: reasonable minds and sensitive hearts, not overstrict, but inclined to virtue, wisdom and truth. In this secularised renegotation of the demands of private desire and public order, the policing role of pulpit and confessional was taken over by the text and its readers.

The cult of sensibility was reinforced in the 1740s by the importation of the fictions of Samuel Richardson (*Pamela*, 1740–1; and *Clarissa*, 1747–9), and later by those of Lawrence Sterne (*A Sentimental Journey through France and Italy*, 1768), who had themselves been influenced by Prévost and Marivaux.[21] In England, such works were perceived as representing the values of merchant-class culture. In France, the cult of sensibility engaged aristocracy as well as bourgeoisie. Diderot's *Éloge de Richardson* (1761) praised a perspective that gave priority to the close-to-home, the everyday and the middle range of society. Richardson's passions, Diderot said, were those of the ordinary reader, and his morality, embodied in vivid, dramatic tableaux and situations, swept readers into empathetic recognition of conflicts and choices that were also their own. Or that they liked to think were theirs: as Diderot recognised, fiction was not simply a way of describing the movement of the world but a means to encourage it into different directions.

One strand of the eighteenth-century novel related, then, to a new sensibility. This was open to passion but also to tenderness, sympathy, and compassion. Its most pleasurable expression was in suffering, and it prized the 'natural' qualities of spontaneity and sincerity. It began its self-definition with the body and the heart, not abstract reason, and its language reflected these priorities. Without necessarily breaking with the grammar and vocabulary of classicism, it pushed these to the limits. Sometimes it went beyond, finding communication in sighs and tears or in silence and gesture. Alongside this strand, another represented the traditional aristocratic culture of the salons, its exclusive codes, strict hierarchies and competitive exchanges. Somewhere between the two ran the multicoloured threads of the libertine novel, that surfaced mid-century as a celebration of pleasures of the body too frank to be accommodated to salon or 'natural' sensibilities. The genre ranged from the light eroticism of Charles Pinot Duclos (*Histoire de Madame de Luz*, 1740; *Les Confessions du comte de* ***, 1741), André-Robert Andrea de Nerciat (*Félicia, ou Mes Fredaines*, 1775) and Louvet de Couvray's popular Faublas cycle, to the more pornographic formulations of the marquis d'Argens's *Thérèse philosophe* (*c.* 1748) and the writings of the marquis de Sade. All of these different discourses of feeling had their own markers.

The cut and thrust of the salon world is well exemplified in Crébillon *fils*'s *Les Égarements du cœur et de l'esprit* (1736–8), the initiation of youth by cynical experience. Language is the instrument of the seventeen-year-old Meilcour's seduction. His gauche silences contrast with the rakish Madame de Lursay's verbal skills, as she teases, charms, and plays on his adolescent passion and fragile self-esteem. Such language never means what it says. It sets a premium on polite forms and correct procedures; within these, it deploys self-interest and spite. Salon discourse is not the language of the heart, which Meilcour's mentor, Monsieur de Versac, dismisses as novelists' jargon. Love in the salons is a transaction and its authentic language is that of the coldly reasoned self-interest in which Versac sets out for the younger man the road to survival. He must disguise his true thoughts and learn to penetrate the disguises of others. He must speak well of himself – modesty is no asset. Most of all, he must speak: the ambition of the salon subject is to be a controlling voice, dominating the conversation, with constant, empty, spiteful chatter.

In Laclos's *Les Liaisons dangereuses*, love is a 'battleground' for a test of individual strength. Theatrical and martial imagery grounds a salon discourse which defines an affair as a power game in which the object is to destroy the opponent. The weapons are wit, reason, familiarity with the rules of the game, and, crucially, a sense of style. With the right stylistic techniques, skilful players will construct a mask to disguise their own intentions, and direct others into supporting roles. Laclos's Marquise speaks with the manipulative voice of the repressed feminine subject whose intellect has been sharpened to perfection by two centuries of silent observation and analysis of the most sophisticated society in Europe.

In contrast, Louvet de Couvray's Faublas cycle (*Une année de la vie du chevalier de Faublas*, 1787; *Six semaines de la vie du chevalier de Faublas*, 1788; *La Fin des amours du chevalier de Faublas*, 1790) declines to take the salon game seriously. Louvet chronicles the sexual and social initiation of his sixteen-year-old Adonis, who wreaks innocent havoc in the salons of Paris, disguised as a young woman, and in his first year in the capital accumulates three mistresses and a wife. Unquestioned stereotypes move in a world of confident clichés in which men enjoy the attack and women the surrender. Louvet's prose style echoes the badinage of eighteenth-century comedy, scattered with titillating euphemisms, evoking with nudges and winks one seduction scene after another, drawing back discreetly from any substantial utterance.

The novel of worldliness, constructed out of closed aristocratic codes, spoke with a self-confidence at complete odds with the relationship of its speakers to history. The language of bourgeois sensibility was also codified. It signalled a body fearful and vulnerable in the present, but with the future in its grasp. Tears, sighs and wounds were the marks of suffering which eventually would demand compensation. The chains of passion, like the chains that bind the multitude in Rousseau's *Contrat social*, would justify rebellion. What gathered strength was a rhetoric of the victim which joined with those other Enlightenment rhetorics of nature and justice. Between them, they would transform the voice of submission into voices demanding power.

The degree of political radicalism in these alternative rhetorics of feeling varied with the time and place from which an author wrote. Marivaux's discourse shows how easily that which seems outside and different can be accommodated into established codes. The sensibility evoked in *La Vie de Marianne* relates to a body less moved by the sufferings of passion and far more sensitive to the pinpricks and putdowns of social exclusion. The voice Marivaux creates for his heroine brings a gossipy lack of seriousness into her experience, an assurance that pains can be mended: this is embarrassment, not humiliation. It operates in a light, fast-moving syntax of short, easy phrases, a self-confessed 'feminine prattle' ('le babil féminin'). Its distinctive feature is an emphasis on the small, precise details of everyday impressions and responses which enable pain to be first focused and then defused.

Prévost's *Manon Lescaut* is more serious drama, which celebrates simultaneously the chains of passion and the chains of authoritarian society, winding both round the fragile, ideal beauty of Manon, as she appears in the opening pages of the text in the prison wagon marked for deportation to the New World. Language here opens up the wider implications of a love affair which is lyrical in the precise sense of the term: it uses techniques that inscribe particular experience as the generic experience of a generation. Manon and des Grieux are representatives of volatile areas of contemporary society whose coming together spawns images of revolt. The Chevalier is the bright younger son of small aristocracy, destined for a career in the Church far beneath his qualities, while Manon is the ambitious young woman stepping from the unmapped fringe of society onto the stage of history. The rationalist analyses of Marianne have no place here. Des Grieux prefers a syntax that creates confusion and self-deceptions, inflating his grievance along with his dream. He builds an image of desire so far removed from possible achievement that it can only be bridged by a delicate language of silence, intense yearning, suffering and desperate, futile physical gesture.

Delicacy is not in evidence in the first part of Rousseau's *La Nouvelle Héloïse*. The precious fire, flames and poison that figure the first experience of sensual love are piled together in a pounding rhetoric that collapses under its own weight into sighs, groans and swoons (in, for example, Saint-Preux's account of the couple's first kiss, Part I, Letter 14). Rousseau's text is a particularly good illustration of the ambivalence of certain rhetorics of suffering. Saint-Preux presents himself primarily as the victim of his passion for his employer's daughter. But in the process of exploring this passion, what he also discloses is his imperialising ego, inventing itself and moving itself to the centre of its world as it articulates the pain of its desire. Saint-Preux, hiding in Julie's boudoir to see his forbidden love, expresses his feelings in language which marginalises Julie, making of her the mere pretext of writing, fetishised away into the scents and softnesses of the cap, kerchief, dressing-gown, slippers, corset that surround him (Part I, Letter 54). At the same time, his rhetoric foregrounds the suitor's 'I' and his devouring sensuality, with a syntax built on the repetition of first-person verbs of feeling that culminates in the delighted recognition that the instruments of power are now to hand: '[J]e te vois, je te sens partout, je te respire avec l'air que tu as respiré. . . . Quel bonheur d'avoir trouvé de l'encre et du papier!' ['I can see you, feel you everywhere, breathe you in with the air you've breathed. . . . what luck to have found paper and ink!']. And it concludes by writing into the rising rhythms of its sentences the approaching footstep which could as well be Julie's father as Julie herself, thrilling less with love than the anticipation of being discovered by the enemy at the heart of his citadel: 'Ô désirs! ô craintes! ô palpitations cruelles! . . .' ['Desire! Fear! How cruelly my heart throbs!'].

The language of feeling developed in Diderot's *La Religieuse* makes its self-assertion in more modest terms. Diderot draws the physical and moral effects of sexual repression produced by the enforced chastity of the convents to which European society consigned younger sons and daughters. With simple, dramatic lucidity, the narrator evokes the desperation of an adolescent self recognising her atrophied sensibilities. Suzanne describes herself slipping into unreason, swooning into unconsciousness as she is forced to the altar, sliding unthinkingly into the manners and gestures of the community whenever she puts on her habit. As with Saint-Preux in Julie's boudoir, the most intimate feelings are shown to be responses to environment. But environment for Suzanne is not a matter of choice, and what she slips into in the convent is not a pleasurable welter of sensation but an icy void of being. As she waits in her cell to discover if the court will release her from her vows, she reports in near-clinical terms, and short, breathless phrases, not emotions but the physical symptoms of panic: '[J]'étouffais, je ne pouvais pas me plaindre, je croisais mes bras sur ma tête, je m'appuyais le front tantôt contre un mur, tantôt contre l'autre; je voulais me reposer sur mon lit, mais j'en étais empêchée par un battement de cœur: il est sûr que j'entendais battre mon cœur, et qu'il faisait soulever mon vêtement.' ['I was suffocating, but I could not speak, I crossed my arms over my head, leaned my forehead against one wall and then another; I tried to lie down on the bed but the beating of my heart prevented me: I could in truth hear my heart beating, lifting my clothing.'].

VI   REVOLUTIONISING THE SUBJECT

The writing of the last decade of the eighteenth century, in the rising tide of Revolution, has often been marginalised in academic histories. Béatrice Didier blames the omission on timidity, which can take many forms: reluctance to defend political revolt, unwillingness to accept interdisciplinary perspectives, and the determination to limit 'literature' to polished texts, which disadvantages the swift compositions of revolutionary moments.[22] Recognition has been reserved for works which appear least touched by the Revolutionary wind, especially the memoirs, novels, and treatises of exiled aristocracy, and those which can shelter under the label of 'pre-Romanticism', pointing away from the moment of disorder.

The Revolutionary decade saw a plethora of printed texts. The freedom of the press decreed by the Revolution (Article 11 of the *Déclaration des droits de l'homme et du citoyen*) started the breakdown of the censorship system. This had major implications for the marketplace. By March 1791, guild printing and bookselling monopolies were abolished, bankrupting the old Parisian publishing houses but making room for other publishers of different kinds of books. The market shifted towards novels and scientific works (especially after 1796, under the Directory) and the ephemera – pamphlets and journals – which were the lifeblood of the Revolution. By the time the censor returned, with Napoleon, the number of Parisian printers had quadrupled and that of booksellers and publishers had tripled.[23]

The legislative processes of the Revolution kept the presses turning. They produced the *cahiers de doléances* that were the prelude to the opening of the Estates-General in May 1789, and then the journals of the factional clubs and societies and the new popular press that disseminated the great speeches and debates of the various stages of the revolutionary process: the Constituent Assembly (July 1789–September 1791) that established the constitutional monarchy; the Legislative Assembly (October 1791–September 1792) that dealt with food riots, the war with Austria and the overthrow of the King; the Convention (September 1792–July 1794) that tried the King and executed him (21 January 1793), purged the Girondins and witnessed the rise and fall of the Jacobins; the Thermidorean Convention (July 1794–October 1795) and the Directory (October 1795–November 1799), which saw the triumphs of the Revolutionary armies under Napoleon and ended with the Bonapartist coup d'état; and finally the Consulate.

The orators of the Revolution had their speeches printed verbatim in *Le Moniteur*, from November 1989 onwards, in the journals of their own factions, or as pamphlets. The elegant speeches of the reforming aristocrat, the comte de Mirabeau (1749–91), appeared in a 5-volume edition (*Collection complète des travaux de M. Mirabeau l'aîné à l'Assemblée nationale, précédée de tous les discours et ouvrages du même auteur prononcés ou publiés en Provence, pendant le cours des élections*, 1791). Jean-Paul Marat (1744–93), whose treatise *The Chains of Slavery* appeared in London in 1774 and who edited the popular broadsheet *L'Ami du Peuple* from September 1789, spoke and wrote with robust but contained violence, cultivating a plain but dignified rhetoric aimed at empowering the *sans-culottes* (see, for example, his 'Dénonciation contre Necker', November 1789). The oratory of Louis-Antoine-Léon de Saint-Just (1767–94) was marked by contrasts: cool, authoritative philosophical demonstration, informal personal address, flashes of Biblical lyricism and fury. His was the devastating phrase that sealed the fate of the King: 'On ne peut point régner innocemment' ['There is no such thing as an innocent ruler'] (13 November 1792). Broadsheets and popular press continued the liberation of language and ideas begun in the Assembly: for example, Jacques-René Hébert's virulently comic anti-clerical *Père Duchesne* (1790–4), or the *Journal de la liberté de la presse* (later, *Le Tribun du peuple ou le Défenseur des droits de l'homme*), published 1794–6 by the Utopian populist François-Noël Babeuf ('Gracchus'), the most ardent advocate of the abolition of private property.[24]

Changed political conditions gave fresh energy to theatre, with audiences who brought their political preoccupations from the streets into the auditorium.[25] Corrupt monarchy was the target in Marie-Joseph Chénier's *Charles IX ou la Saint-Barthélemy* (later retitled *Charles IX ou l'École des rois*), staged in November 1789, a five-act tragedy in verse, claimed by its author to be the first national tragedy written in French. Four years later, under the Terror, Sylvain Maréchal made a symbolic clean sweep of established authority in his popular *Jugement dernier des rois* (October 1793), with a spectacular closing scene in which an erupting volcano blew all the monarchs of Europe, and the Pope, off the face of the earth. A proliferation of new theatres was encouraged by the promulgation in January 1791 of a law ending the exclusive privileges of the Comédie Française and establishing authors' copyright. Freedom was two-edged. The Théâtre de la Nation was closed on 3 September

1793 and the authors arrested for performing 'aristocratic' plays. As with many things, the old order was restored after Napoleon's coup d'état. The Comédie Française was re-established. In June 1806, monopolies were restored and the theatre became the object of government subsidy and control.

The form of most interest was still prose fiction, applied to ever more varied purpose. Already in 1784, Louis-Sébastien Mercier (1740–1814) had said that the novel should deal not only with the analysis of the individual human heart but with the history and ambitions of nations, or should sketch philosophico-political utopias (*Mon bonnet de nuit*, 1784). Mercier's own important prose works (his Utopian novel *L'An 2440, rêve s'il en fut jamais*, 1771; and the anecdotes and observations of his documentary *Le Tableau de Paris*, 1781) expanded with every fresh – and frequent – edition to map the changing manners and ambitions of the time. Madame de Staël's *Essai sur les fictions* (1795) argued that the novel should probe the ways of the 'ordinary' human heart, reserving a special place to the Rousseauist voice of the lonely, passionate soul. Sade's *Idée sur les romans* (1800) demanded realistically written versions of human nature at its least ordinary, under the pressure of extreme circumstance. A final glance at four writers, two who experienced exile and two who stayed in France, indicates some of the ways in which the subject of fiction was positioned between the Revolutionary decade and the turn of the century to counter-revolution.

The writing of Donatien-Alphonse-François, marquis de Sade (1740–1814), presented one very distinctive reformulation of the aristocratic ethos under the pressure of revolutionary change.[26] A voracious reader of Enlightenment philosophies and fictions, Sade generated texts that were shockingly representative of their time. His production casts its shadow over the popular mode of the Gothic novel that appeared at the end of the century (1797–1800), encouraged by translations from the English of Ann Radcliffe and 'Monk' Lewis. Censored and driven underground until their recuperation at the end of the nineteenth century, Sade's figurations of human nature are in their own way as significant as the idyllic versions offered by Rousseau or his best-selling disciple Bernardin de Saint-Pierre (1737–1814) (*Paul et Virginie*, 1788).

As an aristocrat imprisoned under both ancien régime and Revolution, Sade experienced both as subject and as object the effects of absolute power. The theme informs all his work: the novel-chronicle *Les 120 Journées de Sodome*, written in the Bastille in 1784–5 (first published in 1904); the memoir-novel parodies, *Justine ou les malheurs de la vertu* (1787, 1791) and *La Nouvelle Justine, ou les malheurs de la vertu, suivie de l'Histoire de Juliette, sa sœur, ou les prospérités du vice* (1797); the letter-novel *Aline et Valcour* (1793), a family romance intertwining sentimentality and incest; plays; *nouvelles* (*La Philosophie dans le boudoir*, 1795, with its pamphlet-digression on sexual freedom, 'Français, encore un effort si vous voulez être républicains'); and short stories (*Les Crimes de l'amour*, 1800). Sade explored the limits of the human capacity for the self-serving pursuit of desire, and declared them to be non-existent. He ransacked old and new societies impartially to construct scenarios which would allow the strong to do as they liked and confirm the powerlessness of the weak. The feudal dungeons of medieval fortresses, the family where the father's word is law, the web of corrupt regulations spun by the institutions of the modern State (lawcourts, Church, banks) are all safe havens for fantasies of absolute power. In Sade's nightmares of Enlightenment rationality, the would-be omnipotent subject organises and categorises with obsessive precision the details of its dreams, pacing its excitement with calculated changes of register, counterpointing tableaux of debauch with philosophical disquisitions on nature, virtue and crime. The total abjection of the Other is the condition of existence for a subject who will be sole authorising centre of his universe, or who will be nothing, and whose writing style is a monstrous celebration of the observing eye and controlling discourse of the omnipotent author.

Sade offered a version of aristocratic power cast to the margins. Nicolas-Edmé Restif de la Bretonne (1734–1806) was his political opposite, the representative of a marginal group that the Revolution brought closer to the centre.[27] These were the children of the relatively wealthy peasantry, newly-educated and come to the cities to make a career, who helped constitute the middle ground in which revolutionary change was codified and circumscribed by Napoleon in 1804. Restif characterised his sense of himself as having both a private and a public dimension, being a very ordinary representative life lived at a time of great events. He claimed Rousseau for his model, but was acutely aware of their difference: '[J]e disséquerai l'homme ordinaire, comme J.-J. Rousseau a disséqué le grand-homme' ['I shall dissect ordinary man, as J.-J. Rousseau dissected greatness'] (Dédicace à MOI, *Monsieur Nicolas*).

Restif's work offers an instance of how the larger cultural and political themes of the Revolution were assimilated and transformed by a key sector of the Revolutionary crowd.

In Restif's writing, documentary and fiction fed on each other. His 16-volume autobiography *Monsieur Nicolas ou Le Cœur humain dévoilé* (1794–7) charted his journey from the family farm at Saci to boarding-school with the Jansenist Brothers and to printshops in Auxerre and finally Paris. From this diverse background he acquired the skills of observation and story-telling he would later bring to his accounts of the Paris streets. Precise observer and cataloguer of the types and species of the city environment, mixing portraits, tableaux, anecdote and lively dialogue, Restif was a precursor of the Balzacian transformation of the novel into a record of contemporary history. He was in one sense more modern than Balzac, in his constant foregrounding of the process of writing, underlining his awareness that he was engaged in a subjective transformation of history into personal story.

Women are the centre of Restif's work. Much of his writing focused on the organisation of sexuality and the family, which he (like the Napoleonic Code) saw as fundamental to the organisation of the State. The classification and regulation of women in their social and sexual functions – daughter, spinster, wife, mother, whore – were the subject matter of the observations and anecdotes and vivid and vigorous dialogue in *Les Contemporaines* (1780–6), *Les Françaises* (1786), *Le Palais-Royal* (1790), which put the flesh on the bones of the legislative proposals in his *Le Pornographe* (1769), advocating state-run brothels to cement social stability, or in *Le Thesmographe* (1789), sketching new laws on property, marriage and divorce. In all these, securing the status and sexual freedom of men like himself is his first concern. Marriage as bar to sexual freedom is the theme of the novels *La Femme infidèle* (1786) and *Ingénue Saxancour* (written 1786, published 1789). The latter, a graphic fictionalisation of his daughter's struggles to leave a violent husband, is an interesting counterpoint to the incest-fantasies of Restif's pornographic *L'Anti-Justine, ou Les Délices de l'amour* (1798). Restif wrote up a sensuality marked by all the liberties and repressions charted by Rousseau and Sade: frankly obsessive, fetishistic, sadistic, masochistic, and guilt-ridden. In this little man with a large sense of himself, the energies of the Revolution flowed through recognisable ideological channels, dedicated to rampant sensuality, morality and family values: 'j'aimai mes parents, la vertu, la vérité, quelquefois trop le plaisir; jamais le vice' ['I loved my parents, virtue, truth, sometimes I loved sexual pleasure to excess – I never loved vice'] (Dédicace à MOI, *Monsieur Nicolas*, vol. I).

As Restif drafted his versions of the feminine into the supporting roles of his personal script, the feminine was making its own entrance, slipping into other spaces opened up by revolutionary politics. The most noted plea for women's political rights came from the abbé Jean-Antoine-Nicolas de Condorcet (1743–94), in his *Lettres d'un bourgeois de New Haven sur l'inutilité de partager les pouvoirs législatifs entre plusieurs corps* (1787), *Essai sur la constitution et les fonctions des assemblées provinciales* (1788), and, most famous, his essay 'Sur l'admission des femmes au droit de cité' (in *Journal de la Société de 1789*, 3 July 1790). A few women had begun to make interventions on their own behalf, both as groups (through the *Cahiers de doléances des femmes*, submitted to the King in January 1789) and as individuals (Olympe de Gouges, Théroigne de Méricourt, Etta Palm d'Aelders, Claire Lacombe). Others spoke out on general political issues, such as the conservative Orleanist Madame de Genlis, the liberal Constitutionalist Madame de Staël, or the Girondin Madame Roland. The outbreak of war in 1793 put an end to women's aspirations. The newly-established women's political clubs were closed and women barred from public life:

Les mœurs et la nature même ont assigné ses fonctions [à la femme]: commencer l'éducation des hommes, préparer l'esprit et le cœur des enfants aux vertus publiques . . . telles sont leurs fonctions, après les soins de ménage. . . . L'honnêteté d'une femme permet-elle qu'elle se montre en public, et qu'elle lutte avec les hommes? de discuter à la face d'un peuple sur des questions d'où dépend le salut de la République? En général, les femmes sont peu capables de conceptions hautes et de méditations sérieuses.

[Society and nature have assigned women their due functions: to begin the education of men, prepare children's hearts and minds for civic virtues . . . these are their functions, when household duties are done. . . . Does decency permit a woman to show herself in public and compete with men? To stand and argue before the nation about questions on which the security of the

Republic depends? Women, in general, have little capacity for elevated conceptions and serious thought.][28]

(J. P. A. Amar, Rapport à la Convention nationale, séance du 9 brumaire an II, *Le Moniteur universel*, XVIII, 1er novembre 1793)

The statement at least acknowledges that women's subjectivity and functions are on the agenda. From two very different positions, two women writers offered their own versions of what they might be.

Madame de Genlis (Stéphanie-Félicité du Crest, 1746–1830) came to fame as an educationalist and author of moral tales and plays for children (*Théâtre à l'usage des jeunes personnes*, 1779–80; *Adèle et Théodore ou Lettres sur l'éducation*, 1782; *Les Veillées du château*, 1784).[29] This is how she is chiefly remembered in literary histories, though she was at least as widely read and influential in the second phase of her writing career as an author of historical novels, a genre she claimed to have introduced into France in anticipation of the vogue inspired by Walter Scott. An influential member of the Orleanist coterie in the early Revolution, she escaped into exile in time to avoid arrest and execution in 1793. She began writing her fictions while in exile in Berlin, to earn money to live on and also to persuade the Revolutionary government to allow her back into France. The bulk of her production, however, belonged to the campaign to restore counter-revolutionary and counter-Enlightenment cultural values, which began under Napoleon (*Mademoiselle de La Fayette, ou Le Siècle de Louis XIII*, 1813; the Gothic romance *Les Battuécas*, 1816; the satire *Les Parvenus, ou les aventures de Julien Demours*, 1824). Genlis's narratives used melodramatic situations and sensationalised and sentimentalised characters to convey a simple message of the importance of submission to established order. The female subjects they portrayed were entirely within the Gothic stereotype: villainous schemers or pathetic, self-sacrificing victims. In the second role, they were offered as models of conduct for the populace at large. Madame de Genlis wrote in collusion with conventional images of feminine dependency, in the interest of maintaining hierarchies of class. The self-abnegating role she urged on women in her fictions contrasts sharply with the central role she wrote for herself in her autobiography: *Mémoires inédits sur le XVIIIe siècle et la Révolution française* (1825–8).

Napoleon found Madame de Genlis useful, and gave her a

pension. He feared and hated Germaine de Staël (1766–1817).[30] Hostess of a political and literary salon frequented by the liberal French aristocracy, Madame de Staël supported the reforms adopted by the Constituent Assembly, though she drew the line at the replacement of monarchy by popular power. In her political treatises, she argued for moderate Republicanism and an extension of liberty rooted in law, and advocated a particular role for writers and the press in a Republic, to maintain a dissident voice (*Considérations sur les principaux événements de la Révolution française*, written 1812–13, published 1818). She repeated her advocacy of Revolutionary liberties in her novels, *Delphine* (1802) and *Corinne, ou l'Italie* (1807), which offered ground-breaking images of feminine resistance and determination. *Delphine*, a letter-novel set in 1790–2, joined advocacy for the reform of women's condition (the argument for divorce) with a commitment to wider political reform. *Corinne* confronted the question of women's ability to occupy the public stage, with its emblem of the brilliant opera star who focuses the enthusiasm of the Italian people and inspires in them the noblest moral and patriotic sentiments. Despite its romantic structure, the narrative offers a realistic analysis of the limits set by the period to feminine talent. Corinne's genius can only be tolerated in exotic Italy, and on the stage. There is no place for her in the respectable English society to which her suitor, Oswald, belongs. He marries her younger half-sister, Lucile, and Corinne is left to a tragic death.

Two features of Corinne's story distinguished it from the stories of rejected genius, star-crossed loves and blasted futures which, post-Rousseau and post-Revolution, crowded the literary land-scape: the *René* (1802) of François-René de Chateaubriand (1768–1848), for example, or Benjamin Constant's *Adolphe* (written 1807, published 1816). Corinne dies, like her male counterparts, with personal happiness unachieved, but unlike them, she has successes to point to. Her last song celebrates to public acclaim the Utopian city where genius and freedom are for women and men alike. And unlike their stories, her story looks to the future, offering a fresh character for new tales: Juliette, Corinne's likeness, the daughter of the sister with whom she is reconciled. Some of the best hopes of the Revolution are in Madame de Staël's fiction, in the space it creates for a future that will necessarily be linked to an often unhappy past but need not be imprisoned by it. What the next generation of tale-tellers make of that inherited space, and the symbols, forms and subjects with which it is filled, is another chapter.

Part II
The Bourgeois Century, 1815–1914

4

Restoration to Revolution, 1815–48

Writing in 1864 of the thinkers, poets, writers, historians, orators and philosophers of his time, Victor Hugo (1802–85), France's most famous political exile, claimed that 'tous, tous, tous dérivent de la Révolution française. Ils viennent d'elle, et d'elle seule' ['all of them, every single one, are products of the French Revolution. They come from it, and it alone'].[1] Even allowing for the context – Hugo's wish to restate his own Republican credentials and antagonise the government of the Second Empire (1852–70) whose amnesty he had refused in 1859 – his description of 1789 as the zero year of the modern age well reflected the extent to which literary and cultural developments in the nineteenth century issued from the need to come to terms with the legacy of the Revolution and with the extent and pace of change which the Revolution was seen to have inaugurated.[2]

The relationship between the demands in 1789 for constitutional rights and freedoms and the Jacobin radicalisation of 1793–4 was an essential issue for much of the nineteenth century. It was the terrain on which the struggle for control of the state was waged between opposing groups within the middle classes, between those determined to safeguard the gains of the Revolution and those equally determined to expunge its memory. During the first third of the century in particular, an understanding of the past and of its relationship to the present and future became the basis on which to create a positive and coherent programme of values with which to legitimise the appropriation of power in post-Revolutionary France. History became the substance and language of ideological conflict and, therefore, of literature. Writers and historians examined the relationship between historiography and narrative, lyrical or dramatic writing. Alfred de Vigny (1797–1863) believed that history and literature were complementary while Stendhal (pseudonym of Henri Beyle, 1783–42) claimed that *Racine et Shakespeare* (1823–5), his defence of tragedy written in prose and freed from classical rules, was directed at those he called the 'children of the Revolution', who had accompanied Bonaparte on his Moscow campaign and witnessed what he called the 'strange transactions' of 1814, which, after Bonaparte's fall from power, had led to the restoration of the Bourbon monarchy (1814–30).[3]

The histories of France available during the Consulate (1799–1804) and Empire (1804–14) of Napoleon Bonaparte (1769–1821) consisted mainly of work published prior to the Revolution. The Bonaparte regime had no incentive to satisfy the growing demand for historical information as its relationship to the legacy of 1789 was unclear to say the least. With the return of the monarchy, the issues at stake in the understanding of France's past took on a new urgency and the period saw a huge increase in historical scholarship and publication.[4] From this period the idea of historical development gave direction to many forms of intellectual life. This was certainly the case in literature. Hugo's manifesto of Romanticism, the *Préface de Cromwell* (1827), was predicated on a new awareness of the historical nature of reality, in opposition to Classicism's belief in unchanging metaphysical and moral absolutes. During the Restoration, the huge popularity of the historical novel helped to trigger a fundamental shift in the way in which the nineteenth-century novelist represented the world, while the flowering of poetry during the same period is inseparable from the aspirations and anxieties generated by a sense of the changing relationships between self and other in the modern age. Before turning to these literary developments, however, we need to establish other essential elements of the economic and cultural context in which literature would henceforth operate.

II   SOCIO-ECONOMIC CONDITIONS OF LITERATURE

From the beginning of the nineteenth century, the writer's relationship to the activity of writing was obliged to acquire a new basis. Deprived for the most part of the aristocratic patronage or private income which had hitherto made writing an essentially non-commercial activity, writers now depended for a living on the ability to sell their work. However, the economic, political and legal framework within which literature operated made this difficult to achieve. In the interests of the social stability which would (in theory) follow from the creation of a unified national culture, the Empire was as determined to police literature as it was education. Bonaparte's decree of March 1808 sought to impose a military discipline and organisation on the French education system. His decree of February 1810 required publishers and printers to obtain a licence, which for the regime, aware of the role played by printing and publishing in the Revolution, had the double advantage of obliging them to declare their loyalty to the Empire and of limiting their numbers. During the Restoration and July Monarchy (1830–48), the restrictive practices which this system involved became unsustainable as a result of an increased demand for literature from a wider, more diverse public, and because of technological changes which were driving the printing and publishing professions.[5]

In the early years of the century, at a time when advances in literacy were broadening the base of demand for literary material, literature operated within an artisan system of production and distribution.[6] The credit available for investment was small-scale, books cost a lot to produce and to buy, which kept print runs and sales low, and circulation continued to rely heavily on two expedients from an earlier age, *colportage* and *cabinets de lecture*. The *colporteurs* carried in their *balle* everything from the classics of French literature, popular novels, songs and almanacs to works of piety and of scientific vulgarisation but there were obvious limits to the amount that could be carried. In the *cabinets de lecture*, rooms in which books could be read or borrowed on payment of a small fee, the demand, notably for popular novels, outstripped the possibilities of the reading-room system to satisfy it.[7] The change came in the early years of the July Monarchy when developments in the technology of printing and the production of paper made it possible to produce books much more cheaply and to direct larger print runs at specific publics, thereby encouraging distinctions between elite and popular literary forms and changing the nature of the contractual relationships between writers and publishers.[8]

The same technological changes which were resulting in the production of more and cheaper books, combined with the abolition of censorship in the wake of the Revolution of 1830, generated a new economic basis for journalism which also had direct implications for literature. Under the Restoration, journalism and literature were largely separate domains, though they had in common high costs and official controls. On 1 July 1836, Emile de Girardin launched a new daily newspaper, *La Presse*, for which he halved the normal subscription cost, using advertising to make up the difference. The same day, Girardin's rival, A. Dutacq, launched *Le Siècle* on the same basis, triggering a circulation war which, combined with the dependency on advertising revenue, transformed the financial structure of the press. The need to win a wider circulation than that obtained by the traditional *journal d'opinion*, which catered for specific political allegiances, also meant new opportunities for writers as literary talent, now more important than political loyalties or specialised knowledge, became a highly marketable commodity. In this new situation there emerged a new type of versatile writer–journalist, able to turn his hand to different forms of writing, from art journalism to travel literature to scientific or philosophical vulgarisation.

Within literature itself, one of the most significant developments created by the new market in which the press operated was the growth of the serialised novel. Newspaper proprietors, following the lead given by Girardin and Dutacq, turned increasingly to serialisation, with its celebrated formula, 'la suite au prochain numéro' ['to be continued'], in order to attract and retain subscribers.[9] The novelist's reputation and ability to adjust to the readership for, and technical requirements of, this new genre became major issues in the newspaper's marketing policies. Balzac's practice of introducing action with lengthy descriptions of appearance, dress and place was ill-suited to the short segments of plot required by the serial format, but he learned to use this constraint as a way of representing the fragmentation and complexity of modern society. Alexandre Dumas ('Dumas *père*', 1802–70), on the other hand, with his experience of dramatic dialogue and *coups de théâtre* derived from his work in boulevard theatre, achieved phenomenal success in the new form with historical adventures such as *Les Trois Mousquetaires* (1844) and *Le Comte de Monte-Cristo* (1844).[10] Of even greater significance for the future development of the form was *Les Mystères de Paris* by Eugène Sue (1804–57), a novel of the Paris poor and criminal underworld whose serialisation in 1842–3 was the publishing sensation of the nineteenth century. With its larger-than-life heroes and villains, its suspense and unexpected twists of plot, the work became a prototype of popular fiction and its author gave voice for the first time to a mass readership's humanitarian aspirations and socio-political anxieties.[11]

The cumulative effect of all of these changes was that the conditions in which literature was produced and circulated were very different at the end of the July Monarchy from those which operated at the beginning of it. The significance of these changes itself became the subject of *Illusions perdues* (1836–43), which is in several senses the central work of the *Comédie humaine*, the vast series of novels through which Honoré de Balzac (1799–1850) provided his encyclopaedic representation of French society of the Restoration and the July Monarchy.

III   THE DEVELOPMENT OF PARIS

As the cradle of the Revolution and the first Republic, Paris had definitively supplanted Versailles as the seat of French government. The Parisian people's march on Versailles on 5–6 October 1789, which had resulted in the royal family's forced return to take up residence in Paris, was an essential moment in this transfer of power to the capital. To this new political significance, the Empire added a major extension of the city's financial, legal, administrative and cultural roles. The *Banque de France*, founded in 1800, was granted exclusive rights to print money, the Napoleonic code unified the legal system, prefects appointed by the Emperor to the recently created *départements* centralised public administration. The University of Paris was entrusted with administering all institutions of secondary and higher education in Paris and the provinces, in addition to the elite *grandes écoles*, founded during the First Republic to train those who would occupy the upper echelons of the military and civil service.

The development of Paris in the nineteenth century and the transformation of its geography, economic activity and cultural life had profound implications for the ways in which literature was produced and circulated. In terms of urban development, the Empire is usually associated with Bonaparte's grand vision of the city as the new Rome, which his costly and time-consuming wars prevented him from realising. This vision would play an important role later in a quite different context, when Napoleon III (1808–73), Bonaparte's nephew, embarked on the wholesale reconstruction of the city during the Second Empire. Under the first Empire, real, if less spectacular, changes were under way. Although on the Left Bank the Latin Quarter, the Sorbonne and their related activities enjoyed prominent status in the capital's cultural life, there was an imbalance between Right and Left Banks which increased in the early part of the century. In particular, the *Grands Boulevards*, the avenues created by the removal of the eighteenth-century city walls and which ran from the Place de la Bastille to the Place de la Madeleine, were widened during the Restoration to make more room for horse-drawn carriages to drive through streets which, lacking pavements, were as dangerous for pedestrians then as they are now. Tree-lined paths were created along them and benches provided. This combination of better communications and sociability was the key to the boulevards' success. They offered the city's first omnibus system (from 1828) and gas-lighting (1829) and its most frequented theatres and cafés. The Stock Exchange, completed in 1826, was located just off them and from the 1830s the rapidly expanding press had its offices in the vicinity. Bookselling was just one of the trades which moved into the covered passages which linked the boulevards and surrounding streets. Beginning in 1799 with the Passage du Caire, they spread rapidly between 1820 and 1848, stimulating commerce by providing protection from traffic and weather and by fostering a culture of the commodity which would become an essential feature of the representation of modern life.[12] In such ways the capital's intellectual and commercial life grew closer together.

Among the changes which Paris had to contend with during this period, the most serious was immigration. The city's population doubled between 1801 and 1846 to over one million, a demographic explosion with which it was quite unable to cope. The centralisation of public life which has been described was the general context for this development but the largest single factor was the influx of workers drawn to the capital by the prospect of finding work, in particular on the building sites opening up to the west and northwest of the city. They piled into the cheap living spaces in the still largely medieval city centre, in the notorious labyrinth of the quartier du Carrousel situated between the Louvre and the Tuileries and on the Île de la Cité, in the network of narrow, unlit and dangerous streets between the Police Headquarters and the Palais de Justice. Here the population density reached staggering proportions and gave rise to ruling-class fantasies about Parisian low life in which poverty was synonymous with a threat to the social order, and the frisson of excitement at the exotic and unknown combined with the fear of being murdered in their beds.

A less paranoid but perhaps more profound anxiety was that this potential army of the impoverished would find leaders among the frustrated, disillusioned elements of the lower-middle classes who had failed to achieve the legal, medical or administrative careers for which Paris was now the magnet. Literature became a major vehicle for these representations of urban life and for the cliché of *Paris, ville malade* which served to motivate and justify the demolition and reconstruction of the city during the Second Empire.[13]

IV ROMANTICISMS

French Romanticism's forms and phases of development were different from those of its British and German counterparts. In France, classicism enjoyed a more powerful position than in other European cultures for France was a more centralised state and classicism was its official culture, enshrined in the institutions (academies, theatres, Fine Art Salons) which regulated art and literature from the age of Louis XIV. This cultural establishment resisted changes coming from countries with which, for much of the period between the creation of the first Republic (1792) and the battle of Waterloo (1815), France was at war. The result was that Romanticism was able to emerge as an alternative literary and cultural practice only after 1815, when the authority of Neoclassicism had been weakened by its association with the fallen regimes of Republic and Empire. With the restoration of the Bourbon monarchy the political events inaugurated by 1789 appeared to have come full circle and the struggle began in earnest between liberals and conservatives for control of French political and cultural developments.

French Romanticism, therefore, has three main phases, linked to political developments in ways quite different from the British and German forms of the movement. The first (1800–15) is primarily that of writers exiled by the Revolution (émigré Catholic royalists opposed to the rationalist legacy of the Enlightenment, among whom François-René de Chateaubriand was the essential figure) or by the Empire (liberals like Madame de Staël who argued that the new post-Revolutionary age needed a new art) and whose contact with English or German cultures further distanced them from Neoclassicism. The second phase is that of the Restoration period when Catholic and liberal strands gradually converged in opposition to Neoclassicism and to an increasingly reactionary monarchy. In 1830 this aesthetic and political convergence enjoyed a brief honeymoon period when literary revolution (the first performance of Hugo's play *Hernani*, in February) was followed by political revolution (the overthrow in July of the Bourbon monarchy). The honeymoon lasted just the time it took to see through the liberal rhetoric of the new July Monarchy to the economic and political realities of the triumph of the bourgeoisie which the events of July 1830 had sealed. The third phase (1830–48) is that of the aftermath of this discovery. The implications of these new realities for the nature and extent of the writer's responsibility became the central issue. This phase of social Romanticism, as it became known, and the debates it aroused, ended with the defeat inflicted on the Republican idea by conservative forces in June 1848.[14]

From the early eighteenth century, classicism's claim for the universality of the *beau idéal* and the normative system of distinctions and hierarchies which it sustained faced a growing challenge from a new emphasis on the individual and new attitudes to nature and society. The clear and distinct ideas of Cartesian rationalism had been undermined by philosophers investigating the relation between knowledge and the senses, and there was a new emphasis on the importance of feeling and sensibility. Montesquieu and Voltaire had in their different spheres both stressed cultural relativism and diversity to the detriment of classicism's static world view, and Rousseau's work was, as has been seen, profoundly subversive. In 1800, the first unofficial manifesto of the ideas which would be identified with Romanticism appeared when, in *De la littérature*, Madame de Staël applied the comparative method which Montesquieu had developed in his study of the British legal system and analysed the reciprocal relationships between a nation's religion, literature, laws, customs and climate.[15] In doing so, she introduced the comparative history of literature in terms of an opposition between the Latin South and Germanic North, with the Southern classical inheritance derived from Graeco-Roman Antiquity and the Northern Romantic tradition from Christianity and medieval chivalry. Since the creations of the human mind were in her view subject to the law of progress, respect for classical models of perfection had no place in the literature of the modern age, which was free to return to its national source in medieval, Christian France. Such literature would be able to give expression to the complexity of the modern spirit and its tragic sense of an incomplete destiny, which was the source of its melancholy, lyricism and imagination.

Two years later, Chateaubriand's *Génie du Christianisme* reinforced the impact of de Staël's ideas. His praise of Christianity's history, rituals, architecture and contribution to artistic imagination and feeling was very influential, not least because it coincided with, and benefited from, the reconciliation between Church and State enacted in the Concordat of 1802 between Napoleon and the Vatican. Its rehabiliation of the Gothic aesthetic, which the classical had marginalised, was of great cultural significance for it gave increased impetus to a series of cultural trends – historical research into the medieval period, the troubadour craze in poetry, the interest in popular traditions, the preservation of historical monuments – and it underpinned for two decades the association of Catholicism and Romanticism. The text also contained *Atala* (already published separately the previous year) and *René*, two stories of tormented love in exotic American Indian landscapes, which Chateaubriand had extracted from his abandoned prose epic *Les Natchez*. The author's preface to *René*, and Father Souël's closing advice to the story's eponymous hero to get a job and do something useful for a change, provided the reassuring moral frame within which to deploy the ravages of the *mal du siècle*, the spiritual malady of the new age. For René there was no rest from *ennui* nor escape in the 'orages désirés' ['longed-for storms'] from the guilty secret he carried with him in his self-imposed exile (his sister's incestuous desire for him and his sense of responsibility for its tragic outcome). In the course of his lonely wanderings around the world he formulated the essential elements of modern melancholy: passivity, desire for escape and the aspiration towards an unknowable, unrealisable object.[16] From the end of the Bonapartist adventure in 1815, these appealed to a generation disoriented by the defeat of heroic ambition by the forces of mundane social and political realities. In this sense René is the elder brother of such disaffected youths as d'Albert in *Mademoiselle de Maupin* (1835) by Théophile Gautier (1811–72) and of Octave in *La Confession d'un enfant du siècle* (1836) by Alfred de Musset (1810–57).

Despite the misgivings or hostility of the literary establishment during the Empire, these ideas found their ways into the culture of the period. The breakthrough to the second, central phase of Romanticism came in the early years of the Restoration. In 1819,

Hugo created the *Conservateur littéraire*, which became the initial forum for the new sensibility with its support for a Catholic royalist aesthetic programme derived from Chateaubriand and as yet modest in its ambition for renewal of ideas and forms. The following year, Alphonse de Lamartine (1790–1869) published his *Méditations poétiques*, a volume of poetry which was, in his own words, 'classique pour l'expression, romantique pour la pensée' ['classical in expression, romantic in thought'] and whose impact was enormous.[17] In 1823 Stendhal's *Racine et Shakespeare* opened Romanticism's second, liberal front by calling for a new theatre in which prose tragedies addressing modern, national themes would do away with the artificial rhetoric and unities of classical verse drama. His pamphlet formulated the relationship between political and aesthetic renewal which within three years would unite the opposition to the Restoration establishment in both domains. But it was Hugo's gradual move in the course of the 1820s away from his position as official poet of the regime and towards the liberal opposition that enabled the two fronts within the Romantic move- ment, hitherto divided on political and religious grounds, to converge around an explicit declaration of war on Neoclassicism. His *Préface de Cromwell* was the manifesto, his play *Hernani* the performance which secured in the aesthetic domain the victory which the overthrow of the Restoration monarchy in July 1830 appeared to confirm in politics.

The provocative *rejet* in the opening line of *Hernani* – the alexan- drine of line 1 ends with 'escalier', that of line 2 begins with 'Dérobé', thereby separating noun ['staircase'] from adjective ['concealed'] in violation of the requirement that each alexandrine contain complete units of syntax and meaning – may seem the unlikely stuff of literary legend. But the uproar it triggered in the theatre on the play's first night testified to the talismanic virtues of order and balance attributed to the alexandrine in the classical aesthetic. By February 1830 every aspect of this aesthetic was under siege. The threat posed to its prosodic system by Hugo's audacious *enjambe- ment* was accompanied by attacks on its demarcations between 'high' and 'low' vocabulary. Its hierarchy of verse forms was challenged by the revival of the neglected fixed forms of sonnet and ballad, its canon of great authors by the rehabilitation of the sixteenth-century Pléiade poets. In the same way, the boundaries between prose and poetry were challenged in the prose poems of *Gaspard de la nuit* (1842), in which Aloysius Bertrand (1807–41) used the subjects and images of Romantic writing to create a poetic language quite distinct from Romantic prose in its economies and effects and in which Charles Baudelaire (1821–67) subsequently located the origins of the French prose poem.[18] Shakespeare's plays, performed in Paris in the late 1820s by visiting English troupes, contradicted the rigorous separation between the genres of tragedy and comedy central to the classical aesthetic by showing the effects obtained when the former's high seriousness was combined with the latter's lighter tones. This lesson in turn reinforced that of melodrama, in which sublime heroism co-existed with grotesque villainy.

In narrative, a similar fusion of opposites, those of the real and the supernatural or fantastic, redirected the tale of mystery and imagination.[19] Here, important roles were played by Charles Nodier (1780–1844), notably in *Jean Sbogar* (1818) and *Smarra, ou les Démons de la nuit* (1821); by the German writer and musician Ernst Hoffman, whose stories appeared in translation in 1829; and by Prosper Mérimée (1803–70), whose narrator in *Vénus d'Ille* (1841) accumulates clues in an effort to solve a mysterious, violent murder but does not offer the supernatural explanation which his narration invites (the murder of the hero by a statue of Venus).[20] Such subtleties of narrative technique as the creation of realistic effects combined with the presentation of facts which these effects cannot explain has made the tale of mystery and imagination, and Mérimée's story in particular, a privileged terrain for modern studies of narratology.[21]

This commitment to transcend what the Romantics saw as classicism's anachronistic and artificial system of divisions, hierarchies and constraints extended to the other arts. From this period, pictorial and musical analogies became an essential way of thinking about literature. The Romantic commitment to a deeper unity hidden beneath the diversity of artistic forms was expressed in theories of the synthesis of the arts drawn mainly from the German Romantic tradition. Baudelaire's famous sonnet 'Correspondances' (the fourth poem of his 1857 volume *Les Fleurs du mal*) came to be seen as a manifesto for these theories. Music became an increasingly important reference in analysis of the role of sound patterns in poetry, and the visual arts provided a rich source of research into the pictorial and spatial potentialities of poetic language. Indeed some of the nineteenth century's most significant formulations of literary modernity were made in relation to its sister arts (cf. Baudelaire on Eugène Delacroix and Constantin Guys; Émile Zola (1840–1902) and Stéphane Mallarmé (1842–98) on Édouard Manet; Baudelaire and Mallarmé on Richard Wagner).[22]

In this context of the relationships between the arts, another important development during this period was the emergence of the literary genre of art criticism, whose function was to analyse and evaluate contemporary art. Diderot was the first major writer associated with Salon criticism, as it became known.[23] His *Salons*, written between 1759 and 1781 and published together in an 1818–19 edition of his work, made him for most of the nineteenth century the authority for this type of writing. The Salon exhibition was held either every year or every two years but because it lasted in either case only a few weeks, it could not sustain economically an autonomous profession of art criticism. Such criticism was usually produced therefore by writers as a sideline to their main literary or journalistic activities and it gave them a major role, sometimes supportive, sometimes conflictual, in the developments taking place in French painting during the nineteenth century.

Ways in which these different elements of the changing literary landscape during the Romantic period interconnect can be seen in the spectacular growth of travel literature.[24] Travel had grown in importance in the course of the eighteenth century but the combination of political exile, foreign wars and colonial expansion gave travel a new dimension in French life in the decades following the Revolution. Before railways began to transform the possibilities for travel, and before photography gave new visual means of access to the outside world, the writer was an important explorer and transcriber of places the majority could not visit. The Romantics were great travellers, for whether travel meant rejuvenation or a melancholic discovery of the mortality of culture, whether it was a form of escape or an act of faith in the relationship between human and technological progress, it was exploration of the self, of the ambitions and anxieties of modern experience. For Stendhal, Italy expressed the passion and generosity of spirit lost in conformist, utilitarian France; for Musset, Italy and Spain were sources of provocative, erotic stereotypes. The Rhine and its landscapes generated biographical, architectural and political utopias in Hugo's encyclopaedic imagination. Before visiting the Rhine in the late 1830s, he had already played an important part in the development of the Orientalist craze through his collection of poems *Les Orientales* (1829). In 1840 Gautier visited Spain and sent back to the newspaper which was paying his expenses his descriptions of those Spanish customs, dress and behaviour which had not yet been eliminated by the spread of Parisian tastes, and of Spanish art, whose realism was so different from French painting.

Travel often encouraged new forms of writing, such as Chateaubriand's descriptions of American landscapes in *René*, Hugo's reflections on the relationship between history and lyricism in *Les Orientales*, or Gautier's transposition of Spanish paintings in the poems which accompanied the second edition of his *Voyage en Espagne* (1845). And travel exerted a powerful appeal to the Romantic imagination as a metaphor of the self's engagement with, or retreat from, the energies of a dynamic, changing world. When Gustave Flaubert (1821–80) sought to show in *L'Éducation sentimentale* (1869) that, in the 1848 generation, the Romantics' faith in progress had given way to disillusionment, he summarised fifteen years in the life of his main character, Frédéric Moreau, with two words: 'Il voyagea' ['He went travelling'].

* * *

Faced with the conflicting legacies of Enlightenment rationalism and orthodox Catholicism, conscious of living in the age of History, the Romantics aspired to new forms of synthesis. The penetration of the ideas of the *philosophes* is clear in the publication from 1815 of editions of the collected and individual works of Voltaire, Diderot and Rousseau, but the Terror and the period of Imperial authoritarianism which followed necessitated a re-evaluation of rationalist progress. Under the Restoration a major revival of religious vocations and a rapid increase in clerical and lay associations re-established the link between religious and temporal power which once again made entering the Church an important career move. But the restored regime could no more re-establish pre-revolutionary faith than it could pre-revolutionary politics, however much it might have wished to do so. The growth in the study of comparative religion provided other forms of faith for those discouraged by the doctrinal and institutional intolerance of Catholicism (Greek polytheism for the liberal Benjamin Constant (1767–1830), the Muslim faith for Lamartine). The spiritual eclecticism of Victor Cousin (1792–1867) became the religious orthodoxy of the July Monarchy while the social, humanitarian Catholicism of Félicité de

Lamennais (1782–1854) became a major influence during the same period. Combinations of Catholic and secular religion attracted others (Vigny's aristocratic religion of honour, for example).

The need for Catholicism to integrate the new realities of historical and cultural change permeated the work of even the most extreme apologists of counter-revolution. It is true that Joseph de Maistre (1753–1821) and Louis de Bonald (1754–1840) were 'virtual theocrats for whom 1789 was an atheistic revolution' and for whom 'politics was a Manichean struggle in which good would triumph only if the sins of the Enlightenment were washed away by veneration of pope and Bourbon'.[25] On the other hand, their work enabled Catholicism to make contact with intellectual trends in the mainstream of Romanticism. De Maistre integrated the 'crimes' of the Enlightenment and Revolution in a dialectical vision of redemption through blood, a stage in the historical process of divine intervention in human affairs at the end of which lay expiation of original sin and a return to divine unity. Bonald believed that the revelation of religious truth at the beginning of human history was the basis for laws of social harmony and progress.

This type of faith in an eternal, universal tradition founded on divine revelation but evolving in history paralleled Illuminist traditions, which grew in importance in the 1820s and 1830s as Swedenborg's ideas become more available in France. In his system, organic relationships linked matter and spirit, and all phenomena were symbols. Original harmony had been lost through the Fall but could be recovered by the artist/thinker who recognised phenomena's symbolic links to their divine source.[26] This general scheme lent itself to adaptation to any philosophy of history which had progress towards harmony as its objective and gave spiritual direction to the organic models of thought bequeathed by the Enlightenment. Hugo's remark (in *Napoléon-le-petit*, 1852) that, just as human creation had sprung from the word of God, so human societies would spring from the word of man illustrates this fusion of the social, historical and divine which was one of Romanticism's deepest aspirations.

V STAGING ROMANTICISM

As discussed above, Stendhal's *Racine et Shakespeare* and Hugo's *Préface de Cromwell* were essential manifestos in the battle of ideas which the Romantics engaged against Neoclassicism. Despite differences between the two (Stendhal advocated a prose theatre, Hugo the retention of verse), they shared the commitment to a theatre for the modern age, with themes which addressed the nature of history and its relationship to the present. Plays written from this perspective tended to be unperformable in the conditions then obtaining in the French theatre. Hugo's first play, *Cromwell*, with its length (6,000 lines of verse), number of characters and settings and range of voices and tones had no hope of being performed. *Hernani*, a pseudo-Spanish drama of frustrated love, was staged despite the uproar in the theatre and the well-known difficulties Hugo encountered in persuading actors and actresses trained in the classical repertoire to embrace the new rhythms and unclassical language of his play. Musset did not intend his prose drama *Lorenzaccio* (1834) to be performed, which is probably just as well, for quite apart from its theme of political assassination (Lorenzo murders the Duke of Florence in an attempt to change Florentine society), the play shows the expediency and egoism with which this society frustrates the hero's efforts to heal the divisions within himself and intervene positively in the historical process. In *Chatterton* (1835), Vigny showed a poet driven to suicide by a cruel, indifferent and materialist society. As well as handling the staging issues raised by dramatists' confrontations with the values of post-1830 society, the Romantic theatre had to face the general problem of creating its own public out of audiences raised on the classical repertoire and those who frequented the popular boulevard theatre. In *Ruy Blas* (1838), a verse play set in seventeenth-century Spain, Hugo was more successful than most in achieving this.[27] Nevertheless it remains the case that although theatre provided the theoretical terms on which to oppose Neoclassicism, it was in the novel and poetry that French Romanticism achieved the most powerful expression of its commitments and self-doubts.

VI   THE RISE OF THE NOVEL

During the final quarter of the eighteenth century, the novel's evolving forms had reached a new and wider reading public.[28] The upheavals of the Revolution had dispersed many of the arbiters of this public's tastes and the momentous events acted out in the public arena had demanded forms of rhetoric which went well beyond conventional literary categories. In 1797 the translation into French of the most successful English Gothic novels had briefly galvanised the genre in France. Terror endured and virtue triumphant was a potent mixture in the aftermath of Robespierre's fall. The Gothic vogue was, however, soon marginalised by the return to Neoclassical forms and language during the Empire. In literary and cultural terms, the Empire was a transitional period, one of new energies brought under control by a restored high manner. In this respect one of the most significant novels of this period was Constant's *Adolphe*, published in 1816 but written in 1806–9. The novel had obvious roots in the psychological tradition for it shows the motivations of two characters trapped in a situation from which there is no escape. It was also written against the eighteenth-century libertine novel to show the danger of relationships begun without due self-knowledge. But the choice open to Adolphe – between the false freedom of loyalty to Ellénore and the lost freedom of acceptance of social pressures to abandon her – shows Enlightenment individualism faced with the authoritarian constraints of Imperial society. In addition, Constant gave exceptional depth to this conflict between self-alienation and social integration by framing the narrative with a series of readings of Adolphe's account of events (the *Avis de l'éditeur*, the *Lettre à l'éditeur* and the *Réponse*) whose effect is to challenge this account and each other's and therefore to undermine the reader's resolution of the conflicts which the text describes.[29]

As far as *Adolphe*'s critical fortune was concerned, its publication in 1816 was ill-timed. That year marked the beginning of the French infatuation with Walter Scott's historical novels. Translated into French as soon as they appeared, they achieved sales that were enormous for the period and the system of production and distribution available then. For its readers, Scott's writing combined a philosophy of history with a structure of drama. It made the conflicts among the British people intelligible as history and effective as narrative. During the Restoration it was the model of fiction which the aspiring novelist could not ignore.[30]

In *Cinq-Mars* (1826), Vigny aimed to show that Richelieu's defeat of the French nobles, seen in the novel in the failure of the plot organised against the Cardinal in 1642 by Cinq-Mars, had been a major factor in the collapse of the monarchy 150 years later, because it had fatally weakened the nobility upon whom the monarchy's survival depended. To demonstrate this thesis, Vigny departed from Scott's practice by making major historical figures the main characters of his novel. In so doing, he was obliged to portray the psychological balance of power between a few individuals as representative of the power struggles taking place in France at the time. The result is a loss of historical depth. In addition, Vigny was obliged to alter historical facts for psychological purposes, as when he put back the date of the trial of Urbain Grandier by five years in the novel to enable Cinq-Mars to witness it and so justify in part his hatred of Richelieu. In response to criticisms made of this type of historical inaccuracy, Vigny added an important preface to the fourth edition (1829), entitled 'Réflexions sur la vérité dans l'art' ['Reflections on Truth in Art'], in which he argued that truth in the historical novel should be that of human nature and motivation rather than that of facts. Though in these liberties taken with historical realities Vigny's novel went against the grain of Restoration historicism, its adaptation of the Scott legacy ensured a huge success with its first public.[31]

No less successful was Mérimée's *Chronique du règne de Charles IX* (1829), set in 1572, when religious conflict culminated in the St Bartholomew's Day Massacre of 23–4 August. In his preface he argued that the well-chosen anecdote was an economical and effective way of reconstructing historical atmosphere, objective knowledge of the past being in any event impossible. The eighth chapter consists of a dialogue between the reader and the author in which the latter frustrates the former's desire for portraits of historical figures, and the novel ends with the author letting the reader decide how the love story at the heart of the religious divide (between the Protestant Bernard de Cergy and the Catholic Diane de Turgis) should end. The 1572 setting is the means adopted by Mérimée to dress up in contemporary forms of historical costume well-established fictional themes (impossible love, brothers divided) and situations (duels, masked meetings) in order to present his Voltairean anticlericalism and his belief in the permanent conflicts of human feeling between love and hate, fraternity and fratricide.

In 1823, Hugo published a review of the French translation of *Quentin Durward* in which he wrote that Scott's association of history and novel had resulted in the new genre of the dramatic novel, showing the confrontation of opposites: light and darkness, sublime and grotesque. (This opposition would later form the central theme of Hugo's own preface to *Cromwell*.) It was, however, only a transitional form. The novel of the modern age, wrote Hugo, would be an epic novel. His efforts to fulfil his own prophecy are seen in *Notre-Dame de Paris*, published in March 1831 and republished the following year with three additional chapters (Part IV, ch. 6 and Part V, chs 1 and 2). The novel drew together 1482 (in which it is set), 1789 and 1830 into a philosophy of history grounded in the architecture of the cathedral itself.[32]

Hugo's cathedral is a hybrid structure in whose stones the history of knowledge is inscribed. It combines the authoritarian, hierarchical, dogmatic Romanesque and the freer, more modern Gothic spirit and is a monument to the age of change in which the novel is set. Its monstrous genius is Quasimodo, whose deformed body reproduces the building's hybrid form. When he rescues the gypsy, Esmeralda, and shelters her within its walls, he achieves the union of opposites (his ugliness and her beauty) which was the modern form of the divine. Frollo, the demonic priest, is the cathedral's other inhabitant. His passion for knowledge, which he pursues from his hermit's cell in the summit of one of the cathedral towers, is ruined by his sudden, brutal passion for Esmeralda, for which he is eventually hurled by Quasimodo from the cathedral walls. These elements of Gothic fantasy (hunchback, mad priest and beautiful gypsy) were transformed by the chapters added in 1832. Here Frollo explains to two visitors (the king and his physician in disguise) the role of architecture as text of the national memory of the period before the printed word, and asserts that the book will kill the cathedral. Gutenberg's invention of printing, for Hugo's novel, marks the transition from theocracy to democracy, the emancipation of humanity from the control of priests. It is the founding revolution of which the Reformation, Enlightenment and 1789 are the necessary issue.

This relationship between 1482 and 1789 is seen in the connections made in the novel between the cathedral and the Bastille, for both are subjected to the crowd's assault. Just before the cathedral is attacked, Quasimodo sees from its walls a light burning in the room reserved in the Bastille for the king's visits. In the conversation taking place there, the king speaks of his ambition to break the power of the nobles (the theme of *Cinq-Mars*) and Coppenhole warns that the people's hour will come. The representation of the people in *Notre-Dame de Paris* does not suggest a positive outcome to the historically inevitable fate of kings. It is an underclass of destitutes and criminals whose vice, cruelty and primitive instincts place it much closer to the 'dangerous classes' described in much contemporary social writing (and evoked ten years later in Sue's *Les Mystères de Paris*) than to the citizens of the enlightened democracy represented in the Utopian theories of Henri de Saint-Simon (1760–1825), in which the interests of workers and capitalists would be reconciled in a new society scientifically administered by the creators of wealth.[33] In 1831 Hugo's social theories were still evolving. He would return to them much later in *Les Misérables* (1862). In the meantime, the novel's more open, versatile form permitted the dramatic confrontations and historical breadth which could be read but not performed in *Cromwell* and *Hernani*.

For Balzac the period 1815–28 was one of literary apprenticeship, writing hack novels under various pseudonyms, followed by business failure in printing and publishing.[34] Driven by debts to return to writing, he took Scott's model of the historical novel as the basis for *Les Chouans* (1829), the first novel he published under his own name. Set in Brittany in 1799, it is a story of doomed love between Montauron, leader of the Breton forces waging counter-revolutionary war against the Republic, and Marie de Verneuil, republican spy sent to Brittany to seduce and trap him. As in Scott, action is the reflection of geography (the Breton peasants fanaticised by the clergy are an emanation of the remote, hostile landscape), individuals represent socio-political types (Montauran is 'the gracious image of French nobility', Hulot 'the living image of the energetic Republic') and the novel is a dramatic form in which dialogue sustains rapid sequences of action framed by description. But Balzac also represented the power of passion, which, in his view, the puritanical Anglo-Saxon Scott had excluded as too dangerous a theme. In *Les Chouans*, the passions which drive post-Revolutionary society are love, money and power. In his analysis of them Balzac transformed Scott's historical novel into the represen-tation of the historical dimension of the present. The lovers finally attain through their relationship a wisdom which suggests a basis for progress from civil war to national unity. Marie submits through marriage to the authority of her husband; Montauron urges his brother to cease the armed struggle against the Republic. They are, however, trapped in the web of deceptions and betrayals orches-trated from Paris by Fouché, the master spy, and implemented by his agent, Corentin. In the novel's final exchange between Hulot and Corentin it is the spy who has the final word, implying that the virtues of the Republican soldier will be anachronistic in the new France which is emerging from revolutionary upheaval.

Through the writing of *Les Chouans*, Balzac redirected the historical and Gothic novels towards the representation of the real. In *La Peau de chagrin* (1831) he redirected Hoffmann's fantastic tales to the same end. The talisman of wild ass's skin which Raphaël discovers in the curiosity shop gives access to the fantastic reality of Paris in 1830: the mystery, horror and destructive force of its desires. Accepting the skin, Raphaël chooses to descend into the Parisian hell and is consumed by the gratification of desire which the new forms of urban consumption make available. In *La Fille aux yeux d'or* (1834), Paris is explicitly compared to Dante's Inferno. Through each of its five circles (workers, petty bourgeois, liberal professions, artists and aristocracy), money follows its upward movement, separating as it goes masters and slaves of will and desire. Balzac's social and philosophical analysis in his early works developed into an encyclopaedic project to summarise the origins, effects and laws of post-Revolutionary French society, on the basis of an analogy between the human, animal and natural species which he outlined in his 1842 preface to the collection.

The armature of Balzac's vast sequence of novels, *La Comédie humaine*, was provided by the three which have come to be known as the 'Vautrin cycle', due to the presence in each of the escaped convict in disguise whose ambitions and roles drive the narratives of *Le Père Goriot* (1835), *Illusions perdues* (1837–43) and *Splendeurs et misères des courtisanes* (1838–47). The trilogy narrates the success of one young provincial, Rastignac, and the failure of another, Lucien de Rubempré, to master the codes and mechanisms of modern society. In the ever-widening narrative reach, from the Vauquer boarding-house from which Rastignac begins his social climb to the Conciergerie prison where Vautrin's elaborate scheme to marry Lucien into one of the most influential aristocratic families finally comes to grief, Balzac shows the workings of the free market in ambitions and talents which is the new reality of post-Revolutionary culture.

Goriot's cry, 'L'argent, c'est la vie. Monnaie fait tout' ['Money is life. Cash can do anything'], is the ultimate revelation to Rastignac of the source of energy driving this society. Money's origins are corrupt, as are its uses. Madame Vauquer's secret wealth is an accumulation of petty thefts. Goriot's fortune comes from exploiting food shortages during the Revolution and is channelled through his daughters into the dishonest social and financial dealings of their husbands. Money provides the narrative structure of the novel cycle, for its circulation is the means required to propel the upwardly mobile provincial to higher social levels. In *Le Père Goriot*, the still naive Rastignac recoils in horror from the deal proposed by the diabolical Vautrin. At the end of *Illusions perdues*, the defeated and disillusioned Lucien accepts it and triggers the chain of events which in *Splendeurs* exceeds even Vautrin's superhuman control of events.

It was in the course of writing *Le Père Goriot* that Balzac hit upon the narrative device of recurring characters so appropriate to his vision of contemporary society.[35] When, in 1835, readers who were already familiar with Rastignac's social success thanks to *La Peau de chagrin* were taken back in *Le Père Goriot* to his humble origins in the Vauquer boarding house, a whole new dimension of narrator/reader relationships opened up. The effect of inserting the present narrative into past and future ones, the cumulative impact of its economies and repetitions, are striking in the opening pages of *Splendeurs*, which immediately heighten the suspense by implying untold narratives of past, present and future. How has Collin (alias Vautrin, alias Carlos Herrera) engineered Lucien's present position in the time which has elapsed since he saved the young man from suicide at the end of *Illusions perdues*? What stage of Lucien's transformation are readers now witnessing? How will even Vautrin be able to control the talent for failure which Lucien had demonstrated in *Illusions perdues*? The multiple connections between the three novels ensure that when Esther's inheritance arrives only hours too late to save her from the suicide which finally takes the plot out of Vautrin's control, the reader knows that Vautrin, like Goriot, must pay the price for channelling his devotion into a 'son' who is as unworthy an object of love as were Goriot's daughters. Here, the narrative repetitions serve to generalise the corruption of the authority of the father by the moral and social anarchy which, in Balzac's view, the collapse of the old order has initiated.

The device of recurring characters enabled Balzac to develop on a grand scale in *Illusions perdues* and *Splendeurs* the exposé of general principles offered by Vautrin in *Le Père Goriot*. The developing forms of liberal economics and social relations are seen in literary production and distribution in *Illusions perdues* and in sexual desire in *Splendeurs*. Both show the implications for social organisation when Romantic energies are harnessed by market forces. In *Illusions*, poets prostitute their muse to journalists as women are prostituted in the infamous Galeries-de-bois, and promiscuity becomes a metaphor for class and professional relationships in contemporary society. In *Splendeurs*, the alliance between Lucien, the outrageously handsome *arriviste*, and Esther, the stunningly beautiful courtesan (hence her nickname of 'la torpille' ['numb-fish'], explodes class barriers by driving huge flows of cash through them. The deal by which Vautrin, the master criminal, becomes chief of police at the end of *Splendeurs* in exchange for love letters to Lucien from aristocratic women which, if revealed, would threaten state security, is a measure of the fragility of social, moral and legal systems in Balzac's account of the post-Revolutionary world.

In *Le Rouge et le noir* (1830), Stendhal's 'chronicle of 1830', Restoration society is portrayed as having slammed into reverse the energies liberated in 1789.[36] Now the old generation guillotines the new and coalitions of selfish interests block and marginalise youth's aspirations for change. The reversal is such that the death penalty is now the one thing that cannot be bought, and Julien chooses it so as to assume responsibility for having achieved in the private sphere a seizure of power equivalent to Bonaparte's on the battlefield (his double seduction of the wife of a provincial mayor committed to the royalist cause and the daughter of an aristocrat connected with Charles X's plot to replace the Charter of 1814 with the Ordinances of 1830). Julien deliberately masters the lifeless discourse of social and religious orthodoxy to rise in the public sphere; he accidentally achieves the living, authentic language of love to conquer in the private sphere. His success is crowned with a commission as lieutenant in the hussars which frees him to cast off the black disguise of religion and assume the red of his initial military ambition. The campaign successfully concluded was by 1830 a well-charted path of fiction, but when Julien's enterprise is ruined by Madame de Rênal's letter to the Marquis de la Mole, Julien shoots her in church, an act which in the text defies description. Deprived of the external commentary and interior monologue which had made it possible hitherto to distinguish between Julien's private and public selves, the reader is thrown back on motivations which, whether psychological (Julien has taken leave of his senses, is committing a form of suicide) or literary (he is pre-programmed by the premonition of his death discovered in the same church at the outset of the novel), are inadequate to account for the blasphemy of the act and its bungled execution. The failed attempt permits the couple's brief reunion, in which their love is confirmed as belonging in more authentic times. And by undoing Julien's previous strategy of upward mobility, it confers on his solitary confinement the status of a rite of passage to a purer self, in terms of which Restoration society is condemned.

Stendhal never completed *Lucien Leuwen*, on which he worked in 1834–6 and in which he sought to combine a love story with a political satire of the July Monarchy. In *La Chartreuse de Parme* (1839), he returned to his idea of Italy as a theatre of ancient, authentic energies and modern, graceless political intrigues.[37] The work is an anthology of familiar fictional forms (picaresque, cloak-and-dagger, historical and love novels) and characteristically Stendhalian themes (authenticity, energy) and symbols (tower, sky). Fabrice del Dongo, embarked on his search for happiness, grasps nothing of the history unfolding before him in the battle of Waterloo, nor of the political manoeuvres and realignments which develop as a result. He avoids the dangers of inauthentic passions and finds freedom in the Farnese tower, the archetypal prison of love which is the only place where true feeling can still be experienced in the modern world. Balzac wrote an enthusiastic article on the novel but the ambiguities generated by Stendhal's combination of ironic detachment and playful intervention marginalised it in terms of contemporary narrative developments until the end of the century.

The conformism and utilitarianism of post-1830 society triggered a more direct attack in the work of the younger generation of writers, whose initial forays into literature had been in support of the campaign led by Hugo against the classical establishment in the late 1820s. In the aftermath of 1830 some of these writers formed their own ephemeral groups, which became known as the *petits cénacles*. Their Bohemian eccentricities and anti-bourgeois poses and gestures masked a deep anxiety at the marginalisation to which they felt condemned by the ideology which had triumphed in 1830. In the poor and overcrowded areas in the Latin Quarter, scandalous, short-lived groups such as the *Bousingots* and the *Jeunes-France* inaugurated forms of artistic and social dissidence which would characterise the avant-garde for almost 150 years. This Bohemian lifestyle was celebrated in sentimentalised form in the *Scènes de la vie de bohème* (1851) by Henri Murger (1822–61) but its idealisation of so-called carefree poverty was bitterly denounced as inauthentic and reactionary by the radical novelist Jules Vallès (1832–85) in *L'Insurgé* (1886), his novel on the Paris Commune of 1871.

Gautier was the best known member of this early Romantic dissidence. In the preface to his novel *Mademoiselle de Maupin*, he proposed to make a virtue out of art's unavoidable divorce from society and attacked its subordination to bourgeois morality or to social or political progress. Instead, the value of art would lie in its own formal perfection. The artist's work with the materials of the medium would replace Romantic notions of inspiration and lyrical effusions of the heart. The novel itself alternates epistolary and third-person narrative forms to subtle effect in a story of ambiguous sexual identities and the quest for beauty. It was a highly original piece of writing in its time but this originality has always been overshadowed by the preface's manifesto status.[38]

VII WOMEN'S STORIES

One of the most popular writers of serial fiction in the Romantic press, George Sand (pseudonym of Aurore Dupin, 1804–76) has been marginalised by canonical literary histories which have focused on her unrepentantly idealist writing, conspicuously isolated within prevailing realist modes.[39] Certainly, the sentimental pastorals for which, until recently, she was best known, such as *La Mare au diable* (1846), *François le Champi* and *La Petite Fadette* (both 1848), do not show her at her best. In her own time Sand exerted European-wide influence with her humanitarian politics and her advocacy of women's equal rights to the pleasure of passion and the enjoyment of social justice. Novels such as *Indiana* (1832) and *Valentine* (1832) explored in the sphere of private life, in the marriage situation, the problems created by inequalities in class and gender and the conflicting claims of duty and love, and high-lighted the powerlessness of women before the law.

But most interesting, and experiencing a revival in our own times, are Sand's historical novels, which mixed private and public spheres and argued the intimate and vital interest of women in both passion and politics. *Lélia* (1833; rewritten in 1839 to introduce a connection between Lélia's feminist ambitions and social humani-tarian revolution) offered a flamboyant heroine committed to both sensual pleasure and intellectual ambition, advocating both the importance of women's education and wider social change. The text seeks refuge from a corrupt world in religion and nature, but like all Romantic fictions, it carries its own neuroses and obsessions into the alternative world it canvasses. Its real release is in language: lyrical outpourings, repetitions and amplifications, monologues, letters, lakes of words, matching the watery landscapes in which its heroine's sufferings are reflected. *Mauprat* (1835–7), in contrast, offered a gentler female model in Edmée, a reincarnation of Rousseau's supportive, inspiring, passionate and obedient Sophie, who helps mediate the transition from the old feudal world of the robber barons to a post-Revolutionary harmony of mutual respect between classes. Sand covers a wide stage (the province of Berry and its honest peasants, pre-Revolutionary Paris, and an America locked in Civil War, fighting for its freedom) to bring together the elements out of which she invents a Utopian future: political idealism, strength and integrity, and compassion, which she places respectively in the revolutionary *philosophes*, the old nobility and the common people, and women. Style parallels content, to negotiate a consensus between old and new. This is a Gothic novel with all the trimmings, adapted to press enlightened politics and morality; a backward-looking form is harnessed to a progressive vision.

There were limits to Sand's feminism. The *Lettres à Marcie* (1837), which she wrote for Lamennais's *Le Monde*, recommended that Marcie start by trying to get herself a husband; which failing, there was celibacy, an artistic career and, most important, self-education. Sand resisted contemporary feminist efforts to have her stand for the National Assembly in 1848, in a misogynist Republic increasingly addicted to the anti-feminist broadsides of Proudhon. Women, she argued, should not fight for political rights until they had secured civil rights and reform of the marriage laws.[40] Similarly, there were limits to her Christian socialist politics (see *Spiridion*, 1838–9; *Le Compagnon du Tour de France*, 1840; *Le Meunier d'Angibault*, 1845). As the underlying current of the century moved left, she moved right, eventually to join her fellow intellectuals in 1871 in indicting the Commune for its fanaticism while approving the inauguration of Thiers's Third Republic.

More consistent were the politics of Flora Tristan (1803–44), who wrote graphic and realistic accounts of her experiences as a much-travelled activist engaged in socialist and feminist organisation.[41] She was influenced by the feminist and co-operative ideals of Saint-Simon, Charles Fourier and Robert Owen, the philanthropic founder of the factory community of New Lanark. In her turn, she influenced the Saint-Simonist Alphonse-Louis Constant (1810–75), who after her death wrote up her *L'Émancipation de la femme, ou le testament de la paria* (1845) from the notes she left. *Mémoires et pérégrinations d'une paria (1833–34)* (1838) described the visit to Peru which turned her into the champion of the oppressed. It was published with a preface denouncing her husband, from whom she had fled to Peru and was seeking a divorce. *Promenades dans Londres* (1840) was a vivid eye-witness account of the inequalities and squalid degeneracy of English society in the 1830s and its various institutions (prisons, brothels, slums, gasworks, Ascot, the mad-house and the House of Commons). *Union ouvrière* (1843) was a blueprint for a new society, which proposed that change would come through the education of women, since they are the educators of the next generation. *Méphis, ou le prolétaire*, a novel she wrote in 1838, had already urged the need to raise the status of women through education. *Le Tour de France: journal inédit* (written 1843–4) was not published till 1973. This highly personal and immensely readable account of the frustrations of early attempts at workers' organisation included furious portraits of the unhelpfulness of middle-class colleagues and the slow caution of the working classes.

VIII   NEW VOICES AND FORMS IN FRENCH POETRY

In an 1859 article on Gautier, Baudelaire looked back over French poetry during the Restoration, stating that Hugo, Sainte-Beuve and Vigny had at that time 'ressuscité la poésie française, morte depuis Corneille' ['resuscitated French poetry, which had died with Corneille']. The commonly accepted description of eighteenth-century French poetry as a barren waste, followed by a miraculous flowering after 1815, was in fact the invention of the Romantic poets themselves, whose reputations had most to gain from it. The Romantics' wholesale dismissal of poets writing in a quite different context from that pertaining after 1789 gave far too little recognition to the changes which had taken place in poetry during the twenty years prior to the Revolution and which had helped to create the public which their Romantic successors would address to such effect. Some of those who had contributed most to this renewal had become the quasi-official poets of the Empire. Their work had provided the school primers from which the Romantics learned their craft, which was another reason for the pupils to attack their masters.[42]

Despite Baudelaire's dismissive comment, eighteenth-century poetry had produced significant changes in the resources available to poets in the early years of the nineteenth century. For nearly thirty years, between *La Henriade* (1728), his epic poem on religious fanaticism, and his philosophical *Poème sur le désastre de Lisbonne* (1756), Voltaire explored eminently modern themes in a range of poetic forms, recognising the diminishing appeal of the eloquence and mythological subject matter of the classical tradition of dramatic verse for the century's changing reading public. The *Odes sacrées* (1702) of Jean-Baptiste Rousseau (1671–1741) succeeded occasionally in conveying through their rhetorical tone and didactic intent a personal note of suffering and injustice of the kind with which nineteenth-century poets would renew the ode. Enlightenment interest in nature helped to renew the seventeenth-century tradition of pastoral poetry and was reinforced by the taste for nature poetry derived from the translation of James Thomson's *The Seasons* (1826–30). In 1870 Jacques Delille (1738–1813) translated Virgil's *Georgics*, the source of this poetic tradition, and thereafter published a series of volumes on related themes between *Les Jardins* (1782) and *Les Trois Règnes* (1808). Though his descriptive, didactic approach to nature is that of his time, it shows nevertheless the beginnings of a search for the self through nature which the nineteenth-century poets would take much further.[43]

'On peut dater d'André Chénier la poésie moderne' ['Modern poetry can be said to begin with André Chénier'], Gautier said in his *Histoire du romantisme* (1872). Chénier (1762–94) was discovered in 1819, when the publication of his *Poésies* was, according to Gautier, a revelation (p. 256). The circumstances of Chénier's death, guillotined for anti-Jacobinist writing only two days before the fall of Robespierre, fuelled his legend. In his work, the rhythms of the subjective imagination emerge through the mythological references and classical *mot noble*. In this respect, his experimentation with the alexandrine, notably his daring innovations with *enjambement*, was of decisive importance for subsequent poets.[44]

Lamartine, in his preface to the 1849 edition of his work, made the same claim on behalf of his own *Méditations poétiques* that Gautier had made for Chénier. Anthologies of modern French poetry generally begin with one or other of these poets, each seen as the source of the subjective lyric voice which replaced the didactic, descriptive verse of J.-B. Rousseau and Delille as the dominant mode of French poetry from the Restoration. Writing after 1848, when the Romantic movement had entered history, Lamartine and Gautier were primary sources for the terms in which this history was written. The result was that the poetry of Marceline Desbordes-Valmore (1786–1859), whose *Élégies, Marie et romances* appeared in January 1819, was largely excluded, for she brought to the creation of the lyric as the expression of private subjectivity a *feminine* voice which did not correspond to the representation of women as it was established by the dominant male culture of the early nineteenth century. This exclusion remained in force despite the efforts of major poets such as Baudelaire, Paul Verlaine (1844–96), André Breton (1896–1966), Louis Aragon (1897–1982) and Yves Bonnefoy (b. 1923) to secure a central place for the themes and forms of her poetry.

When Desbordes-Valmore did figure in histories of French poetry it was usually in terms of the literary and cultural stereotype of the abandoned mistress or suffering mother pouring out her passionate melancholy in artless verse. Baudelaire helped to impose this version in his July 1861 article 'Marceline Desbordes-Valmore', in which he presented her work as the spontaneous expression of a supposedly natural, eternal feminine feeling. But Baudelaire also identified in her work the voice of female desire and regret, far removed from conventional idealisations of woman constructed during the Restoration and July Monarchy. Her intimate, melancholic poems of family life were overwhelmed by the intellectual ambition of mainstream Romantic poetry. In addition, even during the high point of social Romanticism, no publisher would touch her political poems such as 'Dans la rue', a ferocious attack on the brutal repression of the striking Lyons silk-workers in 1834, which brought together workers and women as victims of the emerging social order. Finally, these themes were expressed by means of a more varied and innovative formal repertoire than that employed by the major poets of the 1820s and 1830s, a point highlighted by Verlaine when he included her in his second series of *poètes maudits*, published in 1888. She created an anxious, self-conscious first-person female voice through which to question the place of woman's poetry and situation within the male-dominated institutions of French writing. It is hardly surprising that there was little audience for such poetry until quite recently.[45]

Lamartine's *Méditations poétiques* was the publishing sensation of the 1820s. Within five years it had gone through twelve editions and sold, if its first publisher is to be believed, an unheard-of 30,000 copies.[46] Writing nearly 30 years later, Lamartine explained this success as the public's spontaneous response to these natural, unmediated outpourings of the soul. Here was a poet expressing sincere, deeply-held feelings about loss, doubt and the passage of time in a language stripped of Neoclassical artificiality and enriched with gentle, musical rhythms. This retrospective, self-interested account omits the extent to which this poetry spoke to the public of the literary salons organised by the returned aristocratic *émigrés* to which Lamartine's family had belonged and to which the poet himself aspired in the early years of the Restoration. The *Méditations* were successful because they were attuned to Royalist, Catholic sentiment as it emerged from the traumas of the period 1789–1815. They suggested its vulnerability, nostalgia for lost permanence, and its fatalistic submission to an unknowable divine purpose and to the anxieties and doubts which flowed from it. They presented these sentiments as springing directly and naturally from the depths of private longing and asserted the universal validity of this individual poetic voice.

'Le Lac', the most famous poem of the collection, commemorates the failed rendezvous at the lac de Bourget in 1817 between Lamartine and Julie Charles. They had met and fallen in love there the previous year but were now separated by the illness from which she would soon die. After the opening stanza, in which the poet asks whether any escape from the inexorable flow of time is possible, the poem is structured by three movements each introduced by the apostrophic 'Ô!' ('Ô lac!' (5), 'Ô temps!' (21), 'Ô lac!' (49)). The use of the apostrophic mode invites nature to participate in their experience and so place their love beyond restrictions of time and space. The poem's treatment of lost love and the passage of time made it, from its publication, a definitive anthology piece of Romantic lyric poetry.

Vigny, born into an aristocratic family and raised in its military values, was, like Lamartine, forced to confront the loss of power of the class to which he belonged. Unlike Lamartine, he never achieved or seriously sought any long-term accommodation with the new order. Instead, he presented his exclusion as that of an authentic intellectual isolated in a society committed to inauthentic values. He practised the short narrative poem of Biblical and historical dramas in which human destiny was enacted, retaining the form's rhyming alexandrine couplets and divisions into successive *chants* but removing its Neoclassical flourishes so as to express an exemplary spiritual isolation. In the poems by which he was best known during the Restoration period – 'Moïse', 'Éloa', 'Le Cor' – he showed that the poet, faced with the enigma of destiny, could preserve moral superiority only through stoic resistance or willed acceptance. Moses curses his election by God for a task from which no respite is granted and which separates him from human contact. Éloa, the angel born of the tear shed by Christ over the tomb of Lazarus, is trapped by the tear she sheds for Lucifer. A victim of the compassion which is her destiny, she is abandoned by God at the very moment Satan appears to be weakened by her innocence, and her fall leaves unexplained Satan's place in the divine scheme. In 'Le Cor', Roland's self-sacrifice at Roncevaux confirms the abnegation, honour and lucidity of the warrior-poet.[47]

Between 1822 and 1828, in the five editions of the collection known from the fourth (1826) as the *Odes et ballades*, Hugo moved from being the voice of Catholic Royalism to become the standard-bearer of Romantic liberalism. In the process, he took the Neo-classical heroic ode, replaced its Greco-Latin myths with Christian themes and adapted its compositional devices more closely to those of the *drame*. The 28 new poems of the third edition (1824) were dominated by the visionary religious themes inspired by his reading of Lamennais, while the preface announced his conversion to Stendhal's definition of Romanticism (in *Racine et Shakespeare*) as modernity and truth and his rejection of classical demarcations between genres. The next edition (1826) saw the introduction of the division between odes, reserved for poems on public themes, and ballads, modelled on the German *Lieder* introduced into France by Madame de Staël, which contained light, picturesque *poésie populaire* of the medieval troubadour tradition popularised by Nodier. This division was accompanied by a new attack on the separation of genres. In 1828, he added new poems and redistributed those contained in the previous editions to create an architecture which was both a retrospective autobiography of his development as a poet during the decade and a history of the Christian account of the world.

After the apocalyptic visions of the odes and the medieval fantasies of the ballads, *Les Orientales* (1829) expressed a third major strand of Romantic poetry, the myth of the Orient.[48] Interest in the East had grown since the late eighteenth century, and the war of independence waged by the Greeks against the Turks had reinforced it. Hugo introduced the collection as 'ce livre inutile de poésie pure' ['this useless book of pure poetry'], which led to its misleading and retrospective baptism as a source for the art-for-art's-sake movement which emerged in the mid-1830s. The formal experimentation evident in such anthology pieces as 'Les Djinns' and the visual, material force of the imagery, in part related to the poet's association with painters during the 1820s, appeared to lend support to this description. In reality, however, in *Les Orientales* Hugo enlarged his repertoire of poetic forms by extending the *Odes et ballades* into descriptive verse. He also continued the shift towards Republicanism that the death of his mother and reconciliation with his Bonapartist father had reinforced. These two elements came together in the myth of Napoleon, which served to focus his evolving theory of the poet, whose genius he saw as an emanation of Napoleonic will.

Drawn into the group of poets, painters and critics gathered around Hugo when he published in January 1827 his review of *Odes et ballades,* Charles-Augustin Sainte-Beuve (1804–69) produced a short-lived but powerful burst of creative and critical writing. His *Tableau historique et critique de la poésie française et du théâtre français au XVIe siècle* (1828) was followed by *Vie, pensées et poésies de Joseph Delorme* (1829) and *Consolations* (1830). The originality of his critical history was not so much his defence of the sixteenth-century poets (who by 1828 had regained favour with the literary establishment) as the parallels he drew between them and the Romantics. In his poetry, Sainte-Beuve was unable to compete with Hugo's drive towards the lyricism of the universal or with the philosophical depth of Lamartine and Vigny. His brief creative burst over, he settled into his role as the founder of the biographical approach to literary criticism for which he is now most remembered and attacked. Nevertheless, his discreet, intimist elegies of private feeling brought new elements – a tone of weariness and urban isolation, a use of pictorial reference and analogy and a rediscovery of the sonnet as an appropriate form in which to express the ramifications of private thought – on which the next generation of poets would enlarge, a point acknowledged by Baudelaire in his letter of 15 March 1865 to Sainte-Beuve.[49]

Support for or opposition to authoritarian regimes, whether those of the Empire or the Bourban monarchy, sustained the tradition of political poetry established during the Revolution and renewed by the publication of Chénier's poetry. The political poems and songs of Pierre-Jean de Béranger (1780–1857) are forgotten now, but in

1830 no contemporary poet enjoyed a wider audience. His patriotic themes, anticlericalism and sentimental, utopian humanitarianism ensured his appeal among all shades of social and political opposition to the Restoration. For the Romantics, his work extended lyricism's range, and its simple rhythms, clear structure and celebration of popular types became part of the moral and intellectual orthodoxy of the liberal bourgeoisie. His reputation began its steep decline almost immediately after his death in 1857, for his facility and sentimentality excluded him from the intellectual and aesthetic ambitions which writing would acquire in the modernist tradition. But the history of French poetry in the first half of the nineteenth century cannot be understood without reference to his work.

The 'Three Glorious Days' of 27–9 July 1830 were a watershed in French history of the nineteenth century. The fall of Charles X, hostile to the Revolution of 1789, and his replacement by Louis-Philippe, the 'citizen King' who had embraced its aspirations, was a turning-point in the emergence of the social and political consensus which, by the end of the century, would secure the victory of the Republican idea. The re-adoption of the Tricolour as France's national flag, the erection of the monument to the 'Trois Glorieuses' on the Place de la Bastille, the revisions to the Charter of 1814 which confirmed the growing secularisation of the State, all confirmed that the political and philosophical values which had triggered the Revolution of 1789 were gaining control of national life.[50]

For the new liberal ruling class, the 'divine surprise' of July 1830 was the discipline of the Paris people. In the immediate aftermath, ruling-class discourse, as if to compensate the people for having used Louis-Philippe to cheat it out of its Republic, praised its political maturity and the restraint with which its force had been directed. The refrain was common among writers too. In Hugo's ode 'Dicté après juillet 1830', published within a fortnight of the events themselves, the people replaced Napoleon as the irresistible force (ocean or volcano) which drove history onward.[51] He called on the Catholic Church, freed from its compromising alliance with the Bourbon regime, to provide a spiritual dimension to the people's wisdom in July 1830 by setting an example of humility. The dissenting voice in the chorus celebrating the people's restraint in July 1830 was that of Auguste Barbier (1805–82). As if in response to Hugo's ode, Barbier published in September 1830 'La Curée', a bitter denunciation of the betrayal of the people by the bourgeoisie, who had used the people's courage to open their own doors to power. He published this and other poems on the July Revolution in his volume *Iambes* (1831), whose title was a reminder of the continuing relevance of Chénier's poetry of political opposition. He followed this with *Il Pianto* (1833), a defence of Italian nationalism, and *Lazare* (1837), poems of sympathy for the victims of the English Industrial Revolution. In the three collections, Barbier created a pessimistic vision of humanity imprisoned in a world without values, and exhausted his indignation and poetic range. Yet for forty years the expressive and controlled power of his images and rhythms made him a major poet of the Romantic period and an essential link between the political poetry of Chénier and Arthur Rimbaud (1854–91).[52]

With its stereotypical heroes and heroines acting out fantasies of passion, jealousy and revenge in the imaginary local colour of Mediterranean settings, its wide range and playful virtuosities of language, tone and metre, Musset's first collection, *Contes d'Espagne et d'Italie* (1830), reproduced in one volume many of the developments in French poetry during the 1820s.[53] But it already contained signs of the fractures within the self and between self and world which the Revolution of 1830 would exacerbate and which would make the lyrical and narrative dramatisation of the divided self the major theme of Musset's subsequent poetry. Written in the immediate aftermath of the July Days and published in October 1830, 'Les Vœux stériles' recounts the sense of exile from, and nostalgia for, the fusion of aesthetic and ethical values which made Ancient Greece the paradise lost to the modern world. In his poetry of the early 1830s, this loss was projected in various characterisations, notably that of the displaced, libertine aristocrat Jacques Rolla ('Rolla', 1833) who, ruined by gambling and having spent his last night with a 15-year-old girl forced by poverty into prostitution, takes leave of the world through poison – but not before denouncing Voltaire and Enlightenment values for being as bankrupt as himself.

For Musset, the July Revolution merely confirmed that these values had been hijacked by a selfish, materialist bourgeois liberalism. In his poetry, his response was to raise the drawbridge on the failures and disappointments of the public arena and explore, through the solitary pain of sexual betrayal, the same hunger for, and lack of belief in, self-knowledge. In his cycle of four poems, 'Les Nuits' (1835–7), the poet engages in dialogue with his muse and with the seasons. This familiar rhetorical ground serves to intensify the dysfunction between the organic rhythms of growth and renewal in nature and the turmoil of the poet's elation and despair. For Musset, alienation and solitude are the natural home of the lyric subject in the post-1830 world.

The transitional nature of the work produced by the new generation of poets who began writing in the closing years of the Restoration is seen in Gautier's *Poésies* (1830).[54] The collection combined the legacy of Neoclassical diction with themes (time, nature, the Gothic) and forms (elegy, ballad, meditation) clearly identified with Romanticism. Such explicit use of derivative elements freed Gautier to concentrate on other possibilities made available to poetry in the course of the 1820s. *Poésies* contains a wide range of experimentation in line length, stanza structure and rhyme as well as Gautier's first attempts at the descriptive, visual poetry for which he became so widely reputed. A range of factors (his early training as an art student, the impact upon him of Hugo's *Orientales*, the social and cultural developments which were bringing writers, painters and musicians closer together at that time) encouraged him to develop what became known as *transposition d'art* poetry, in which the poem represented the subject and/or manner of visual art. Gautier, one of the most important art critics of the century, was one of the major practitioners of this poetic mode.

He republished the *Poésies* two years later in *Albertus*. The poem which gave its name to the new volume and which consists of 122 stanzas of 12 lines each (11 alexandrines and a final octosyllabic line) is a tongue-in-cheek anthology of the fantastic, satanic and aesthetic strands of Romanticism. It has the world-weary dandy's pact with the devil, extraordinary journeys, miraculous transformations and juxtapositions of the comic, horrific and grotesque. In a sense, it was the manifesto of the *petit cénacle*, the expression in ironic mode of its collective gestures. But its themes of the idealist destroyed by the quest for the ideal, of appearances as the only reality and of lucid cynicism as the only virtue gave serious direction to the growing disillusionment of the 1830s. Its formal values established Gautier as one of the most inventive prosodists to emerge from within the Romantic movement. In *La Comédie de la mort* (1838), the formal initiatives and period themes and accessories remain but the tone is more sombre. Faust, Don Juan and Napoleon represent three forms of the despair and martyrdom that inevitably follows the deluded human aspiration to ultimate power, for which art is the sole antidote. Gautier celebrates the great artists of the past whose work makes up for the inadequacies of the present and offers the poet the compensations of a craft mastered.

In the context of the increased calls for commitment which followed the Revolution of 1830, Hugo published *Les Feuilles d'automne* in December 1831. The preface argued for a less direct definition of authenticity for the artist than that of involvement in political struggle, stressing instead the relationship between knowledge of the self and an understanding of the world, between private loss (the passage of time and the grief of bereavements and marital crisis) and the questions asked of political and religious systems. The opening poem, 'Ce siècle avait deux ans . . .', states, in its famous definition of the poet as an 'écho sonore' ['sonorous echo'], that the poet's autobiography is also the story/history of the mysterious origins and purposes of human experience. Through social intercourse with family and friends, the contact with nature, and the memories and associations which these trigger, the poet investigates the power of the imagination to explore the inspirations and terrors of the unknown. The images and rhythms of poetic language are the means by which the dark, limitless, Babel-like architectures of the universe can be brought to the surface and mastered.

Between *Les Feuilles d'automne* and *Les Chants du crépuscule* (1835), the political and cultural climate emerging in the wake of the change of regime had, for Hugo, darkened; he and his contemporaries found themselves in the ambiguous half-light of a society suspended between dusk and dawn, past and future. 'Dicté après 1830', the first poem chronologically, was an optimistic ode to reconciliation between antagonistic forces within French society: bourgeoisie and people, liberty and force, religion and anticlericalism, Napoleonic myth and the insurrectionary crowd. Five years later, hope has given way to anxiety, expressed in the dominant metaphor of darkness challenging sunlight. Hugo's first poems on the misery of the people, his fears of impending explosion, his lament for the age's lost freedoms and wasted youth, bring together in the first half of the collection his anxieties for France's political and spiritual future. These fears are dispelled and harmony re-established in the second half by the revelation of love and the emotional equilibrium achieved between the opposing happiness with wife (Adèle) and mistress (Juliette Drouot), tenderness and passion, innocence and desire. This clarification brings with it a renewed faith in the poet as echo. The final two poems complete the spiritual journey: the love for Juliette allays doubt and the fidelity of Adèle replaces half-light with clarity.

Two years later, in *Les Voix intérieures*, he extends his theory of the poet as echo in the direction of impersonal poetry through Olympio, the poet's alter ego. A sequence of poems provides an anthology of Romantic attitudes on nature as source of love and faith, as succour and terror, and as the repository of human feeling and divine mystery. Domestic poems celebrate children as the link between poetry, love, nature and the divine. Poems of the streets confirm the artist's right to distance from direct commitment. As the political hopes invested in the July Monarchy have not survived subsequent events, Hugo urges the rich to remember the sacred duty of charity and the poor the sublime consolations of prayer, two pillars of July Monarchy ideology which would remain in Hugo's subsequent work. These inner voices heard, the poet returns to the theme of doubt in 'Pensar, Dudar', which inaugurates the sequence of dialogues with alter egos (his deceased brother, Olympio, the Muse) through which is re-affirmed the poet's heroic obligation to express the totality of human experience, nature and world, known and unknown. This more pronounced emphasis on the metaphysical nature and ambition of the poetic experience is taken further in *Les Rayons et les Ombres* (1840).

* * *

The period covered in this chapter was one of profound changes in the writer's relationship to the past, to the literary practices derived from it and to the terms in which the relationship with the public was conducted. The Romantic movement's challenge to classical aesthetic and cultural norms provided the framework for the changes which were effected, which led to a major extension of the literary sphere. The emergence of the historical novel reflected the new instability of political regimes and responded to a public desire to understand the crisis of authority this instability had produced. During this period Balzac created what would later be seen as the dominant form of the realist novel by adapting for the representation of contemporary society the means by which Scott's novels appeared to have resurrected the hidden meaning and purpose of history. In *La Comédie humaine*, he created an aesthetic system whose range and structure corresponded to the contemporary desire to see human society as a totality which could be categorised and described like that of animal and plant life, but his own novels showed this society to be a theatre of conflicting ambitions which no authority could circumscribe. The claim to represent modern society, the narrative practices which this encouraged and the economic and technological changes taking place created a new public for the novel and enabled it to displace poetry as the dominant genre. The poet now became the most vulnerable figure in a literary landscape shaped by new social and economic realities and identified himself as an important focus of resistance to the values which these realities signified. The *petits cénacles* of Romantic poets provided early examples of the poet as outcast, and this function would in turn engender an alternative authenticity of the avant-garde within this system of literature.

By the end of this period, *la bataille romantique* was over but its legacy was just beginning. This is why Baudelaire could assert provocatively in his *Salon de 1846* that Romanticism was 'art moderne, – c'est-à-dire intimité, spiritualité, couleur, aspiration vers l'infini, exprimées par tous les moyens que contiennent les arts' ['modern art, – that is intimacy, spirituality, colour, aspiration to the infinite, expressed by all the means which art possesses']. In the aftermath of 1848 this legacy would have to be addressed.

5

Reactions to Revolution, 1848–71

I   CONSERVATIVE PROGRESS

In June 1848 Republicanism's universalist ideal collapsed in class conflict and conservative reaction.[1] Louis-Napoleon's coup d'état of December 1851 reinforced the victory of these conservative elements. During the 1850s his regime enjoyed a period of strong economic growth, of which the development of the railways and the rebuilding of Paris were the most visible signs.[2] Technocratic modernisation was the Second Empire's big idea. The enormous prestige of science and technology fuelled the faith in economic and social progress which would eliminate class antagonisms and political upheavals and generate the apolitical cultural consensus to which the regime aspired.[3] Saint-Simon's fusion of religion and social science in *Nouveau Christianisme* (1825) had created powerful disciples, including the Emperor himself, committed to the creation of a modern entrepreneurial society. Auguste Comte (1798–1857), in his *Cours de philosophie positive* (1830–42), had created a philosophy of science confident in its power to establish absolute truths on the basis of observation and experimentation and to provide a rational basis for social organisation. Hippolyte Taine (1828–93), in his *Histoire de la littérature anglaise* (1864), extended this approach into cultural history, arguing that this could be established on a scientific basis through study of the 'race', 'milieu' and 'moment' (the inherited personality, environment and historical situation) of the writer. To novelists, Taine's formula offered a model for the observation and description of human behaviour with which to extend Balzac's ambition to represent the mechanisms of modern society; to poets, it offered values such as objectivity, impersonality and historical reconstruction with which to replace what were considered to be Romanticism's sentimental outpourings of the soul.[4]

During the Second Empire, literature's public was significantly extended by the growth of literacy, itself consequent on the expansion of primary education, where the battle for control of young French minds began in earnest between supporters and opponents of religious education. In addition, technological changes were making available new possibilities for the publication and distribution of literature. The regime sought to remain in control of this changing situation. Already in 1850, the increasingly conservative Second Republic had introduced a tax on newspapers publishing serial novels in an effort to counter what it saw as the threat posed by the wider access to novels that serialisation had created from the mid-1830s. The extraordinary impact of Eugène Sue's *Les Mystères de Paris* was still fresh in the memory. The Second Empire reinforced the existing mechanisms of censorship with controls over distribution. Printed materials destined for the provinces now required an official stamp, for the emerging railway network and the station bookstalls for which Hachette had obtained the franchise were creating new means of circulation for literature. Predictably, censorship was a double-edged sword, resulting in court cases (notably those brought against the 'immorality' of Flaubert's *Madame Bovary* and Baudelaire's *Les Fleurs du mal*, both in 1857) which brought the regime little credit but which no doubt encouraged self-censorship in authors, publishers and distributors.

With increased literacy, the targeting of particular audiences became more sophisticated. New collections flourished, particularly those aimed at younger readers. The new demands for school textbooks and for scientific and technological vulgarisation of all kinds played a major role in the growth of some of France's major publishing houses (Larousse, Hachette, Flammarion, Armand Colin). In 1857 Hachette launched its *Bibliothèque rose*, with moral tales for children and adolescents. The collection's providential author was the hugely successful Comtesse Sophie de Ségur (1799–1874), whose stories became essential reading for the younger members of this widening public.[5] In 1862 Jules Verne (1828–1905) published *Cinq semaines en ballon*, the first of the Extraordinary Voyages whose success testified to the age's sense of wonder at the scientific advances of the time and at the forces of the natural world against which science was pitted.[6]

During the Second Empire, the growth of the press created for many writers a source of income and an opportunity to develop forms of writing which would be appropriate to the growing readership for creative and critical literature. As during the July Monarchy, press owners also responded with technical and commercial initiatives to the advances in literacy and the growth in demand for information created by these advances.[7] The most important of these was the creation in 1863 of *Le Petit Journal*, forerunner of the modern tabloid. Here, the key to commercial success was the daily diet of *faits divers* (news items), notably crimes and court cases. These in turn obliged the serialised novel to respond to the greater authenticity that such items possessed. It was on one such *fait divers* that Émile Gaboriau (1832–73) based *l'Affaire Lerouge* (1866) and, in doing so, created the French detective novel in which the detective's scientific methods and powers of deductive reasoning eventually unmask the villain.

The *Petit Journal* alternated Gaboriau's novels with those of Pierre-Alexis Ponson du Terrail (1829–71), the most successful serial novelist of the Second Empire, whose most famous fictional character, Rocambole, appeared in nearly thirty novels and gave his name to a type of plot ('rocambolesque'), in which rapid and barely credible sequences of events were sustained by the author's talent for the creation of suspense. Paul Féval (1816–97) created a gallery of both heroic and odious characters in novels of Breton folklore, socio-political comment and criminal adventures through which he promoted a conservative ideology of paternalism, family values and the importance of elites in a changing society. The success of such writers was based on the degree of complicity they established with a new, popular readership which, with the *Petit Journal*, had for the first time its own newspaper and its own literature. In its breathtaking accumulation of mysteries revealed and resolved, this literature showed the complexities of modern social reality to be reducible to a few simple, reassuring and easily assimilated oppositions (good/evil, reward/punishment, oppressor/victim and so on).[8]

II NEW NOVELS

In Gustave Flaubert self-imposed social exile and the commitment to the craft of fiction merged to generate one of the most powerful literary myths bequeathed by the nineteenth century to the modern period. By the time of his death, the 'hermit of Croisset' was already widely considered the founder of the modern French novel and his position has been consolidated since by each redefinition of modernity. In his early work he practised autobiographical writing in which he exploited characteristic Romantic themes (death, madness, *ennui*, exoticism) and forms (the fantastic, historical and philosophical *conte*). In *Madame Bovary* (1857) and *L'Éducation sentimentale* (1869), this Romantic legacy is presented as an obstacle to the individual's adaptation to new social and historical realities, yet these realities are themselves shown to be sordid, ugly and unworthy of respect. Between Romantic illusions and reality's disillusionment, the one true value was art itself. Flaubert's radical scepticism set the romantic and realist positions against each other, and the language through which he did so became for him the means and end of writing.[9]

By the mid-1850s, when Flaubert was working on *Madame Bovary*, Balzac's *Comédie humaine* was the major literary reference for the emerging realist movement. *Mœurs de province*, the subtitle to *Madame Bovary*, was a clear reference to Balzac's novels of provincial life and the reference underlines the extent to which Flaubert turned the model against itself. Faced in her dismal provincial life with the mismatch between desire and experience and the misrepresentation of both by the fraudulent language of received wisdom, Emma attempts to force her experiences into the literary stereotypes of Romantic passion and adultery. When she is finally obliged to recognise the extent of her misreading, she commits suicide rather than give up her dream of a life and love story lived in an ideal idiom. Her fall takes her hapless husband and innocent offspring with it (Charles dies of grief and Berthe is sent to work in a cotton mill); its counterpoint is the elevation of the pragmatic opportunist Homais to the *Légion d'honneur*. Flaubert was hauled before the courts in 1857 for not providing in the text a clear narrative viewpoint from which to condemn Emma's confused perceptions. Instead he juxtaposed individual idiolects to ironic effect (the Homais/Bournisien confrontations and the *Comices agricoles* scene have become classics) and replaced the fiction of an omniscient narrator with the shifting representations created by *style indirect libre*. In this free indirect style the boundaries traditionally separating the voices of narrator and character became indistinct and thereby opened up new possibilities for the ironic presentation of character and event.[10]

In *L'Éducation sentimentale*, Flaubert further complicated the difficulties encountered in the writing of *Madame Bovary* when he brought the practices of fiction he had created there to the historical novel. In Flaubert's novel, set in the events of 1848, the Balzacian model is again dismantled. Where Balzac associated private and public events to demonstrate the purposeful agency of history, Flaubert linked the sentimental education of Frédéric Moreau and the doomed Revolution of 1848 in a shared failure of purpose. The failure is all the more obvious because the chronology of convergence between personal and political crises is so clearly established that even Frédéric himself notices it: 'Je suis la mode, je me réforme' ['I am following fashion and reforming']. The nineteenth-century myth of Paris as the cradle of the Revolution has become unintelligible.[11] The city is now a place of disorientation and the Revolution a collection of bit parts for ham actors and posers. The ironic juxtaposition of rival discourses used to such effect in *Madame Bovary* now links 'patriots' and 'reactionaries' in a shared failure to transcend a limited, selfish vision and establish a positive, collective basis for action. Motivation itself is problematic, for action is more often the result of accident than volition and the characters themselves are as much disconnected fragments as cumulative determinations. The catalogue of failed initiatives culminates in the political meeting in the gloriously-named *Club de l'Intelligence*, when the comrade from Barcelona intervenes in Spanish. Frédéric's exasperated response – 'C'est absurde à la fin! Personne ne comprend!' ['But it's ridiculous! Nobody can understand a word he's saying!'] – leads to his own ejection from the meeting and, with it, from any productive relationship with the public sphere. In *L'Éducation sentimentale* history as progress has indeed descended into farce.

The nature of Flaubert's achievement in *L'Éducation sentimentale* can be seen when it is compared with that of another major novel of the Second Empire with an historical subject set in the capital: Hugo's *Les Misérables* (1862), written in two stages between 1845–8 and 1860–2.[12] In Flaubert, political action is pointless confusion or selfish expediency; in Hugo it is collective, universal drama. In Flaubert, history is empty repetition; in Hugo it is the realisation in the human sphere of a vast spiritual adventure, represented by the links established in the novel between Napoleon, Valjean and Christ. *Les Misérables* is a profoundly religious work, an epic of the people redeemed in which social and political conflict is resolved through the higher spiritual purpose of which it is part. Valjean's fall and rehabilitation are those of Satan in *Fin de Satan*, on which

Hugo worked before returning to *Les Misérables*. Paris in the novel is the new Jerusalem, in which the revolutionary tradition finds its true dimension and purpose. This is the reconciling, universal Republican vision at its most all-embracing.

Hugo's religious vision of the people and his definition of misery made the novel an enormous success from the moment it appeared despite, or because of, the fact that it ran counter to the realist trends that were leading to more materialist approaches to the representation of the poor in the French novel. Edmond (1822–96) and Jules (1830–70) Huot de Goncourt had already published widely on the life and art of the eighteenth century when they turned to the novel.[13] As aristocrats and aesthetes displaced in the bourgeois century, they looked on the lower classes with curiosity and distaste, as a combination of the exotic and the degenerate and, as such, a vehicle for the display of their own refinements of perception and style. As congenital bachelors they looked on women as pathologically given over to lethal, instinctual urges. In the preface to their fourth novel, *Germinie Lacerteux* (1865), they argued that in the modern scientific age the lower classes had a right to be represented in fiction and this novel, with its scandalous subject, detailed documentation *sur le terrain* and medico-sociological claims, presented itself as modern fiction's most advanced form. The heroine was based on their own servant, Rose, whose death in 1862 had led to the brothers' shocked discovery of her double life of lovers, debt and alcoholism and to her role as a model for their case study of the working-class female species. Their narrative style combines a morbid fascination for what they saw as the manifestations of a civilisation in post-aristocratic decline and the aesthetic distance of the connoisseur handling a specimen of a foreign culture. Its stylised, self-conscious neologisms, rare words and emphasis on the order of sensations became known as *écriture artiste* and have been seen as a parallel to Impressionist innovations in painting.[14] For this reason the Goncourts now occupy a greater position in the history of French narrative styles than in that of the novel itself, where their achievement has been overtaken by that of Émile Zola.

Zola considered *Germinie Lacerteux* to be a major moment in the development of modern, scientific fiction. He had arrived in Paris from Aix in February 1858 at one of the high points of Haussmann's transformation of the city and appears to have sensed almost immediately the significance for his future writing of the political and economic factors at work there. He quickly made contact with centres of literary, artistic and intellectual development in the capital and began to gravitate towards opponents of the Empire. He worked for nearly four years from March 1862 for Hachette, a centre of progressive ideas, where his discovery of the work of Taine and Littré reinforced his adherence to the new religion of science and technology which dominated this milieu. He took these commitments with him into his journalism of the mid-1860s, in which his articles in defence of Manet reveal his developing theories of literature rather than a real understanding of Manet's painting. He was by this time working on his first major novel, *Thérèse Raquin* (1867), to whose second edition the following year he added an important preface in which he claimed for the novel a scientific objective. This modern version of the fateful triangle, in which the lovers murder the husband, applied to two human beings the sort of case study that surgeons carried out on a corpse. The novel portrays the logical, inevitable collision between a 'nature sanguine' (Laurent) and a 'nature nerveuse' (Thérèse), each the product of a given environment and education. At the beginning of their relationship, their two temperaments complement each other in a positive, enriching equilibrium of desire satisfied. Once this equilibrium is shattered by the remorse which follows the murder, they are trapped in a logic which compels each to destroy the other.

In *Thérèse Raquin* Zola brought together the scientific ambition and the scandalous realities of contemporary culture which would form the basis of the vast fictional project whose broad lines were already clear in his mind by the end of the Second Empire. Begun just as the regime was collapsing, and written with the hindsight which this collapse provided, *Les Rougon-Macquart*, a 20-novel cycle forming what Zola called a natural and social history of a family under the Second Empire, aimed to demonstrate the natural and social laws regulating the private and public behaviour of a representative family unit whose heredity, milieu and social interactions constituted the raw data for Zola's 'scientific' novel. The analogy with the scientific experiment was misleading, however, for despite the emphasis on documentation, investigation and so-called laws of behavioural psychology, the novel cycle would derive its power and range from the novelist's interpretation of the energies which drove the world. This combination of the scientific and subjective, first practised in *Thérèse Raquin*, would make Zola the most powerful figure in the French novel for the remainder of the century and the undisputed leader of the Naturalist movement with which he became identified.[15]

III   POST-ROMANTIC POSITIONS IN POETRY

There is a sense in which, if Napoleon III had not existed, Victor Hugo would have had to invent him. The coup d'état of 2 December 1851 released the poet from the ambiguities inherent in his relationship with the July Monarchy and consummated his break with the political classes with whom in 1848 he had shared a distaste for the Second Republic and support for the presidential ambitions of Louis-Napoleon. The defeats and humiliations which in 1849–51 accompanied his slow but sure progress towards the Republican opposition, together with his accumulated grief at the death of his daughter and that of Juliette Drouot, freed him for the exile whose idea was already present as an undercurrent of his work of the 1830s and 1840s. *Châtiments* (1853) is the first result of this clarification. On the one hand, it is a collection of political poems written to accompany *Napoléon-le-petit*, his prose attack on the new regime; on the other, it is the first of a series of volumes, including *Les Contemplations* (1856) and the first series of *La Légende des siècles* (1859), which extend the religious and philosophical implications of the new political realities.

In *Châtiments*, Hugo appointed himself the guardian of the Republican flame with a rhetoric of no compromise designed to secure the moral ground on which to base his present authority and future interventions in the public sphere. The poems narrate the journey from the darkness of the night of 2 December ('Nox') to the light of the Empire's inevitable defeat ('Lux'). The banishment of the poet is the act of martyrdom which sustains Hugo's messianic myth of Fall and Redemption, his Biblical parable of humiliation and ultimate deliverance. Christian and secular religions, Jesus and Voltaire, Charity and Progress, all merge to define the true political and spiritual dimension and purpose of the French Revolution. As in earlier collections, history in *Châtiments* is the ground of meaning and of the poet's responsibility; it stands by his side as he brands the Emperor-criminal with the mark of his crime ('L'homme a ri'). Hugo draws on a wide range of old and new models (from the Bible, Juvenal and Dante to Barbier and Béranger) to energise the poetic tradition henceforth ranged, through him, against Napoleon III, and invokes a variety of verse forms and strophic and line structures with which to give voice to its resistance.

Though many of the poems of *Les Contemplations* were written before his exile and are rooted in the events and texts of Hugo's experience in the late 1830s and 1840s, the creative burst of lyricism triggered by *Châtiments* produced in *Les Contemplations* its most complete and representative expression in Hugo's work. The collection demonstrates the power and scope of poetic contemplation when the Romantic poet's self-regarding gaze moves outwards to embrace the entire forward movement of creation, using every voice at the poet's disposal: lyric and epic, universal and everyday, tragic and grotesque. The destiny of the individual poet is here indissolubly tied to the world's ultimate historical and metaphysical destination. The solitary, exemplary resistance to Napoleon III is a modern reiteration of the defeat of Cain, with, at the end of the struggle, the redemption of evil itself in creation's return to its source in God. At the centre of the book, the personal tragedy from which the representation of these finalities is derived and around which their elements find their alloted place in the thematic structure of the text, is the father's grief for his lost daughter. His poetic biography is divided into *Autrefois* (1830–43) and *Aujourd'hui* (1843–56), two equal halves, one before, the other after, her death. The memory of her presence in his life is followed by the power of her intercession in his living death of exile. Each division contains three sections or 'books', and each book defines an essential theme of the spiritual itinerary opened, divided and completed by the father's conversations with his daughter. Through the six books, the history of humanity and its place in the divine order yields to the power of the poet's language, to the relentless forward drive of his rhetoric. In the antitheses, enumerations and personifications which translate his sense of the forces with which humanity is engaged, the poet becomes the voice of the world.

More perhaps than any other single volume, *Les Contemplations* offers a compendium of the ambitions and interrogations of French nineteenth-century culture as it sought to establish consensus around the Republican extension of the values of the Enlightenment. More than any other it asserts the poet's central place as the priest of the new age, as the means of intercession between the world and the unknown forces which shaped public and private destiny. Hugo truly did espouse his century, its passion to know, to confront the terror of mystery, to impose order and discipline on new forms of knowledge and on the range and complexity of modern experience. The confrontation between his colossal imagination and the system of French poetry which he inherited and transformed portrays at local level the general forces at work in the culture of his time. Developments in French poetry subsequent to Hugo's work in exile created reservations about his achievement, its epic scale and apparent facility, but if contemporary and subsequent poets saw themselves in part as writing against Hugo, it was, from *Les Contemplations*, on his terms and with his sense of the possibilities of poetry.[16]

* * *

For Charles Baudelaire, disappointment with the outcome of the Revolution was in proportion to the hopes he had invested in it. Napoleon III's coup d'état sealed their fate.[17] In a letter of 5 March 1852, Baudelaire wrote that the events of 2 December had finished him with politics and, by implication, with the wider hope that poets might re-establish their connections with the public, which for Baudelaire had been such a feature of the great flowering of French poetry during the 1820s. Released from this illusion, he returned to the search for knowledge of self and other begun before 1848 but this time with new guides. As he put it in his *Journaux intimes*, 'De Maistre et Poe m'ont appris à raisonner' ['De Maistre and Poe taught me how to reason']. De Maistre's social and historical pessimism and his authoritarian religious and political mysticism founded on expiation gave Baudelaire's own world view a powerful theological credibility from 1852. In his reading and translations of Poe, he found support for his contempt for the utilitarian, positivist humanism of the Second Empire and his belief that critical lucidity was central to the act of writing.

Expelled from paradise by original sin, exiled in the city by the alienation of modern life, the poet was, as he wrote in the poem 'L'Héautontimorouménos', a 'faux accord' ['false chord'] in the 'divine symphonie' ['divine symphony'] torn, like his reader, between what he called the double postulation of God and Satan, between nostalgia for lost innocence and the embrace of evil. A 'vorace Ironie' ['voracious irony'], the bitter laugh of the defeated, was the essential voice of this permanently divided and displaced self but, expressed in the language of poetry, it might produce in the reader's imagination a terrible and cleansing beauty. Its realisation would imply, however, a new programme for lyric poetry and it was the dialogue he conducted in the late 1850s with Hugo's poetry of exile and with the lyricism of Théodore de Banville (1823–91) which enabled him to achieve it.[18]

In *Les Fleurs du mal*, woman is, as so often, the other term of the lyric equation. Baudelaire's poet is confounded by her mystery and the instability of roles and transactions generated by the multiple forms of his desire. At one extreme, there is the child/sister/ sovereign of the 'Invitation au voyage' with whom the poet would journey to an ideal landscape of sensual and spiritual fulfilment, whose topography of pleasure is evoked by the verse structure of the lullaby and by the networks of sound and rhythm created by rich rhymes, assonance and alliteration, all drawn closer together by the short lines. At the other, there is the mistress of 'À une Madone', whose alleged faithlessness galvanises the poet's infernal self-loathing into fantasies of pornographic violence and revenge which expand through the images, syntax and rhythms of the alexandrine couplets, pausing briefly at the typographic space following line 36 in order to give maximum impact to the final act, in which the poet hurls the seven knives of the seven mortal sins into her heart with the climactic thuds of the final three symmetrical hemistichs. Between these two extreme representations of woman, as a means to a return to an original ecstatic unification of self and world and as the instrument of a diabolic annihilation of both, the poet attempts to negotiate the ambivalent signs (hair, perfume, gesture, expression) she places along the various paths which connect the 'spleen' of everyday reality with the longed-for 'ideal' of reunion with the divine origins of being.

Closing his *Salon de 1846*, Baudelaire described Paris as 'féconde en sujets poétiques et merveilleux' ['rich in poetic and marvellous subjects'], the exemplary location for what he called 'l'héroisme de la vie moderne' ['the heroism of modern life']. This heroism was another illusion lost in 1851. During the Second Empire, virtually the entire city centre was razed to the ground in the name of progress, which Baudelaire despised. New wide boulevards, favourable to more rapid communications required by changing economic forms of production and distribution of goods (not to mention military control of the urban space), were carved through the old overcrowded working-class and Bohemian districts of the Île de la Cité and the Latin Quarter. The fecundity of this new environment for the poet was undiminished but disorientation, surprise and jostling confrontation were its new forms. Paris was now littered with the human and material debris of change, peopled by other existences as displaced, alienated and marginalised as the poet's own. It was therefore an appropriate site for his search for contact with others in order to restore wholeness to his sundered, fragmented self.

On the loose among the urban crowd, the poet was a *flâneur* ['stroller'] who enjoyed the incomparable privilege of being at once self and other, free to engage in and disengage from what he called its sacred prostitution of the soul, but no longer able to control the signs through which this exhilarating but dangerous intercourse was conducted. Like nature in his programmatic sonnet 'Correspondances', Paris is a forest of symbols emitting confused words, triggering chance collisions with people, memories and lines of poetry. In his trilogy of Paris poems written in the late 1850s and dedicated to Hugo ('Le Cygne', 'Les Sept Vieillards' and 'Les Petites Vieilles'), Baudelaire represents with extraordinary force the pleasures and terrors, the commitments and retreats involved in the desire for the sacred prostitution of self in others and shows this desire achieving instead only a circular journey back to the solitary confinement of the self.[19]

As France's most famous exile, Hugo was present between the lines of 'Le Cygne' and was its natural dedicatee. Indeed Baudelaire told Hugo in a letter of September 1859 that he had written 'Les Petites Vieilles' after reading several of his poems. But whatever truth these (and other) external factors may contain, Baudelaire's relationship to Hugo at this time springs from deeper sources. He can only have dedicated and sent these poems to Hugo because he was quite aware that in them he had successfully risen to the challenge of Hugo's domination of the French lyric tradition, that he had taken this tradition at the point at which Hugo appeared to have made it his own and had given it a decisive new direction. His was not Hugo's physical, political exile across the sea but the internal, existential isolation of the modern city poet, not the heroism of Hugo's lyric ambition as we have seen it but the ambiguity and mystery of modern experience.

By the same token the homage to Banville published in the *Revue fantaisiste* in August 1861 was accompanied by his implicit recognition that this new direction he had imparted to the French lyric went beyond that of this 'parfait *classique*' ['perfect *classical poet*']. In *Les Cariatides* (1842) and *Les Stalactites* (1846) Banville had expressed his distaste for what he saw as the materialism of July Monarchy society by means of a cult of beauty inspired by Greek sculpture, and for what he saw as the excesses of Romantic sentimentality by means of a cult of verse form of which rhyme was the key. In the *Odes funambulesques* (1857), his sensibility is expressed in verse of great technical virtuosity. For Baudelaire, however, Banville's less multi-dimensional lyric voice could not reach the depths or heights of modern experience. He remained a 'classical' poet whose commitment to earlier lyric forms restricted expression of a complex modernity.

Baudelaire's ambition to express the simultaneous attraction towards opposing poles of human experience is seen in two central but seemingly opposed features of his prosody: his renewal of the French sonnet and his development of prose poetry. These provide on the one hand a concise and highly regulated fixed form to which the Paris theme is largely extraneous (only two of the *Tableaux parisiens* are sonnets), and on the other a new as yet unregulated form which was essential for the Paris theme. Almost half of the poems of *Les Fleurs du mal* are sonnets and they display a wide range of experimentation with the form's regular strophic system based on the rhyme scheme *abba abba ccd ede* (or *ccd eed*). The sonnet combined flexibility with mathematical precision, and the aesthetic and intellectual virtues of concision with the capacity to express a wide range of tone and mood. Its internal division into octave and sestet (and the range of expressive possibilities which resulted) invited endless permutations of the relationship between what he called, in *Fusées*, the two fundamental literary qualities: surnatural-ism and irony. In the sonnet's structure itself, the one's expansive, generalising movement could be challenged by the other's bitter, critical lucidity. From their combined struggle for mastery of the poet's psyche, Baudelaire created the distinctive, post-Romantic lyric voice.[20]

Despite this achievement and no doubt to some extent in reaction to the disciplines of the sonnet, Baudelaire began to explore in a second, uncodified poetic medium themes and lyric movements whose expressive potential he had realised in verse. For Baudelaire, the challenge of the prose poem was that of the dynamic but poten-tially lethal absolute freedom it offered the poet, who must seek to achieve the expressive power of verse while relinquishing the system of rules and constraints which structured and directed his creativity. Writing prose counterparts to his own poems was a logical place to begin the exploration of this uncharted territory of prosody, but in the ambition, described in his preface to *Le Spleen de Paris*, to achieve 'le miracle d'une prose poétique, musicale sans rythme et sans rime' ['the miracle of a poetic prose, musical without rhythm and rhyme'], the primary motivation came from the city and its innumerable intersecting relationships. Baudelaire's experience of the modern city stimulated his search for alternative forms with which to organise the fragmentations resulting from its colliding energies and complex socialities. His prose poems display an enormous range of tones, forms and structuring devices and they made available to his successors forms of experimentation which would decisively redirect theories and practices of the poetic.[21]

* * *

Gérard de Nerval (1808–55) represents in an extreme form the Romantic subject's search within the self for a source of identity which might heal the breach between self and world, subject and object.[22] He projected himself into a series of Biblical and mythological ancestries in an effort to re-establish contact with the harmonies of an earlier age, with the aim of making them available again to the present one. In *Voyage en Orient* (1851), the Romantic travelogue became a reconstruction of the imagination's journey through the world of private myth. *Sylvie* (1853) shows the withdrawal into the memory of the self in search of an illusory ideal. *Les Filles du feu* (1854) is a group of short stories which explore through a range of narrative forms his myth of the feminine and the magical places associated with women. To the end of *Les Filles du feu* he added *Les Chimères*, a short collection of sonnets which appear to form an elliptical commentary on *Les Filles du feu* and on one another, as they trace the tensions between loss and hope, between the darkness which inhabits our tomb-like world and the light which penetrates it.

Nerval's sense of the range and depth of these tensions in the modern age found the perfect vehicle in the sonnet form, in its combination of tight discipline and subtle flexibility. The quatrains create between one another a structure of relations which the tercets can then reinforce, oppose or enlarge, and their interplay is the poet's demonstration of his role, carried over from the Romantic into the post-Romantic era, as the privileged voice of these hidden realities. One very simple example would be that of 'El Desdichado', where 'Je suis . . .', which opens the quatrains, is inverted in 'Suis-je . . . ?', which opens the tercets. This sets up the opposition in syntax and prosody between assertion and uncertainty of identity which will in turn be resolved in the final rhyme of the poem 'Orphée/fée', where the poet achieves self-definition in Orpheus (the source of poetry itself in Greek mythology) and self-knowledge in his successful conclusion to his Orphean quest.

Nerval's last work, *Aurélia* (1855), brings together his familiar themes and myths in the search for the loved woman and the pardon which will enable their reunion. In the final sequence, entitled 'Mémorables', the narrator methodically retraces and explores his dreams, which, together with his description of the sonnets of *Les Chimères* as written in what he called a *supernaturalist* dream-like state, was later seized upon by the Surrealists as a model for their own exploration of the unconscious. Seventy years after his death, Nerval's poetry finally found the place within the mainstream of modernist developments which the complexity of his inner world and of the persona invented to describe the self had prevented him achieving during his lifetime or in its immediate aftermath.

* * *

In his preface for the 1849 edition of his poetry, Lamartine had claimed that single-handed he had brought poetry down from Parnassus and made a gift of it to everyone. The Parnassian movement, as its name suggests, sought to return it to Parnassus, the sacred mountain in ancient Greece where Apollo and the Muses resided. In the late 1850s, a group of young poets in Paris who frequented the Left Bank cafés and literary salons gathered around Catulle Mendès (1841–1909), publishing their work initially in various ephemeral reviews and then in the three collections entitled

Le Parnasse contemporain (1866, 1871, 1876). Like many such movements, this one was united less by a specific programme than by a shared hostility to what its members saw as the facile subjectivity of the poetry of Lamartine and Musset and by their commitment to the poem as an internal harmony of sound and sense. Hugo and Gautier represented the acceptable face of the Romantic tradition, the former for the descriptive aesthetic of *Les Orientales* and the cosmic ambition of his exile poetry, the latter for his refusal to accept a utilitarian or social function for art. Banville's commitment to the expressive beauty of verse forms and techniques was an essential model. But it was the poetry of Charles Marie René Leconte de Lisle (1818–94) which gave the Parnassian movement its sense of identity, cohesion and authority.[23]

For Leconte de Lisle the Revolution of 1848 was a personal and collective failure. His own candidacy in the elections turned to farce and the Fourierist Utopianism which he had espoused from the mid-1840s proved no match for Louis-Napoleon's ambitions. He turned instead to poetry and to ancient Greek and Indian cultures.[24] The *Poèmes antiques* of 1852 and their manifesto preface asserted that study of the history of religion and myth were essential if the poet were to recover the means to transcend the worn-out subjectivity of Romanticism. By immersing the self in the spiritual sources of Greek and Indian poetry, which had given voice to the age and its gods, the modern poet could provide the example of a new collective spirituality with which to oppose the materialism and individualism of contemporary society.

This sense of a lost age of plenitude and harmony which it is the poet's duty and honour to resurrect in the modern world through the poem's formal perfection creates the particular tonality of Leconte de Lisle's poetry, in which despair almost but never quite overwhelms faith in regeneration. The sublime example of the Venus of Milo (in the poem of that name) creates anguish that the poet did not live at that time and place, but the poem concludes with the prayer that its beauty will generate modern counterparts. The tension between defeat and affirmation is reinforced by the poem's formal rigour, the precision and balance of the alexandrines, and the reinforcement of the strophic structure by syntax. The enormity of the poet's obligations is the subject of the *Poèmes barbares* (1862), which narrate humanity's fall from the grace of the pagan, pantheistic Eden described in the *Poèmes antiques* into medieval cruelty and torture. Christianity, with its inquisitional violence and institutionalised betrayal of Christ's example, is the major villain. Its destruction of nobler religions than its own has led to the long night of the modern age, bereft of faith and ideals. The Darwinian fatalism of this relentless decline is charted in precise, detailed, highly visual descriptions of slaughter and destruction. The ideal of impersonality to which the poet subscribed on the intellectual level is, however, often opposed by the sensuality of description and by a horrified fascination with the violence they display. Much of the power of his famous animal poems, for example, derives from just this tension between fascination and aesthetic distance. In the cultural vacuum created by the end of the Romantic movement, the range and ambition of Leconte de Lisle's poetry, and its commitment to the search for formal perfection, exerted a powerful attraction on the younger generation of poets.

Gautier adjusted more easily than Leconte de Lisle to the regime introduced by the coup d'état. Already in the mid-1830s he had rejected the idea of socially useful or politically committed literature and this association with art-for-art's-sake was a distinct advantage under a regime whose cultural policy aspired to a broad apolitical consensus. *Émaux et camées* (1852), whose very title evoked a poetry of carefully-crafted enamels and cameos, opens with a sonnet, 'Préface', in which the poet claims to have written the collection impervious to the political storms raging outside his window. His commitment to the impassive, timeless serenity of ideal beauty found its model in the sculpture of ancient Greece, in which perfect form was fashioned from the recalcitrant materials of stone or marble, and his poem 'L'Art' (1857) became a manifesto of this essential ideal of Parnassianism. Following his death in 1872, Gautier's reputation was compromised by the prestige he had enjoyed as a major figure of the Second Empire literary establishment and by the greater seriousness with which subsequent poets appeared to have pursued the Parnassian ambition.

One of the privileged subjects for the representation of statuesque beauty and pure contour was the female nude. Whether in his poetry or art criticism, the forms of his desire for this model of perfection show the relationship between writing and the post-1848 world. 'Le Poème de la femme' displays the male fantasy of the ideal woman in an extended metaphor of the poem of her beautiful body, in which each pose and each presentation of her nudity is a new stanza. As an actress, she is skilled in performing the cultural representations of woman which fuse life and art and which respond to and provoke male desire (striptease artist, painter's nude, queen of the harem, odalisque); as a poet, he is skilled in using the constraints of the verse system to stimulate new performances of familiar rituals. Her display of her body in the gestures and poses fixed by cultural stereotype permits his display of metaphorical and prosodic variations. Both displays climax in the description of her perfect statuesque and painterly forms aroused by her performance as sexual object to a pleasure so extreme that she expires. This most stereotypical of male fantasies reinforces the poet's virtuoso performance in transforming stereotype into a skilfully-worked *objet d'art*, a tribute to craft at a time when craft was seen to be threatened by emerging forms of mass production. But it also displays the extent to which poetry was embedded in cultural forms and rhetorical practices, and in this respect too *Émaux et camées* is an essential text of nineteenth-century poetry.

In his *Odes funambulesques* (1857), Banville fused contemporary subjects and non-traditional forms (twelve of the poems are described as 'occidentales' in an affectionate parody of Hugo's *Orientales*) with fixed forms of the fifteenth, sixteenth and seventeenth centuries (such as the rondel, triolet and virelay) to create a telling and at times profound marriage of the lyrical and the burlesque.[25] These fixed forms used few rhymes but this constraint, contrary to the aspiration for greater prosodic freedoms which the generation of 1830 had brought to poetry, made them a perfect instrument for Banville's verbal games. Similarly, the themes and rhythms associated with these forms could achieve powerful effects of caricature when directed at some object clearly unworthy of them. Debureau, the inventor of the Pierrot figure of the Théâtre des Funambules, is the model in the *Odes funambulesques* for the poet as clown, walking the tightrope above the crowd or leaping up towards the stars. These poems of artistic and social life in Paris of the 1840s and 1850s are period pieces, graceful pirouettes the poet performs before the surface reality of the city. Though there is little of the depth of contact with its life or modernity that characterises Baudelaire's *flâneur*, it would be wrong to see these poems as mere pretexts for verbal ingenuity. Banville returned to pre-classical forms for the sources of a lyrical tradition stripped of what he felt were its Romantic insincerities and positivist ambitions, and promoted poetic forms which were both conservative in their respect for rules and audacious in the flexibility these rules permitted. For subsequent poets as diverse and as essential to modernity as Mallarmé and Laforgue, the lesson would be an important one.

* * *

During the final third of the nineteenth century, Parnassian values continued to enjoy great prestige within the French poetic establishment, as two examples will illustrate. The first is the acclaim which in 1893 greeted *Les Trophées*, a collection of sonnets by José-Maria de Heredia (1842–1905), whose formal disciplines and symmetries provided the framework for images of visual beauty in historical or natural settings.[26] The second is the award in 1901 of the first Nobel Prize for Literature to the minor Parnassian poet Sully-Prudhomme (pseudonym of René-François Armand Prud-homme, 1839–1907), whose scientific and philosophical poetry in didactic epic form is now largely forgotten. Yet by the mid-1860s the challenge to the Parnassian domination of French poetry was already under way in the work of Paul Verlaine.

In *Poèmes saturniens* (1866), Parnassian historical and mythological themes and decors co-exist alongside nocturnal, autumnal or nostalgic evocations ('Nevermore', 'Chanson d'automne') whose rhythms and sound patterns blur the contours of thought and feeling. In Verlaine's second volume, *Fêtes galantes* (1869), Parnassian principles are abandoned and a new poetic voice is created. The volume's title derived from the eighteenth-century painters of aristocratic leisure, particularly Watteau, whose work had enjoyed a major revival during the Second Empire.[27] By 1869 the *fête galante* and the Italian *commedia dell'arte* themes associated with Watteau were little more than conventional decors, which Verlaine used to explore systematically the power of poetic form to evoke the hesitations and fragilities of feeling. Of the twenty-two poems, only two, 'Pantomime' and 'Fantoches', have the same permutation of line length, rhyme scheme and strophic structure, and their identical formal system and shared subject (the amorous games of *commedia dell'arte* characters) serve to underline their opposite conclusions on the thematic level. This diversity of poetic forms corresponds to the wide range and sharp transitions of a modern, nostalgic imagination sensitive to feelings whose source is lost to the memory but whose impact shapes the present. In *Fêtes galantes* this diversity results in a promotion of the seven- and eight-syllable lines at the expense of the alexandrine which dominates the *Poèmes saturniens*. The shorter lines, with their rhymes closer together, their more flexible rhythms and greater use of *enjambement*, permitted a much wider range of tone and mood than the Parnassian alexandrine, with its oratorical, declamatory effects. The association of modern sensibility and formal originality in *Fêtes galantes* gave this work an essential role in post-1870 developments in French poetry.[28]

6

The First Inter-War Years, 1871–1914

I NATURALISM'S NARRATIVE CLOSURES

On 4 September 1870, the Second Empire collapsed in the wake of the crushing French defeat at Sedan, which brought the Franco-Prussian war to an end. No sooner was the Third Republic proclaimed in its place than a new phase of the struggle between conservative and radical forces for control of the Republic was enacted in the ferocious civil war of the Paris Commune. In the final 'bloody week' of 22–8 May, the radicals who had seized power in the capital ten weeks earlier were massacred by government troops advancing across Paris from the west of the city.

The gravity of the events between the declaration of war on 19 July 1870 and the brutal repression of the Commune had the effect of mobilising writers to explain the disasters which had befallen the nation. With few exceptions, they described the Commune as the inevitable consequence of military defeat. Though interpretations of this defeat varied – from calls for France's moral re-armament as a prerequisite for revenge on Germany to fatalistic pessimism at the nation's eclipse as a cultural as well as military force – writers were by and large united in their demonisation of the Commune. From the outset it was the object of derision or vicious abuse whose violence precluded constructive literary responses.[1] In the novel and short story, the systematic depiction of the Communards as animals or drunken rabble and of their repression as a moral crusade in defence of civilisation was hardly conducive to renewal of the genres. The negative portrayal of characters condemned by heredity or milieu to ridiculous or odious actions was a sign of an impasse which was both ideological and narrative. The refusal to recognise any political and social project in the Commune, and the transfer of its meaning to a metaphysical terrain of conflict between the forces of light and darkness, constituted a denial of the

158

positive hero whose powerful interventions in history had been a feature of the novel written on the Balzacian model.

This narrative closure is clear in Zola's novel on the events of 1870–1, *La Débâcle* (1892), the penultimate novel of his *Rougon-Macquart* cycle. As early as 1 July 1871, Zola had described the trajectory this cycle would take as a closed circle. The fall of the Empire had given him, he said, the terrible and necessary dénouement of his work.[2] In *La Débâcle* Zola sought to demonstrate the implacable Darwinian laws in terms of which, he argued, France had been obliged to endure the twin catastrophes of military defeat and civil war in order to expiate the greed, desire and selfish ambition which had poisoned Second Empire society. The natural processes of social evolution, halted in the crossfire of imperial arrogance (the Franco-Prussian war) and radical folly (the Commune), were reactivated by the elimination of non-viable or diseased forms (Napoleon III, Rochas, Maurice). Recovery would be achieved when the nation returned to its spiritual roots in the natural rhythms, labours and submissions of rural or provincial life (Jean, Henriette), far removed from the manic, disruptive energies of the capital. In 1892, Zola's version of the lessons of 1870–1 had powerful resonance for the Third Republic, anxious to steer a course between the radical challenges of Right and Left. By this time the closed circle of his naturalist aesthetic, scientific models and conservative social and political theories had become Republican orthodoxy.

Zola had arrived in Paris in 1858 to find the capital in the throes of physical, economic and cultural change, a society cut loose from its spiritual moorings by its rapid transition to consumerism. His *Rougon-Macquart* cycle portrayed his strong attraction to, and fear of, the energies rising from the lower levels of society to challenge, corrupt or overthrow enfeebled or outmoded elites. In *La Curée* (1872), Saccard swoops on Paris like a bird of prey in the wake of Louis-Napoleon's coup d'état, sublimating sexual energy in a frenzy of property speculation while his wife Renée, morally and emotionally unhinged by her search for ever more refined forms of pleasure, has an incestuous affair with her stepson Maxime, whose ambiguous sexuality denotes the degeneration of a family and society exhausted by a legacy of instability. Nana (*Nana*, 1880), born in the year of the coup d'état and dying on the eve of Sedan, espouses the Second Empire's chronology of pleasure and decay, breaking out from her working-class origins in poverty and vice

(*L'Assommoir*, 1877) to circulate her infected currency of desire to the highest levels of society, whose defences collapse before this (male fantasy of) rampant female sexuality.

A similar social upheaval takes place but with positive results in *Au bonheur des dames* (1883), in which Octave Mouret, the draper's assistant from *Pot-Bouille* (1882), wipes out the old forms of commerce by manipulating the sensual urges triggered in middle- and upper-class women by his department store's *démocratisation du luxe*. Here a harmonious social order is re-established when the irresistible force of Mouret's all-conquering energy meets and submits to the immovable object of Denise's modesty and *douceur*. This union of positive masculine and feminine intelligences creates within marriage and society a benevolent paternalism whose effect is to counter the havoc wreaked in private and public affairs by the necessary elimination of all non-viable forms of human activity.

The vulgarisation of contemporary theories of evolution, heredity and pathological behaviour gave Zola a powerful thread with which to tie together the multiple strands of his cycle of novels. The detailed documentation served to put flesh on the bones of the central idea established from the outset in each novel. The example of deductive reasoning helped him to organise and structure the material. These well-known features of his writing reflected the encyclopaedic ambition in the scientific culture of his time and reinforced the authority of the narrative voice as it centralised and totalised the natural and social history of the Rougon-Macquart family.

At the same time, characters such as Saccard, Nana and Mouret manifest the almost limitless possibilities for the generation and circulation of energy available in the new consumer society of the Second Empire. In their headlong flight forward, they reflect the fascination and unease that Zola felt with the increased scale and pace of change which scientific and technological progress had made available. They are counterparts to the huge machines which consume, destroy or run amok in the *Rougon-Macquart* cycle. The still in *L'Assommoir* exercises its malevolent influence on Gervaise's doomed slide into debauchery and death. In *Germinal* (1885), the mine, like the Minotaur of Greek legend, devours its daily ration of workers but Étienne Lantier, the leader of their fight against their class enemies, survives its final catastrophic explosion as a sign of the force for life which emerges from death. The unmanned train hurtling out of control in *La Bête humaine* (1890) is the technological amplification of the deadly primitive urges released by sexual desire in Jacques Lantier, its driver, and carries off the soldiers destined to become cannon-fodder in the battle between old and new civilisations at Sedan.

At the centre of the forces at work in modern society, Paris is a huge stomach (*Le Ventre de Paris*, 1873), a gigantic brothel (*La Curée, Nana*), a poisonous fluid or life-giving blood (*L'Argent*, 1891). It is a vast bodily function continually threatening to ruin the mechanisms of social control. Throughout the cycle the forces of life and death are locked in a struggle of Biblical proportions. In Zola's language, the historical and universal, social and natural, scientific and poetic vie for control of a fictional project whose conservative and radical tendencies dramatise the contradictions within which Republican ideology operated in the early years of the Third Republic.

The publication of each volume of the *Rougon-Macquart* cycle, particularly after *L'Assommoir* in 1877, strengthened the identification of Naturalism with Zola's practice of the novel. The creation of the Médan group of young writers (which met regularly in Zola's home in Médan, bought out of the proceeds of *L'Assommoir*) and the publication of the *Soirées de Médan* (1880), a collection of stories on the war of 1870, and of the collections of Zola's theoretical essays which appeared between 1880 and 1882, made Naturalism the most powerful literary movement of the early years of the Third Republic.[3]

The major revelation of the *Soirées de Médan* was *Boule de suif* by Guy de Maupassant (1850–93), a tart-with-a-heart tale of a virtuous prostitute who, under the pressure of her travelling companions, submits to the demands of a Prussian officer. In this harsh indictment of the gulf between the words and deeds of 'respectable' society, the prostitute achieves a reversal of values which leaves her as the sole guardian of a true *ordre moral*. Her action is nevertheless powerless to transform the values of the inauthentic society from which she is excluded and into which she seeks to integrate herself. This type of thematic reversal woven into a structure of patterns and transitions (in this case the ternary distribution of journey, halt, journey) would become trademarks of Maupassant's technique in six novels and over 300 stories. His Naturalism, outlined in his text 'Le Roman', which precedes *Pierre et Jean* (1888), pursued the details of gesture, tone and expression which betray the greed, selfishness, hypocrisy and cruelty that lurk below the surface of everyday social forms. Founded on philosophical despair, his Naturalism is central to his tales of mystery and imagination, notably *Sur l'eau* (1876), *La Peur* (1882), *Lui?* (1884) and the two versions of *Le Horla* (1886 and 1887), in which everyday objects take on malevolent powers which gradually overwhelm the mind's rational defences. The supernatural is internalised in the obsessions which lead to hallucination, madness and death and suicide but which leave the texts with its mysteries unresolved.[4]

II HISTORY AS FICTION

In 1864, Hugo had considered the French Revolution to be the defining event of modern history. In exile he had had time to reflect on the nature of the revolutionary moment whose forward drive had, from his point of view, been so shockingly reversed by the Second Empire. The return of the Republic and the civil war which followed raised essential issues for him; in particular, the meaning of revolutionary violence and the role, in that tradition, of Paris, described in *Quatrevingt-treize* (1874) as the 'enormous pendulum of civilisation', now cradle of the Revolution, now theatre of savage civil war. In 1872, such questions could be seen in a broader historical perspective, for that year was the tricentenary of the earlier fratricidal conflict which culminated in the St Bartholomew's Day massacre of Protestants by Catholics.

In *Quatrevingt-treize*, begun in 1872, the apparent aberration of history's alternating advances and retreats is resolved in terms of a higher truth of divine origin.[5] The cannon which breaks free from its fastenings and demolishes everything in its path is tossed by the boat, which is tossed by the sea, which is tossed by the wind, whose source is God. Likewise, the great figures of the Revolution are depicted as no more than waves of the ocean, mere scribes of the text of which God is the author. Knowledge of the divine form of revolutionary truth depends on the rejection of the human form of revolutionary law. Lantenac, the leader of the counter-revolutionaries, is transfigured when he places the lives of three children above his political commitments. His gesture liberates Gauvain for the same transcendent act of clemency, to which he sacrifices himself. Just as Lantenac saves the children, so Gauvain, by saving Lantenac, his political enemy but also his grandfather's brother, is true to the Revolution's ideal, that of humanity, symbolised by the family. It is for this future, explicitly founded, the text says, on the authority of the father, that Gauvain sacrifices himself. By contrast, Cimourdin, who puts ideological purity above humanity, executes Gauvain, his pupil and spiritual son, but by killing himself at the same moment he too is saved. Their two souls fly off together, the shadow of the one mingling with the light of the other in a mystical resolution of conflict. Playing in the dungeon, the children rip out the pages of *Saint-Barthélemy*, a history of the event which symbolised the tyranny of absolute monarchy and served to justify revolutionary violence for supporters of 1793. The text of the massacre is reduced to a swarm of paper butterflies borne off on the breeze to disappear in the heavens. In *Quatrevingt-treize*, historical reality is transcended in a quasi-religious ideal of revolutionary truth and justice.

Only from 1880, when the Third Republic felt secure enough to amnesty those who had fought on the side of the Commune, did it become possible to represent positively the events of March–May 1871. In *L'Insurgé* (1886), the third volume, after *L'Enfant* (1878) and *Le Bachelier* (1881), of his autobiographical trilogy of novels, Jules Vallès (1832–85) described the Commune as the great federation of sorrows, from whose defeat the future might yet be born. Here, the convergence of personal experience and historical reality is carefully structured: seventeen chapters on the period from 1862 to Sedan, seventeen from Sedan to the end of 'la semaine sanglante' ['bloody week'] (which alone occupies chapters 29–34), with chapter 35 as an epilogue which leaves open the hope that the spilled blood of the workers will usher in a new era. The first half of the text establishes the narrator's political commitments: an equal hatred of the Empire and the official, parliamentary Left. The second shows the divisions and disorganisation which ensure that the radical Left is crushed by the government forces ranged against it from 18 March 1871 but also the narrator's discovery of himself in extreme moments of solidarity and danger. In addition, the Commune liberates in him the full force of language. For the rhythms, structures and images to represent it, he draws on his experience of journalism. The work fuses classical and popular culture in short segments of text in which fragments of dialogue, exclamations, puns and detached noun phrases jostle one another in the increasing urgency of the dramatic events. In 1886, Vallès attempts to renew in language the insurrectional message.[6]

In *Bas les cœurs!* (1889), the anarchist sympathiser Georges Darien

(1862–1921) used autobiographical material more obliquely than Vallès to express similar feelings of contempt for the Second Empire and for Third Republic repression of the Commune. Here, the first-person narrative is that of a twelve-year-old, Jean Barbier, growing up in Versailles between the declaration of war in July 1870 and the defeat of the Commune ten months later. The military and political situations during this period are the catalyst for his discovery of the hypocrisy, cowardice and self-interest of the bourgeois family to which he belongs and, through its members, of the Versailles mentality responsible for the brutal repression of the Commune. Versailles is the dead culture of the past, represented in the park's formal gardens, with their puny, imprisoned, regimented vegetation. Paris is represented in the limited forms of the child's experience and imagination as the source of freedom, whose blood-red sky represents, as it does for Vallès's narrator in *L'Insurgé*, the refusal to submit. Its radical tradition is present through the appropriately-named Merlin, whose counsel and strictures enable the child to develop in the course of the narration from an object of bourgeois paternalist indoctrination into a young adult subject to whom is entrusted the legacy of insurrection.[7]

Immediately prior to the First World War, Anatole France (pseudonym of Anatole Thibault, 1844–1924) returned to the central theme of the late nineteenth-century historical novel, that of the nature of revolutionary violence, in *Les Dieux ont soif* (1912), which is in some respects a response to Hugo's historical evasions in *Quatrevingt-treize*. Set in the period of the Terror between April 1793 and July 1794, it recounts the elevation of a failed painter, Gamelin, to the Revolutionary Tribunal, from where he dispenses revolutionary justice with increasing fanaticism until he achieves the martyrdom by which all religions are nourished by sharing in the fall of the Robespierre faction. His mistress, Élodie, watches him with fascinated horror, appalled and aroused by his blood-lust. Revolutionary justice is shown to be merciless, indiscriminate and dishonest, spilling blood but only temporarily interrupting the transactions of bankers and prostitutes, which, once the Terror is over, resume their control of public life. One of the most effective historical novels in its seamless interweaving of private and public affairs, *Les Dieux ont soif* also extends the author's sceptical, disillusioned analysis of French society in his novels dealing with the Dreyfus Affair (see below, pp. 178).[8]

III   POETICAL OPENINGS

After the innovative themes and forms of *Fêtes galantes*, Verlaine's next collection, *La Bonne Chanson* (1870), emphasised instead the poet's desire to anchor life and work in more conventional practices following his engagement in 1869 and marriage the following year. The arrival of Arthur Rimbaud (1854–91) on Verlaine's scene in 1871 put an end to this short-lived stability. In the context of the emotional turmoil and poetic emulation their relationship produced, Verlaine composed his most important collection of poems, *Romances sans paroles* (1874). The title of the collection implies that in this poetry sound is more important than sense, that its language suggests more than it signifies. Taken with the fact that in the year of its publication, Verlaine also wrote the manifesto poem 'L'Art poétique', with its emphasis on 'De la musique avant toute chose' ['Music above all else'] and the role of the imparisyllabic line (the *vers impair*, with its uneven number of syllables) in the creation of this 'music', *Romances sans paroles* has acquired an essential place in Verlaine's work as the volume in which his representation of ill-defined emotional states and acute sensitivity to the sound structures of French verse achieve their most effective match. Dream-like landscapes mirror the poet's sense of inner exile and the contours of the self dissolve in unstable forms of feeling. These wordless songs have the transparent, restless fluidity of the water-colours which gave the title to one section of the volume.

In these poems Verlaine brought together a number of rhythmic elements with which to tone down the sharp metrical outlines of standard prosody. The privileged position enjoyed there by the eight- and twelve-syllable lines made the imparisyllabic line intrinsically suitable to the evocation of imprecise, uncertain emotional states but Verlaine reinforced this effect with others, such as the occasional use of feminine rhymes throughout a poem instead of the standard practice of alternating masculine and feminine rhymes, the use of internal rhyme and assonance to make sound patterns reverberate across the length of the poem, the extensive use of *enjambement* to blur the contours of the line, and the use of the mute 'e' to prolong fragile echoes. Though there is nothing inherently musical about such procedures, their combination and concentration in *Romances sans paroles*, and appropriateness to the feelings evoked, created an audience for the poems when the publication of a second edition in 1887 coincided with the emergence of the Symbolist movement.

The poet's conversion to Catholicism while serving his prison sentence for the attack on Rimbaud dominates the following collection, *Sagesse* (1880). Here, the peace of his new-found faith, though profound, is never secure and the range of feeling woven into the unmistakable rhythms of his verse gives these poems a spiritual depth which enabled them to play a prominent role in the literature of the Catholic revival in the final phase of the nineteenth century.[9]

Even as Verlaine's *Fêtes galantes* appeared, Rimbaud was embarking on a far more radical attack on the rhetorical, political and cultural forms of his time. His poetry, written between the ages of fifteen and twenty-one, was, from its beginnings in 1869, deeply anti-Bonapartist in content, while the use it made of contemporary caricature also subverted models of political poetry practised by Hugo, Barbier and Coppée.[10] The collapse of the Empire and the crisis of the Paris Commune brought to the surface of Rimbaud's writing his rage against the multiple forms of contemporary repression – sexual, cultural and aesthetic. In his manifesto letters of 13 and 15 May 1871, he set out his programme to bring all the forces of reason and unreason to bear on his effort to turn himself into a poetic and political visionary through a 'long, immense et raisonné *dérèglement* de *tous les sens*' ['long, immense and reasoned *disordering of all the senses*']. Here, the attack on the subjective lyricism of Romantic poetry and the sculptural perfection of Parnassianism expands into a utopian liberation from the limitations of the self. In his famous 'JE est un autre' ['I is an other'], the Cartesian subject is released from its identity, set free to bathe in what Rimbaud called (in 'Le Bateau ivre') 'Le Poème de la mer' ['Poem of the sea'], the ocean of vision reached by abolishing the artificial boundaries between subject and object, language and perception. By submitting to language's potential to free the imagination from recalcitrant reality, the poet joins up with the Parisian workers fighting at that very moment to free themselves from the hated bourgeois order. As he wrote in his letter of 15 May 1871 to Paul Demeny, the poet was 'un multiplicateur de progrès!' ['a multiplier of progress!'].

Rimbaud did not invent this visionary ambition for poetry – as has been seen, it is present in much of Hugo's poetry and in Baudelaire's description of the spleen and ideal of modern reality – but he took it further than anyone before him and he invented new forms with which to express it. In 'Le Bateau ivre', his extraordinary poem of visionary experience expressed through the metaphor of the boat breaking its moorings to sail into unknown seascapes of senses and mind, the alexandrine strains under the pressures created by the intense visions of freedom; in 'Qu'est-ce pour nous, mon cœur, que les nappes de sang', it is severely undermined, particularly in Rimbaud's handling of the caesura after the sixth syllable. 'Chant de guerre parisien' is a declaration of war on the conventional language of poetry. 'Voyelles' subjects the tightly-knit sonnet form to the mystery of origins and purposes, to new types of vocabulary and to the power of the raw material of language to generate unimagined combinations of the visual and verbal. 'Bonne pensée du matin' forms an irregular pattern of lines of different syllable counts. In 'Larme', rhyme has become approximate. 'Bannières de mai' is written in blank verse, 'Marine' in unrhymed lines of different lengths.

Une saison en enfer (1873) is a series of prose fragments in which the poet dramatises the permanent contradictions and vicious circles of his psychological and emotional life. It is a bitter pilgrimage through the illusory freedoms and real captivities which his culture has made for him and the history of his efforts to find in poetry the means to express and relieve his anguish. The hope of recovering the innocent eye of childhood or the serene vision of Oriental philosophy is defeated by the Western rationalism and intellectualism he has inherited. Alone and derelict, the poet is engaged in an endless struggle with reality. In *Illuminations*, written sometime between 1871 and 1875 but published only in 1886, discontinuous fragments of prose and verse create blasphemous celebrations of (self-)destruction, a powerful and willed formal order at the service of the disorder which is the foundation of our conscience and which no principle of coherence can stabilise.

If Rimbaud uses the prose poem to create flashes of insight illuminating correlations and tensions between the visible and invisible, Lautréamont (pseudonym of Isidore Ducasse, 1846–70) used it to deconstruct from within the very idea of poetry. In *Les Chants de Maldoror* (1869) and *Poésies* (1870), he subjected the ideals of Romantic poetry to exasperated subversion. *Les Chants de Maldoror* consists of six cantos, each divided into stanzas, which defy conventional categories of prose and poem. They form a largely disconnected series of sadistic and angry narratives and digressions in which every form of Romantic faith in the absolute is rerouted through provocation and parody, and in which Lautréamont reworks his vast reading of Gothic horror and serial novels.

Running through this baffling sequence of Maldoror's confrontations with the divine, human and animal realms is the question of
literature itself. The Romantic lyric poet, whose intellectual and
emotional states were the source of meaning, is deleted. Themes,
styles and sequences of text are lifted from the 'great authors' of
literary and scientific texts and the reader is summoned to embrace
the freedoms and dangers of an imagination without limits.
Maldoror and *Poésies* constitute a virtuoso intertextual performance
outside any definition of poetry the nineteenth century could recognise and which remained unknown until the Surrealists discovered,
in this work's subversion of writing from within, an essential
model for their own efforts to transform literature.[11]

In *Les Amours jaunes* (1873), Tristan Corbière (1845–75) presented
dismay and self-directed derision in a poetic language quite distinct
from that of Parnassianism.[12] His poems have the unstable rhythms
of the language of his native Brittany and the Paris streets. The use
they make of appositions, antitheses and word play creates sharp
shifts of meaning through juxtaposition of seemingly unrelated
feelings to produce their distinctive effect of carefully controlled
free association. The work went unnoticed until Verlaine discovered it in 1881 and selected Corbière as one of his *poètes maudits*. A
similar fate befell the first edition of *Le Coffret de santal* (1873) by
Charles Cros (1842–88), in which the poet expresses the sensuality
and duplicity of love and anguish at the passage of time and in
which insecurity and cynicism make themselves felt through the
conventional forms of appeal and seduction.[13] Cros's mastery of the
multiple effects of the octosyllabic line and fixed forms he most
favoured results in delicate but profound hesitations between
reality and fantasy, humour and despair. His poems share with those
of Verlaine an analogy with music, its sound patterns, refrains and
non-descriptive meaning. The work of Corbière and Cros was characteristic of that produced in the early 1870s at the margins of
French poetry where the Parnassian ideal of stable, definitive form
appeared unable to assimilate language or articulate feelings which
were outside the recognised terms of high culture but which were
necessary to express the constantly shifting sands of modern experience. This marginalised activity is also to be found in the noisy
and heterogeneous talents who gathered in such ephemeral groups
as the *Vilains Bonshommes* founded in 1871, the *Hydropathes*,
founded in 1878, and the *Club des zutistes*, founded in 1883.[14]

With the publication of the third volume of *Le Parnasse*

contemporain in 1876, the challenge to the Parnassian domination of French poetry found focus. The editorial board consisting of François Coppée (1842–1908), Anatole France and Banville rejected, among other poems by Cros and Verlaine, Mallarmé's 'L'Après-midi d'un faune', which the poet published as a separate volume the following year. Mallarmé's early masters were Hugo, Gautier, Banville, Poe and Baudelaire but from 1864 he embarked on his poem 'Hérodiade', and his study of what he called the mysterious science of poetic language.[15] His aim was, he said, to represent not the object, but the effect it produced, but his efforts to achieve this new poetic language of effects led to his spiritual crisis of 1866–8. In the course of it, his loss of faith in language as a necessary relationship between word and idea, his loss of religious faith and his discovery of the idealist tradition in the work of Hegel led him to conclude that the poet must abolish in poetry the forms of the real world and his subjective responses to these forms as a prerequisite for realising an absolute Beauty of which the mysterious science of poetic language was the only possible form. As he later wrote, poetry was a process of *elimination*, created by the 'disparition élocutoire du poète, qui cède l'initiative aux mots' ['the elocutionary disappearance of the poet, who yields the initiative to words']. He therefore set out to abolish the everyday, discursive, linear forms of language and the meanings displayed through them by an authoritative author–subject. In their place, he created an exceptionally dense and elusive geometry of sound and meaning in which words, released from their conventional syntax and function, inter-reverberate on every level of poetic language. In Mallarmé, poetry became a constellation of structured sound and sense, whose effect is to generate and postpone meaning simultaneously. He took Parnassian impersonality and the cult of perfection to lengths which undermined its other aspirations to definition and sculptural form. A comparison between the published version of 'L'Après-midi d'un faune' and two surviving earlier versions confirms that already in 1876 a new era of writing was under way.[16]

IV ANTI-POSITIVIST REACTIONS: DECADENCE AND SYMBOLISM

In the final third of the nineteenth century, at the very time that the different forms of scientific humanism appeared to dominate

Republican ideology (most visibly in the field of public education), spiritual and religious traditions experienced a major revival.[17] From the Romantic period onwards, these had not ceased to provide for writers a system of values with which to challenge the optimistic faith in progress through science. But from 1870–1, quite apart from the self-doubts generated by military defeat and civil war, many writers felt increasingly alienated by the emergence of what they considered to be an anonymous, ugly, industrial mass society, and saw in spiritual and religious values a necessary form of social and political authority. Papal denunciation of the errors of modernity (atheism and democracy) in the Syllabus of 1864 and the proclamation of Papal infallibility at the Vatican Council of 1870 were signs of a renewed offensive on the part of the Catholic Church against anticlerical Republican democracy. New forms of German idealist philosophy also became available during the 1870s with translations of Arthur Schopenhauer (1788–1860) and Éduard von Hartmann (1842–1906). The former described reality as our representation; the latter as the creation of an impersonal force and intelligence which he called the Unconscious.[18] Henri Bergson (1859–1951) renewed the French spiritualist tradition from 1889 when he published his *Essai sur les données immédiates de la conscience*, in which he sought to free thought from positivist determinism and materialism by describing reality as a ceaseless flow perceptible by intuition rather than by practical, rational intelligence.[19]

The first major collective form of this anti-positivist culture was the decadent movement, which burst onto the French scene in 1884.[20] Its Bible was *À rebours* (1884) by Joris-Karl Huysmans (1848–1907).[21] Huysmans began as a disciple of Zola, writing Naturalist fiction (*Marthe, histoire d'une fille*, 1876; *Les Sœurs Vatard*, 1879; 'Sac au dos' in the *Soirées de Médan*; *En ménage*, 1881) but the distance he was placing between himself and Naturalism was already clear in his art criticism of 1880, in which he praised the work of the painter Gustave Moreau, who became, thanks to *À rebours* and despite himself, one of the exemplary artists of Decadence. In *À rebours*, Des Esseintes, a rich, neurotic aristocrat, closes his door on modern society to indulge his private fantasies, pleasures and terrors and to share those of kindred spirits in the visual arts – the narratives of castration and revenge he detects in Moreau's treatment of the Salomé theme or the fantastic dream visions he experiences in the drawings of Odilon Redon – and in

literature – the Latin decadence, the tales of Jules Barbey d'Aurevilly (1808–89) and Edgar Allan Poe, and the alternative poetic
tradition represented by Baudelaire, Verlaine and Mallarmé. When
this attempt to escape the modern world becomes life-threatening,
he must return defeated to the Paris he despises.

Durtal, the novelist hero of *Là-bas* (1891), is writing a medieval
fantasy of violence and retribution (purportedly a historical novel
based on the exploits of Gilles de Rais, the legendary Bluebeard)
and investigating black magic in contemporary Paris. The fusion of
mysticism and sexuality, the seductions of legend, and the detailed
documentation on the proliferation of mystical sects in Paris in the
late 1880s combined to produce a heady romance with a powerful
air of authenticity, ensuring the novel's immediate success. But
already by the time it appeared the decadent vogue was on the
wane and the Symbolists were asserting their authority over the
Parisian avant-garde.

Barbey d'Aurevilly contributed significantly to decadent sensibility by carrying forward into Third Republic culture major elements
of the Romantic revolt.[22] First, he was identified with a philosophy
of dandyism (through his essay *Du dandysme et de George Brummel*,
1845) from which the representation of the decadent as solitary
exquisite in pursuit of refined sensations was in part derived. Secondly, after his conversion to Catholicism in 1846–7, Barbey
adopted de Maistre's views on the universality of evil and, faced
with the 'double postulation' described by Baudelaire (the need to
choose between God and Satan), chose the latter, for the fictional
possibilities which the representation of the supernatural and of
sadistic, blasphemous transgression of moral values made available
(in *L'Ensorcelé*, 1854, and *Les Diaboliques*, 1874). Thirdly, his extreme
right-wing Catholic monarchism was an important strand of the
late nineteenth-century Catholic and conservative reaction in which
Decadence played a significant transitional role.

Though other writers gave expression to essential elements of the
decadent spirit and its relationship to late nineteenth-century political, sexual and religious ideologies – Jean Lorrain (1855–1906),[23]
Octave Mirbeau (1848–1917),[24] Pierre Louÿs (1870–1925),[25] Joséphin
Péladan (1859–1918)[26] – the pursuit of ever more bizarre, neurotic
or violent sensation could not occupy for long the mainstream of
literary developments. The movement was soon seen as a very
partial response to the philosophical and aesthetic shortcomings of
Naturalism.

In a manifesto article of 18 September 1886, Jean Moréas (1856–1910) used the term Symbolism to describe the aesthetic theories and practice of young writers grouped around Mallarmé.[27] As Moréas defined it, Symbolism opposed the materialist ambition of Naturalist literature, the Parnassian description of beauty and Decadence's pursuit of rare sensations, which was seen as little more than an exacerbated form of Naturalism. Though in fact Symbolism, as practised by many members of the group, was less opposed to Naturalism, Parnassianism and Decadence than it liked to think, it nevertheless appeared in 1886 to offer an alternative programme, poetic practice and leader. The programme was the search for the absolute. The poetic practice was suggestion, since the absolute could not by definition be described directly. The leader was Mallarmé, who by 1886 had already produced a small number of dense, mysterious and highly crafted poems.

Des Esseintes's pursuit of refined sensations in *À rebours* had included reading the poetry of Mallarmé, and the novel played an essential role in increasing the audience for his poetry within the Parisian avant-garde. Another essential element was the founding in January 1885 of the *Revue wagnérienne* by Édouard Dujardin (1861–1949) and Téodor de Wyzewa (1863–1917). Though, as far as the Symbolists are concerned, it is difficult to distinguish between responses to Wagner's music and the readings of this music established by Baudelaire and others, it is clear that Wagner 'ravished the symbolists with his treatment of the remote and the legendary, the mystically erotic and the esoteric; likewise his insistence on the artist as priest, his emphasis on the need to mythologise the historical, his concept of the fusion of the arts and the use of the leitmotif'.[28] Escape from present into past, real into dream, history into myth, much of Symbolism's local colour between 1886 and 1895 is Wagner-based in one form or another. But in a broader context too, Wagner's impact was essential. For many Symbolists, his theory of Total Art (the idea that the definitive art form would be that which united the arts at the point at which their individual limits touched) merged with Baudelaire's theory of correspondences and reinforced the prestige of music as literature's role model for indirect rather than direct forms of expression. In the theatre, the Wagnerian emphasis on mysticism and ritual encouraged wide-ranging experiment in all aspects of stagecraft; in poetry, Wagner's interweaving of musical fragments and use of the leitmotif contributed to the emergence of the *vers libre* (free verse), and in the novel, led to what became known as the stream-of-consciousness technique.[29]

Free verse was the culmination of the process by which nineteenth-century French poets had sought to loosen the rhythmic system of the classical alexandrine, to make it more responsive to the expression of the individual poet's sense of place in the changing realities of nineteenth-century experience. Traditionally, the alexandrine's mandatory caesura on the sixth syllable had the effect of dividing the verse line into two equal metrical and syntactic units of 6 + 6 and classical poetry had derived its effects from within this structure. At the end of the eighteenth century, Chénier had occasionally used an alexandrine in three measures (4 + 4 + 4) instead of two (6 + 6), which the Romantic poets, Hugo in particular, had taken further, both for the expressive potential of the rhythmic flexibility it offered and as part of a campaign against classical prosody. Post-Romantics such as Verlaine, Rimbaud and Corbière had extended this attack on the traditional alexandrine through a range of devices including the *vers impair*, single-gender rhyme sequences and so on. Despite these developments, the two defining features of regular verse – rhyme and syllabic regularity – were still in place in 1885. In 1886 these two remaining features were overthrown.

In the early 1870s, Rimbaud had already written two poems in free verse, 'Marine' and 'Mouvement'. In 1886 they appeared in *La Vogue*, an avant-garde literary review which supported the Symbolists. In the months which followed, the review's editor Gustave Kahn (1859–1936) and his friend and fellow poet Jules Laforgue (1860–87) gave the final shove, publishing in *La Vogue* their own work and that of others (Laforgue's translations of Walt Whitman) in which lines of different numbers of syllables were combined indiscriminately and in which rhyme was no longer the necessary determiner of the stanza's structure. In the short term, Kahn's poetry (published in volume form the following year as *Les Palais nomades*) was the more influential of the two for it was a period piece of Symbolist themes and language.[30] From the end of the century, however, it was Laforgue's work, with its association of a modernist aesthetic and prosodic innovation, that proved to be the more powerful model for the new poetry.

In the late 1870s, Laforgue's reading of Schopenhauer and Hartmann had reinforced his view that the human will was dominated by impersonal cosmic forces which left it powerless to transform the ugliness and pointlessness of modern experience. The poet's only option was to adopt the dandy's playful ironic detachment, mocking his own desires and despairs. The poetic language appropriate to this persona required a new aesthetic, one which was in accord with Hartmann's Unconscious, Darwin's transformism and the work of Helmholtz (the German scientist whose work on colour perception contributed to the development of Impressionism). The aesthetic theory described the relationship between the isolated feeling and the whole life of the unconscious of which it was part, between the melody and the symphony; the existing models were Baudelairean correspondences, Wagnerian leitmotif and the Impressionists' organisation of brushstrokes on the picture-surface.

In *Les Complaintes* (1885), *L'Imitation de Notre Dame la lune* (1886) and *Derniers vers* (published posthumously in 1890), Laforgue developed the flexible poetic language these relationships required. To the themes which served as the vehicle for his pessimistic vision (the clown, Hamlet, the sun–moon opposition) he brought the rhythms of popular song, the language of the boulevard and the ironies of the decadent spirit. Incongruous puns, colloquialisms, invented words, literary parodies, the juxtaposition of different registers and tones, all bring a sense of improvisation and chance collision to poetry's description of modern experience. Decadent in its themes and tones, adopted by the Symbolists for its metaphysical interests and formal innovation, modernist in its extension of poetry's language and field, the work of Laforgue is one of the most complete representations of French late nineteenth-century writing.[31]

The Symbolist movement concerned itself primarily with poetry and theatre and generally dismissed the novel as an inferior genre suitable for realist ambitions and mass audiences. Nevertheless, the Symbolist novel represented an important early phase of the anti-Naturalist reaction because its idealist commitments had implications for narrative technique.[32] If, for example, the world was our representation (Schopenhauer) and/or the expression of the Unconscious (Hartmann), new narrative forms were required to show how the self created the world or manifested the unconscious. Successes here were few, for, by refusing the idea of the novel as history, the Symbolist novel too often reduced characters to abstractions and action to contemplation of an ideal without development. But in *Bruges-la-morte* (1892), Georges Rodenbach (1855–98) created, through the narrator's identification between his adored deceased wife and the moribund city's canals, rains and mists, a fatal labyrinth of true and false correspondences which renewed the tale of mystery and imagination and provided a model for an intermediate, indeterminate fictional form, that of the poetic novel.[33] More significant in historical terms, Dujardin's use of the interior monologue in *Les Lauriers sont coupés* (1887) was an attempt to adapt Wagnerian procedures to narrative technique. The events of one evening are experienced through the narrator's consciousness. Thoughts are presented with minimum syntactical development, and themes return architecturally in the manner of the Wagnerian leitmotif. Dujardin himself referred to this analogy between Wagner's musical motif and the short successive phrases produced by free association in the narrator's mind. James Joyce read the novel as a young man and later generously recognised it as a model for *Ulysses*.[34]

V   AFTER SYMBOLISM

In 1891, even as the Symbolist movement reached the high point of its audience within the Parisian avant-garde, the reaction began against what were seen as its gratuitous obscurities, its verbal idiosyncracies, and its foreign (that is, German) sources. Some abandoned Symbolism's philosophical idealism in favour of a return to modern, urban inspiration. Others joined the growing numbers who were converting to Catholicism during this period, among whom Huysmans, Léon Bloy (1846–1917), Paul Bourget (1852–1935), Paul Claudel and the influential critic Ferdinand Brunetière (1849–1906) were notable examples.

Mallarmé himself continued to administer his public persona through his literary relationships, his elegant and witty circumstantial verse and beautiful correspondence, while pursuing in his private writing the ambitions he had set himself from the late 1860s. With his belief in the virtue of poetic language, he had been obliged to address the impact of Wagnerism in France. In an essay, 'Richard Wagner, rêverie d'un poète français', and a sonnet, 'Hommage [à Wagner]', both written in 1885, he recognised the scale of Wagner's achievement but declined to see in his music the realisation of the definitive work of art to which he aspired and to which he referred, in his autobiographical letter to Verlaine in 1885, as 'Le Livre'. He therefore pursued his lonely journey towards the 'cime menaçante d'absolu' ['menacing peak of the absolute'], which he felt Wagner had only half-scaled.

As an example of the steepness of the climb which the reader of Mallarmé must face, we may look briefly at 'À la nue accablante tu'. S/he may recognise the structure and shape of the octosyllabic sonnet before beginning to read the poem and wonder how the lack of punctuation relates to whatever preliminary expectations this recognition may create, but this data, such as it is, is provisionally set aside when the reading begins. The discontinuities of syntax in the first quatrain are so powerful that we are obliged to move back and forward along the line of verse while units of syntax are asserted and arrested in turn and we struggle to find bearings in the blank semantic spaces between them. Is 'nue' a cloud or a naked woman, 'tu' a personal pronoun or the past participle of 'taire', 'basse' an adjective or a noun, 'À' the preposition or present tense of 'avoir'? These questions are put on hold while other forms of the poem's operation are interrogated: the visual and phonetic prominence of the four-syllable 'accablante', framed by mono-syllables which share the same /y/ vowel; in each line the creation of complete, self-contained word-chains and between each line the 'slavish echoes' of internal and external rhyme which override this independence; the harmonies and conflicts between the semantic, metrical and phonetic patterns; the lack of punctuation, which might otherwise restrict the creative workings of these relation-ships. The reader carries forward as best s/he can these multiple suggestions until sudden, relative clarification is achieved in line 5, when the first quatrain is recognised grammatically to be in antici-pated apposition with 'naufrage', the subject of the single sentence the poem forms.

Shipwreck's familiar scenery of disaster, loss and hoped-for survival gives us our first serious purchase on the poem. When the verb and direct object of which 'naufrage' is the subject arrive in line 8, this theme of wreckage takes its place within the sonnet form's familiar structuring procedures. The passage from quatrains to tercets traditionally brings a new departure to the theme and 'Ou cela . . .' introduces an alternative proposition to that of lines 1–8. But does 'cela' mean 'that' (demonstrative pronoun) or 'concealed' (past historic of 'céler')? As the tercets unfold, they envelop mystery within mystery, forming patterns of syntax and sound through whose relationships is produced the endeavour the poem has evoked without naming. The Mallarméan poem ends the conventional linearity of reading and institutes in its place new strategies for the creation of meaning.

The shipwreck in 'À la nue accablante tu' was taken up again in Mallarmé's extraordinary final work, *Un coup de dés jamais n'abolira le hasard* (1897).[35] Here he reclaimed the alternatives through which nineteenth-century French poetry had sought to extend or replace the classical tradition – analogies with music and the visual arts, prose poetry, free verse – and transcended them in an entirely new form. Through eleven double pages the words which compose the single enunciation of the poem's title are displayed in their own large capitals and around them Mallarmé creates rhythms of typeface and blank space through which themes, images and stages of thought reverberate, obliging the reader at each stage to carry forward multiple forms of linear and spatial reading all at the same time. The antagonisms of mind and matter, of the consciousness which aspires to definitive, intelligible structures and the hasards of the human condition – its unstable thought, language and material reality – which ruin the aspiration, are displayed as a permanent wager by the form of the poem itself. *Un coup de dés* is a *cas limite*, a poem at the outer reaches of the nineteenth-century's exploration of the French poetic tradition and which preserves intact, a hundred years on, the challenge of Mallarmé's exceptional ambition.

VI   THE DREYFUS AFFAIR

In 1889 the centenary of the Revolution was celebrated with the building of the Eiffel Tower, a monument to the faith in scientific progress which had for most of the century underpinned the Republican ideal. With each year the possibility of a monarchist restoration was receding. Early 1889 saw the collapse of the attempt by the populist General Boulanger to organise into an alternative electoral force the disparate groups of radicals and conservatives excluded from power by the moderate Republican consensus which increasingly formed the political establishment of the Third Republic. In this situation, Pope Leo XIII recognised the need for the Catholic Church to reach some *modus vivendi* with the Republic, while the Republic recognised the value of a more tolerant Church as an ally against socialism and anarchism. The result was the reconciliation between Church and Republic known as the *Ralliement*. Though there was support for the policy among moderate Catholics and Republicans, its effect was to radicalise those on both sides who were hostile to it. These elements came into their own with the Dreyfus Affair, which crystallised the return of writers to the contemporary public arena in the aftermath of the Symbolist movement.

In 1894 Alfred Dreyfus (1859–1935), a Jewish officer, was convicted of spying for the Germans on the strength of a memo, allegedly written by him and discovered in a wastepaper basket in the German Embassy. For over three years, his family, convinced of his innocence, strove with little success to bring the injustice to the attention of the public. On 13 January 1898, in *L'Aurore*, the Parisian daily edited by the former radical deputy and future Prime Minister Georges Clemenceau (1841–1929), Zola published his famous open letter 'J'accuse', addressed to the President of the Republic, accusing the French High Command of an anti-Semitic plot to pervert the course of justice. The authorities had no choice but to prosecute France's most famous living writer. The Dreyfus Affair now began in earnest. The Catholic and anti-Semitic press launched a fierce counter-attack and soon French political life was polarised between Dreyfusards, who saw the conviction as a militarist, clerical plot against Truth and Justice, the defining virtues of the Republic, and anti-Dreyfusards, who saw it as a Judeo-masonic socialist conspiracy to undermine the authority of the army and the unity and continuity of the nation which they believed the army to embody. The Affair galvanised the anti-Semitic energies of the far Right into the creation of proto-fascist leagues, of which the *Action Française*, organised by Charles Maurras (1868– 1952), was the most important. Their opponents responded with leagues of their own in defence of Republican values, notably the *Ligue pour la Défense des Droits de l'Homme*. Clemenceau coined the term 'intellectuels', to describe those who supported the petition in *L'Aurore* in favour of revision of the Dreyfus verdict and among whom writers and teachers dominated. The twentieth-century concept of the committed intellectual was therefore another essential offshoot of the Dreyfus Affair.

The Affair triggered exceptional interest among writers.[36] Zola, in *Vérité* (1902), saw it as a struggle for justice: the scientific age against the forces of obscurantism. Anatole France, notably in *Monsieur Bergerat à Paris* (1901) and *L'Île des pingouins* (1908), denounced the anti-Semitism, nationalism and royalist subversion which the Affair had revealed and which, in his view, threatened the Republic. In *Jean Barois* (1913), the first novel by Roger Martin du Gard (1881–1958), composed entirely in dialogue form, the Affair plays a pivotal role in the recognition of the need to defend the Republican ideal. In *Jean Santeuil*, written c.1895–9 but published posthumously (1952 and 1971), and in *À la recherche du temps perdu* (1913–27), Marcel Proust (1871–1922) linked the Affair to ethical issues and the problem of identity. The most prominent anti-Dreyfusard writer was Maurice Barrès (1862–1923), a Boulangist deputy in 1889 and author of a trilogy of novels, *Le Culte du moi* (1888–91), which narrated the effort to construct the self in the context of the intellectual crisis of the *fin de siècle*. In *Les Déracinés* (1897), he showed the failure of seven individuals uprooted from their native Lorraine to establish a viable form of action in a society weakened and confused by democratic rationalism. The novel became a major reference for extreme right-wing nationalist and anti-Semitic ideology.

VII   THE NOVEL IN CRISIS?

By the end of the century, the oppositions we have seen to the positivist interpretation of the world – whether in the form of idealism, subjectivism, spiritualism, Catholicism, the Unconscious or permutations of these – had resulted in a widely-perceived sense of crisis in the novel, whose prestige had been so closely bound to faith in the view of the world which positivism had underpinned. On the one hand, the advance of literacy continued to widen the audience for so-called popular fiction.[37] On the other, the sense within the literary community that the Naturalist novel had reached an impasse was directing attention towards alternative narrative approaches.[38] Two of the younger writers associated with Mallarmé's Symbolist group – André Gide (1869–1951) and Paul Valéry (1871–1945) – wrote parodies of the novel which were light-hearted in tone but whose implications remained with them throughout their writing. The subject of Gide's *Paludes* (1895) is its narrator's laughable efforts to write *Paludes*, an early example of Gide's use of the *mise en abyme* technique in which a major theme or structural element of the text is reproduced in reduced form within the text itself and whose effect is to problematise the nature of writing. Valéry's *La Soirée avec Monsieur Teste* (1896) portrays a 'hero' who does nothing, whose purely theoretical activity denies the basis on which the nineteenth-century novel operated. The idea that the world was our representation had spread with the vulgarisation of the ideas of Schopenhauer and had the effect of displacing the centre of interest from the world to the self. Barrès's trilogy, *Le Culte du moi*, represented an important early attempt to create narrative forms for this reflection of the world through the subjective mind.[39]

Symbolism had sought to define new directions for the novel and, however modest its achievements, it had placed the idea of a poetic novel firmly on the agenda. Relationships between poetry and prose had been actualised by the powerful development in the second half of the nineteenth century of the prose poem, whose flexibility lent itself to the expression of the new complexity and diversity of modern experience. Similarly, Symbolism's role as a conduit into the cultural mainstream for various theories of subjectivity in art had important implications for critical writing. For example, Remy de Gourmont (1858–1915), famously committed to Schopenhauerian idealism, pursued its consequences for literature and literary criticism. In his short stories and novels, the idealist perspective and the philosophy of Egoism he associated with it, gave a distinctive inflection to his representations of the relationship between sexuality and artistic creativity. In his critical writing he developed a theory of poetic criticism which foregrounded the subjectivity of writer and critic, expressed in form, which later made him one of the major influences on Anglo-American New Criticism.[40] Having also written on the art criticism of the Goncourts, he contributed to the presence of their so-called impressionistic effects in the debate about the poetic novel. He was, therefore, an important theoretician of what he saw as the shared aesthetic function of novel and poem to reveal the mysterious, shifting depths of the inner self in its contact with the world and the reader. For this, the novel's conventional intermediaries, plots fixed in linear time and characters accomplishing significant action, were expendable.

Among the multiple forms of theory and practice in the poetic novel during the immediate pre-war years, it was *Le Grand Meaulnes* (1913) by Alain-Fournier (pseudonym of Henri Alban Fournier, 1886–1914) which achieved the most powerful fusion of narrative and poetic effects.[41] This is a novel of initiation, of the quest for happiness with its rites of passage, joys and illusions, a fairy tale with its princess of the mysterious domain, a story of adolescent friendship with its unspoken desires, a journey through the landscapes of memory to a lost paradise of childhood, followed by return to the mediocrity of reality. Throughout, the theme of disguise serves as alibi for the desire to transcend the real and live in the imaginary. However dated these effects may now appear, this work's themes and narrative forms (the use of multiple voices through which the real is fragmented) reveal the transitional phase reached on the eve of 1914 by the post-naturalist novel.

VIII   POEMS DOWN TO EARTH AND UP TO HEAVEN

In the final years of the century and in reaction to the Symbolist movement, poets returned to nature, the city, or God. Francis Vielé-Griffin (1863–1937) confirmed in *La Clarté de vie* (1897) the return-to-nature theme which exercised a powerful appeal in the closing years of the century, as did Francis Jammes (1868–1938), in the lyrical free verse of, for example, his *De l'Angélus de l'aube à l'Angélus du soir* (1898). Elsewhere, the emphasis was on the energies of the modern city, as in the poems of Emile Verhaeren (1855–1916), one of the essential figures of francophone Belgian literature, or on forms of collective experience, as in *La Vie unanime* (1908) by Jules Romains (pseudonym of Louis Farigoule, 1885–1972). The poets of the *école fantaisiste*, particularly Jean-Paul Toulet (1867–1920) in *Contrerimes* (published 1921), made full use of the resources and new freedoms of French prosody to express the modern sensibility.[42]

Among the poets of the Catholic revival, Claudel, in *Cinq grands odes* (1910), celebrates the place of poetry in the divine and human order. The poet becomes the priest who discovers through poetic inspiration the nature and meaning of divine action in the world, and finds his place in God's universe. By taking possession of the self and world in language, he renews the poet's historic role as the community's voice and gives form to divine revelation. Charles Péguy (1873–1914) expressed in *Ève* (1913), an incantation of nearly 2000 quatrains written in sonorous, rhythmically distinctive alexandrines, a mystical and combative patriotism in which the spiritual and historical dimensions of human experience are fused. Jesus reminds Eve of her paradise lost and of the great moments of the Christian story, of the Redemption which remains to be completed but which is threatened by the false prophets of modernity.[43] As nineteenth-century certainties were undermined, and French culture entered into new collective transformations, the renewal of the relationship between Catholic tradition and the modern world was one of many key areas where the individual poetic voice, redefining the poetic role, felt itself called on to contribute to the direction of change.

Part III
A Century of Transformations

7
Changing Language and Changing Worlds

[C]'est dans la seconde moitié du XIXe siècle, à l'une des périodes les plus désolées du malheur capitaliste, que la littérature a trouvé, du moins pour nous, Français, avec Mallarmé, sa figure exacte: la modernité – notre modernité, qui commence alors – peut se définir par ce fait nouveau: qu'on y conçoit des utopies *de langage. Nulle 'histoire de la littérature' (s'il doit s'en écrire encore) ne saurait être juste, qui se contenterait comme par le passé d'enchaîner des écoles sans marquer la coupure qui met alors à nu un nouveau prophétisme: celui de l'écriture. 'Changer la langue', mot mallarméen, est concomitant de 'Changer le monde', mot marxien: il y a une* écoute *politique de Mallarmé, de ceux qui l'ont suivi et le suivent encore.*

[(I)t is the second half of the nineteenth century, one of the grimmest periods of calamitous capitalism, that literature finds its exact figure, at least for us Frenchmen, in Mallarmé. Modernity – our modernity, which begins at this period – can be defined by this new phenomenon: that *Utopias of language* are conceived in it. No 'history of literature' (if such is still to be written) could be legitimate which would be content, as in the past, to link the various schools together without indicating the gap which here reveals a new prophetic function, that of writing. 'To change language', that Mallarmean expression, is a concomitant of 'To change the world', that Marxian one. There is a *political* reception of Mallarmé, of those who have followed him and follow him still.][1]

In the middle of the nineteenth century, in a process discussed in the previous section, literature became an institution in its own right, by courtesy of the market and its politics. From then on, there were two kinds of writing. One kind, literature proper, was the province of an elite of writers and intellectuals, who wrote in the first instance for each other. The other kind was produced for the audiences of the mass market, passive consumers of ideologies generated by the elite. But it was not until the middle of the twentieth century that the situation was recognised, the changed status of literature analysed, and the right questions asked about the distinctive nature of literary language (for which Roland Barthes coined the term *écriture*). Between the change and its perception lies a history of economic, social and philosophical changes that ended with an association of politics and language that would in itself be an instrument for further change. Modernity begins with the generation of Mallarmé.

What came of that generation was a long sequence of transformations which this chapter traces in a number of selected areas. An overview of the audience and centres of intellectual production in the twentieth century is coupled with an account of some main points of reference in the development of twentieth-century thinking. This is followed by reviews of developments in prose fiction, poetry and theatre. The end comes with two fresh beginnings: women's writing, and francophone literature.

* * *

The history of twentieth-century France is one of a society where people at all levels were becoming increasingly capable, as producers, consumers or both, of taking part in the processes of intellectual production. Milestones on the long march of popular education included the law establishing free primary education, 16 June 1881, and the law of 28 March 1882 making it compulsory and removing religious instruction from the curriculum in favour of civic morality and solidarity. Literary studies played a part in the school curriculum, as a medium for the teaching of Republican values. In the period 1928–33, measures were passed to make state secondary education free and compulsory. The school leaving age was raised to fourteen in 1936 by the Front Populaire government; in the 1960s, it was raised to 16. Attempts were made to extend the class base of students proceeding to higher study. Comprehensive secondary schools were founded in the early 1960s. The Haby reforms of 1977 set up mixed-ability classes in the comprehensives and pointed towards more practical, scientific, and less theoretical curricula. Numbers in higher education expanded, from 122,000 in 1939, to 247,000 in 1960 and 612,000 in 1968.

State interventions also took place in other areas of national culture. In 1945, a Service des Lettres was created within the Direction Générale des Arts et Lettres, and in 1946 a Caisse Nationale des Lettres appeared (which became in 1973 the Centre National des Lettres). Ministers of Culture made their mark. In the 1960s, under de Gaulle, André Malraux built the Maisons de Culture, multi-purpose arts centres. Under Mitterrand, Jack Lang (Minister of Culture 1981–6) channelled funds for the first time to encourage both high and popular culture.

As the literate educated public grew in number, so did the centres of intellectual influence. In the 1880s, the Sorbonne, under the bibliographer Gustave Lanson, became a powerful centre for literary study alongside the Académie Française. From the start, the Sorbonne competed with the *grandes écoles*, where powerful new minds gathered: the École Normale Supérieure (Bergson, Sartre, Nizan, Althusser, Foucault, Macherey, Lacan, Derrida, Bourdieu), the École Pratique des Hautes Études (home of the structuralists Lévi-Strauss, Lacan, Barthes – who in the mid-1960s wiped the floor in debate with the traditionalist literary critic from the Sorbonne Raymond Picard), and the Collège de France (Bergson, Barthes, Lévi-Strauss, Foucault, Benveniste). Publishing expanded, taking over from the academy as the dominant field in the 1930s. New publishing houses, often associated with journals, constituted alternative centres of intellectual activity.

The 1880s had seen the first proliferation of avant-garde little magazines, chief among which was the *Mercure de France*, founded by Alfred Vallette and Remy de Gourmont in 1890. The publishing house and journal of the *NRF* (*Nouvelle Revue Française*) appeared in 1908, the little magazines of the Surrealist movement in the 1920s and 1930s, and the magazines and publishing houses of existentialism in the 1940s: *Les Temps modernes* and *Critique*. In the 1960s came the socialist, Marxist or Maoist collectives such as *Tel quel* and *Change*. After that point, intellectual hegemony began to shift to the media, but there is still a substantial degree of overlap and mutual reinforcement between those who run the electronic media, the press barons and the publishing houses, fostered by the operations and demands of the market.

The promotional activities that began in the late nineteenth century with the celebrated puffs worked up in collusion by journalists, critics and publishing houses appeared in different form in the 1920s, in the marketing strategies for book and author promotion evolved by the publisher Bernard Grasset (author of *La Chose littéraire*, 1929). They swept up the Prize Book system that developed after the establishment of the Swedish Nobel Prize for Literature in 1901 (Prix Goncourt, 1903; Prix Fémina, 1906; Prix Renaudot, 1926; Prix Médicis, 1958). Their present centre is the radio and television book programmes that famously boost an author's sales. The *nouveaux philosophes* of the mid-seventies, for example, such as Bernard-Henri Lévy and André Glucksmann, exploiting contemporary disillusionment with Marxism, owe much of their success to media hype.[2]

As intellectual production has expanded through the century, ways of thinking have undergone radical change. Mallarmé's generation saw a proliferation of competing ideas. As was seen at the end of the previous section, it carried the seeds of those reconceptualisations of the subject and its relation to the world which were shortly to flower in the domains of philosophy, psychology and politics. Linked with these were changes of economic and social structures and changes of the perspectives in which these structures were viewed and understood; all of which would lead eventually to a redefinition of the nature of perception itself.

Of all the new intellectual phenomena that emerged in the *fin de siècle*, it has arguably been the sciences of psychology and psychoanalysis that have since proved of most significance. Welcomed in the first instance throughout Europe as an instrument of normalisation and repression, psychology rapidly found itself supplying both writers and the reading public with matter for both salacious and censorious investigations into tabooed and transgressive areas. Jean-Martin Charcot's accounts of hysteria (*Iconographie photographique de la Salpêtrière*, 1876) and Alfred Binet's studies of fetishism ('Le Fétichisme dans l'amour', 1887) helped spawn whole strands of Naturalist and Decadent literature focused on neurasthenic states, hysteria, fetishism, criminality and perversion. The work of Sigmund Freud (1856–1939) filtered only slowly into this environment, but as its implications became clear it transformed the scene.[3]

Freud's version of psychoanalysis, the 'talking cure', was applied with a conservative intention to cure aberrant behavioural symptoms and restore patients to family and social norms. But behind it lay revolutionary structures of thinking. Freud theorised the importance of the drives, especially the sexual drives, in the formation of the subject. He presented the centre of personality formation as the Œdipus complex (the interplay of the child's movements of desire towards father and mother, a way of envisaging the processes of repression and identification through which the individual's gender identity is formed). He offered an analysis of how the unconscious and its desires and repressions could be seen at work in the patterns of language and the workings of dream. The 'Freud season' in Paris began in 1922. Translations of major works followed: *Introduction to Psychoanalysis* and *Psychopathology of Everyday Life* (both in 1922), *Three Essays on the Theory of Sexuality* (1923), *Beyond the Pleasure Principle* (1927), *Civilisation and its Discontents* (1934).

In the 1920s, psychoanalysis was a central interest for Gide and the *NRF* group. But it was the Surrealist movement that was chiefly responsible for taking Freud's ideas into the wider public domain, and for adapting them as a means to artistic creation, with the emphasis not on normalisation but on disruption. Through the Surrealists, Freudianism was placed in explosive combination with the revolutionary enthusiasms rippling through Europe after the Russian Revolution of 1917. André Breton and Aragon called hysteria the greatest poetic discovery of the latter part of the century, and transformed it into a poetic act. Breton's evocation of 'convulsive' beauty in his novel *Nadja* (1928) made of hysteria a style (a new kind of syntax, obsessively focused on the image) and a subversive form. The decadent *femme fatale* found herself revived and infused with modern energy, as the emblem of the seductive and productive relationships to be spun between sexuality, criminality and death.

In 1932, Jacques Lacan (1901–81) brought a materialist dimension into psychoanalysis with the publication of his thesis *De la psychose paranoïaque dans ses rapports avec la personnalité*. His originality in this work was to study both the unconscious of his patients, through their fantasies, and their social situation within their families and, through the family, with society in general. In Lacan's account of the subject, paranoia was not simply approached as an illness but explained in terms of the social structures within which it was generated. Welcomed by his Surrealist and Marxist contemporaries, Lacan was viewed with suspicion by the analytical community. In the course of the 1960s, Lacanian ideas of the subject, developed in the light of Saussurean linguistics and disseminated in the seminars he launched in the mid-1950s (published from the mid-1970s), overtook Freud in setting the agenda for the intellectual and literary avant-garde.

The 1930s were still predominantly philosophically rather than psychoanalytically inclined. The intellectual scene was dominated by renewed interest in the work of the German philosopher G. W. F. Hegel (1770–1831), inspired by the seminars given by the Marxist Alexandre Kojève (1902–68) at the École Pratique des Hautes Études (1933–9), which were attended by influential intellectuals including Lacan, Georges Bataille and Jean Paulhan. Kojève's commentaries spoke to a generation watching the rise of Hitler and Stalin who, like Hegel observing Napoleon, felt they were living at the 'end of history'. They wanted to reflect on the movement of history and the meaning of revolutions, to contemplate the themes of tyranny and violence, and to understand as the founding matter of history those class struggles which, Kojève argued, Hegel had figured in his celebrated explorations of the relationship of master and slave. Kojève turned Hegel's idealist concept of history as the manifestation of the World Spirit into an understanding of history as the effects of human consciousness, which took different forms at different moments. What Kojève emphasised was the transformative action of humanity in the world.[4]

Kojève's Hegel influenced the development of atheistic existentialism, matching the aspirations of a generation looking for levers of social, political and personal change. Already in 1932, the Communist Paul Nizan (1905–40), in *Les Chiens de garde*, was demanding that intellectuals should take political responsibility for their ideas. The sense of urgency sharpened with the experience of the right-wing riots and demonstrations of January and February 1934 which led to the formation of the Front Populaire (the gathering of the forces of the Left against fascism). As fascism extended its grip, from the overthrow of the Spanish Republican Government in 1937 by Franco's rebels to the defeat and occupation of France by Hitler in 1940, commitment became an imperative.

Existentialism is most generally associated with the group that formed around Jean-Paul Sartre (1905–80), Simone de Beauvoir (1908–86), Albert Camus (1913–60), Nizan and Maurice Merleau-

Ponty (1906–61).[5] Beauvoir's treatises *Pyrrhus et Cinéas* (1943), *Pour une morale de l'ambiguïté* (1947) and *L'Existentialisme et la sagesse des nations* (1948) made a significant contribution to the doctrines she elaborated jointly with Sartre. These however remain better known through Sartre's texts: *L'Être et le néant* (1943), *L'Existentialisme est un humanisme* (1946), which built on the thought of the German philosophers Martin Heidegger and Edmund Husserl, and *Critique de la raison dialectique* (1960), which took the discussion into the sociological field. *L'Existentialisme est un humanisme* argued for a humanist understanding of the power of individual subjects to make their own and the collective destiny. In a flurry of now-famous phrases, it declared that existence comes before essence and that God does not exist. There is no divinely-created 'human nature' to predetermine human action. Humans determine themselves, by their choices, and in the process of choosing they extend or limit free choice for others. Sartre characterised the human condition as one of absolute freedom and total responsibility, experienced as a burden of anguish, abandonment and despair by subjects who are always conscious of the limits set to their chances of achieving the results they want. Even so, they must commit themselves and act out their commitment. The emphasis throughout the text was on the subject in society, the individual living in a world of 'inter-subjectivity', and Sartre was elaborating a brief to fuel collective action for change.

Albert Camus's *Le Mythe de Sisyphe* (1942) took a different tack, declaring the death or otherwise of God an irrelevancy. Camus discussed the 'absurd', which was, he said, the gap between the human desire for things to be reasonable, and the fact that the world simply will not fit itself into human categories of reason. In another now-famous phrase, he asked whether thought could live in the deserts that come of knowing a need for clear meaning that will never be satisfied and facing the fact that the only reality humanity knows is death. For Camus, the appropriate response to this knowledge was not anguish but revolt, which would bring with it a sense of personal liberation and enhanced passion for life.

Maurice Merleau-Ponty developed the work of the phenomenologist Husserl, but replaced Husserl's focus on abstract consciousness with one on the consciousness of living bodies engaged in the world of history. *La Structure du comportement* (1942) and *La Phénoménologie de la perception* (1945) proposed that the perceiving subject itself structures, rather than simply describes, what it sees, and that the subject exists not in isolation but as a working part of the totality of interacting structures that constitute the form of the real. After Merleau-Ponty, it became easier to conceive of the subject–world relationship as a fluid, constantly-developing whole, rather than in terms of the brutal causality of mechanistic notions of subjects moved by external stimuli. Another of his legacies was the critical awareness of how individuals' ways of looking at things shape the 'truth' of what they see. He argued that what individuals can 'know' depends upon what they are, and that moral theory begins with psychological and sociological self-critique.

From the mid-1960s, the existentialist concept of the subject as a responsible, self-critical agent in history began to come under attack. Structuralism, developed in the academy, not, like existentialism, through journal groups linked to practical immediacies, set the terms of debate.[6] The movement that started with the work of Ferdinand de Saussure (1857–1913), founder of structuralist linguistics (*Cours de linguistique générale*, 1916), spread rapidly to all other disciplines. It was especially visible in literature, through the criticism of Roland Barthes, Gérard Genette and Tzvetan Todorov, and in the social sciences. The ethnologist Claude Lévi-Strauss (b. 1908), seeking to establish general laws underlying social and cultural practices, produced texts which transformed Western culture's sense of itself: *Tristes Tropiques* (1955), *Anthropologie structurale* (1958), *La Pensée sauvage* (1962), *Mythologies* (1964–71) (vol. 1, *Le Cru et le cuit*).

Structuralism starts not from the concept of the 'real', which is arguably unknowable, but from the concept of the sign, by which elements of the 'real' (the *referent*) are represented in discourse. Saussure distinguished two elements in the sign: the *signifier*, which is the visual or auditory mark that carries the representation, and the *signified*, which is the image or idea being represented. He pointed out that the relation between the two is an arbitrary one. Words are human constructs, not natural carriers of meaning.

Structuralist thinking does not start with individual phenomena or terms but instead understands these in their relationships within a system, seeing them as in fact constructed by those relationships, which set up the *differences* between them. Individual systems in their turn are not isolated; they only exist, function and have meaning in relation to other systems. The word uttered by individual speakers ('parole') makes no sense outside the whole language system, involving the particular grammar, syntax, semantics ('langue') they implicitly invoke every time they speak. In this way of thinking, meaning does not come from an individual author or subject, a unique point of origin, but is generated by a system, that is, a complex of structures. The contrast with existentialism is absolute, and has given rise to central debates on the existence of free will and individual responsibility.

Structuralism brought with it some productive new methodologies of study, which have transformed disciplines. Phenomena, it urged, should be considered both synchronically and diachronically: that is, within the working system that constitutes them in the present, and also through the layers of prior states – their history – that have generated the present formation. Positivist 'explanations' of phenomena simply in terms of their generation by isolated causes are no longer feasible.

An initial difficulty with structuralist thinking was that it paid too much attention to the search for universal patterns in the systems it was addressing, and too little to material details of fact. Working on adjacent lines, the *Annales* history movement managed to develop the same awareness of the interactions of fields of endeavour without the tendency to reductive abstraction. Named after the journal founded in 1929 by Lucien Febvre and Marc Bloch, the movement continues to grow in importance, and has produced such major figures as Robert Mandrou, Philippe Ariès and Fernand Braudel. *Annales* history is concerned with the analysis of *mentalités*, that is, mindsets and sensibilities, and it charts the exchanges between economic base and cultural phenomena, the local detail of everyday life and the broader movements of political and social economy, which generate the living social organism.[7]

The ground-breaking structuralist analyses of literature and culture were provided by Roland Barthes (1915–80), first professor of literary semiology (the science of signs) at the Collège de France. *Le Degré zéro de l'écriture* (1953) gave stimulating accounts of how writers are constituted in the changing languages of their societies (anticipating Barthes's later, more radical accounts of the 'death' of the author) and evoked, too, another future central theme of Barthes's work: the political nature of all language. His 1977 inaugural lecture argued that language has inscribed within it the multitudinous powers within society that both make speech possible and set its limits. Literature, he added, was liberating in that it involved the 'displacement' of language, staging the play of words. *S/Z* (1970) described a text that does this as a 'writerly' text, in contrast with a 'readable' text, which merely conveys a message. Barthes's reader is expected to work with a text to develop its meanings, not behave as a passive consumer. In *Mythologies* (1957), a founding text of contemporary cultural studies, Barthes applied semiological analysis to sign-systems of contemporary culture. In *Le Système de la mode* (1967), he explored the varying significance of fashion.

A second structuralist generation acknowledged its debt to Lévi-Strauss and Lacan, whose *Écrits* appeared in 1966, and moved on into ever more delighted disruptions of the 'certainties' of Western thought. This generation has been characterised as proclaiming the end of philosophy (by which it means rationalist metaphysics), and as developing a Nietzschean genealogical method of analysis (which involves explaining not the contents of a discourse but the political, economic, psychological conditions of its production).[8] It stressed the historical relativity of all intellectual categories and rejected the idea of absolute truth for that of truth as historical product. Its members share a distinctive style, marked by the cultivation of paradox, complexity and difficulty and the cult of the marginal. They follow Barthes in declaring the death of the subject and presenting 'individuals' as products of language and ideology.

How linguistic and institutional discourses generate the subject was the theme of the studies of the relations between power and knowledge offered by Michel Foucault (1926–84). *Folie et déraison: Histoire de la folie à l'âge classique* (1961) investigated the institutionalisation of madness. *Surveiller et punir. Naissance de la prison* (1975) analysed the development and function of the prison system. Three volumes, beginning with *Histoire de la sexualité, I: La Volonté de savoir* (1976), explored the politics of sexuality. Foucault's work was often based on debatable interpretations of history, but his methodology was subversive and stimulating. His lecture 'Nietzsche, Freud, Marx', delivered at *Tel quel*'s Cérisy conference in July 1964, identified the three presiding geniuses of contemporary thought, defining their importance in ways they themselves might have been reluctant to recognise, as men who changed thinking on the nature of the sign and its interpretation, and who were the first to declare that there are no absolute meanings, only interpretations. In *Les Mots et les choses: une archéologie des sciences humaines* (1966), he presented a radical version of how ideas are generated: not so much, he argued, by individual thinkers as by the historical moment. Foucault's foreword to the English translation of that text spoke of what he called a positive unconscious of knowledge, an underlying structure or set of rules of formation that at any one period generates all intellectual and scientific production (what he called an *episteme*). The book closed with the famous proclamation of the death of Man.[9]

The work of Louis Althusser (1918–90), Marxist philosopher and Communist activist, brought together Marxism, structuralism and Lacanian psychoanalysis in a seminal article, 'Freud et Lacan', published in 1964. Althusser's attack on humanism, *Pour Marx*, appeared in 1965, together with *Lire 'Le Capital'*. *Lénine et la philosophie* and *Marx devant Hegel*, based on lectures delivered in February 1968, were published in 1969. Althusser's contribution to debate was the concept of *ideology* as the essential dimension of all societies and that which, basically, constructs all subjects.[10] Ideology for Althusser was not simply what people thought, but a matter of material practice, a condition lived through at the level of the unconscious. In his words, it is the imaginary relation of individuals or groups to their real conditions of existence. Ideology is inscribed in people through the institutions that organise their lives, such as churches, family, educational system, trade unions ('Idéologie et appareils idéologiques d'État', *La Pensée*, June 1970). Althusser's disciples, Étienne Balibar and Pierre Macherey, added literature to the list, for its role in the reproduction of the so-called 'national' common language, which was actually, they said, class-divided, and for the central part it played in the middle-class educational system (Pierre Macherey, *Pour une théorie de la production littéraire*, 1966).

The work of Jacques Derrida (b. 1930) is a long meditation on language, text, writing and speech, whose project is to destabilise confidence in the concepts of language, truth and subject (*L'Écriture et la différence*, 1967; *De la grammatologie*, 1967; *Glas*, 1974; *La Carte postale de Socrate à Freud et au-delà*, 1980).[11] 'Truth' for Derrida is replaced by 'meaning'. Meaning is not an absolute but an effect created out of the matter of a text by readers who interweave with it their own interpretations. 'Significance' is a better word than 'meaning', since it represents the limited gesture towards meaning which is all that can be managed. A Derridean approach to a text is not motivated by the intention to 'interpret' it (that is, winkle out some inner truth), but to foreground the uncertainty, ambiguity and indeterminacy of meaning within it. Derrida has challenged what he sees as the central weaknesses of Western culture: its 'logocentrism' (the belief that some ultimate word or reality is the foundation of thought and experience) and its 'phonocentrism' (the belief that speech is more 'true' than writing, because it seems to be delivered by a single author and to place its hearers in the 'presence' of 'meaning').

Derrida has also foregrounded the role of *difference* in producing significance. First-generation structuralism understood the differences that generate meaning as binary oppositions (either–or differences: black defined as not-white). Derridean post-structuralism turns attention to shades of grey, speaking of the 'slippage' of meanings. A sign works because it carries within it a 'trace' of all the other signs that weave the net that generates the particular shade of meaning that, just for the time being, is focused, for its immediate users, in that sign. (The argument is easier to understand by looking at the poetic practice that is its creative precursor. Rimbaud's 'Voyelles', for example, dramatised the process of making meaning which Derrida describes in abstract and analytical terms.) Finally, what is true of language is for Derrida equally true of the subject, who has no absolute existence but exists only as a process, a constant *différance*, a flickering hesitation.

The importance of such thinking for an understanding of the context in which contemporary literature operates can be seen by looking at the avant-garde journal *Tel quel*, founded in 1960 by Philippe Sollers (b. 1936), which mirrors the progress of post-war Parisian intellectual fashion. Politically uncommitted at the start, interested chiefly in the *nouveau roman*, the journal moved to support the Communist Party until around 1970 and then spent the 1970s moving in and out of Maoism. Its key figures are now locked into the American university conference circuit.

The volume *Théorie d'ensemble*, published by the collective in 1968, crystallised the thinking of a significant formative moment. The reference points of past and present influence were indicated as Lautréamont, Mallarmé, Marx and Freud, and Foucault, Barthes, Derrida, Lacan and Althusser. An article by Foucault, 'Distance, Aspect, Origine' (first published in *Critique*, November 1963), redefined the practice of creative writing, not as representation but as the production of 'la nervure verbale de ce qui n'existe pas, tel qu'il est' (p. 9) ['the verbal ribbing of that which does not exist, as such']. More helpfully, it also characterised some features of the new writing. These included the replacement of proper names by pronouns or generic nouns (the man, the woman), and an emphasis not on presenting events but on representing their construction, foregrounding not the story itself but the movement from one level of narration to another, the connections (or indeed the blanks) between statements, ideas, thoughts and objects.

Barthes's contribution, 'Drame, Poème, Roman' (first published in *Critique*, 1965) redefined both history and subject as being, like language, 'jeu de structures' ['interplay of structures']. Derrida reprinted the lecture on 'La Différance' he had given on 27 January 1968 to the Société française de philosophie, with its call to consider a text not as conveyer of a message but as a model of working language. Julia Kristeva, writing on 'Problèmes de la structuration du texte' and 'La Sémiologie: science critique et/ou critique de la science', called for the term 'literary' to be reserved for texts whose *raison d'être* is to communicate the concept of meaning as a construction, and something which is constantly deferred. She wanted literary studies in future to concentrate on texts written since the end of the nineteenth century, such as Joyce, Mallarmé, Lautréamont and Roussel, and to seek to understand the mechanics of modern discursive systems and establish models of general contemporary social practice.

The whole volume pointed to the beginning of a debate within contemporary literature which matches in importance the eighteenth-century controversy over whether fiction is a truth or a lie. It marked a welcome renewal of focus on form. It bore witness to the movement to destabilise the overconfident and authoritarian subject of Gaullist society, and to break some of the barriers isolating that individualist subject from awareness of its part in the interplay of the social whole.

These ideas became a two-edged sword as political circumstances changed in the course of the 1970s and especially the 1980s, when the hesitant, divided subject turned from an instrument of resistance into a tool of reaction. Fashionable thinking is now postmodernist, accelerating down the track of structuralism and post-structuralism to foreground its own version of the proposal that history and meaning only exist through the structuring perceptions of their observers, themselves structured by the present moment from which they observe. Postmodernism problematises not only all totalising concepts but also all values: notions of human community, consensus of meaning, individual and collective progress. Progress in particular has been dismissed as a fiction of Enlightenment reason, one of the grand narratives of history by which the past has been misled (Jean-François Lyotard, *La Condition postmoderne*, 1979).

Postmodernism collapses the hierarchies of discourse, between, for example, elite, official, mass and popular cultures. It exposes the hollowness of the institutions through which modern society is constructed, debunking their pretensions to authority. But it is not interested in disposing of them completely, and has nothing to put in their place.[12] Iconoclastic gesture, irony, parody and pastiche are the forms in which it lives. Postmodernism presents the human condition as a game, in which the board and the rules always come from somewhere else; and the players, apparently, prefer it that way. The analyses by Jean Baudrillard (b. 1929) of contemporary consumer society and its construction and manipulation through the sign-systems of the media (*Le Système des objets*, 1968; *La Société de consommation*, 1970; *Pour une critique de l'économie politique du signe*, 1972; *Les Stratégies fatales*, 1983), originally Marxist, latterly resigned, have been influential in propagating the notion of a society with no alternative but to live on surfaces.[13]

Against the quietism fostered by some extremes of postmodernist thought are to be set recent signs of a resurgent interest in thinking the human subject in terms that might renew confidence in the human capacity to engage productively with society and to effect changes for the collective as well as the individual good. This trend has emerged particularly in the context of debates over questions of human rights. In 1972, casting round for a radical alternative, the philosopher Gilles Deleuze (1925–95) and the psychoanalyst and left-wing political activist Félix Guattari (1930–92) published *L'Anti-Œdipe: capitalisme et schizophrénie, I*, attacking post-structuralism for still being locked, they claimed, within old rationalist categories, and looking for more radical analyses that might intervene in existing power structures in order to change them.[14] Michel Foucault's last work returned to the question of the relation between individual subject and society to produce an account of the exchanges of Ancient Greek society that pointed to a very different ethic of both self-cultivation and collective loyalty (*Histoire de la sexualité, II: L'Usage des plaisirs*, 1984). The work of Pierre Bourdieu (b. 1930), founder of the study of the sociology of knowledge, and one of the few Marxist innovators of the 1960s to have successfully maintained through the 1980s both his Marxism and the relevance of his work to the changing contemporary situation, has always remained wedded to the conviction that the world is understandable, and that the purpose of understanding it is to change it. *Homo academicus* (1984), studying the structural constraints to conservatism built increasingly into the academic world, speaks of the need for academics to grasp the constraints of the system that has generated them in order to grasp responsibility and freedom within it.

8

Changing Forms and Subjects

I   THE NOVEL

1914–39: New Ideas and Forms

The most profound challenge to the Naturalist legacy in the novel came from Marcel Proust (1871–1922) in *À la recherche du temps perdu* (published 1913–27). All of Proust's early work was in one form or another a preparation for this novel, which he began writing in July 1909.[1] Reading Ruskin had confirmed his sense of the over-riding importance of art; translating him had reinforced the apprenticeship of writing also evident in his pastiches of the style of major French writers.[2] In the fragments of *Jean Santeuil*, he described the pleasure derived from identifying elements common to sensations in the past and present. In *Contre Sainte-Beuve*, what began as an attack on the biographical approach to literary history developed into a series of autobiographical texts in which essential characters and themes of *À la recherche* were developed towards their final form. Just as the critical work extended into episodes of fiction, the novel incorporated across its length an analysis of the nature of literature, ending with the narrator's discovery of the means to write the novel which Proust was drawing to a close.

The search for lost time is the search for the permanence and coherence of human identity.[3] Predicated on the essential truth announced at the outset that 'nous ne sommes pas un tout matériellement constitué, identique pour tout le monde' ['we are not a materially-constituted whole, identical for everyone'], but that 'notre personnalité sociale est une création de la pensée des autres' ['our social personality is the creation of the thoughts of others'], it is a lifelong journey through the damage which the passage of time inflicts on knowledge of the self and others. Fashionable upper-class Parisian society of the Third Republic is the arena for the meaningless and inauthentic action whose false values and empty rituals replace knowledge in a world subjected to time. Extending Flaubert's ironic deconstruction in *L'Éducation sentimentale* of Balzac's energised city, Proust shows characters and events as reference points for rituals of social acceptance or exclusion which are vicious and intensely comic at the same time. The Dreyfus Affair is an 'erreur mondaine' ['social gaffe'] through which Madame Verdurin loses ground in the social race; the First World War demonstrates the stupidity of the baron de Charlus's conversation. History is refracted through, and reduced to, the shifting and ephemeral anecdotes of society gossip.

If time condemns social aspirations and relationships to a meaningless formalism, it is no less destructive of love. Since time renders knowledge of the self and others impossible, love in *À la recherche* is a doubly sterile delusion of power, a projection of imagination and desire onto others which always carries the seeds of its own destruction. Each major relationship (Swann with Odette, the narrator with Albertine, Charlus with Morel and so on) repeats the same infernal sado-masochistic sequence of pain inflicted and endured, of a desire for mastery which fuels jealousy and provokes lies and silence.

Only at the end of the novel does the narrator realise that the experience of society and love, worthless in itself, finds its necessity in art. Real without being imprisoned in time, ideal without being devoid of reality, the sensations experienced in the Guermantes courtyard convene past and present in what the narrator describes as time in the pure state, abolishing contingency and the fear of death. The lessons of the madeleine and Martinville steeples episodes in *Combray* can at last take their true place in this self-discovery and in the literary project which flows from it, in the synthesis of sensation and memory in which the necessary relationship between past and present may be demonstrated. Metaphor and simile, which annul restrictions of time and space and fuse abstract thought and physical sensation in a single association, provide an essential linguistic counterpart to this victory over the negative effects of time.

Proust's novel is a compendium of fictional models, its whole extending far beyond the sum of their parts: realist (its socio-historical analysis); psychological (its involvement of the reader in the narrator's introspective response to experience); developmental (the narrator's sentimental education from childhood to middle-age); confessional (first-person revelation of a life); Wagnerian (its length, and the strategic role of themes and symbols linked by the leitmotif technique). It offers an extended history of its own creation as the narrator eventually abandons the example of the false artists and aesthetes (Swann, Charlus) for the lessons of the true (Vinteuil, Elstir, Bergotte) and, in the novel's circular structure, decides at the end of *Le Temps retrouvé* to write the history of a narrator becoming a writer. Each volume reproduces the same sequence of the aspiration to an ideal world of essential terms followed by the confrontation of this ideal with the reality of experience. The repeated failure of this confrontation brings the narrator to the very brink of defeat – from which victory is snatched in the closing moments of the quest. At the centre of this vast cycle, the Proustian narrator moves between the multiple levels of past and present experience, reflecting on the nature of narrative in ways which have offered subsequent writers enormous potential to extend the means of fiction.

The work of André Gide (1869–1951) is dominated by the conflict between the desire for authenticity and the moral, intellectual and social systems which oppose it.[4] Following the death of his father in 1880, Gide was raised by his mother and his Scottish governess in an intense Protestant austerity. In the mid-1890s he undertook two journeys to North Africa, during which he experienced what he felt to be a spiritual rebirth through the discovery of his homosexuality, the life of the senses and openness to experience. These discoveries intensified the conflict between self-denial and desire for experience with which he had struggled throughout adolescence. In the course of his life this conflict between the temptation and the fear of desire, between submission and resistance to authority, took many forms and Gide used the act of writing to analyse its contradictions critically and thereby deliver himself from them. Each of his books, he said, carried within itself its own contradiction.

In Gide's *récits*, a first-person narrator confronts with varying degrees of lucidity and self-deception the consequences of an ethical choice taken to destructive limits. In *L'Immoraliste* (1902) Michel sacrifices his wife to his theory of immoralism. Formulated five years earlier in *Les Nourritures terrestres*, this philosophy of *disponibilité* and of freedom from external moral constraints had as its object the search for God, deemed the source of all experience. In *L'Immoraliste*, it has become a self-serving cult of force and independence which leaves the narrator with anguish and doubt. *La Porte étroite* (1909) re-enacts the destructive outcome of *Les Cahiers d'André Walter* (1891), Gide's first published work. Alissa's mystical ideal of virtue and self-sacrifice in the name of a silent God lead to desperate solitude and ultimate tragedy. In *La Symphonie pastorale* (1919), the pastor's deception of self and others leads Gertrude to the fatal despair of the knowledge of sin without the knowledge of forgiveness; her death highlights the dangers of the pastor's self-interested interpretation of the Scriptures, choosing between a religion of law and one of love. In these *récits*, the use of the first-person narrator paradoxically achieves what Gide called the height of objectivity, because without authorial intervention, the narrator, recounting experience in her or his diary and letters, unwittingly betrays the self-deception and sophistry which kill. For this reason Gide referred to his *récits* as 'ironic' books. The difficulty of self-knowledge implies a permanently critical, ironic mode of writing.

This ironic mode found its fullest development in Gide's *soties*, a term taken from the medieval popular comic play in which actors masqueraded as fools. *Paludes* (1895), his satire on Symbolist attitudes to the relationship between art and life, and *Le Prométhée mal enchaîné* (1899), his modernised version of the Greek myth in which Prometheus discovers immoralism, illustrate its possibilities but its most powerful demonstration comes in *Les Caves du Vatican* (1913), an hilarious spoof adventure story of an alleged abduction of the Pope and his replacement by an imposter. Composed at the height of the Catholic revival, this ferocious satire of uncritical allegiance to systems of belief centres on the Vatican cellars, under-ground passages which link the residences of the true and fake Popes and so serve as a metaphor for the unfathomable distinctions between appearance and reality and for the threat of the counterfeit in every area of experience, from Protos's disguised crooks to Lafcadio's false *acte gratuit*. As in his *récits*, Gide in *Les Caves* makes the problematics of writing central to the burlesque escapades. Autonomous pantomime characters, shifting narrative points of view, a decentralised and open-ended plot structure, a profusion of coincidences and word-play represented Gide's most sustained subversion to date of the nineteenth century's practice of the realist and psychological novel.

In this respect it was an essential preparation for *Les Faux-Monnayeurs* (1926). This was the only one of his texts which Gide described as a novel, for he tried to fulfil there the encyclopaedic ambition of Balzac and Zola to depict modern society (which Gide saw as threatened by inauthenticity at every level) while showing at the same time the conflict between the reality of this society and our representation of it. In *Les Faux-Monnayeurs*, the moral focus of the *récit* and the narrative innovations of the *sotie* are combined and multiplied. The threat of the counterfeit provides unity across the range of characters and themes (Bernard and the family, the Oliver/Édouard couple and homosexuality, Passavant and writing) while the narrative system unpacks realist conventions of linear time, fixed characters, absolute knowledge and closed structure. The multiple narrative points of view created by these procedures are themselves displaced by the *mise en abyme* technique which shows Édouard writing *Les Faux-Monnayeurs* and keeping a diary, the *Journal des Faux-Monnayeurs*, and an 'author' intervening in the text to judge his characters, as does Gide himself.

Gide was also the most prominent founder member in 1909 of the *Nouvelle Revue Française*, which became, particularly from 1919, when Jacques Rivière (1886–1925) took over as director, one of modern France's most famous literary reviews. Despite the review's commitment to independence from political programmes, Gide was passionately involved with some of the central moral and political issues of his time and ours – homosexuality (*Corydon*, 1924), the failures of colonisation (*Voyage au Congo* and *Retour du Chad*, 1927–8) and those of Stalinism (*Retour de l'URSS*, 1936). His experimentation with new narrative practices, though complex and somewhat contrived, his use of narrative to work through the contradictions and potential dangers of intellectual systems, his continued reflection on the nature of autobiographical writing in the diary he kept throughout his life, all stemmed from his sense of the importance of self-knowledge at a time when the systems of thought which had underpinned the literature of the nineteenth century were losing credibility. For these reasons, his work makes an essential contribution to the development of twentieth-century sensibility.

The Great War and its Aftermath

The work of Proust and Gide provided from the 1920s two of the most important models of the implications for narrative practice of the re-examination of that positivist ambition which for much of the nineteenth century had given literature coherence and direction. By then, however, these issues had been engulfed by the catastrophic devastation of the Great War (1914–18).

The sense that the entire European cultural tradition had been dishonoured by the war was widely felt; Paul Valéry expressed it powerfully in his famous essay of 1919, *La Crise de l'esprit*.[5] Despite the unprecedented scale of the slaughter, certain writers found it possible to view the war positively, transforming it into a nostalgic ideal of heroic comradeship and purification through sacrifice. But at the other end of the cultural spectrum, one faction of the avant-garde saw it as the justification of its contempt for the culture responsible for the industrialised carnage in the trenches, and an opportunity to unite the European avant-garde in the great task of destroying through derision the rationalist tradition on which bourgeois language and culture was based. This faction formed the Dada movement in Zurich in February 1916. Its main activity however took place from 1920 in Paris where its leading figure, Tristan Tzara (1896–1963), linked up with the French pre- and post-war avant-gardes and, in particular, with the *Littérature* group, created in 1919 by André Breton (1896–1966), Louis Aragon (1897–1982) and Philippe Soupault (1897–1990) and quickly reinforced by Paul Éluard (1895–1952) and Benjamin Péret (1899–1959). Together they channelled Dada's provocative and nihilistic agitation in the direction of the Surrealist programme of literary and political revolution.

The wave of euphoric nationalist and revanchist sentiment which greeted the declaration of hostilities in August 1914 was soon confronted by the atrocious facts of the trench warfare into which the conflict settled from its first winter. Public ignorance of the realities of modern warfare, and the divorce between these realities and the official propaganda emanating from incompetent and deceitful military and political authorities, created, for writers seeking to describe authentically the experience of the trenches, the problem of finding words for what was unprecedented, and literally unspeakable. Though there were some reference points in the French novel tradition to help them – the description of the battle of Waterloo in Stendhal's *La Chartreuse de Parme*, that of the battle of Sedan in Zola's *La Débâcle*, for example – the sheer scale and horror of the carnage called for new types of description of death, mutilation and survival and a wider range of linguistic registers, incorporating dialect, slang and obscenity. Limited points of view and episodic, disjointed sequences of events displaced the purposeful actions of linear narratives, which were inappropriate for the sudden catastrophes visited upon soldiers unable to comprehend the forces that a modern technological civilisation had unleashed upon them.

The two most famous novels of the Great War, *Le Feu* (1916) by Henri Barbusse (1873–1935) and *Les Croix de bois* (1919) by Roland Dorgelès (1886–1973), offered different responses to the chaos. Despite the censorship to which its initial serialisation in a left-wing review was subjected, *Le Feu* outraged conservatives, but its strong fusion of documentary realism and pacifist, internationalist vision of a society of equality and brotherhood made it a huge critical and commercial success.[6] *Les Croix de bois* recounted the fear, suffering and will to survive which marked day-to-day life in the trenches, where horror was displaced by moments of intense release and humour. Unlike *Le Feu*, *Les Croix de bois* contained little political analysis or vision and this distinction between the two novels also characterised the post-war directions taken by the authors. Both before and after joining the Parti Communiste Français (PCF) in 1923, Barbusse played a leading role in efforts to create a collective revolutionary consciousness among intellectuals, notably through the reviews *Clarté* and *Monde*, of which he was the founding editor (in 1919 and 1928 respectively), and through his contribution to the debate on proletarian and popular literature.[7] In *Le Réveil des morts* (1923), Dorgelès vented his sense of outrage that the society which had survived the war was failing in its moral obligations to the war dead. Having done so, he turned to writing travel literature and escapist, nostalgic chronicles of an idealised and carefree bohemian life in pre-war Montmartre.

The Inter-War Years

In the novel the end of the war triggered a wide range of responses. Not surprisingly, anti-war sentiment was prominent among them, while the implications of the war for religious faith, spiritual values or cultural and intellectual issues of the sort raised by Valéry in 'Crise de l'Esprit' also became important themes. At the same time, other novelists responded to a powerful public need to draw a veil over 1914–18, and this led to a sharp increase in the production and consumption of thrillers and of travel and adventure novels. Exotic geographical, historical and social locations had in any case long since been the staple diet of popular and escapist fiction. In the post-war euphoria of the *années folles,* the adventure novels of Pierre Benoît (1886–1962) achieved huge sales.[8]

On another level, novelists whose work came into the imprecise and wide-ranging category of the poetic novel again took up pre-war criticisms of what were considered to be the artificial and superficial observation and organisation of external reality in Naturalist fiction. The 1920s novels of Jean Giraudoux (1882–1944) contained sequences of loosely-related episodes which showed the poetic sensibility's subjective transformation of everyday life. This formula, in which the mechanisms of prose poetry and fiction collaborated within the narrative structure, was a focus for much discussion of narrative theory during this period.

The most important group of novels referred to at that time under the term 'poetic novel' was that of the regional *roman rustique,* which tapped into a demand for something more profound than the conventional pastoral of rural local colour. The desire to escape modern urban industrial society through a return to the values of a mythical *France profonde* reflected the wish to re-establish contact with more stable rhythms associated with the ancestral relationship between people and land, far removed from the brutal contingencies of modern history. André Chamson (1900–83), with his historical novels of the Cévennes (published 1925–8), and Maurice Genevoix (1890–1980), with *Raboliot* (1925), were important figures in this development, but it was in the work of the Swiss francophone novelist Charles-Ferdinand Ramuz (1878–1947) and that of Jean Giono (1895–1970) that the regional novel briefly appeared central to the intellectual and formal developments taking place in the novel of the period.

In Ramuz a lyrical and mystical vision of the mysterious forces in nature which both threaten and enhance those in contact with them was expressed in distinctive verbal rhythms and syntactic disjunctions. In a cycle of novels known as the Pan trilogy (published 1929–30), Giono created a myth of rural life in which the ancestral gestures and rhythms of day-to-day experience confront the mysterious forces of nature. In *Le Grand Troupeau* (1931) he returned to his loathing of war. As is indicated by the metaphor of the flock contained in the title, the novel contrasts apocalyptic scenes of soldiers led like lambs to the slaughter with descriptions of the cyclical continuities and force of life within peasant society. The interwoven themes and images of war and land bring to the surface the relationship between anxiety about the nature of modern experience and the values for which the regional novel of the 1920s was the vehicle. Nevertheless, the novel retains a guarded optimism that the force of life exemplified in peasant society will overcome even as violent an assault on its values as that of the Great War.[9]

It was no coincidence that in 1931 Giono returned to the theme of war or that he depicted it then as an essentially totalitarian phenomenon. After an initial rush of war novels of the 'lived experience' type, the Great War began to serve as a metaphor for the post-war world it had engendered. An early case in point is that of *Le Diable au corps* (1923), in which Raymond Radiguet (1903–23) showed, through an affair between an adolescent and a young woman whose husband was fighting at the front, the premature cynicism of an adolescent growing up in the exceptional situation created by the war. The youth's calm amoralism and the negative portrayal of the female characters created a huge *succès de scandale* at a time in the early 1920s when 'official' accounts of the war were stressing heroism, self-sacrifice and just revenge.[10]

As the 1920s progressed, the growing impact of the ideological systems of Communism and National Socialism drew intellectuals in every sphere towards contemporary historical and political issues. The publication of *La Trahison des clercs* (1927), in which Julien Benda (1867–1956) denounced what he considered this betrayal of the intellectual's responsibility for detached speculative thought, and the reaction his work provoked, crystallised this trend. Any hopes Benda might have had of convincing his fellow-intellectuals of the need to withdraw to some ivory tower of pure ideas were ended by the economic and political crisis triggered by the Wall Street Crash in 1929. The Great Depression and its political consequences created for many writers the sense of living after one war and on the verge of another, and refocused their interest on the nature of modern history and its origins in the Great War.

The Great War is the first of the four locations in which Louis-Ferdinand Céline (1894–1961) situated his *Voyage au bout de la nuit* (1932), in which modern life is depicted as a sinister farce played out initially in the military context of war and later in the economic and social context of peace. In this radically pessimistic variation on *Robinson Crusoe*, dehumanising victimisation exercised by a ruling elite is the general law in all four locations (trenches and military hospital, African colonies, American factories, Parisian suburbs) down whose long, dark night the protagonists, Barmadu and

Robinson, wander. In his second novel, *Mort à crédit* (1936), the death is that of the *petite bourgeoisie* to which the narrator's family belongs, while the credit is that of the new technological economy which is the source of its ruin. The novel recounts the narrator's hopeless childhood and adolescence, spent in growing conflicts with his family. This second novel took further than the first Céline's efforts to inject into the literary tradition the energy and authenticity of popular spoken French and slang and his experimentation with expressive, stylised punctuation. The scandalous nature of the themes and language in both novels, and the predominantly socio-political readings they encouraged, notably in view of Céline's notorious pro-fascist sympathies immediately before and during the Second World War, were originally the basis of his reputation. Later, *nouveau roman* experimentation in the 1950s and 1960s helped to promote awareness of his subtle and complex reworking of the Proustian legacy in the French novel.[11]

The ironic reversal of the values of the Great War from heroism to farce is also present in the work of Pierre Drieu la Rochelle (1893–1945). Leading the charge at the battle of Charleroi in October 1914, Drieu had apparently experienced a mystical, purifying vision of the union of intellect and action, after which life in post-war Paris appeared as one of cultural and political decline. In the title story of his collection *La Comédie de Charleroi* (1934), heroism has become a 'comédie', farcically ill-adapted to the forms of modern warfare, which reduced heroes to cannon-fodder, and irrelevant to the post-war world order, in which the USA and the Soviet Union were replacing the old European empires. In the story, a middle-aged narrator speaking at an unspecified time in the 1930s tells of his return to the battlefield in 1919, in the course of which he had recounted the 1914 battle to the mother of his fallen comrade. Through the interplay between these three narrative moments, Drieu shows how the war prefigures the unviable, divided society created in Europe by the advanced industrialised civilisation of the post-war years. As the collection was appearing, Drieu was finding his own solution to the problems it raised: the fascist riots of February 1934 precipitated his conversion to the fascist cause. The intellectual itinerary of the fascist is the subject of his novel *Gilles* (1939).[12]

Les Thibault (1922–40) by Martin du Gard illustrates a different aspect of the impact on fiction of the retrospective assessment of the Great War. Planned in 1920 as a modern version of the classical chronicle of the lives of two antithetical brothers, the cycle traces the development of Jacques and Antoine Thibault in relation to the pre-war values of their authoritarian father. The final volume, *L'Été 1914* (1936), marks the eruption of modern history, in the form of the declaration of war, into the private destinies of the brothers. Within a conventional naturalist technique, Martin du Gard presented an analysis of human relationships deepened by his study of Freudian descriptions of sexuality, and by what Camus called a 'shared misery', in which the subject is both limited and empowered by its recognition of the force of collective realities.[13] As such, he appears in histories of French literature as a transitional figure between the nineteenth-century Naturalist and the mid-twentieth-century existentialist novels.

The nature of collective experience is central to the other major novel cycle of the inter-war period, the 27-volume *Les Hommes de bonne volonté* (published 1932–46), in which Jules Romains tried to integrate the theories of unanimist collective realities developed in his pre-war poetry (see above, p. 181) with an account of history in the making, based on the realist model.[14] The two volumes (15 and 16) which deal with the battle of Verdun are thematically and structurally central. They illustrate unanimist principles in the sense that the sum of the limited and distorted individual narrative points of view before and during the battle is less than the whole, transcendent overview of their collective relationships. The cycle of novels strikes an uneasy balance between fatalistic submission to contingent, uncontrollable forces and faith in the possibility of individual action which might channel these forces in directions beneficial to the collectivity.

By the mid-1930s one of the clearest signs of the heightened awareness of the novel's engagement with modern history was that of the complex, difficult relationship between the Surrealists and the French Communist Party.[15] By that time Aragon was the sole survivor in the Party of those members of the group who had joined in 1927, and his support for the theory of socialist realism alienated them still further. Aragon used the term to describe *Antoine Bloyé* (1933), the first novel by his fellow Communist Paul Nizan (1905–40). Whereas Aragon considered socialist realism to be the means to bring together the political and cultural levels of revolutionary struggle, Breton thought it a sterile dogma indicative of the Party's subservience to Stalinist cultural orthodoxy. In *Pour un réalisme socialiste* (1935), Aragon claimed that the Surrealists had sought to submit Marxism to Freudian theory without regard to socio-economic conditions. But like Breton (in *Nadja*, 1928), he was the author of a classic Surrealist prose text.[16] In *Le Paysan de Paris* (1926), a narrator creates from chance encounters and observations triggered during visits to the Passage de l'Opéra, scheduled for demolition, and the Buttes-Chaumont gardens, a collage of dialogues, memories, inventories and newspaper cuttings which reinvent the city as an adventure of the imagination. With his conversion to socialist realism, Aragon did not, however, simply abandon the effort to create a new type of novel which *Le Paysan de Paris* had represented.

During the 1930s Aragon published *Les Cloches de Bâle* (1934) and *Les Beaux Quartiers* (1936), the first two of a cycle of novels which would be called *Le Monde réel*. *Les Cloches de Bâle* shows the condition of three women in French society between 1897 and 1912 (the latter being the date of the Basle Congress of European Socialists, which gave the novel its title). Diane de Nettencourt is a high-class prostitute whose life illustrates the corruption, duplicity and waste inherent in the bourgeois capitalist system. Clara is the emerging proletariat and Catherine represents that sector of the bourgeoisie that tried and failed to rebel against its class through social and political education. In contrast, the epilogue introduces the German militant Clare Zetkin as a model of the new emancipated political woman. In *Les Beaux Quartiers*, the classical fictional device of two brothers following opposing paths, one towards wealth and power, the other towards left-wing political commitment, is used to represent pre-war Paris, its *Belle Époque* decadence and its political agitation. The novels have a political objective absent from *Le Paysan de Paris* but draw on a variety of narrative forms and tones already present in Aragon's work of the 1920s.[17]

The other essential figure of French socialist realism, the militant novelist and journalist Paul Nizan, had already established his Communist credentials with his attacks on colonialism in *Aden Arabie* (1931) and on the idealist philosophical tradition of the French university system in *Les Chiens de garde* (1932) when he published *Antoine Bloyé* (1933).[18] This novel recounts the life of a railwayman who betrays his working-class origins in favour of integration with the petty bourgeoisie and pays, through alienation and solitude, the price of his lack of political lucidity. His life is analysed by his son, compassionate towards his politically uneducated and manipulated father but aware, as a committed

Communist, of the ideological mechanisms which have led him to betray his class. This problem of the complexities and self-deceptions of political commitment, and the consequent need for lucid self-criticism, is taken further in *La Conspiration* (1938), Nizan's most accomplished novel.[19] He broke with the French Communist Party in September 1939 following the signing of the German–Soviet non-aggression pact and was, as a result, denigrated as a traitor by the Party (and, in particular, by Aragon).

The commitment to socialist realism created difficulties for Communist novelists working within a culture which had not yet carried out its own revolution and whose reading public was therefore from the Marxist point of view an accomplice to the forms of sophistry and mystification by which the ruling class maintained its position. The need to show the development of the proletarian class consciousness from which revolution would spring, to analyse the economic and historical factors which produced the situation in which characters found themselves, and to show how the forces of reaction worked from mysterious centres of power to frustrate the emergence of a revolutionary situation – all these created difficult issues of narrative technique in a culture in which pre- (or counter-) revolutionary narrative traditions were so strongly established.

It is hardly surprising, given the pressure of circumstances, that Aragon and Nizan made use of mechanisms readily available in the French nineteenth-century realist tradition, even though it represented the triumph of the bourgeois ideology to which they were opposed. These mechanisms included the use of the Balzacian omniscient narrator, able to relate individual action to the wider socio-historical context; the description of places and objects onto which a Marxist perspective of economic determinism might be grafted; the creation of characters as types representative of class commitments; and the representation of the city and its streets and buildings as signs of the social organisation enacted there. As a result, Aragon and Nizan were attacked for relaying a revolutionary message through conservative narrative techniques, and the serious-ness with which they struggled with the issues of narrative tech-nique and the interest of the solutions they brought were overlooked.[20] Only from the mid-1950s did different historical circumstances make it possible to consider these issues from new perspectives. These included Aragon's own fiction from 1956, and Nizan's rehabilitation, begun in 1960 with the famous preface by

Jean-Paul Sartre (1905–80) to a new edition of *Aden Arabie* and extended by the rediscovery of *Chiens de garde* in the student upheavals of May 1968.

In addition to their political novels, Nizan and Aragon were essential figures in the controversies which in the course of the 1930s increasingly polarised French intellectuals. If, at the beginning of the decade, the 'spirit of 1930' was for many of the younger generation of intellectuals still a largely-unfocused rejection of contemporary political and social structures, by the mid-1930s polarisation had taken place on political lines. The choice appeared clear between the communist/socialist rapprochement, which led in 1936 to the election of the Popular Front government under Léon Blum, and the conservative Right, which aligned itself with the fascist opposition to this development. The outbreak of the Spanish Civil War in 1936 was a defining moment in this process of polarisation in the period leading up the Second World War.[21]

The work and political activity of André Malraux (1901–70) was directly involved with these events and the issues they raised.[22] Like Gide in the Congo, Malraux had discovered in the Far East the decline of European culture, and in the alien gaze of the colonised he saw reflected the crisis of Western bourgeois individualism (*La Tentation de l'Occident*, 1926). With the death of God there was no universal human nature created in His image and likeness. There was only the human condition, the tragic state of being in an unstable world. With no prospect of an afterlife, the choice was either to reconcile oneself to living in a meaningless world of atomised subjectivities or to struggle to create new meanings through revolt against the tragic vision of human destiny.

For those who chose struggle, the historical situation in which they did so made available a further choice between individual and collective action. In Malraux's novels the characters who act seek either to project into the world the values of self-realisation or to submit these values to a collective discipline which will transform political and social reality for the group with which they identify. The tensions between the two forms of action, between what Malraux presents as the anarchist urge to be and the communist urge to do, underpin the structure as well as the ideological and ontological debates which the novels enact. In *La Condition humaine* (1933), the representatives of both types of action within the revolutionary community engaged in the Communist uprising in Shanghai in April 1927 are doomed in advance, victims of the political expediency of the Communist International in Moscow, which sacrifices them to its own wider strategy of class alliances with bourgeois parties. In this situation the dichotomy between being and doing is transcended only negatively, in the faith in the value of martyrdom, and the belief in the right to choose how one dies, which unite the two groups.

The vision of hope, tragic in *La Condition humaine*, is epic in *L'Espoir* (1937), in keeping with the fact that in 1937 the outcome of the Spanish Civil War was still uncertain. Between the anarchists whose commitment to a personal ethic of immediate and absolute freedom leads only to the lyrical illusions of the initial phase of the conflict (Part I), and the Communists whose collective discipline and organisation, however important strategically, threaten the ideals for which the war is being waged, certain characters (Manuel, Magnin, Garcia, Scali) represent in different forms the ambition to produce effective military and political action which embodies an idealism of liberty and fraternity.

For Catholic novelists the essential issue during this period was not the death of God but the mystery of His existence. In the work of François Mauriac (1885–1970), the certainties and doubts of modern Catholic faith and, in particular, the difficult relationship between free will and divine knowledge, underpin the theory and practice of fiction.[23]

With *Le Baiser au lépreux* (1922), a tragic allegory of marital incompatibility whose conflict between creative and destructive dynamics can be resolved only in self-sacrifice, the essential themes, types and settings of Mauriac's fiction are in place. In *Thérèse Desqueyroux* (1927), Mauriac explored technical and ontological issues involved in the relationship between author and character. On the one hand, Thérèse extends the movement towards the greater psychological indeterminism of characters which Mauriac (like Gide before him, notably in *Les Caves du Vatican*) had seen as the legacy of Dostoievsky and the Russian novel, and which might express what Mauriac thought of as the illogicality of life. On the other, she inherits the Jansenist predestination which imprisoned Phèdre in a logic of destructive action. In the stifling, claustrophobic physical and moral landscape of the materialistic provincial society in which much of Mauriac's fiction is set, her solitary confinement, real and symbolic, concentrates the tensions of her struggle to find, within the narrow range of freedoms created for her by Mauriac's subtle, flexible use of narrative point of view, her essential but indefinable self in the face of the destiny which drives her to destroy herself and others.

In a sequel, *La Fin de la nuit* (1935), Mauriac attempted to write the happy ending of her redemption but stopped short because, as he put it in his preface, he was unable to *see* the priest who would receive Thérèse's confession. The Communist Nizan saw this as the resistance and protest of the novelist against the theologian, proof that the aesthetic demands of Mauriac's system of characterisation blocked the religious apologetics and that this impasse devalued his fiction and theology. The existentialist Sartre saw it as an example of Mauriac's bad faith, denying freedom to his characters to create themselves, through his authorial omniscience, and disguising this denial by means of the ambiguities of his narrative point of view.

Georges Bernanos (1888–1948), unlike Mauriac, sided with the traditionalists against the modernists in the controversies which divided the Catholic Church in the 1920s, and, more than Mauriac, he drew for his fiction on themes central to the Catholic revival at the turn of the century. He stressed the metaphysical reality and power of evil, the need for a militant faith with which to sustain the relentless struggle against it and the importance of willed submission of the self to God's hidden purposes. In *Journal d'un curé de campagne* (1936) the curé of Ambricourt keeps a diary which recounts his own version of Christ's agony on the Way of the Cross. Like Christ, he experiences the anguish of physical and moral suffering through a series of struggles against multiple forms of darkness (his own illness, the incomprehension of the villagers, loneliness, the temptation of suicide). In this novel, thematic elements and stylistic features present from the beginning in Bernanos's fiction (the importance of childhood, the relationship between natural and supernatural, and between physical and spiritual) achieved a new depth through the use of the first-person diary form, both because of the confrontation it permitted between the priest's experience and the trials of his faith, and through its erasures and omissions, which suggest the priest's anguish at the invisibility of God.[24]

Despite their holding different viewpoints, both Mauriac and Bernanos found in the reality of faith a firm framework within which to explore the limitations of nineteenth-century models of the psychology of individualism. In exploring the complexity and difficulty of faith, they confirmed their own commitment to this

individualism. One result of this was that both distanced themselves (albeit in different ways and to different degrees) from what
they saw as the failure of the Catholic Church to dissociate itself
from fascism. This relationship between Christian commitment and
the craft of fiction was one manifestation of the growing recognition by intellectuals during the 1930s of the need to break down the
barriers between action, writing and professional or confessional
philosophy.

Benda and Nizan had taken prominent parts in this debate but in
the final years of the inter-war period it was Sartre, versed in the
German philosophical tradition from Kant to Heidegger and a
committed atheist, who produced in *La Nausée* (1938) the most
wide-ranging attack on the philosophical system which underpinned the French novel.[25] In a world which the lack of religious
faith leaves bereft of inherent structure and necessity, the relationships in which we invest meanings – those between words and
objects, objects and people, body and mind, past and present –
prove to be no more than reassuring conventions designed to keep
at bay the arbitrary nature of existence. The narrator, Roquentin,
experiences a series of panic attacks at his discovery of existence
without meaning or necessity, until he finally understands, listening
to the jazz song 'Some of these Days', that art exists in a radically
different form from that of other objects. Whereas objects simply
exist, brutish and shapeless, art *is*; human creativity can set up
a model of a coherent, necessary world, simply by practising
variations of form, on a theme of its own choice. Existence precedes
essence, but art brings both together. The philosophy of existentialism, of which Sartre was, from the publication of *La Nausée*, the best
known representative, required the individual to recognise and
accept the terrible but empowering freedom of contingency. The
outbreak of the Second World War in September 1939 would give a
dramatic new relevance to existentialism's ambition to fuse writing,
thought and action in the world.

After 1939: Commitments and Interrogations

In May 1940, the German army swept through Northern Europe,
reaching Paris on 14 June. The invasion brought an end to the
eight months of phoney war which had followed the declaration of
hostilities on 3 September 1939. It triggered a mass French exodus
southwards during the summer of 1940 and, in association with

these dramatic events, a substantial literature of primarily documentary interest.[26] Following the armistice, the literature of collaboration returned to simple explanations already familiar from the débâcle of 70 years earlier. Crushing military defeat was no more than France deserved for the decadence of the pre-war years. The experience was an opportunity for self-appraisal and renewal or for a return to the supposedly essential virtues of traditional, rural France.

Among the most famous literary figures associated at the time with the Vichy regime, collaboration took different forms and involved various levels of commitment. *La Solstice de juin* (1941) by Henry de Montherlant (1896–1972) contained themes which supported collaborationist ideology, but in his own life Montherlant placed the lucidity and independence of the creative writer above collaboration. Drieu la Rochelle became the editor of Gallimard's prestigious pre-war literary journal the *Nouvelle Revue Française*, which published during the period 1940–3 a mixture of pro-Vichy polemic and ostensibly apolitical literary criticism. Céline produced a series of ferocious anti-Semitic pamphlets. The journalist Lucien Rebatet (1903–72) was Céline's equal in anti-Semitism and wrote a violently anti-Republican account of the final years of the Third Republic, *Les Décombres* (1942). But it was Robert Brasillach (1909–45), as editor of the fascist *Je suis partout*, who most consistently promoted the fascist cause and who, along with Drieu, paid the heaviest price when the liberation of Paris in August 1944 ushered in the *épuration*, the purges of collaborators, real or invented. Montherlant was investigated but simply forbidden to publish for a year. Céline fled into exile in Denmark. Rebatet, condemned to death in 1946, was reprieved and, in the course of the six years he spent in prison, wrote *Les Deux Étendards*, a novel on his sentimental education into cynicism and disillusionment. Drieu committed suicide and Brasillach was executed by firing squad after a trial which became a focus for the post-war debate on the responsibilities of the writer.

The literature of resistance grew slowly at first in a country divided (until November 1942) between the Northern, occupied zone and the Southern, 'free' zone administered from Vichy.[27] For the reasons we shall see, poetry was the exception. In fiction, the emergence of Resistance sentiment achieved a significant breakthrough with the creation in 1941 of the clandestine *Éditions de Minuit*, whose editor, Vercors (pseudonym of Jean Bruller,

1902–91), wrote and published the collection's first novel, *Le Silence de la mer* (1942).[28] In the novel, silence is the most powerful form of passive resistance to the occupier and the most eloquent expression of the victory of French humanist values over a hateful ideology. Silence thwarts the efforts of the francophile German officer von Ebrennac to blur the distinctions between friend and enemy and forces him to face the evidence of his self-deception.[29]

In the area of active resistance, *Pilote de guerre* (1942) by Antoine de Saint-Exupéry (1900–44) showed the efficacy in the context of war of the intellectual and spiritual humanism developed in the adventure of aviation, with its heightened awareness of the interdependence of the individual and collective and of the contrasting beauties of earth and sky. These themes were already in evidence in his pre-war novels (notably *Courrier Sud*, 1928, and *Vol de nuit*, 1931).[30] In *Drôle de jeu* (1945), Roger Vailland (1907–65) created one of the major novels of the Occupation years, with its analysis of the nature of Resistance and language in occupied Paris.[31]

Under the Occupation, literature was primarily one branch of the political and military activity of collaboration or resistance. With the liberation of Paris and the end of the war it returned to its more specialised forms of intervention in the cultural domain. The immediate post-war period was dominated by the existentialist sensibility (see above, pp. 190–2), in which concepts such as commitment, responsibility and situation, erasing the boundaries between philosophy, literature and action, had acquired enormous prestige through the Resistance effort. The publication of *L'Être et le néant* (1943) and *L'Âge de raison* and *Le Sursis* (both 1945), the first two volumes of his intended trilogy of novels *Les Chemins de la liberté*, and the first performances of his plays *Les Mouches* (1943) and *Huis Clos* (1945), made Sartre a paradigm of this sensibility. No sooner was Paris liberated than he began working to establish in the cultural domain the existentialist values which he hoped would prevent a return to the bankrupt values of the pre-war Third Republic he had attacked in *La Nausée*.[32] He set about founding a literary review, *Les Temps Modernes*, whose first issue appeared in October 1945 and in which he outlined the theory of *littérature engagée*, which he then revised and expanded in *Qu'est-ce que la littérature?* (1947).

Within the theory of *littérature engagée* the relationship between commitment and literature, between political and aesthetic freedom, remained a difficult issue, but as the post-war period settled into Cold War confrontation between the United States and Soviet Union, the search for a third way between the two blocs led Sartre to engage his theories of situation, choice and action on behalf of the Rassemblement Démocratique Révolutionnaire (RDR) launched in 1948. His departure from the group in October 1949 was a clear sign of the dissensions undermining the unity of purpose which the Resistance effort had encouraged. Another was his disagreement with Camus following the publication of the latter's *L'Homme révolté* (1951).

As the author of *L'Étranger*, *Le Mythe de Sisyphe* (both 1942) and *La Peste* (1947), and as a journalist who had worked in the Resistance movement, Albert Camus was a major figure in the post-war literary debate. Since he too rejected the prospect of an afterlife and believed that the only certainty was death, the essential issue was how one lived with this knowledge. Awaiting death in his cell, Meursault (*L'Étranger*) discovers through his confrontation with the priest the meaning of the absurd and with it the knowledge of the significance of the present when it is emptied of that form of resignation which is hope for the future.[33] In *La Peste*, this lesson acquired on the individual level takes collective form through the allegorisation of the experience of the Occupation. Faced with the moral and metaphysical absurdity of arbitrary, unjustified suffering, the only choice is between solitude and solidarity, and the only solution is revolt. The journalist Rambert initially refuses solidarity, only to discover through his experience of a child's death the obligation of collective resistance. Putting into practice Camus's own reformulation (in *L'Homme révolté*) of the Cartesian *cogito ergo sum*, 'I revolt, therefore I am', he joins Rieux and Tarrou in their ethics of service. Human happiness, the goal of ethics in a world without God, is a ceaseless struggle against the forces of the plague and cannot be achieved alone.

Transposed into the political philosophy of *L'Homme révolté*, the two fundamental values of revolt – happiness and freedom – placed Camus at odds with Marxism's commitment to scientific models of historical materialism, which for Camus led inevitably to political and intellectual terrorism. The result was a public dispute with Sartre, more closely identified with the Communist cause, and the relative decline of Camus's reputation in literary, intellectual and academic circles in which Communist sympathies were still powerful. When this dominant position of Marxist thought began itself to be called into question, notably from the late 1970s, Camus's critical fortune enjoyed a strong revival. The critical and commercial acclaim which greeted the publication in 1994 of *Le Premier Homme*, the strongly autobiographical novel on which Camus was working in the year prior to his death, powerfully re-affirmed this revival.

Sartre's withdrawal from the RDR and his break with Camus confirmed that the sense of common purpose which had brought writers together during the Occupation was being eroded by their post-war dissensions in the political sphere. At the same time, the legend of the French Resistance was serving as an important source of legitimacy for the coalition of left-of-centre parties in government during the Fourth Republic (1946–58) and for de Gaulle, who was returned to power in May 1958 to resolve the Algerian conflict. Significantly, certain major texts intended to project the forms of the *prise de conscience* that occupation and resistance had produced were not completed. Sartre had intended *Les Chemins de la liberté* to provide a more collective destination for the escape from contingency than Roquentin's Proustian idealisation of art in *La Nausée*, but though the third volume, *La Mort dans l'âme*, appeared in 1949, the fourth and final volume, *La Dernière Chance*, remained unfinished. In the face of the difficulties encountered in determining a practice of the novel which would reconcile existentialist freedom and Marxist theory, Sartre's faith in *littérature engagée* declined in favour of more direct political commitments and a critique of literature which led him towards autobiographical writing (*Les Mots*, 1953). Similarly, Malraux failed to complete *Le Combat avec l'ange* and Aragon rewrote *Les Communistes*, publishing the definitive version only in 1967.

Committed writing remained a powerful idea among the left-wing intellectuals from whom the Resistance movement had drawn its main support. But with the emergence of the Cold War, writers on the political Left were increasingly faced with the choice between responsibility for a general commitment to humanist values on the one hand and allegiance to a particular party line on the other. Communist writers were expected to adhere to an increasingly intransigent Stalinist orthodoxy of socialist realism which left unresolved the difficult problem of the relationship between form and content in literature. Though several major novelists practised forms of socialist realism in the early post-war period (notably Roger Vailland and Pierre Courtade[34]), the Soviet invasion of Hungary in 1956 and the beginnings of de-Stalinisation in the Soviet Union further weakened its credibility.

The legend of the French Resistance was relayed through a wide range of popular cultural forms until the late 1960s – until, that is, the first post-war generation reached maturity and de Gaulle, baffled by the events of May 1968 and defeated in the referendum of April 1969, withdrew from political life. In the novel, however, this myth of the Resistance as national unity, heroism and self-sacrifice was challenged from an early stage after the end of hostilities. The novels of Roger Nimier (1925–61), *Les Épées* (1948) and *Le Hussard bleu* (1950), proposed a distinctly unheroic reality of collaboration and offered a sardonic, disillusioned commentary on the humanist commitment of much writing of the immediate post-war period. Marcel Aymé (1902–67) in *Uranus* (1949), set at the time of the Liberation, presents the Resistance ideal as an official dis-course to which lip-service must be paid in order to stay healthy at a time when the country is embroiled in vicious settlings of political scores and when the Resistance groups are now rivals for power. In *Au bon beurre* (1952), Jean Dutourd (b. 1920) ridicules the opportunistic switching of allegiances as supporters of Vichy and Pétain seek to establish Resistance credentials with which to turn the *épuration* to their own advantage. In these texts the universal humanist ideal central to the Resistance message confronts the sordid realities of the *années noires*.[35]

The most radical challenge in fiction to the dominant humanist ideal of the post-war years, however, came in the work of Samuel Beckett (1906–90).[36] Growing up as a Protestant in Dublin was an early experience of life at the edges of a world in change. This was reinforced from 1928 by his move to Paris where he made contact with the brilliant, cosmopolitan avant-garde gravitating around James Joyce and fostering wide-ranging literary experimentation. In Beckett this was filtered through his readings of literary and philosophical tradition (most notably Dante, Proust, Joyce, Descartes, Pascal, Sartre, Wittgenstein). He began writing short stories, poems, essays, translations, and produced his first novel, *Murphy* (1938), which went largely unnoticed in the immediate pre-war context. His wartime experience in the Resistance confronted him with the bankruptcy of the ideals which European culture claimed to uphold and in 1943, whilst in hiding, he wrote his last novel in English, *Watt*, a comic investigation of the 'meaning of unmeaning' which would dominate his subsequent work.

In the immediate post-war years Beckett's writing flowered in an extraordinarily productive period which included *Mercier et Camier* (1946, published 1970), his trilogy of novels, *Molloy*, *Malone meurt* and *L'Innommable* (1948–9, published 1951–3), and, for the theatre, *En attendant Godot* (1948, performed 1952). In *Molloy*, two monologues recount two symmetrical searches, Molloy's for his mother, Moran's for Molloy. Both peter out in atrophy and the impossibility of discovering the source of meaning and being. The text makes the same forward journey towards an ending which may or may not be merely another false departure. Imprisoned in the chain of being whose law is unexplained suffering and in the arbitrary, self-contained system of language whose relationship to the world is a mystery, the desire for silence and urge to speak are all that remain. In *Malone meurt*, Malone invents absurd doubles so as to sustain a flow of words with which to keep the game in motion on the unlikely chance that some break through the barrier of language into meaning will occur. In *L'Innommable*, the first-person narrator dismisses all previous selves and their pointless searches, and struggles on through new and increasingly grotesque incarnations in which words, emptied of their traditional claim to narrate and invent, are voices in the mind, saturating the silence yet without belonging to the self. Beckett's trilogy conveyed in unique depth the philosophical and literary interrogations of modern experience and, in doing so, facilitated the wide-ranging challenge to the novel tradition emerging in the 1950s as existentialism's relationship with literature began to lose credibility.

New Novel Commitments

Existentialism's influence waned as dissension increased among writers associated with it, as did the public desire to draw a veil over the bitter divisions of the Occupation and *épuration*. Emphasis in the novel moved away from political and ethical commitments towards concerns about language and narrative technique. These had been central issues in the work of Proust and Gide and were a significant legacy of French translations of the Russian novel, but the political crisis from 1930 had made them appear less urgent than engagement with the ideological divisions with which Europe was confronted. In practice, however, novelists with a political, religious or philosophical position to convey were led more, not less, to address questions of narrative technique. Céline had explored the use of fractured narratives and innovative language and syntax. The novels of the socialist Aragon and of the fascist Drieu la Rochelle had illustrated ways in which an apparently unproblematic representation of perceived truths about the world may be undermined by the language of fiction with which they are represented.

The 1930s had also seen the discovery by French writers of a whole series of major American novels in translation, beginning in 1931 with Faulkner's *Sanctuary* and continuing with the works of Hemingway, Dos Passos, Steinbeck and Caldwell. The techniques associated with these novels – simultaneity of action, narrative fragmentation and impersonality, and the assimilation of forms of popular culture such as the cinema and the detective novel – whether seen as symptoms of the alienation of modern civilisation or of the freedom enjoyed in a culture unfettered by literary traditions, were gradually assimilated into French narrative practice. Malraux's *L'Espoir*, with its rapid shifts of narrative focus, is a well-known case in point. Sartre considered Dos Passos's *U.S.A.* a model for the integration of history and fiction and adopted in *Les Chemins de la liberté* certain of its technical features, such as the simultaneous presentation of events. In *L'Étranger*, Camus used narrative procedures derived in part from Hemingway to show that the model of psychological interiority used by the prosecuting counsel to secure the death penalty for Mersault entirely failed to explain Mersault's action.

Wider intellectual developments in science and philosophy had also undermined the positivist relationship between consciousness and the world from which nineteenth-century realism had derived its mimetic ambition. The phenomenology of Merleau-Ponty, with its emphasis on the subjectivity of perception and representation, was providing an alternative philosophical context for fiction to that of the German philosophy on which existentialism had drawn. By the early 1950s a substantial body of narrative theory and practice operating within a changing intellectual framework was available to novelists hostile to the concept of existentialist *littérature engagée* and ready to embark on a new phase of experimentation.

By the end of the decade, this experimentation had achieved a collective status in what was by then known as the *nouveau roman*.[37] The term was adopted as a means of grouping together novelists whose writing during the 1950s appeared to share a determination to work out in the practice of fiction the implications of the cultural and intellectual changes which had taken place in the period

1930–50. As is frequently the case with literary labels, the term referred more to a series of shared objections to traditional forms of the novel than to any common programme of writing. The new novelists rejected the plots, characters, linear chronologies and omniscient narrators of the nineteenth-century tradition, which had expressed that century's belief in a knowable, representable world of which man was the centre and purpose. From this perspective the existentialist committed novel was no more than the latest form of this outmoded anthropomorphism and was dismissed in favour of a commitment to explore, from within, the theoretical and practical issues involved in the production of fiction from the raw materials of impressions, perceptions and feelings. Characters, far from denoting real people in a real world, were the supports on which to hang the exploration of mental states and the production of language. The *nouveau roman* sought to forge a new relationship between writer and reader on the basis of their complicity in the adventure of writing, an adventure in which the creation of narrative becomes in a self-referential way the subject of narrative.

Not surprisingly, this radical departure from a literary tradition in which the novel was expected to enact serious ethical or political dilemmas judged to be central to the human condition was initially attacked as antihumanist or dismissed as a self-indulgent game. The new novelists (notably Robbe-Grillet in *Pour un nouveau roman*, 1963) responded that to oblige the human mind to recognise that the world has no inherent meaning or stability on which to base identity, knowledge or absolute moral values, to free it from complacent acceptance of the comfortable falsehoods it prefers to these difficult truths, was a profoundly political act and more authentically humanist (in the widest sense of dealing with the reality of human experience) than the committed literature to which it was opposed.

In the early novels of Alain Robbe-Grillet (b. 1922), a narrator's eye charts the material world in meticulous detail, either investing it with obsessions or desires or travelling across its impenetrable surface.[38] The traditional role of description – that of establishing relationships between an observer and a meaningful universe – is dispensed with in texts which at the same time rework some of the novel's most stereotypical genres and myths (the detective story and the Oedipus myth in *Les Gommes* of 1953, the novel of adultery and the colonial novel in *La Jalousie* of 1957). In *Dans le labyrinthe* (1959) a complex network of narrative paths and passages link three labyrinths, those of an anonymous town, a delirious character's mind, and an author's creation of a text. At specific junctions in the text the reader is moved from one labyrinth to another and continually obliged to re-establish bearings as the signposts operative at one narrative level (the soldier's fear and alienation in his efforts to deliver his parcel) suddenly stop working in another (the text's foregrounding of its own manoeuvres). From *La Maison de rendez-vous* (1965) Robbe-Grillet's novels combine and interrogate the fictions triggered by the most powerful collective myths (sado-masochistic eroticism, political revolution, secret agencies), cultural objects (paintings, poems, musical arrangements), mathematical figures (triangles, circles). Within each text the construction of meaning is provisional, frustrating the reader's search for reassuring fictions with which to counter the anxieties and unintelligibilities of modern experience.

The work of Michel Butor (b. 1926) represents in even wider terms this continual exploration of the nature of writing. Beginning with novels, each of which explored new forms of fiction's internal architectures, and with literary criticism distinguished by its cosmopolitan range, Butor's writing extended into other forms of aesthetic and cultural production (including music, painting, utopian philosophy, ethnography, dreams), each relationship a new exploration of language's capacity to produce and organise text. In his first four novels, he focused on the nature of fictional time and space.[39] In *Passage de Milan* (1954), which reconstitutes twelve hours in the lives of the inhabitants of a Parisian block of flats, the simultaneity of chronology and architecture structures the narrative. In *Emploi du temps* (1956), the narrator keeps a diary in an attempt to understand the physical and psychological geography of a city which threatens to envelop him in its labyrinthine streets and multiple layers of time between present and legendary past. *La Modification* (1957) explores the mechanisms of second-person narration and the relationship between internal and chronological time. In *Degrés* (1960), the attempt to recount the hour of a school lesson forces the narrator to face up to the extent to which experience evades language and to the consequential need to invent the real.

On her own admission, the entire work of Nathalie Sarraute (b. 1900) was present in embryonic form in her first novel, *Tropismes*, published in 1939 but largely unknown until its second edition (1957).[40] Tropism is the response of an organism, especially a plant, to an external stimulus and Sarraute used the term as a metaphor for the intense, pre-verbal psychological activity situated on the edge of consciousness and of which the family unit is the most common and most powerful trigger. In Sarraute, the family is the theatre for the ceaseless movement of advance and retreat produced when two centres of tropistic life enter into contact with each other. In each novel Sarraute takes up the challenge to create a verbal form for these indefinable movements, an internal 'sub-conversation' which negotiates with that public, social discourse whose polite, formulaic platitudes are designed to neutralise its complex, elusive and potentially explosive energies. These negotiations do not produce characters or plots of the type the traditional psychological novel displayed, nor the laws of an essential self grounded in involuntary memory on behalf of which Proust had challenged the earlier practice of the psychological novel. Instead they reveal a new type of psychological material, with the invention of a language for the basic, instinctive urges of attack and defence, embrace and rejection, which constitute the power struggles in which human beings are ceaselessly engaged.

The publication of *Moderato cantabile* (1958) drew Marguerite Duras (1914–96) into brief and provisional association with the *nouveau roman* group, for the novel marked a break with the more traditional forms of characterisation through which her earlier work had represented woman's struggle against the confinements of patriarchal society.[41] The experiment was the vehicle for a more radical refusal of such authoritarianism. The piercing cry which interrupts the music lesson in *Moderato cantabile* triggers a series of encounters between Anne Desbaresdes and Chauvin which, through the imaginary reconstruction of the murder in the café, lead Anne gradually to destroy her conformist, externally imposed social self in order to attain an absolute form of freedom and self-knowledge. *Le Ravissement de Lol V. Stein* (1964) takes the formal experimentation and, with it, the understanding of woman's emancipation a stage further. Abandoned by her fiancé for another woman, the heroine is so entranced by the power of the love she feels between them that she experiences abandonment as a form of liberation. Released from the prison of her socially-defined role as member of a couple into a new and creative loss of identity, she is free to share as observer in the mystical, total power of lovers' passion.[42] The loss of identity, the breakdown into fragmented states of mind which this self-effacement produces, is expressed through the silences or gaps which frustrate meaning and narration but in which the narrative voice seeks to translate the unknown of female experience.

The novels of Claude Simon (b. 1913) show the continual search for narrative procedures able to describe the inscription in the present of the multiple forms of memory (personal experience, family archive, collective history) and the ways in which the language which effects this fusion of present and past time in turn generates and structures the production of narration.[43] Thematic elements common to the sequence of novels embrace the major themes of modern writing (the nature of time, the presence and displacement of desire, the awareness of death), but with each novel, Simon deepens his analysis of their role in the operations of the mind and in the processes of writing itself. A brief comparison between, for example, Malraux's *L'Espoir* and Simon's *Le Palace*, in which an experience of the Spanish Civil War forms the common narrative base, demonstrates the extent to which Simon's fiction abandons the existentialist values sustaining that of Malraux in favour of a fatalistic initiation into the lack of human control over cycles of history repeating themselves regardless.

Simon's central work, *Histoire* (1967), draws together the strands of the exploration of the past contained in the earlier novels. Through the description of a collection of postcards sent by the narrator's father to his mother and the evocation of a twenty-four hour period in the narrator's life, the text constructs a complex collage of language in which the tension is sustained between representation of human feeling in search of an ever-elusive auto-biography and the capacity of language to produce text through its own material, non-representational associations.[44] Hence Simon's departure from the traditional conventions (chapters, paragraphs, punctuation), which served to organise works of fiction but are quite inadequate to address these operations of the mind and language.

The sustained analysis of universal themes of fiction gives Simon's work an epic range and power lacking in other members of the new novelists group. His increasingly radical reflection on the act of writing has taken his work beyond fiction in the accepted sense, beyond representation of the events of personal or collective memory to the play of language itself, as it defers satisfaction of the aspiration to stable definition and meaning. Instead, the text is structured on the basis of internal formal design, in a manner related to the modern painting with which Simon is so familiar.

The unpredictable exploits and failings of memory are also an important element of the work of Robert Pinget (b. 1919) for they combine to generate narrative sequences which unfold, miscarry, return, lead in other directions or nowhere, scraps of conversation in which the act of speech is as central as the content.[45] In *L'Inquisitoire* (1962), a half-deaf servant is interrogated about his masters, and the wanderings through the labyrinth of his memory, prompted by the questioning, lead to no resolution of the enigma but to a reconstruction of the process of story-telling. Pinget's increasingly refined exploration of the nature of narrative voices bears the mark of his friendship and collaboration with Beckett. Claude Ollier (b. 1922) used some of the most familiar narrative forms (the colonial novel in *Mise en scène*, 1958; science fiction in *La Vie sur Epsilon*, 1972) to undermine the description in traditional fiction of the narrator's relationship to the world and to the act of writing.[46] Claude Mauriac (1914–96, son of François Mauriac), whose critical texts *L'Alittérature contemporaine* (1958) and *De la littérature à l'alittérature* (1969) made him one of the most informed commentators on contemporary writing, built on his study of Proust (*Proust par lui-même*, 1953) to show the nature of subjective time through the structure of fiction itself, notably in *Le Dîner en ville* (1959) and *La Marquise sortit à cinq heures* (1961). The eleven volumes of his memoirs, *Le Temps immobile* (1974–91) constitute a vast reflection on the nature of sensation and memory.

* * *

Public perception of the 'new novelists' as a coherent group continued through the 1960s and 1970s but their work increasingly diverged. Simon (*Les Géorgiques*, 1981) and Sarraute (*Disent les imbéciles*, 1978) continued to produce work of major importance by extending the intellectual and formal parameters established in their work of the 1950s. With *Mobile* (1962) and *6 810 000 litres d'eau par seconde* (1965), Butor abandoned the novel in favour of freer forms of textual production. Robbe-Grillet and Duras turned increasingly to film-making and the possibilities it offered for the creative interplay of their written and filmic texts.[47] But quite apart from the intrinsic value and interest of their work, the impact of the original group of new novelists in an increasingly mediatised French literary and educational environment has been significant.

Their active and productive relationships with the institutions of literary criticism and the teaching of literature in higher education both in France and abroad has ensured a wide circulation of their commitment to a more creative role for the reader in the practice of fiction and encouraged the fundamental reappraisal of the work of earlier novelists which has taken place since the 1950s, notably under the impulse of the *nouvelle critique* with which the *nouveau roman* was initially associated.

As the 'new novelists' pursued their different practices of fiction, other experimental writing parallel to theirs created an analogous group identity. In November 1960, a group of writers and mathematicians committed to research into literary forms with the potential to generate new types of writing formed Oulipo (the *Ouvroir de littérature potentielle*).[48] Its most important member was Raymond Queneau (1903–76), its (subsequently) most important recruit Georges Perec (1936–82). In 1959, when he achieved the huge success of *Zazie dans le métro*, a modern Parisian version of *Alice in Wonderland*, Queneau had been a major literary figure for nearly thirty years. In 1933 he had published his first novel, *Le Chiendent*, which he began as an attempt to translate Descartes's *Discours de la méthode* into spoken French. This attempt to end the linguistic divorce between academic philosophy and the language of the streets was another example of the ambition to transform philosophy from a theory of knowledge into a committed analysis of existence and was contemporaneous with Céline's radical extension of narrative language. In addition, its playful yet serious combination of mathematical constraints against which to construct fiction – the text consists of 91 (7×13) sections – made it a precursor of Oulipo experimentation, which in 1960, as *Le Chiendent* had already done in 1933, sought to reject the twin legacies of Jarry's 'science of imaginary solutions' (which he called pataphysics) and Surrealism's automatic writing.

The Oulipo writers did not of course discover the idea that formal constraints stimulate rather than obstruct creative writing but they took it to far greater lengths than before. Their arbitrary phonetic, syntactic and alphabetical restrictions made enormous demands on the writer's ingenuity and had two main effects: first, to reaffirm the capacity of language to create texts from within its own operations and thereby shape our perceptions of reality; secondly, to free the writer from the obligation to create politically or philosophically committed literature, which for the Oulipo group was a far more alienating constraint. Perec's *La Disparition* (1969) is a novel written without a single 'e', the most common letter in French, while the same vowel is the only one used in *Les Revenentes* (1972). His *La Vie mode d'emploi* (1978) is an astonishing construction based on a mathematical puzzle known as the Magic Square, thought to have been first used by Dürer, the German Renaissance painter and engraver, of which Perec used a specially-adapted form.[49] Though such fiendish ingenuity is not in itself inherently literary, Perec combined it with an exceptional knowledge of a wide range of writing, and a powerful desire to explore the anguish of the human condition.

Perec's first novel, *Les Choses* (1965), was subtitled 'une histoire des années soixante' ['a story/history of the 60s'], a study of the consumer ideology which for a young Parisian bourgeois couple, Jérôme and Sylvie, replaces political commitment as the form of their relationship to society. They fail to get involved in the central political issue of their youth, the Algerian War, and instead define themselves in relation to the objects of bourgeois desire as they appear in the advertisements in *L'Express* magazine. *Les Choses* is closely related to Barthes's study of social signs in *Mythologies* for it shows the way in which the most everyday objects are invested with meaning and participate in an economy of signs. Perec does not condemn consumer society (though with the advantage of the hindsight provided by the events of May 1968 it was widely believed that he had done so) but encourages the reader to recognise the form of its manipulations, something Jérôme and Sylvie fail to do. *Les Choses* was followed by two entirely different works, the hilarious *Quel petit vélo à guidon chromé au fond de la cour?* (1966) and the dark *Un homme qui dort* (1967), by the period of involvement with Oulipo and its formal and linguistic acrobatics, and by the post-Oulipo writing of his final years.

The unity within the diversity of these and other Perec texts is located at a deeper level, in the autobiographical condition of the writing, but it must already be obvious that with Perec this relationship is exceptionally complex. In *W ou le souvenir d'enfance* (1975) he stated that his writing was born out of the horror of the war in which his father was killed in 1940 and the concentration camp into which his mother disappeared in 1943. Dedicated to the 'E' which disappeared from *La Disparition* and to the homophonous 'eux' of his lost parents, it explores the relationship between autobiography and literary reconstruction, which has itself become a significant development in the contemporary novel. The oblique fragments of a remembered and imagined relationship with his parents are forms of his inner need to address the personal grief of their loss and the universal grief of the holocaust through writing, the decisive sign of presence in the world. This association of personal anguish and passion for the creative power of language gives Perec's work a depth and range which make him one of the essential literary figures of the century.

* * *

By the late 1960s, just as the *nouveau roman* had established itself as the French novel's official avant-garde, taught on university syllabuses as the culmination of the experimental, self-referential tradition of fiction going back to Proust and Gide and representing what now appeared to be the central twentieth-century trend, it was caught in a crossfire of new developments: on the one hand, a return to story-telling and myth-making; on the other, more radical forms of experimentation. The commercial and critical acclaim which greeted the rewriting and re-siting of the Robinson Crusoe story by Michel Tournier (b. 1924) in *Vendredi ou les limbes du Pacifique* (1967), resulted from Tournier's use of a very familiar narrative to produce a powerful contemporary criticism of Western society's consumer culture and express a renewed aspiration to alternative forms of spirituality.[50] The re-working of the literary and philosophical traditions of Defoe's novel through contemporary theories of the material imagination and structuralist analysis of myth met a demand for the novel of ideas which for those unsympathetic to *nouveau roman* experimentation had been unanswered since the passing of the existentialist novel.

In his subsequent writing, Tournier continued to develop his interest in the German metaphysical tradition, which he had studied in Tübingen after the Second World War, exploring the themes of the ogre (*Le Roi des aulnes*, 1970), twinship (*Les Météores*, 1975), the Magi (*Gaspar, Melchior et Balthazar*, 1980), Gilles de Rais and Joan of Arc (*Gilles et Jeanne*, 1983) and exile (*La Goutte d'or*, 1986). Tournier described these narratives of quest and initiation by ordeal as a 'mystic Naturalism'. On the one hand, he makes full use of nineteenth-century narrative procedures (description, character, plot). On the other, this Naturalism serves texts which, though historically located (*Le Roi des aulnes*, for example, set in 1938–44, reworks allegorically some of the most sinister episodes of the Second World War), present themselves as re-narrations of a timeless story, in which the novelist explores alternative forms of sexuality and social organisation.

Other forms of rejection of the technocratic direction of Western culture can be found in the work of Jean-Marie Le Clézio (b. 1940), notably in *L'Extase matérielle* (1967), *La Guerre* (1970) and *Désert* (1980).[51] His characters share an intense commitment to the value of life and to reconciliation with the self and the natural world, continually threatened by the destructive elements of modern, technocratic civilisation. In *La Guerre*, the aggression of modern cities induces panic and a desperate nostalgia for an ideal, lost world in which to experience a purifying calm. It is the world from which Lalla, the heroine of *Désert*, is exiled to Marseilles, whose wretched squalor fails to extinguish the light and purity of her desert origins, to which she eventually returns. To the spiritual light of such communion with the elements of the natural environment corresponds the author's intense observation of the world and a prose style of diversity and virtuosity with which to inscribe its depth of meaning for a public increasingly insecure about the implications of technological advance.

Tournier's use of intertexuality and Le Clézio's poetic description of detail may be said to participate, albeit tangentially, in experimental forms of writing with which in the 1950s and 1960s the *nouveau roman* was identified. In contrast, Patrick Grainville (b. 1947), associated with Tournier and Le Clézio in the use his fiction makes of myth, is well known for his contempt for the *nouveau roman*, which he dismissed as introverted and self-seeking.[52] His best known novel, *Les Flamboyants* (1974), links up with neo-Romantic primitivism and its myth of Africa, seen as the repository of ancient and more authentic force and physicality lost to the degenerate rationalism of Western, Christian culture. In Grainville's work, this otherwise well-worn literary theme is renewed by the sheer drive of his language. In its excess and vitality it evokes the transformative energies of the erotic imagination which are released when the individual makes contact, beyond the constraints of modern experience, with the submerged but still vital forces of earlier cultures.

* * *

Another and more explicit opposition, from within, to the official modernism of the *nouveau roman* was forming in the late 1960s around the review *Tel quel*, founded in 1960 as an extension of the anti-existentialist context to which the *nouveau roman* had contributed. By the end of the decade, the *roman tel quel* had taken *nouveau roman* experimentation a stage further and replaced the production of *fiction* with the production of *text*. For over twenty years, *Tel quel* was the essential focus for the discussion of experimental writing and its relationship to radical contemporary literary, psychoanalytic and political theory.

It was in his fourth novel, *Drame* (1964), that Philippe Sollers extended the *nouveau roman*'s deconstruction of traditional fictional forms.[53] The text alternates first-person and third-person segments of poetic prose in which a divided subject observes and narrates the production of narrative, and its relationship to the mysterious experience of identity, language and engagement with the world. The conventional linearity of narrative is abandoned for the spatial configurations of the chessboard, whose sixty-four squares are represented in the sixty-four segments of text. Compensating for this loss of sequence, on which narrative representation was traditionally based, is the freedom to explore the power of language to generate text. The political and cultural crisis of May 1968 encouraged the *Tel quel* group to situate the act of writing in relation to the revolutionary project (*Théorie d'ensemble* 1968), and to explore the link between literary and political avant-gardes in a variety of ways throughout the early 1970s. Sollers's *Nombres* (1968) staged in its text an opposition between what *Tel quel* saw as the productive, dynamic language of the Chinese ideogram and its domesticated Western counterpart, at a time when Mao's Cultural Revolution and the American crisis in Vietnam had given this opposition a powerful political reality. *Lois* (1972) and *H* (1973) continued this experimentation with the material nature of language. By the second half of the 1970s, however, *Tel quel* had broken with Marxism and was turning again to America, since 1945 the most important initiator of avant-garde practices in the arts.

From his intense involvement for over a decade with theoretical and practical issues relating to the nature of the avant-garde, Sollers finally concluded that the avant-garde in advanced Western societies had failed to effect social transformation and that its organic relationship to the dominant culture would prevent it from ever doing so. His conclusion marked the end of a tradition, which can be traced back to the first-generation Romantics, of the writer seeking to achieve transformation of the world through the revolutionary literary act. In 1983, the year in which *Tel quel* was dissolved, Sollers published *Femmes*, an American journalist's narration of erotic experience, the rise of feminism and the cosmopolitan extensions of mediatised cultural happenings. Within weeks, the *enfant terrible* of post-war French writing was up there on the bestseller lists.

May 1968: Structures in the Streets

In many respects *Tel quel* was the post-war equivalent of Surrealism's pre-war attempt to bring together literary and political change. This explicit effort at convergence was only one of the forms in which the events of May 1968 impacted on French writing. Though these events failed to achieve direct political transformation of French society (the legislative elections of June 1968 returned the largest-ever Gaullist majority), they played the crucial role of bringing to the surface underlying tensions in many areas of French private and public life, with far-reaching consequences for literature.

One such consequence, the raising of feminist consciousness, is discussed in detail below (see pp. 276–93). Another was the revision of the official history of the war period which accompanied the end of the Gaullist phase of the Fifth Republic. Huge amounts of historical material began to appear which shed light on the hitherto hidden realities of the *années noires*.[54] For novelists who belonged to the generation born during or immediately after the war, this historical revisionism was intimately related to a search for the self: these hidden realities were those of their own parents' experience of war and Occupation, which official history had silenced.

This search made the work of Patrick Modiano (b. 1945) one of the most significant examples of 1970s writing.[55] Driven by his own cosmopolitan Franco-Jewish background to go in search of origins and to explore the collective memory, real or imaginary, of the Occupation, and by his profession to locate himself in relation to his predecessors in the novel, Modiano wrote a trilogy of novels (*La Place de l'Étoile*, 1968; *La Ronde de nuit*, 1969; *Les Boulevards de ceinture*, 1972) which show characters moving through a shadowy world of false names, false papers and blurred identities, biographical and moral. Marginal, stateless people slip in and out of roles of collaboration, black marketeering and Resistance as much by accident as by design (a theme also prominent in the film scenario Modiano wrote with Louis Malle for *Lacombe Lucien*, 1974). *Villa triste* (1975) inaugurated a new phase of his writing in which echoes of the Occupation period remain but in which the emphasis shifts to a more general quest in search of lost time. It is of course the Proustian theme but without the Proustian revelation of the transcendent significance of art. Building on the fragility of memory's lost traces and false trails, Modiano creates novels in which the conventions of detective fiction, autobiography and the psychological portrait are set against each other in ways which reflect the hesitations of the modern subject in the face of the unfathomable reality of experience.

The events of May 1968 themselves became the subject or context of fiction. Through them, the question of the literary mediation of specific political and social events was now raised in terms of the wide-ranging developments in French fiction since the 1950s.[56] Pascal Lainé (b. 1942) was a teacher in a *lycée technique* during the events and in his second novel, *L'Irrévolution*, he shows a teacher's efforts to communicate to working-class children in a small provincial town the revolutionary spirit and project of May 68. Their refusal to be enlisted in the political programme of this representative of a class-based culture foreign to their own obliges the teacher to recognise the inauthenticity of his political discourse, his collaboration with a system he claims to despise and, by extension, the failure of a revolution which the participants had no interest in realising. He discovers his own existentialist bad faith in a post-existentialist age in which humanist solutions of the type proposed by Sartre or Camus seem no longer credible. The working-class children are victims of the historical division in French society between those who participate in the dominant culture and those who are controlled or marginalised by it, a division increased by post-war consumerism. The novel placed in the context of May 1968 questions already raised in *B. comme Barrabas* (1967) about the difficulty of self-knowledge and the ambiguities of narration. In *La Dentellière* (1974), Lainé extended his analysis of the failed experiment in class communication by showing the doomed relationship between Pomme, a passive, silent drudge in a hairdressing salon, and Aiméry, a privileged student of the École des Chartes, who undertakes to mould her in terms of the cultural stereotypes of femininity within which male image-makers imprison women. His inability to gain purchase on Pomme's unfathomable, inarticulate self is mirrored in the very visible and highly self-conscious shifts of narrative tone and viewpoint which confront the reader with the artificial nature of the construction of identity through language. In subsequent texts Lainé continued this exploration of narrative practices by re-working literary models (Queneau, Proust, the eighteenth-century libertine novel).

Novelists of wide-ranging ideological and narrative commitments responded to the events in one form or another in their fiction. The neo-Romantic libertarian agenda of May 1968 was expressed in Duras's *Détruire, dit-elle* (1969), in which a conventional bourgeois married woman discovers revolt and freedom from the conventions and fears of her class. In Sarraute's *Vous les entendez?* (1972) the events provided a wider theatre for the generation gap, which is encapsulated in the contrasting reactions of seriousness and laughter between a father and his children to an *objet d'art* the father is proud to own. At the other extreme of narrative practice, the traditional novelist J.-L. Curtis (1917–95), in *L'Horizon dérobé* (1979), showed young people disillusioned with the society of their parents, participating in the events as a final youthful fling before taking their allotted place in this society. The humanist convictions of Robert Merle (b. 1908) are seen in *Derrière la vitre* (1970), in which, in the Arts Faculty of Nanterre, where the events of May 1968 began, a new generation of would-be revolutionaries dream of an alternative fraternal society.

* * *

The French novel since 1980 can be seen as pursuing the engagement with post-war social and cultural change which the events of May 1968 had so dramatically brought to the surface. The problematical relationship between writing, knowledge and history appears to underpin its most significant trends.[57] New narrative domains have developed from widely differing points of origin. The particular importance of women's writing, and of francophone literature, will be considered in more detail below. Both are renewing French narrative's themes and forms. The growth of gay writing, itself stimulated by the changes in attitudes to sexuality which followed 1968, was reinforced by the AIDS crisis – most notably in

À l'ami qui ne m'a pas sauvé la vie (1990) by Hervé Guibert (1955–91).[58]

Alongside these very visible general signs of the changing narrative field, there were in the course of the 1980s some revealing individual developments. We have already seen Sollers drawing a line in 1983 through the avant-garde and, by implication, through the writer's relationship to the world with which the avant-garde project had been associated. In 1984, Duras's *L'Amant* became the publishing event of the year, achieving sales usually associated with the bestseller thriller or adventure market. It did so because it brought together an author who was one of the historical figures of French post-war writing, a series of contemporary literary, political and cultural issues (the search for female self-knowledge and self-representation, woman's relationship to eroticism and to political change, the colonial experience, the nature of autobiography), and a literary form which told an apparently simple story without abandoning the subtleties of characterisation and of motivation associated with Duras's work. The media's ability to package literature delivered a huge commercial success reinforced on the critical level by the award of the Goncourt prize for the outstanding French novel of the year. Not surprisingly, the screen adaptation followed. In 1985, Claude Simon was awarded the Nobel Prize for literature and thereby received consecration for his continued exploration of the problem of narrative and of the individual's difficult relationship to history, so powerfully renewed in *Les Géorgiques*. These and other examples suggest that the distinction between 'serious' and 'mass' fictional forms has to some extent been eroded and that the forms and implications of the experimentation introduced in the post-war period have become assimilated by the reading practices of a wider public.

The 1980s saw the emergence of a number of novelists who, when taken together with Modiano, might be said to have best expressed both the dominant modern sense of the subject deprived of presence and universality of meaning and the conscious decision to open literature to the contemporary culture of popular and mass art forms. Jean Echenoz (b. 1956) weaves together narrative models drawn from the forms of popular fiction (detective and spy novels, science fiction and comic strips) in exuberant, at times hilarious, narratives (notably *Cherokee*, 1983; *Lac*, 1989; *Nous trois*, 1992), but the proliferating adventures and comic-book characters reproduce the incoherence of a world in which the subject seems to have lost control over events. Daniel Pennac (b. 1944) is best known for his four-part cycle of novels (*Au bonheur des ogres*, 1985; *La Fée carabine*, 1987; *La Petite Marchande de prose*, 1989; *Monsieur Malaussène*, 1995) in which we find the same narrative energy, naive characterisation and use of popular forms as in Echenoz but with a slightly more optimistic sense that despite the mendacity and inauthenticity of the world, despite the multiplicity of false trails in modern experience, the possibility of creating meaning and ethical purposes survives. This sense permeates Pennac's superb essay on the pleasures of reading, *Comme un roman*, which was a huge commercial and critical success on its publication in 1992. Sébastien Japrisot (b. 1935) is a good example of the genre writer (exponent of the detective novel such as *Piège pour Cendrillon*, 1965, which plays with the conventions of the genre) who has emerged as a major novelist, particularly with *Un long dimanche de fiançailles* (1991), a quest narrative on the themes of war and memory.

In a postmodern age deprived of universality, the novel may be adopting less heroic stances and more self-reflective irony. And it seems possible that this general trend has been to some extent reinforced by the socio-political context of recent years, in which the socialist project which triumphed in the presidential and legislative election victories in 1981 has been forced from 1983 to face the economic realities of internationalised money markets and in 1986–8 to accept 'cohabitation' with the conservative political parties. In politics and literature, confrontation with the realities of the modern world was in the 1980s a difficult narrative. Be that as it may, the re-invigoration of narrative through its extension into mass forms – the detective novel in particular – offers a potentially powerful source of renewal.

* * *

The path through some of the major trends in French post-war fiction leads us to the threshold of a new century, in which the creation of fictions is likely to be subjected to conditions quite different from anything experienced so far. The French novel, particularly since the Revolution, has to some extent always been technology-driven, so it is certain that the mediatisation of Western culture and the revolution in information technology on which it is now embarked will transform the means and modes of fiction. Some of the implications are already evident; for example, the demise of the concept and practice of the avant-garde as it evolved in the early stage of the nineteenth century out of the cultural developments associated with the Revolution. The literary and cultural space which this classical avant-garde occupied has, like every other public space, been occupied by the media, whose capacity to transform all cultural products into spectacle was seen in the extraordinary impact of the televised book programme *Apostrophes*, France's most popular television programme between 1975 and 1990.[59] Just where the information superhighway will take the novel, where the Internet's transformations of narrative's themes, forms and modes of production will leave the tradition established by the writers discussed above, in what forms it will generate reassessment of the history of the French novel traced here, is of course a matter of conjecture. The narration of the relationship of world and subject will continue but in forms which remain to be seen.

II POETRY AND ITS PURPOSES

Poetry of the New, 1914–39

In the closing years of the century, reaction to the Symbolist movement in poetry most frequently involved a return to the modern, urban world. Its increasingly complex, fragmented reality was a source of both excitement and anxiety.[60] The very elements which offered the hope of renewal also frustrated the self's aspiration to stability and unity. In the poetry of Guillaume Apollinaire (1880–1918), a rootless cosmopolitan background reinforced a sense of fragmented identity. On the one hand, this created an elusive search for the self expressed in tender melancholy or nostalgic melody. On the other, it encouraged an aggressive commitment to the new, particularly from 1904, when Apollinaire's contacts with avant-garde painters and poets gave him a pivotal role in the efforts to create verbal and visual forms appropriate to the new century, and to the new world that scientific and technological change was creating.[61]

The dominant feature of *Alcools*, a selection of his poetry written between 1898 and 1913, is a multi-directional lyricism which weaves together the self's search for meaning in mythical, mysterious landscapes of Symbolist inspiration and in the associations and discontinuities of modern urban experience. The dominant theme is that of the journey, which may be in time or space, through personal or collective memory, and may be liberating adventure or aimless wandering. Such thematic links between the poems emphasise the range of voices used. Lost love is evoked with haunting simplicity in 'Le Pont Mirabeau', in which the poignant refrain softens the transitions between pain and resignation. 'La Chanson du Mal-Aimé' retains the range and intimacy of the private feelings of desire, anger and pain in a vast historical and mythological epic in which the disconnections between episodes are balanced by the formal continuities of rhyme scheme, strophic structures and repetitions. In 'Zone', the industrial landscape at the edge of the city, where the poet wanders between sensations and memories, and the combination of free verse and rhyme or assonance, denote the tensions between familiarity and insecurity which characterise the modern city. The proliferation of ready-made sights and sounds simultaneously invites and frustrates personal revelation. As in the Cubist painting of Pablo Picasso (1881–1973) and Georges Braque (1882–1963), who sought to represent the complete structure of the object and its relationship of volume and space by juxtaposing different views of it in interlocking planes, in 'Zone' the use of the historic present tense, which displays past and present in a single moment, and of abrupt shifts between first-person and second-person pronouns produces an interplay of fragmented, discontinuous selves in a modern collage of human feelings.

The poems of *Calligrammes* (1918) form a diary of the poet's immediate pre-war days, the mobilisation and his experience of the war. The title of the volume refers to the picture poems, in which the typographical phrase mimes the visual form of the object represented. Mallarmé's *Coup de dés*, republished in 1914, had made such experimentation topical but Apollinaire's picture poems had other terms of reference in Cubist painting, on which he had already published *Les Peintres cubistes* (1913), and in the work of Sonia and Robert Delaunay (1884–1979 and 1885–1941 respectively), which he had baptised Orphism in 1913.[62] Words take on a pictorial function through graphic arrangements and multiple typographies and the poet draws heavily on the sound patterning of alliteration, assonance, onomatopoeia and repetition to extend the forms by which meaning is produced in ways analogous to Cubist collage. In

'Lundi rue Christine', the juxtaposed fragments of conversation create montage effects reinforced by links of sound and theme. In the visually more conventional poems, Apollinaire exploits the expressive potential of the relationships between free and traditional verse and draws on all the resources of vocabulary, sound and rhythm to represent the real experience of war in its modern and mythical dimensions. In the final sequence, the more experimental forms become less frequent, the tone more measured. The final poem, 'La Jolie Rousse', takes stock of the journey accomplished and pleads for tolerance for the avant-garde poet searching for a new language.

Apollinaire's support for Orphism was only one of the productive exchanges between literature and painting in which the Delaunays were involved and which were central to definitions of modernism in the immediate pre-war period. The catalogue of the 1913 Berlin exhibition in which Robert Delaunay showed ten of his *Windows* series contained the first published version of Apollinaire's poem 'Les Fenêtres', republished five years later in *Calligrammes*. Delaunay then produced a simultaneist poem–painting on Rimbaud's *Alchimie du verbe* (1914). In 1913, Sonia Delaunay illustrated the six-foot-long folding sheet of twelve panels which contained *La Prose du Transsibérien* by Blaise Cendrars (1887–1961).[63] Labelled the 'first simultaneous book', it recounts in free verse the multiple forms of the modern world and their relationship to the journey of memory. With Cendrars, as with Apollinaire, the formal invention is not gratuitous. Its abrupt shifts of tone, rhythm and voice produced by the accelerating rhythms of real and imagined journeys register the poet's efforts to synchronise external stimuli and inner world and the excitement and anguish created by a confrontation from which only provisional stability can be achieved.

Among the group of writers and painters who, along with Apollinaire and Cendrars, worked side by side in Montmartre in the immediate pre-war years, Pierre Reverdy (1889–1960) and Max Jacob (1876–1944) made, in quite different terms, major contributions to the poetic theory and practice of modernity. For Reverdy, poetry was to be found 'dans ce qui n'est pas' ['in that which is not'],[64] in a solitary, often anguished exploration of everyday experience. Confined within the walls of a room or the limits of a garden, the poet looks for meaning and purpose in the diffuse and shifting presence of reality. In poems such as those in *Ardoises sur le toit* (1918), fragments of language combine the suggestive power of images with that of unusual and seemingly random typographical arrangements to create a quiet but profound tension between aspiration and disappointment. Jacob's prose poems of *Le Cornet à dés* (1916), on the other hand, are verbal pyrotechnics. Contemporary political and artistic topics, the poet's memories, reading, verbal games, pastiches of literary genres and tones, all crackle in the associative logic of language. Both poets were associated with contemporary developments in painting. Jacob described his work as Cubist realism.[65] Reverdy's essay 'Sur le cubisme', published in the newly founded avant-garde review *Nord–Sud* (1917), provided a theoretical framework for analogies between Cubist painting and literature.[66]

Essential features of what came to be seen as the modern spirit of French poetry were therefore in place before the outbreak of the First World War. The war's impact on poetry was as profound as it was on the novel but less direct. There was no French equivalent of the great flowering of English war poetry. Among the three poets who had sought in the pre-war period to open the poetic to the new and the everyday, Apollinaire was alone in doing so in the context of the war itself.

In some ways, the most important poetry written during the war was that of a poet who wrote by disengaging himself from contemporary events. In 1919 Paul Valéry described the First World War as the failure of European culture, yet he wrote his major poetical work, 'La Jeune Parque', at the very time the world seemed to be going up in flames.[67] He had embarked on the poem in 1912, when, encouraged to revise his early work for publication, he had returned to writing poetry after a twenty-year absence. In the early 1890s he had published poems in Symbolist reviews, and frequented Mallarmé, whom he worshipped, but he gave up literature after the spiritual crisis he experienced during the night of 4–5 October 1892. Its upshot was his decision to focus on the power of the mind to observe thought and feeling in action rather than to make these thoughts and feelings the object of literature. It gave him an intellectual method through which to recover from what he considered to be the destructive effects of thoughts, feelings and images on his sense of self. The critical writing which resulted has made him one of the foremost French intellectuals of the century, while the poetry written after his long silence is one of the most profound reflections on the nature of poetic language itself.

The subject of 'La Jeune Parque' (1917), a dramatic monologue of over 500 lines, is the self-questioning consciousness as it feels its way through a night-long struggle with conflicting experience and aspiration (sensuality and abstraction, desire and memory) towards the dawn light of harmonious self-knowledge. The complex thematic modulations, as Valéry called them, are themselves reinforced by the formal constraints derived from his commitment to classical prosody. Hostile to many early twentieth-century manifestations of the modern (Freudism, Marxism, feminism, Cubism, Surrealism), he rejected such recent developments in French prosody as free verse in favour of the classical alexandrine, whose rigour and expressive potential of sound patterning combine in the poem as both creative process and drama of the intellect. The poems of *Charmes* (1922) maintain the intellectual ambition in a wide range of forms and registers of exceptional technical virtuosity. The most famous poem of the collection, 'Le Cimetière marin', originated according to the poet in purely formal considerations (the expressive potential of the ten-syllable line, its use in six-line stanzas themselves organised in terms of thematic contrasts), around which he modulated the movements of the mind in its dialogue between light and darkness and its ultimate celebration of life.

Such commitments and procedures could hardly have been more removed from those of the Surrealist movement which dominated French poetry of the inter-war years. The revulsion felt by certain writers at the slaughter of the First World War strengthened the ambition to channel avant-garde literary activity towards a wider transformation of culture and society. They aimed to do this by unleashing desire and its forms of expression against the rationalist ideologies which in their view constrained or censured freedom. This would enable a new fusion of the real and the imaginary, a surreality, to be created to transcend the system of oppositions and hierarchies which this discredited Western ideology sustained. The Surrealist movement was the result of a series of connections: the meeting in 1917 of Aragon, Breton and Soupault, their shared discovery of Freud's work on the unconscious operations of the mind, their reading of nineteenth-century poets who had in their different ways practised forms of poetic language outside the didactic, Parnassian aesthetic (notably Baudelaire, Nerval, Lautréamont, Rimbaud, Mallarmé, Jarry), their contacts with avant-garde activity in Paris, and their meeting with Tzara, whose effect was to radicalise their opposition to the dominant culture. Thanks primarily to Breton, its chief theoretician and publicist, and despite (or because of) doctrinal disagreements and conflicts of personalities, Surrealism created a collective impetus which made it a major source of literary and cultural developments between the wars. From Paris, it spread quickly abroad, becoming the first truly international avant-garde movement.[68]

Language and linguistic experimentation were a central focus of Surrealist activity. To the alternative nineteenth-century tradition of poetic language noted above, the Surrealists added Reverdy's description of the poetic image and their understanding of Freud's work on dreams. In 1918, in *Nord–Sud*, Reverdy had defined the image as a pure creation of the mind, the juxtaposition of two more or less distant realities. The more distant the relationship, the greater the image's power. This definition substantiated Lautréamont's description of the poetic beauty of the chance encounter, on a dissecting table, of a sewing machine and an umbrella.[69] Freud's work on word association and dreams had suggested that a huge, untapped source of pre-rational mental activity was readily available. In the *écriture automatique* ['automatic writing'] of *Les Champs magnétiques* (1920), Breton and Soupault showed that when the rational mind's control over the instinctive urge to verbalise was removed, powerful repressed energies were released into language in the form of free verbal play. Such free association with the sounds and meanings of words would reveal the Surrealist dimension of the imaginary hidden within the real, the extraordinary hidden within the everyday of modern experience. As the Lautréamont example had shown, such verbalisation was intensely visual, hence Surrealism's impact on painting.

Not surprisingly, given the ambition, present in the Surrealist project from the outset, to extend this liberation into every aspect of cultural and social life, the Russian Revolution of 1917 became a crucial reference point for the revolution in literature. In 1927 the group's leading figures (notably Aragon, Breton, Éluard) joined the PCF (Parti Communiste Français), but the need to reconcile Marx and Freud – political transformation and the Surrealist commitment to liberation from intellectual and cultural constraints – remained a source of powerful tensions. The Marxist subordination of the latter to the former obliged Surrealists sooner or later to choose between the two. Breton's second manifesto (1929) showed the extent of dissensions within the group on this issue and though he re-stated his faith in the necessary relationship between Surrealism and revolution, relationships between him and the Communists were increasingly strained. In 1932 Aragon chose the Party, rather than the Surrealist, line; three years later Breton's *Position politique du surréalisme* consummated the divorce between the group and the Party. The emergence of the fascist threat in the 1930s nevertheless ensured that Communists and Surrealists remained allies in practice if not in theory.

Many of the major poets of the period were marked in one way or another by the Surrealist movement, usually adapting it to their own commitments and forms of expression. Paul Éluard (1895–1952), one of its founders, embraced wholeheartedly its liberation of the imagination but submitted its discoveries to the constraints of theme and the disciplines of rhythm.[70] His work contains some of Surrealism's most powerful images but their power derives less from their exploration of the unconscious *per se* than from the relationships they establish in the poem with other forms of human experience and the network of thematic and formal associations in which they participate. His poetic voice is a highly personal one but even in his free verse the familiar rhythms and patterns of the French poetic tradition can usually be discerned behind it. He brought to poetry his sense of the wonder of everyday experience and his conviction that the language of poetry could be liberated by and for everyone. The element common to these features of his work was his conviction that love was the source of the imagination's most creative, transformative energies and of the individual's most profound moral and political choices; love, for Éluard, was a truly revolutionary force. In *Capitale de la douleur* (1926) and *L'Amour, la poésie* (1929), love may bring the anguish of solitude and loss of self, but it is the ecstatic celebration of love shared which provides in both collections the most memorable verse. In 'La Courbe de tes yeux fait le tour de mon cœur', the sensations of light, water, wind and air generated by the eyes of the loved woman trigger in the poet both an intense erotic intimacy and an unlimited expanse of feeling.

Despite increasing internal dissensions within the Surrealist group, Éluard took part in collective efforts such as the poems of *Ralentir travaux* (1930), written with Breton and René Char (1907–88), and the automatic writing of *L'Immaculée Conception* (also 1930), on which he again collaborated with Breton. Like Breton, he was expelled from the Communist Party in 1933 but from 1936 the Spanish Civil War and his friendship with Picasso led him towards poetry of a collective humanism (*Cours naturel*, 1938; *Donner à voir*, 1939). This transition to a more explicitly political poetry led to Éluard's break with Breton in 1938 but would form the basis of his inspiring Second World War and Resistance poetry.

Among the earliest members of the group, Bejamin Péret (1899–1959) and Robert Desnos (1900–45) illustrate the diversity of poetic practices and intellectual commitments the Surrealist movement embraced during the inter-war years. Péret remained the most intransigent in terms of its original aesthetic and political ideals, and the most loyal to Breton's conduct of the movement. His unswerving contempt for all the forces which oppress, and a complete faith in the power of the imagination to liberate, fuelled the explosive mixture of vicious satire, burlesque verve and absurd linguistic and logical games which characterise his poetry (*Je ne mange pas de ce pain-là*, 1936). Like other Surrealists, Péret's anarchist faith led him to oppose Communist political orthodoxy, in his case by actively supporting Trotsky against Stalin, but his political commitment extended to fighting in Spain against Franco from 1936. Desnos, in *Rrose Sélavy* (1922–3), a collection of word-games which he claimed to have written in a transatlantic séance with the artist Marcel Duchamp, took Surrealist experimentation with hypnosis and automatic writing further than most, using with humorous, subversive and highly poetic results every manner of word- and sound-play to generate images and ideas outside the control of logic. In *À la Mystérieuse* (1926), he channelled this exceptional verbal virtuosity towards the poignant search for an inaccessible love. Surrealism's public commitment in 1927 to the PCF alienated Desnos, who was too much of an individualist to subscribe to any political programme, and his poems of *Corps et biens* (1930) represent his summary of his Surrealist years. Despite such divergent trajectories, both Péret and Desnos in their different ways later played significant roles in the French Resistance.

As important early members like Desnos and Queneau broke with the group in the late 1920s, there were new arrivals, notably René Char. He participated in the group's activities (working with Breton and Éluard on *Ralentir travaux*) and this participation, though brief, made a lasting impact on him. It was brief because he was soon uncomfortable with group formulae for poetry; it was lasting because Surrealism's central belief in the power of poetry to transform human existence was one he never abandoned. Though the poems of *Le Marteau sans maître* (1934) were written during this phase and appeared under the aegis of the Éditions surréalistes, they show that Char was already moving on. In Surrealist terms they present themes (such as poetry as mystery and spiritual combat) and forms (such as the prose poem) which were not inherently Surrealist and whose power would be reinforced by Char's experience of the Second World War.[71]

For poets indifferent to Surrealist performances of automatic writing or opposed to their assault on the fixed forms of the poetic tradition, poetry continued to represent an intellectual and spiritual journey, closer to Hugo than to Breton, in a language organised into recognised patterns of sound and image. *Anabase* (1924) by Saint-John Perse (pseudonym of Alexis Saint-Léger Léger, 1887–1975) is, in its author's words, an 'expédition vers l'intérieur', a journey into the interior through vast, undefined spaces of nature and memory. It is a rare example of a modern epic poem, weaving together the history of a people and of a poet, an Eastern and mental landscape.[72]

Jules Supervielle (1884–1960) possessed a Surrealist sense of the imagination's magical transformation of the real, but in collections such as *Gravitations* (1925) and *La Fable du monde* (1938), the vastness of his exploration of time and space has greater affinity with Romantic poetry than with Surrealism. It differs from Hugo in the humour and lightness with which this exploration is recounted, even if certain poems do express the poet's alarm for a world which appears to have broken from its moorings.[73] More often, however, this cosmic vastness finds a human scale in the organic relationships between the animal, vegetable and mineral universe. Supervielle's imagination performs a vast humanist embrace of the world, taking in the most distant stars and the most familiar objects. Despite the intense desire for understanding, there is a deep innocence and gentleness in his work; despite the difficulties of understanding, there is no rage or despair. In formal terms, Supervielle appears to move effortlessly between regular or fixed forms, free verse and the *verset* (a short sequence subdivided like the Biblical text), in which the choice of form and patterning is determined by the nature of the poetic substance to be expressed. It is a very deliberate, crafted relationship between thought and rhythm quite opposed to Surrealist experimentation with automatic writing but which has won for Supervielle an audience which seems certain to grow.

Henri Michaux (1899–1984) began writing in the ambiance of

Surrealism in the sense that it was his discovery of Lautréamont's work in 1922, followed by that three years later of contemporary painting (Klee, Ernst, Chirico), that precipitated his faith in the transformative energies of verbal and visual signs. Compulsive in his commitment to voyages of discovery within and outwith the self, to experimentation of all kinds (in the borders between prose and poetry, the narratives of European myths, the visual arts, linguistic research, drugs), he invented landscapes which were war-zones for the raging contradictions of his fragile, fragmented self. This experimentation seeks to liberate the unknown within the self and results in a poetry of relentless, turbulent, occasionally fluid rhythms. Michaux is in this respect a distant relation of the Rimbaud of the 'Bateau ivre' and the prose poetry. His utopian hallucinations are more private than those of Rimbaud, and they lack the latter's political project. But they have a lucidity in which humour plays an important part and whose effect is moving as well as alarming.[74]

Like Michaux, Francis Ponge (1899–1988) was largely unclassifiable in terms of inter-war poetic practice, though for quite different reasons. He began writing, he tells us, as a result of the difficulties he encountered when, having tried and failed to express himself, he tried, and failed again, to describe objects. He decided to publish his accounts of these failures to describe. The result was *Le Parti pris des choses* (1942), in which Ponge confronts the difficulty of description and, in the process, transforms the reader's perceptions of the object described and of the nature of the language involved. The liberating potential of this repeated renewal of language and perception would echo down the twentieth century. Published in 1942, the collection was one example of the effort made by a Resistance poet to reclaim the language from the German occupier. In the post-war period, it (and subsequent Ponge texts) was identified in what became a trend of poetry devoted to the description of the visible world, in opposition to the Surrealist legacy of the imagination. Later still, it was adopted by the *Tel quel* group as a model of language's power to generate text.[75]

The Second World War

The period of Occupation and Resistance witnessed a remarkable revival in the public fortunes of poetry in France. Hardly had the armistice been signed than poets hostile to it began to circulate poems clandestinely.[76] Given the circumstances, poetry had obvious advantages over other forms of literary production. It used less paper and print. It could be memorised and transmitted orally. Its concision, density of language and use of symbolism and allusion gave it more powerful forms of expression than prose and made life difficult for censors. Moreover, there is a sense in which poetry is by its very nature oppositional, that 'good poetry is by definition protest and resistance, and cannot thrive on resignation or acceptance of the status quo'.[77] On the other hand, its effectiveness as an instrument of resistance depended on the reader recognising her or his place in a community of language and culture which the poetic tradition embodied. For this reason poets who were committed to the Resistance tended to abandon the introspective and esoteric forms of expression which since the late nineteenth century had distanced much contemporary poetry from its potential audience. Instead, they returned to more familiar rhythms, forms and language likely to prove more accessible to the wider public they now wished to reach. Some poets (Péret, for example) believed that political poetry was a contradiction in terms and refused to write during these years; others (Reverdy, Char) continued to write but refused to publish until after the war. But many poets wrote, circulated and published work which, taken together, redefined the relation between poetry and the circumstances in which it is written.[78]

The extreme situation of 1940–4 provoked in many poets a deep sense of outrage and revolt, and the challenge to create forms of poetic language capable of communicating these feelings to others. The extent of their moral and political commitment and the engagement with language that resulted from them led in many cases to poetic creativity of exceptional range and quality. The outstanding example was Aragon, who, after a decade in which his greatest creative effort had been invested in the novel, launched with *Le Crève-cœur* (1941) a collection of volumes of poetry and critical writing on poetry which made him during this period an essential voice of Resistance poetry.[79] Other poets who, like Aragon, had been associated with the Surrealist movement from its beginnings, were also actively committed to the Resistance cause. In the case of Éluard, the experience of Occupation and Resistance strengthened the humanist themes present in his poetry of the 1930s (such as faith in a universal fraternity, or the power of the mediation of love), while in 'Liberté' he created the single most famous Resistance poem. Desnos's clandestine poetry celebrated liberty and castigated oppression in a poetic language which drew heavily on the rhythms and tones of popular speech and for which he ended up in a concentration camp, where he died.

As leader of the Basses-Alpes section of the Forces françaises combattantes, Char played a significant part in the Resistance effort and the work published in 1948 under the title *Fureur et mystère* tells of his fury at the obstacles which historical reality was placing against the poet's ambition to transform the real, and of the mystery which poetic language projects into the present. Prose poems, notes on clandestine activity, poems of Provence and Alsace landscapes are followed by what Char calls the 'poème pulvérisé' ['pulverised poem'], fragments of emotion and sensation from which language seeks to establish a basis for a universal community of feeling. The distinct tensions Char's poetry creates made him one of the essential figures in post-war French poetry. From a non-Surrealist perspective, the Catholic poet Pierre Emmanuel (b. 1916–84) sought to establish the relationship between the historical reality of the war and human destiny in its ambition for the divine. In these and many other cases, the experience of Occupation and Resistance led poets to reformulate their understanding of the relationships between poetic, political and spiritual aspirations.[80]

In 1941, Aragon's anger at the phoney war of the winter of 1939–40 and at the débâcle of June 1940 was expressed in the poems written in the twelve-month period from October 1939 and published in *Le Crève-cœur*. Their impact was enormous for they not only found words for the feeling of calamity which had engulfed the French in June 1940 but also demonstrated Aragon's conviction that poetry could help to regenerate the values of national unity and common culture necessary to overcome the sense of hopelessness and isolation which had resulted from the débâcle. In addition, this national poetry derived much of its emotional force from the poet's love for his wife, Elsa Triolet. Their enforced separation was a source of despair and anger, a form of death comparable to the collapse of unity in national life. So, in 'Les Lilas et les roses', their separation and the news that Paris has fallen to the Germans are '. . . les deux amours que nous avons perdus' ['. . . the two loves we have lost']. But their love was also an affirmation of the solidarity at the heart of private and public life which fascism could not defeat. This reciprocal relationship between his love for Elsa and for his country remained a major theme in the two collections which followed, *Les Yeux d'Elsa* (1942) and *La Diane française* (1944).

One of the ways in which Aragon sought to represent love as a profoundly political response to fascism was to adopt the forms of medieval courtly love poetry. In this tradition of twelfth-century 'amour courtois', the knight placed his courage at the service of love and was loved in return, since his virtues were both a homage to his lady and a service to the Court community of which he was part. This 800-year-old poetic tradition seemed contemporary to Aragon in the early 1940s for it promoted the social values of the feminine over fascism's cult of masculine force. It was one example of the attempts made by poets to recreate the sense of national unity vital to the Resistance effort by drawing on France's geography, history and culture. In their poetry, French placenames appear repeatedly – Paris, inevitably, but also towns, villages, provinces and rivers. The most famous example is 'Oradour', by Jean Tardieu (b. 1903), written when news reached him in Paris of the atrocity perpetrated against the inhabitants of the village of Oradour-sur-Glane on 10 June 1944. Tardieu's poem made the name of the village synonymous with horror itself through the relentless rhythm of its repetition across the text.[81] Similarly, historical reference and analogy was used to sustain the idea of the nation in the face of Nazi myths of superiority founded on race. Multiple references to the Middle Ages, whether historical or literary, remind the reader of the emergence at that time of a French national culture. Joan of Arc is invoked as an earlier representative of the struggle for sovereignty; the Revolution and its Marseillaise, the Paris Commune and its Internationale contribute their exploits, martyrs and anthems to the values of international brotherhood and resistance to oppression. A wide range of literary references drawn from high and popular forms underline this sense of a community of culture at a time when the culture appeared to have collapsed in the face of Nazi aggression.[82]

For poets the most powerful instrument of resistance was, however, the language itself, and the most urgent need seemed to be to reclaim it from collaborators who were placing it at the service of an alien, destructive ideology. For many poets, this involved returning to the traditional rhythms of French poetry, to forms of versification anchored in the collective memory, in order to adapt them to the contemporary experience of defeat and resistance. This effort to create modern rhythmic patterns from within established ones took place at every level of the system of versification, from the use made of the most familiar fixed forms and line lengths to the organisation of stanzas and the creation of rhyme.

Once again, Aragon's poetry contains many examples. In *Le Crève-cœur*, for example, he uses a wide variety of stanza structures, ranging from the most familiar, the quatrain ('Le Temps des mots croisés' is made up of thirteen quatrains in cross rhyme, *abab*), to the less familiar, such as the stanza of six lines (*sizain*) in 'Zone libre', nine (*neuvain*) in 'Pergame en France', or ten (*dizain*) in 'Le Poète international'. The same poem may combine several different stanza structures (cf. 'Vingt ans après', 'Les Amants séparés') to exploit the sharp changes of rhythm and tone which such combinations may reinforce. 'Tapisserie de la grande peur' is an unusual case of a single-stanza poem of 32 lines, in which three four-line sequences of embraced rhyme (*abba*) are interrupted by a sudden switch to four lines in cross rhyme (lines 13–16), followed by a return to the embraced rhyme pattern for the rest of the poem. The effect of the sudden switch is to give an exceptional emphasis to the word in the rhyme position of line 15, where the break from the embraced rhyme scheme adopted up to that point is recognised. This emphasis which the word ('rapaces') derives from the rhyme scheme is added to that from the phonetic patterning in which it is also involved (with 'Espace', 'passe' and the other elements in /a/ and /s/). This is only one small example among many in the same poem in which Aragon uses the different levels of the French verse system to evoke the sense of panic which accompanied the *exode* from Northern France in June 1940.

The two most common line lengths in the French system are the alexandrine and the octosyllable. In his essay 'Crise de vers', Mallarmé had called the alexandrine 'la cadence nationale' ['the national cadence'], and the war poets used it for the history of shared feelings and rhythms it brought with it. Equally, the flexibilities which nineteenth-century poets from Hugo onwards had brought to its traditional 6/6 structure gave precedents for expressing profound feelings by showing a line's rhythm pushing against the alexandrine's well-established rhythmic constraints.[83] The octosyllable, on the other hand, had been a feature of more popular poetic forms and the war poets used it to connect their poetry to the familiar rhythms of folk song, with its emphasis on the spoken word, which lodged in the reader's memory. The *vers impair*, whose virtues Verlaine had extolled in his poem 'Art poétique', could be used in combination with the standard twelve- or eight-syllable line to create effects of emphasis or surprise through the switch between even and odd line lengths (as in Éluard's 'Faire vivre', in which the change to seven syllables in the final three lines of the poem underlines the sharp change of theme and tone on which the poem closes).

Fixed-form poems such as the sonnet, which had undergone a spectacular revival in the nineteenth century, also had deep roots in the collective memory. The dilemma facing Resistance poets in negotiating the relationship between expression and constraint was central to the ways in which the French sonnet worked, and its concision and familiar rhyme schemes made it easier to memorise. Jean Cassou (1897–1986) wrote his *Trente-trois sonnets composés au secret* (published in 1944) while in solitary confinement and their profound humanist values emerge more powerfully from the poet's respect for the constraints of the regular sonnet form. Desnos, on the other hand, in his sonnet 'Le Legs', which was published in the 1943 anthology *L'Honneur des poètes*, and opened with a reference to Victor Hugo, France's most famous nineteenth-century political exile, used an irregular rhyme scheme in the quatrains (*abba* in the first, changing to *baab* in the second) to reinforce his contempt for the Nazi leaders and French collaborators named there. Aragon adopted the earlier fixed forms of the *complainte* and *romance* for the same purpose of drawing upon familiar forms and reminding readers of the human and national values invested in these forms.

For Resistance poets, the problems of poetic language varied according to whether the poem was written as a private expression of feeling, without the intention to publish, or whether the aim was publication and, if so, whether this publication was intended to take legal or illegal form. Many poets wrote work of all three types but of the three, the attempt to publish a Resistance poem legally created particular problems, since the poet was obliged to choose themes and terms which censors would fail to recognise as an expression of resistance but which the poem's intended audience would identify as such. In this way, every contraband poem published represented a small victory over the forces of oppression. In this, as in many other aspects of Resistance poetry, Aragon played a major role, both by placing contraband verse in a French literary tradition (that of medieval troubadour poetry in which the lover declares his feelings to the lady under the nose of the husband, who fails to recognise the message), and by the examples he provided in his own poetry. To quote just one case in point, 'Santa Espina', in *Le Crève-cœur*, contains on one level a religious theme to which the authorities could hardly object and, on another, references to the Spanish Civil War and Catalonian anthems which would be unmistakable for those who had taken part in activities in support of Republican Spain's struggle against Franco.

Some Post-War Directions

The euphoria which greeted the liberation of France was of short duration. As was the case in the French novel, the ideals which had fuelled Resistance poetry were no match for the realities of the *épuration*, for the political expediencies surrounding the creation of the Fourth Republic, or for the ideological divisions which culminated in the Cold War. Symptomatic in this respect are the bitterness evident in Aragon's poems in his *Nouveau Crève-cœur* (1948) and the decline in his own position from the quasi-official status of *poète national* he had enjoyed at the Liberation. Though the publication of war poetry continued into the early post-war years, and though it was in some cases work of major significance (Char's *Fureur et mystère*, for example), it appeared at a time when the energies which the themes and forms of French war poetry had derived from the collective nature of resistance to oppression were receding. Poets withdrew once more into their more private spaces, where poetry could resume its broader historical development along the paths opened up in the latter part of the nineteenth century and which the events of 1939–45 had interrupted. In this respect, two collections of poetry published in the immediate post-war period signalled this renewed distance between the private and public spaces of poetry. The first, published in 1945, was the Pléiade edition of the complete works of Mallarmé, whose status in the post-war theory and practice of French poetry would not cease to grow. The second, the following year, was *Paroles* by Jacques Prévert (1900–77), whose poems of the everyday, liberating in their spontaneity, anarchic in their humour, full of the sights, sounds and rhythms of the street, have become classics of popular culture.

The major pre-war figures and the poets who had emerged during the war wrote on into the later stages of the century. Saint-John Perse, in *Vents* (1946) and *Amers* (1958), pursued his dialogue with the elements, and their relationship to human mortality and desire. In *Épreuves, Exorcismes* (1945), Michaux continued, as the title suggests, to develop his practice of poetry as exorcism of the obsessions and terrors of his private self; but from the post-war years, it is his interest and experimentation in different visual art forms which, more than his poetry, represent the new departures in his work. In *Babel* (1951), Pierre Emmanuel renewed his ambition to practise what he called the spiritual exercise of poetry, in this case a mystic contemplation of the rise and fall of humanity's Promethean ambitions.

Among the poets who began publishing in the post-war years, Yves Bonnefoy (b. 1923) has been the major revelation. In *Du mouvement et de l'immobilité de Douve* (1953) he explores the indispensable presence of death at all the transactions of experience. It is the common fate whose recognition is the essential prerequisite of knowledge. The poet's task is to find words with which to describe the presence of things permanently threatened by disappearance. In the poem, Douve is an enigmatic female figure who progresses through stages of death towards what the final section of the work calls the 'true place' of meaning in the material world, towards that sense of plenitude which the consciousness of mortality heightens. At certain moments experience of the natural world can be so intense as to fill the consciousness with an intimation of immortality, and poetry seeks to stabilise, however briefly, these hints of transcendence. This search for what Bonnefoy calls 'presence' and for the relationship between it and the language of poetry has been the focus of all his creative and critical writing.[84]

Philippe Jaccottet (b. 1925) published in the 1950s two volumes of poetry (*L'Effraie*, 1953, and *L'Ignorant*, 1958) in which the world is perceived in the fragile beauty of its surfaces, elusive and enigmatic. His work shares with that of Bonnefoy this intense focus on the real, which aims to discipline the unfettered imagination of the Surrealist legacy and to oblige poetic language to respect the smallest elements of the real, which are poetry's subject. As in Bonnefoy, such attention to the here and now seems to invite the belief in some form of permanence, however far removed, however circumscribed by the interrogative forms his language takes. It appears as a pale shadow of the Romantic faith in the correspondences between the external world and the ideal. In the late twentieth century, Jaccottet seems to imply, such permanence could at best be provisional. Modern poets can no longer claim to reveal the meaning of the world as confidently as predecessors did but, despite the limitations of subjectivity, they can still manifest in language the means to involve others in human and social vision and ambition. Jaccottet took this further in *Airs* (1967), brief, limpid poems modelled on the Japanese *haiku*, in which fleeting sensations of nature open out onto the poet's interrogations of the meanings such beauty might contain.[85]

The seriousness with which this search is conducted remains even when the means appear to be playful. The Oulipo experimentation practised in the novel (see above, pp. 229–31) took place in poetry too, notably in the work of Jacques Roubaud (b. 1932). His *Trente et un au cube* (1973) is, as its title suggests, a collection of 31 poems, each with 31 lines, each with 31 syllables, themselves distributed on the basis of a Japanese poetic form, the *tanka* (5 + 7 +5 + 7 + 7). In addition, the poems openly recycle texts of different types, French and translations into French, in what amounts to an anthology of post-war experimental practices. But the seriousness of the game as a reflection of the power of language to rewrite itself, of the role of formal constraints in the process of writing, can be seen in the context of Roubaud's other efforts in the theory and practice of poetry, in particular his important study of French versification (*La Vieillesse d'Alexandre*, 1978) and his contribution to the publications of the *Change/atelier* group, which included the definitive version, edited by Mitsou Ronat, of Mallarmé's *Un coup de dés* (1980).

It would not be difficult to find other examples of the faith which post-war poets continue to retain in poetry's power to trace a spiritual or philosophical journey from which to bring back alternative representations of being in the world. The work of Eugène Guillevic (b. 1907), Jacques Dupin (b. 1927), Michel Deguy (b. 1930) and Jean Daive (b. 1941), who, from different points on the generational and intellectual map, pursue the search for what Guillevic described (in *Vivre en poésie*, 1980) as the sacred in everyday life, provides further cases in point. This faith sustains the great vitality of contemporary French poetry. With hindsight, the intellectual upheavals which have taken place in the French cultural field since the late 1950s have tended to reinforce and generalise the terms of the discussion of the means and ends of poetry which Mallarmé formulated one hundred years ago. The 'initiative' which he 'ceded to words' has become the new orthodoxy. Yet this initiative has resulted not in a Surrealist vision of total freedom or automatic writing but in the continuing interrogation by poets of the relationship of modern experience to the language of poetry, of the nature of this language, and of its relationship to the French poetic tradition, its fixed forms, its systems and practices of versification. The one essential post-war cultural and political development which as yet lies outside these terms is that of women's writing (see below, pp. 276–93). As far as poetry is concerned, it is clear that a substantial number of French women are currently writing and publishing poetry and it may well be that the events of May 1968 were a defining moment in this development. Yet contemporary French poetry appears not yet to have engaged with the issues within feminist debate (for example, the distinction between 'écriture féminine' and 'écriture féministe').[86] Whether (and, if so, in which ways) this new voice of French poetry will enter and redirect the mainstream of French poetry is another question for the future.

III THEATRE: LANGUAGE IN PERFORMANCE

The Current of Change

Twentieth-century French theatre, said Jean-Louis Barrault (1910–94) in his *Réflexions sur le théâtre* (1949), is a protean form, reflecting a society that lives between two currents. One current pulls it to the past, described by Barrault as the great bourgeois epoch whose close we sometimes seem to be living, and is responsible for the prolonged life of conventional theatre and the 'boulevard' play. The other directed towards a still-undefined future, rushes forward to create channels of its own, towards dramatic forms still in the making.

This second current, starting up in the 1890s and given strength and direction in the early twentieth century by the attack on commercialism launched by the director Jacques Copeau (1879–1949), has transformed concepts of theatrical place and space, the roles of actor, director and playwright, acting styles and directing techniques, the relation between written text and performance and the relation between public and play. One of the few collective experiences still remaining to a fragmented society, theatre has become a rallying-place for avant-garde challenges to conventional ways of seeing. Increasingly materialist in its concept of itself – preoccupied with presenting the human body in its multiple and active relationships with the living world – seeking to liberate the imagination and the senses, theatre dispenses an excitement totally different from that of the cinema, whose challenge from the early years of the century forced it into radical self-examinations.

Antonin Artaud (1896–1948) argued the superiority of the theatrical over the cinematic image, which, he said, however poetic, is only film, and fixes imagination in a single visual form. Theatre allows imagination to pursue its own images and, most important, its medium is living matter, with all its challenges and resistances (*Le Théâtre et son double*, 1938). Paul Claudel, writing in 1929, had already seen further. Film for him was another creative resource, alongside music, poetry and action, to release the audience's imagination from the limits of the real. Film could open up the fixed décor of the stage to project the shifting variations and possibilities of dream ('Note sur *Christophe Colomb*', 30 December 1929).[87]

From the start of the modern period, theatre was on the move.[88] Narrowly bounded from the mid-nineteenth century by boulevard theatre and the Comédie Française, its spaces expanded to include the privately run little theatres of the 1880s (which reappeared in the 1950s and 1960s), State-subsidised drama centres, the open-air festival venues pioneered by Jean Vilar (1912–71, founder in 1947 of the Festival d'Avignon), working factories, with their hastily improvised stages (again pioneered by Vilar, in the 1950s) and in 1968, the streets. From the 1910s, a steady process of decentralisation marked a search for wider audiences in the popular classes. Jacques Copeau (1879–1949) moved his Théâtre du Vieux-Colombier from the boulevards to the Latin Quarter in 1913. His book on *Le Théâtre populaire* (1941) argued for the need to break with Paris altogether. In 1945, Jeanne Laurent, in the socialist Ministère des Beaux-Arts, moved drama to the provinces by establishing the Centres Dramatiques Nationaux. In the 1960s, under de Gaulle, André Malraux followed with the Maisons de Culture. Pompidou swiftly turned off the tap after the events of May 1968. It was switched on again in the early 1980s with Mitterrand as President by Jack Lang, Arts Minister in a socialist government with a programme of political reform based on regionalisation.

Acting styles evolved to reflect the shift away from the notion of individual 'star' performance and towards ensemble production. The single-author script was no longer the sole mover of the drama. Body language, mime and mask, or the equally potent language of objects, were held to communicate more complex meanings, more effectively, than the word alone. Eastern theatrical traditions could offer whole languages of gesture and movement which attached different meanings to the different kinds of movement of different parts of the body, reaching the same complexity and subtlety as the West had brought to the elaboration of its verbal codes.[89] Performance became a collaboration between actors, playwright and director in which the latter increasingly took the major part, inventing and disseminating new acting techniques.

Jean-Louis Barrault's *Réflexions sur le théâtre* gives a glimpse of the networks of influence and mutual reinforcement which grew out of Jacques Copeau's school. Barrault studied with the actor-director Charles Dullin (1885–1949), whose teaching emphasised the body and its expressive powers and the importance of the mask. Dullin introduced him to the ideas of Copeau, the Russian director Constantin Stanislawski and the scenic designer Edward Gordon Craig. From Craig, he acquired the notion of theatre as a collective craft where the actor shares the work of carpenter and electrician, helps with costume design and learns how the music works. He learned about mime from the actor Étienne Decroux, formerly of Dullin's troupe, and developed his own techniques of breath-control and gesture. Barrault's first production, *Autour d'une mère* (1935), based on William Faulkner's modernist novel *As I Lay Dying*, was an exploration of the expressive powers of the body, which filled the stage with controlled movement, stylised gesture and non-verbal vocal sound.

The exceptional actor or actress continued to be a focal point in the production, with such stars as Louis Jouvet, Barrault himself, Madeleine Renaud, Gérard Philipe, Edwige Feuilllère. But the later 1960s and early 1970s saw productions collectively devised by the acting group, whether working with a text or improvising their own themes. New relationships were established with the audience, or rather, the various audiences to which different productions were addressed.

Alongside these changes ran a continuing discussion of the relationship between the written playtext and performance. This has caught up many of the twentieth century's other debates on the origins of authority, the relations between writing and speech and between tradition and innovation, and (that false dichotomy inherited from the eighteenth century) whether understanding comes through reason or the senses.[90] More often than not, the best twentieth-century dramatic performances have been generated in negotiation with a script. A poet who can write for the page cannot necessarily transfer his talents to the stage, as Symbolist theatre discovered in the 1890s with plays by Verlaine, Mallarmé, Laforgue. But dramatic poetry, written for the human body to unleash the energies of language as part of a total discourse incorporating gesture and sound, breath-rhythms and body movements, and underlining the connections of speech and action, is quite another matter.

Stepping Stones

In the period 1870–1920, the commercial theatre waxed fat on the continuing popularity on the boulevards of the farces of Georges Courteline (1858–1929) and Georges Feydeau (1862–1921), limiting its investment in new work to plays such as Edmond Rostand's tragi-comedy in verse, *Cyrano de Bergerac* (1897). Innovation came first from neighbour countries in Northern Europe through such diverse influences as Wagner, Ibsen, Strindberg and Maeterlinck, channelled through the little theatres of the Symbolist and Idealist movements. Home-grown Idealist drama consisted mostly of minor productions by minor playwrights, often with occultist sympathies (Villiers de l'Isle-Adam, Jules Bois, Joséphin Péladan), which foregrounded the text at the expense of performance.

Two dramatists from this period set the perspectives for twentieth-century theatre. In works such as *Partage de midi* (written 1905, staged 1948), *L'Annonce faite à Marie* (staged by Lugné-Poë, 1912), *Le Soulier de satin* (written 1919–24, published 1929, and staged 1943), the Symbolist Paul Claudel (1868–1955) dedicated his talents to the revival of the religious and political ideologies of the Right. For Claudel, spiritual and material worlds were joined in close communion, and his drama, built on Catholic doctrine and symbol (the Fall, the Cross, redemptive sacrifice, reparatory suffering, the Communion of Saints, the Providential direction of History), aimed to remake the connections between them in the contemporary imagination. The Wagnerian influence is strong in his work. In a programme note dated 30 December 1929, for the Berlin production of his play *Le Livre de Christophe Colomb*, he pointed to Wagner's interest in the subtle connections of rhythm and sonority that link the spoken word with music and enable the artist to transport his audience out of their present into a narcotic other-world of his own creation. In the 1930s, Claudel added to this discourse the techniques of the sacred lyrical drama of the Japanese Nô theatre, with its emphasis on ritual gesture, liturgical costume, and the use of the Chorus to provide a doubling commentary on the action ('Le Festin de la Sagesse', *La Revue de Paris*, 1 July 1938).

Claudel's theatre came into its own in the 1940s. Its search for a dramatic language which could make plain the tragic tensions between despair at a stifling present and longing for a liberating future is exactly that of the left-wing political drama of Sartre and Camus, who admired Claudel's work in this respect despite their antipathy to his religion and his politics. Jean-Louis Barrault, by then at the Comédie Française, was the first to realise the potential of his work and to stage Claudel's two evocations of star-crossed love, the epic and spectacular *Le Soulier de satin* (performed 1943) and the more intimate psychological drama, *Partage de midi* (performed 1948). Barrault's actors were excited by the technical challenges of a language which married mime and diction, the 'breathed' character of Claudel's prose-poetry, the loaded meanings to his words, and the drumming rhythms of his lines. The audience was, to Barrault's delight, overwhelmingly receptive to innovations which marked an energising reorientation of the theatrical enterprise.[91]

Equally influential, but set at the opposite political pole, was the work of Alfred Jarry (1873–1907), whose monstrous farce *Ubu roi* (1896), in a single two-night run, unleashed anarchy.[92] This parody of Shakespeare's *Macbeth*, set in a parody of Poland, was a provocative onslaught on the Third Republic, indicted for its small-mindedness, obsession with money and power, blinkered positivism, worship of technology and disregard for humane values. Two years before the Dreyfus Affair, the play stirred the same mud and released the same poisons. In his theoretical statements on drama, written mostly in 1896–7 ('De l'inutilité du théâtre au théâtre', 'Réponse à une questionnaire sur l'art dramatique', 'Questions de théâtre'), Jarry presented theatre as a visual, performative act, in which decor, mime and masks were as important as words. The puppets and robots who gesture and fawn mindlessly around the grotesque tyrant Ubu are the human wreckage on which the ballooning, predatory ego feeds. At the same time, for the fantastic horror of the play to achieve its full dimension, Jarry needed to depict the wreck of language, the gap between the words of modern culture and the meaning they create. Ubu's pompous rhetorics, parodies of medieval epic, Shakespeare, and Racinian tragedy, contrast sharply with his venal, cowardly and cruel acts. Jarry dramatised the processes by which culture is taken captive by an opportunistic bourgeoisie.

There are formal analogies between Jarry's work and that of his closest contemporary, Guillaume Apollinaire, whose verse play *Les Mamelles de Tirésias*, staged in 1917 under the tag 'drame surréaliste', bolstered its comedy with music, acrobatics and Chorus. But his direct heirs for both form and political intention were the Dadaists and Surrealists, who emerged in the 1920s and then again in the 1960s: Roger Vitrac, for example, whose *Victor, ou les Enfants au pouvoir* (1928) was revived in the 1962–3 season and who with Artaud was co-founder of the Théâtre Alfred Jarry in 1926.

In 1920–40, a stylish commercial theatre, fed by the prolific pens of Jean Cocteau (1889–1963), Jean Giraudoux (1882–1944) and Jean Anouilh (1910–87), produced much entertaining formal innovation but little substance. Isolated against this lightweight backdrop, Antonin Artaud identified a demand from the younger generation, against the establishment grain, for a culture which could reconnect human sensibility to historical event. Modern youth, he said, was opposed to bourgeois capitalism and like Karl Marx was sensitive to 'le déséquilibre des temps où monte la personnalité monstrueuse des Pères basée sur la terre et sur l'argent' ['the unbalance in times when the monstrous personality of the Fathers, founded on money and land, is on the ascendant'].[93] In response to that demand, he proposed his own concept of a Theatre of Cruelty. This theatre was not necessarily cruel in the sense that it staged violence and crimes, though it often could. (Artaud's own play *Les Cenci*, 1935, rewrote the exploration by that other revolutionary, the English poet Shelley, of murder and incest within the patriarchal family.) Rather, its cruelty lay in tearing an audience away from the conventions that pad the edges of everyday existence and confronting it with the terrible thrill of being alive, part of the blind, zestful drive of creation ('Lettres sur la cruauté', 1932). Such a theatre required a new dramatic language, seen in action in the body-centred ritual forms of the Balinese Theatre in Paris in 1931. This became the basis of Artaud's radical rethinking of theatrical form and function in *Le Théâtre et son double* (1938), whose impact was only felt on its reissue in 1944 and which fed powerfully into the New Theatre of the late 1950s.

Theatre, Artaud argued, like plague, should shake its audiences with paroxysms of feeling, push them (in imagination) to extreme gestures and disclose repressed depths of eroticism, cruelty and violence. It was essentially a symbolic form, producing a double of reality, probing the myths and fables of the cultural inheritance to evoke their dark underside ('Le Théâtre et la peste'). Words in such a theatre played a supporting role to the spectacular. The stage was a space to be filled with the concrete language of drama, which addresses itself to the unconscious, through the senses ('La Mise-en-scène et la métaphysique'). Creating the 'blaze' of energies and images which constituted ideal drama required a synthesis of music, dance, mime, vocal intonation, architecture, lighting and decor.

In the 1940s and 1950s, the drama of Jean-Paul Sartre and Albert Camus plunged theatre directly into history and politics.[94] Sartre's writing for the theatre doubles his political trajectory from optimistic faith in the revolutionary potential of France and Europe to deep disillusionment. *Bariona* (1940), written and staged in Sartre's prisoner-of-war camp, celebrated the collective rise of the local people to save the Holy Family from the Roman legions. *Les Séquestrés d'Altona*, produced in 1959 to indict French policy in Algeria, showed the impotence of individuals locked into family, nation, and a Europe bankrupted by past collusions with tyranny. All his plays deal with the problematic relation of character to historical situation, and with the individual subject's ability to turn intellectual desire for change into effective action. Their aims are theorised in *Qu'est-ce que la littérature?* (1947) and in the articles and interviews collected in *Un théâtre de situations* (1973). A Sartrean play is written to demystify conventional notions of human nature and motivation and to show how individuals are constructed by the situation – the complex of private, political, ideological and material relations – in which they are placed ('Forger des mythes', June 1946).

Serious bourgeois theatre continued to formulate its studies of contemporary issues as accounts of the psychological crises of the classically constituted hero (for example, the plays of Henry de Montherlant, *La Reine morte*, 1942; *Le Maître de Santiago*, staged 1948; *Port-Royal*, 1954). Sartre's analyses started from a situation in crisis, posing conflicts of moral and political values ('Pour un théâtre de situations', November 1947). Within that situation, individuals, caught in new lights and perspectives, confronted or dodged their contradictions and made or failed to make the choices that change worlds. Such a concept of character was meat and drink, as Barrault noted, to the modern director, concerned with the representation of the cross-currents of body language and speech. Sartre described the challenge of writing for popular theatre as one of re-establishing the connections between word and action ('Théâtre populaire et théâtre bourgeois', September–October 1955) and gave careful attention to the technical problems involved in giving contemporary colloquial dialogue a capacity for precise significance that could match the language of classical drama ('Forger des mythes'). Every word uttered in the theatre should itself be an act: 'une manière d'agir . . . serment ou engagement ou refus ou jugement moral ou défense des droits ou contestation des droits des autres' ['a mode of action . . . an oath, a commitment, a refusal, a moral judgement, a defense of rights or a challenge to the rights of others'] ('Le Style dramatique'). Conversely, the written word needed the actor's gesture to complete its movement towards meaning.

In *Qu'est-ce que la littérature?*, Sartre argued that all writers must recognise the class standpoint from and to which they speak, and commit themselves to the cause of the oppressed. A play must find the appropriate myths to make visible the formative conflicts and preoccupations of its audience, generating an understanding that can be turned into political action. The myths could be, as in *Les Mouches* (staged 1943), a new version carved out within the shell of Ancient plots. More often, his plots were modern, encapsulating in vivid (melo-) drama those moments of confrontation and choice that were part of everyday life in post-war Europe. *Huis clos* (1944) brought together in a Hell of eternal futility three characters who limited their horizons to private life, and selfishly built their own happiness at the cost of the lives around them. *Morts sans sépulture* (1946) presented an arrested Resistance group, facing torture and death, struggling to fix their choices for the greater public good. *La Putain respectueuse* (1948) raised the issues of racist and sexist oppression. *Les Mains sales* (staged 1948) dramatised the failure of a young middle-class intellectual to break with his idealist conditioning and make choices which would further collective freedom.

Albert Camus's dramatic career began with the theatre collective he helped found in Algeria in 1937. For his models, he looked not to Brecht but to Shakespeare, the Spanish Golden Age and French Classicism and, among contemporaries, the novelist Faulkner, whose *Requiem for a Nun* he adapted for the stage. In all these periods, he saw a moment of major historical change, poised between present despair and future unknown and presenting a cluster of inevitably tragic choices. In their representative authors he prized the ability to represent those tragic tensions with heroic simplicity. His first text, written with the collective in 1936, *Révolte dans les Asturies* (published 1962), an account of the repression of the miners' rebellion in the Spanish Civil War, was banned from production. Its experimental features included a stage that surrounded the audience, locking them into the action, a stylised emphasis on the group (miners and ministers in opposition) rather than the individual actor, mimed battle scenes, and some skilful interplay of sound and presence. Radio news voice-overs, tracking the revolt and its defeat, indicated the dominance of distant Barcelona, and a closing scene of disembodied, imprisoned voices in the dark gave a powerfully lyrical presentation of crushed hope. Later work, more severe philosophical investigations of political problems, was less exciting dramatically. *Caligula* (written 1936–9, performed 1945) was an exploration of the meaning of freedom in an Absurd world, and of the tensions that exist between the individual's power to exercise his freedom and the freedom of others. *Les Justes*, which opened in 1949, explored the question of whether murder can be politically justified, comparing the different responses of a group of terrorists in 1905 in theory and in practice.

The 1950s and 1960s saw an acceleration in the dual emphasis on performance and politics, encouraged by a fresh wave of influences from abroad. The Piccolo Teatro de Milan, which in 1949 put down the first marker for a Marxist and materialist political theatre, returned regularly to Paris through to the 1960s. Brecht's Berliner Ensemble arrived in 1954, with its techniques for engaging the audience's enthusiasm while also positioning it to consider a case from a distanced, objective perspective (the 'alienation effect'). The Théâtre des Nations welcomed performances by the Peking Opera in 1955 and by Japanese Nô companies in the 1950s and 1960s. In 1959, Joan Littlewood presented the work of Brendan Behan and her own *Oh What a Lovely War*. The 1960s saw translations from the English New Theatre of Harold Pinter, Edward Bond, John Osborne, Tom Stoppard and Arnold Wesker. Piscator was directing in Paris in the 1950s, and his *Political Theatre* appeared in French translation in 1962. The American Theatre anarchist collective, with Judith Malina and Julian Beck, touring Europe in 1964–8, appeared at the Théâtre des Nations. In 1966, Jerzy Grotowski of the Warsaw Theatre Laboratory came with his 'poor theatre', in which the sole means of representation was the actor's body.

In France, the first impulse was to seek to re-address tradition and turn it to serve the needs of the present. Jean Vilar, director of the Théâtre National Populaire (1951–63), and Roger Planchon, founder of the Théâtre de la Cité in Villeurbane, an industrial suburb of Lyons, offered productions of Racine, Molière and Shakespeare which reconstructed the original historical reality explored by these dramatists and added a second dimension that explored conflicts in contemporary France. But in France as in England, it was new plays that gave directors such as Vilar, Roger Blin, Barrault and Jean-Marie Serreau their greatest stimulus and made the mid-century French theatre a place where major critiques of power relations and practices were being undertaken at the level of structures and language. The great dramatists of the Absurd – Genet, Beckett, Ionesco – embraced the flow of that second, innovatory current of theatre identified by Barrault and declared its philosophical and political implications. In the theatre of performance, concepts of authority and meaning are completely transformed. 'Meaning' is not a noun, a message, a truth to be handed over on a plate. 'Meaning' in this theatre is a verb, a process of construction, an act of making made afresh from moment to moment. Meaning can be seen and understood on stage, modelled within given, pre-constructed forms, but not definitively lodged in any. It is a working congeries of many discourses, mutually transformative, and all showing their constructed nature, their status as human productions. To a culture still committed to rationalist and religious absolutes and to notions of essential structures and unchanging truths, Absurd drama presented the liberating alternative of an Absurd universe. In the beginning was not the Word; beginning is speaking and seeing.

The first signs of change appeared at the end of the 1940s in the first representations of the alternative world of Jean Genet (1910–86), *Les Bonnes* (staged 1947) and *Haute Surveillance* (1949). In his lyrical evocation of the murderous venom of the maidservant-sisters, and the snarling criminals in the death cell, Genet presented original and shockingly celebratory emblems of the eroticism and violence whose repression constitutes the limits of the bourgeois order. The Surrealist philosopher and prose-writer Georges Bataille, in a review of *Haute Surveillance* on its publication in 1949, wrote of the power of Genet's theatre to rediscover in the forbidden places of the modern world the sacred thrill and heroic grandeur of classical tragedy, which had slipped, he said, out of the reach of a mediocre bourgeoisie.[95]

Genet's lyrical drama is a production of the lived relations of power between individuals and between individuals and society. These relations, political and economic in their origins, are seen, in the tradition of Artaud, as experienced most profoundly in the erotically-charged myths and symbols by which a culture lives. A culture focuses and displays or conceals its repressions, fears, desires and latent powers in certain images, which then become forms through which the culture can be manipulated. These forms, perceived as 'natural', are in fact constructions, ideological illusions which individuals live without questioning. All power, Genet told an interviewer, shelters behind some kind of theatricality, and only the theatre, the place of avowed illusion, has the means to lift the veils.[96] The erotic dressing-up games in the brothel (*Le Balcon*, published in 1956 and first produced in 1957), the play-rehearsals undertaken by blacks for the entertainment of whites (*Les Nègres*, first performed 1959), and the criss-crossing of screens over the stage of the Algerian War (*Les Paravents*, published 1961, first staged by Roger Blin in 1966) are so many emblems of the illusionary processes by which participants in a society collude to create the society's self-image.

'Comment jouer "Les Bonnes" ', Genet's preface to the published text of *Les Bonnes* (1947), explained that the function of theatre was to externalise in scenic images and rhythms the buried processes of individual and social dream. To this purpose, scenic techniques and acting style must blend realism and artifice, introducing an edge of surrealism that frees convention-blunted perceptions for new kinds of understanding. Sartre spoke of the 'whirligigs' of a drama that disorientates spectators, tossing them to and fro from the true to the false and the false to the true (*Saint-Genêt: comédien et martyr*, 1952, Appendix 3). Genet had wanted the women in *Les Bonnes* to be played by adolescent boys, as part of a process of stylisation which could turn the women from individuals into symbols of femininity and so release the spectators from preconceptions and let them think creatively about the feminine function. The feminine is a central concept in Genet's work, representing that repressed, marginalised and dependent element in the psychological and social unit which colludes with and reproduces its own subjection but is also a potential source of hostile energies, permanently on the edge of revolt.

One of the great conjuring-tricks of ideology is its presentation of everyday life as a harmonious order. The jarring contrasts and discrepancies set up by Genet's drama scar and crack this smooth surface. In *Les Nègres*, the disruption comes in the foregrounding of the acting, the make-up, the masks, and also in the mixing of linguistic registers, juxtaposing the colloquial and the lyrical, in which the blacks make their challenge. Invisible gaps and divides in society are made visible. In *Le Balcon*, the brothel's clients and visitors (the Judge, the General, the Bishop) act out their fantasies in what look like discrete private rooms but are all essentially the same space. When the social battle-lines are drawn, the establishment figures line up together on the balcony and the real divide is disclosed, between those on high and the anonymous crowds struggling off-stage, out of the reckoning.

The collaboration between Samuel Beckett (1906–89) and Roger Blin on *En attendant Godot* (1953), staged at the Théâtre de Babylone, marked the opening of another potent investigation into the capacity of drama to reformulate the relationship of meaning and form, glossed by discreet reference to the deep structures of self-deception, exploitation, collusion and illusion which have shaped Western civilisation.[97] Like the full-length stage plays that followed, in French and English (*Fin de partie*, 1957; *Krapp's Last Tape*, 1958; *Happy Days*, 1961), and then the ever-shorter pieces written for stage, radio and television (*Cascando*, written 1962; *Eh Joe*, produced in 1966; *Not I*, premiered in 1972; and *Catastrophe*, in 1982), *Godot* was an experiment that put the spotlight on discourse. Or more accurately, it explored the relationship between discourse and the referent: that is, the universal silence which human perception, movement and speech punctuate into significance.

Beckett's genius was to marshal the left-over materials of the theatrical tradition – a minimum of décor, a diminishing number of characters, and a ragbag of rhetorics – into a set of relationships and exchanges which, realised in the rhythms of performance, model the absurd void of significance that constitutes the lived present of European culture. Habit, and the patterns of familiar routine, Beckett's dramas demonstrate, give the illusion of order, direction and sense to contemporary life. Speakers mouth rhetorics moulded around concepts – God, Reason, Nature – without substance. Life's lack of any absolute structure is modelled by the movement of the dramatic performance.

Beckett's plays play at stretching and shrinking time and space. Passing the time is the object of his characters, as it is the sole object of life demystified of religious absolutes and orientations. Time goes fast or slow depending how it is lived. The movement of the world is fixed by the situation of its speakers. Clov, the servant in *Fin de partie* (produced 1957), turns on Hamm, his master, refusing to differentiate 'yesterday' from any other day, when all days are equally grey and empty. In *En attendant Godot*, the destitute friends Vladimir and Estragon congratulate one another on a well-timed exchange of dialogue that has filled at least a minute with distraction. In the same play, Pozzo, the capitalist exploiter fallen on hard times, defines life as a fleeting awareness, empty of human feeling (a woman gives birth straddling the grave, light flickers, then darkness falls again). Objects, sparsely placed in this devastated world, are points in which meaning can be located. Radishes, turnips, boots keep people going in a literal sense (*En attendant Godot*), as well as in the sense of providing a subject to talk about. Winnie's handbag and toothbrush (*Happy Days*) perform the same function, as does, more ominously, her revolver. In the hands of the masters, both objects and language are politicised and turned into instruments of control. Pozzo rules through his whip, watch and food hamper; Hamm, with his whistle and his key to the food cupboard.

Beckett manages his world of frightening absurdity with black humour, humanly lurching between the grotesque and the sublime. Life, says Estragon, is a circus. As Beckett stages it, it is knock-about farce, shot through with cruelty, pain and terror. Terror comes with the realisation that being is self-authoring and self-perceiving (a recognition process brilliantly mimed in the silent comedy *Film*, 1963), and with the acknowledgement of the shortness of the time which the human voice has to find itself (*Breath*, 1969). At the end of the day, confronting the terror head-on is the heroism of the ordinary human. The light goes out on Krapp, playing over to himself the tapes of his past life, as he teeters on the brink of seeing what he is and has been, embracing it, and letting it go.

From a conservative and idealist position, Eugène Ionesco (1912–94), Romanian-born, settled in Paris from 1938, offered a critique of contemporary rhetoric superficially similar to Beckett's but different in its intentions and in the corrosive despair by which it is animated.[98] Ionesco denounced the stereotyped, robotic nature of modern society and its inhabitants, reduced to absurdity by their identification with their social functions, not human beings but effects of ideology ('Le Rôle du dramaturge', *Notes et contre-notes*, 1962). His black comedies, brilliantly visual, staged the monstrous absence of meaning from the forms that claim to communicate it. *La*

Cantatrice chauve (first produced 1950) displayed the absurdity of language, the arbitrary nature of grammar and syntax, the lack of correlation between sound and sense, and the conventional nature of the narrative forms by which all these elements are constructed into a semblance of meaning. Ionesco emphasised the deceitfulness of the 'story', with its assumptions of a beginning, a middle and an end, which cocoons listeners in the prejudice that coherence and meaning exist. In his own plays, storyline was replaced by layered sequences of intensifying panic, where the real toppled over the edge into the disproportions and distortions of nightmare ('Entretien avec Edith Mora', *Notes et contre-notes*). The old couple in *Les Chaises* (1952) are gradually pushed off-stage by a proliferation of empty chairs. In *Amédée ou comment s'en débarrasser* (1954), a corpse swells to fill the stage. Panic breeds violence, not least in those who hold power. The teacher in *La Leçon* (1951), who kills his pupil with the language of authority, belongs to the same totalitarian impulse that in *Rhinocéros* (1960) takes over the whole world, leaving one solitary romantic standing symbolically in a crumbling house.

None of this ground-breaking new work was political in the simple, dogmatic sense. The work that declared itself political did not have the same intellectual and dramatic force: that of Arthur Adamov (1908–70), for example (*Paolo Paoli*, 1957), or the plays of Armand Gatti (b. 1924), which are interesting for their attempts to make the audience a working part of the production (*Chant public devant deux chaises électriques*, 1966, on the execution of Sacco and Vanzetti; *V comme Vietnam*, 1967; *Les Treize Soleils de la rue Saint-Blaise*, 1968, written in collaboration with the audience during the May events; and *La Colonne Durruti*, 1974). The 'théâtre panique' or 'théâtre de cérémonie' of Fernando Arrabal (b. 1932) is effective as spectacle but less so as political analysis, from *Le Cimetière des voitures* (1958) to the scatalogical black humour of *L'Architecte et l'Empereur d'Assyrie ou Joseph K tenté par la mégalomanie* (staged 1967).

After the Events

May 1968 took theatre onto the streets.[99] A meeting organised by Roger Planchon in his Villeurbane theatre led to the 'Declaration of Villeurbane' that cultural action should be an exercise in politicisation and must invent ways to help a public accustomed to impotence to practise creativity and freedom of choice. Theatre unions took part in the general strike, demanding changes in theatre administration. The predictable government withdrawal of subsidies for popular and political theatre provoked further demonstrations.

The independent troupes who came to prominence from late 1969 in the regions and Paris made significant advances in improvisation, collective creation and audience participation. Jacques Kraemer's Théâtre Populaire de Lorraine, founded in 1963, dramatised the crises associated with the iron and steel industry (*Splendeur et misère de Minette la bonne Lorraine*, 1969; *Les Immigrés*, 1972). André Benedetto's Nouvelle Compagnie d'Avignon, founded in 1966, gave a dramatic voice to such issues as Occitanian independence, the Vietnam War, revolution and class struggle. In Paris, the Théâtre de l'Aquarium, a student company turned professional in May 1970, satirised urban exploitation and the abuses of the press. Jérôme Savary's troupe, Le Grand Magic Circus et ses animaux tristes, embarked on a series of riotous productions, subversive in their sheer exuberance.

Of all such companies, the most influential and successful was Ariane Mnouchkine's Théâtre du Soleil, founded in 1964, which first established its distinctive identity in *Les Clowns* (1969), a production built up through a process of individual and collective improvisation, with its thematic centre the relationship between actors and their society.[100] Mnouchkine's multi-stage spectacular presentations swept the audience into the actors' critique of the contemporary State. The latter was attacked at its Revolutionary foundations in *1789, La Révolution doit s'arrêter à la perfection du bonheur* (1970), which offered from fairground trestle stages a panoramic, carnival analysis of the origins of the Revolution and its take-over by the bourgeoisie in 1791. *1793, La Cité révolutionnaire est de ce monde* (1972) recreated the private lives of commoners in a revolutionary community and contrasted their disappointed aspirations with the triumphalist claims of bourgeois history. *L'Âge d'or* (1975), plotted on the struggles of an immigrant worker, satirised the materialism of modern France.

The emphasis on collective creation from the 1970s onwards resulted in the temporary marginalisation of the writer. At the beginning of the eighties, David Bradby has noted, the important names in French theatre were still those of directors: Barrault, Planchon, Mnouchkine, Chéreau, Vincent, Vitez.

Recently, women directors and writers have become more

numerous.[101] Their work is marked by a common motif of resistance to the confinement of meanings in rigid forms and categories and to the definition of an authoritative subject centre. Marguerite Duras's *India Song* (1972), which received its first performance in England in the summer of 1993, constructs a complex web of dialogues between voice-overs, voices off-stage, sound and music, combined with the spectacle of silent actors on-stage to model the slips and shifts of gendered desire (male and female, homosexual and heterosexual). Duras has also directed her own play, *Savannah Bay* (1983). Simone Benmussa, playwright, director and editor of the *Cahiers Renaud-Barrault*, is especially interested in turning non-theatrical texts into theatre. Her own *La Vie singulière d'Albert Nobbs*, adapted from George Moore's study of transvestism, appeared in 1977, and *Enfance*, adapted from Nathalie Sarraute's memoir-dialogue, in 1984. But Benmussa is best known for her adaptation and direction of Hélène Cixous's *Portrait de Dora* (1976), on which she comments in *Benmussa Directs* (1979). For this performance, different stage levels, voice-over, film projections and lighting effects were used to catch the swirl of significations around the split subject that is Dora: the shifting subject positions, complex interrelations of male and female desire, the overlapping time-planes of Dora's dream-recollections and Freud's crude interrogations. The movement of representation aims to displace Freud from the spotlight, prising away from him control of his case-study narrative and releasing Dora from the object-status in which it scientifically imprisoned her.

The most adventurous of the women directors remains Ariane Mnouchkine, though her adaptations of Shakespeare in the early 1980s and her attempts at contemporary epic have been criticised for allowing history to fall back into myth and for sacrificing analysis for an over-simplifying single vision. Her productions of Hélène Cixous's dramatisations of the Cambodian catastrophe (*L'Histoire terrible mais inachevée de Norodom Sihanouk, roi du Cambodge*, 1985) and the making of Gandhi's India (*L'Indiade*, 1987) were not helped by texts which themselves seem to have exchanged feminist ambition for myth-making and gesture.[102]

Published plays were still few in the early eighties, but the situation was eased by subsidies from Jack Lang's Ministry, to help young writers. Two dramatists have dominated in recent years, both advocates of the written text. In his preface to the collection of dramatic commentaries developed in his seminars held in the 1980s at the universities of Paris III and Paris VIII (*Écritures dramatiques: Essais d'analyse de textes de théâtre*, 1993), Michel Vinaver emphasised the double nature of the dramatic text, which is produced both for representation and for private reading, and where spoken word and action are intimately connected. His closing pages, however, gave primacy to the text: 'l'œuvre est tout entière dans son écriture même, et l'écriture n'est pas quelque chose qui change en cours de route' ['the work is entirely in the writing, and the writing is not something that changes as you go along']. Bernard-Marie Koltès (1945–89) included in the Notes to the text of *Roberto Zucco* (1990) an impressioned plea for more new plays to be staged and fewer rewrites of the classical repertory, and a statement that the room for collaboration between writer and director (in his case, Chéreau) is limited to the narrow space between the points when the writing is finished and rehearsals begin.[103]

From his first play, *Aujourd'hui, ou les Coréens* (staged 1956), to his most recent, *L'Émission de télévision* (1990), Michel Vinaver (b. 1927) has produced multi-layered political drama, which recognises the construction of so-called private experience by the webs of political and economic discourse. The marketing ethos and its transformations of the world of work and the individual subject inspired both the comic epic *Par-dessus bord* (1969) and the shorter *Les Travaux et les jours* (1980). The legal system is the focus of *Portrait d'une femme* (1988), where the heroine confronts judge, lawyers and witnesses in Court, object of an interrogation that emphasises the theatrical and constructed nature of her experience. Actors change costume and scenery in full view of the audience. Juxtaposed sets make it possible to offset against each other dialogues between different sets of characters and to use flashbacks to build up a picture of the complex machinery of the patriarchal State that has made of Sophie the prisoner in the dock. *L'Émission de télévision* (1990) evokes the anxieties generated around individuals who must redefine themselves as they cross the gulf between the world of work and the no man's land of unemployment, and who suddenly find themselves called to account not only by the stereotyping machinery of law but by the even more powerful machine of the media. No music, no scenery and a minimum of props leave language in full possession of the stage. Stage-directions specify the movement of lighting over different parts of the stage to indicate fragments of a reality made of various times and places: 'Un peu comme si le spectateur, muni d'une télécommande, zappait face à l'espace du jeu' ['As though the spectator is zapping the playing space with a channel-changer'.]

Vinaver articulates and mobilises the anxieties of audiences caught in the sticky, quivering webs of contemporary life, which become substantial matter for analysis through the language of his drama. As the examining magistrate and would-be orchestrator of the action in *L'Émission de télévision* comments: 'En cinq jours, j'ai vu des situations basculer / Je travaille une matière vive' ['I've seen situations turn upside down in five days; I work on living material']. Koltès, in contrast, again in the Notes to *Roberto Zucco*, rejoices in the capacity of theatre to refuse the weight of the so-called real. For him, like Genet, theatre is the only place that does not claim to be real life. Rather, 'C'est comme le lieu ou l'on se poserait le problème: ceci n'est pas la vraie vie, comment faire pour s'échapper d'ici?' ['It's the place where you can pose the problem: this isn't real life, how do we get out of here?'].

Koltès's plays give glimpses of the possibility of other realities, admittedly inaccessible, but whose evocation briefly lifts the darkness of the prisonhouse. *Combat de nègre et de chiens* (1983), set in colonised Africa, evokes the tantalising world of the enslaved black that itself defies definition but defines and denounces the limited horizons of its brutal and impotent white masters. (There is always, notes Koltés, a black lurking at the edge of his dramas – an intimation, we should understand, of an Otherness which is never the reassuring reflection that the gazer in the mirror thinks he can see.) In these and subsequent playful exercises in moral and political paradox (*Quai ouest*, 1986; *Dans la solitude des champs de coton*, 1987), Koltès's representative character is not the magistrate but the criminal, the mad murderer–hero Roberto Zucco, climbing onto the prison roof, slipping past the guards, demonstrating and creating a new logic of existence, seductive and liberating. Against playwrights who explore the 'Why?' of a narrative, its rationale, Koltès argues for the importance of simply showing the 'How?', taking an empty space, setting in it an unexpected collocation of characters, and seeing what develops.

The result is a concept of theatre which is in every sense play with the logic of language. The dialogue is a comic match for Molière's, simultaneously pastiche and parody, catching with a discreetly unifying hint of lyrical movement the precise inflections and distinctive styles of individuals who are chiefly performers of social functions (sons and mothers, big brothers and little sisters, prisoners and guards, slaves and masters). But alongside the fun is a distinct sense of awe at the ability of language to model the constraints of time and space, and this, increasingly, was what Koltès tried to stage. Out of his own dramatic experience he reinvented the classical theatre of speech and presence:

> [J]'ai découvert la règle des trois unités, qui n'a rien d'arbitraire, même si on a le droit aujourd'hui de l'appliquer autrement. En tous les cas, c'est bien la prise en compte du temps et de l'espace qui est la grande qualité du théâtre. Le cinéma et le roman voyagent, le théâtre pèse de tout notre poids sur le sol.

> [I have discovered the rule of the three unities, which is by no means arbitrary, though we are entitled nowadays to apply it in different ways. In any event, the distinctive feature of theatre is the account it takes of time and space. Cinema and novel can go travelling; theatre stands us full square on the ground.]
>
> (Notes to *Roberto Zucco*)

9

Starting Fresh

I WOMEN/WRITING/WOMEN

In 1979, Julia Kristeva caught the excitement of a generation of women confronting collectively, for the first time, the challenge of authorship. In her article 'Le Temps des femmes', she wrote of the 'expectation' charging the air as women took up their pens: what, people were asking, would they write that was new?[1]

In the course of May 1968, women activists in the student movement became aware that in radical and revolutionary groups, just as much as in the establishment structures they were attacking, the levers of power were in the hands of men. Women had to find their own ways of formulating their criticisms of the old world and their blueprints for the new.[2] The MLF (Mouvement de Libération des Femmes), officially founded in 1970, generated a mass of feminist journals and newspapers, most collectively produced, such as *Libération des femmes: Année zéro* (a special issue of *Partisans*), *Le Torchon brûle*, *Les Cahiers du GRIF*, *Questions féministes* (whose editorial board included Simone de Beauvoir and the socialist feminist Christine Delphy). A new publishing house, Éditions des femmes, was launched by the group Psych et Po (Psychanalyse et Politique), under the leadership of Antoinette Fouque. Popular mass-market journals such as *Elle* found that readers now dreamed of more than just marriage and motherhood. New publications such as *Marie-Claire* were an acknowledgement of the buying power of the new women. Book publishers were even slower to recognise the new market than their English and American counterparts. Even so, houses such as the Éditions de Minuit and the Éditions du Seuil, and even that great stalwart of station bookstalls, Le Livre de poche, now include some of the best new women's writing on their lists.

There was little warning of this sudden flowering. From the

276

1920s onwards, the few women with something distinctive to say generally said it within the same perspectives and spaces as their male contemporaries: Nathalie Sarraute, for example, or – initially, at least – Marguerite Duras (both discussed above), or Marguerite Yourcenar (pseudonym of Marguerite de Crayencour, 1903–87), who in 1980 became the first woman to be admitted to the French Academy.³ Yourcenar's psychological and historical novels are the creations of a woman who saw and lived beyond the limits her society set but who still observed certain discretions. Sexuality was an issue for her, but there was no question of introducing a contestatory feminine centre to her writing.

Alexis, ou le traité du vain combat (1929) presented the confession made to his wife by a middle-aged man who had finally acknowledged his homosexuality and was leaving for a new life. It was written with an almost precious reticence of language, as was *Anna soror* (1981), a narrative of incestuous passion between a brother and sister. Political and philosophical issues interested her equally. The historical novel *Mémoires d'Hadrien* (1951) was an idealisation of imperial values, a nostalgic gesture of liberal humanism in and for a Europe struggling to come to terms with the end of Empires. *L'Œuvre au noir* (1968), which won the Prix Fémina, counted the painful cost to the individual scholar-scientist who must pursue the search for truth in a war- and plague-torn Europe emerging from medieval barbarism. Difference interested her from a historical or geographical distance (*Mishima ou la vision du vide*, 1980). But already the difference of female subjectivity was emerging in her work, obliquely, as an issue. Yourcenar spoke, for example, in the Notebooks appended to the *Mémoires d'Hadrien*, of the constraints on her choice of structural perspective: 'Impossibilité aussi de prendre pour figure centrale un personnage féminin, de donner, par exemple, pour axe à mon récit, au lieu d'Hadrien, Plotine. La vie des femmes est trop limitée, ou trop secrète. Qu'une femme se raconte, et le premier reproche qu'on lui fera est de n'être plus femme' ['It would also have been impossible to take a female character as my central figure, to make Plotina, for example, the axis of my tale instead of Hadrian. Women's lives are too limited or too secret. If a woman talks about herself, the first complaint will be that she is no longer a woman']. Yet without Plotina, who, Yourcenar's novel says, concealed Trajan's death for several crucial days, and then emerged from the death chamber to declare that Trajan had named Hadrian his successor, Hadrian would not have been

Emperor and the pax Romana would not have been forged. Yource-nar's writing registers women's collusion in the suppression of women's voice and agency from the political and cultural account.

Election to the Academy was never on the cards for Simone de Beauvoir (1908–86), who foregrounded the inequities of the femi-nine condition.[4] Her single most influential work, *Le Deuxième Sexe* (1949), scored a *succès de scandale* in a France where women had just been granted voting rights on equal terms with men (in 1944, as a gesture of gratitude from de Gaulle for women's work in the wartime Resistance). An even bigger storm was raised by its trans-lation and publication in the United States in 1953, at the height of the post-war drive to push working women back into marriage and motherhood. In 1956, the Holy Office placed the book on the Index.

Beauvoir offered a two-part philosophical investigation into the concept of 'woman' in Western culture. Women, she argued, have been figured throughout recorded history as man's Other, mirrors of men's fears and desires, never as subjects in their own right. She challenged the concept of an 'essential feminine': 'Woman' was simply a category constructed by men. She punctured the myths of the feminine produced in men's sciences (biology, psychoanalysis, history) and in their fictions. She traced the malformations of female experience through childhood and adolescence, into the constrictions of marriage and motherhood. Women were alienated instruments of reproduction, who needed to become economically independent subjects, with careers and minds of their own. For this, they required the co-operation of men, who were equally crippled by the inequitable relations between the sexes.

Le Deuxième Sexe declared that few women to date had given signs of artistic genius, because of the limited nature of their experi-ence. Beauvoir's own writing was a model of how women could broaden their experience. Her work covered a range of genres: philosophical treatises (*Pyrrhus et Cinéas*, 1944; *Pour une morale de l'ambiguité*, 1947), plays, novels and autobiography. From the *Mémoires d'une jeune fille rangée* (1958) to *La Cérémonie des adieux* (1981), she provided a commentary on her personal life and career, at the same time as she wrote that life into the wider contexts of family and peer relations, social patterns, political conflicts by which it was structured. Her novels show how choices of perspective and direction of ambitions can close or open lives. Women's experience can be deadlocked into the personal and domestic (*L'Invitée*, 1943;

La Femme rompue, 1968) or opened out to share the possibilities of the age.

Les Mandarins (1954, awarded the Prix Goncourt) rewrote Beauvoir's near-split with Sartre and her affair with the American novelist Nelson Algren into an exploration of the questions confronting the Parisian intellectual after the Liberation: what role the intellectual could play in the reconstruction of European social order, how to handle divisions on the Left, what relationship could be sustained with the Communist Party after the discovery of Stalin's labour camps. With Sartre, she came late to collective politics, in the 1930s, in a situation polarised between fascism and the Popular Front. From that time, her personal development increasingly required her active involvement in national and international struggles. *La Longue Marche* (1957) described her visit to Mao's China in 1955. She protested in the street demonstrations against de Gaulle's Algerian interventions, right up to the settlement of 1962. She sat on the Russell Tribunal on American war crimes in Vietnam and supported the student uprisings in May 1968.

Her engagement with the women's movement began in the sixties, supporting Colette Audry's campaign on contraception and abortion, which in 1967 secured the legalisation of contraception. In 1967, speaking in Nasser's Cairo, she attacked Egyptian sexism, dismissing the traditional defence that Islamic law prescribed female subordination as brusquely as she had dismissed similar Catholic pretentions in *Le Deuxième Sexe*. On 5 April 1971, she was a co-signatory of the pro-abortion manifesto published in *Le Nouvel Observateur*. In 1972, she became president of the pro-abortion association Choisir, and took a leading role in the Bobigny trial, in defence of a working-class mother who had helped her 17-year-old daughter obtain an abortion. (The first law permitting abortion was introduced provisionally in November 1974 and finally confirmed in November 1979.) In 1972, Beauvoir formally acknowledged the existence of a distinctive women's politics and made a specific commitment to the feminist as distinct from the socialist struggle. She did not however separate the two in effect: *Les Belles Images* (1966), her satire of middle-class consciousness inside the Gaullist cocoon, registers the gathering presence of the feminist debate as part of its anti-capitalist critique.

Women writing in and since the sixties come from a wide range of backgrounds and speak to equally diverse audiences.[5] United by a common sense of oppression and desire for freedom, they can differ radically in the ways they formulate that desire. For convenience, they can be roughly categorised into two groups, divided precisely by form. The language women writers choose to speak and the kind of relationship they consequently establish with readers can be very different. Some writers are more accessible than others. They adopt discourses close to that of conventional realism, addressing in familiar terms the material practices of everyday life and identifying for themselves a constituency of average middle-class and working-class women, with the aim of creating feminist awareness and solidarity across a wide base. A kernel of Utopian dream or a shield of ironic humour points to the possibility that things could be said very differently. Theirs could be called a reformist style, especially when compared with the radical explorations of a smaller number of writers, who have taken further the proposition that the conventional concept of 'woman' is a fiction of masculine discourse, and argue that for the feminine to be conceptualised in its own right a new language has to be invented. The division is focused in *La Jeune Née* (1975), in the debate between the journalist and essayist Catherine Clément (b. 1939) and the prose fiction writer Hélène Cixous over whether a feminist critique can use the inherited language of Western rationalist culture, constituted within patriarchal priorities and hierarchies, or whether women should seek to remake the language of 'hysteria' (womb-madness), the term used by patriarchal speech to hustle contentious femininity back into its 'own' sphere. There are few rights and wrongs in this debate: if words are weapons, then different weapons do different jobs.

The women's liberation movement started with the first kind of writing, direct address to an audience, catching the popular imagination by speaking the receiver's own language. The best-selling autobiographical novels of Albertine Sarrazin (1937–67) spoke directly of freedom to a whole adolescent generation. *L'Astragale* and *La Cavale*, published simultaneously in 1965, and *La Traversière* (1966), all set in the 1950s, told the story of a gifted and rebellious student who runs away from school and family into a life of petty crime and a love affair with another young criminal. Imprisonment, escapes, recapture are the fabric of her life, until the release that comes with the publication of her first novel. The attraction of Sarrazin's work was double: the realism of her presentation, and its allegorisation of the feminine condition as an imprisonment in the institutions of society. The energy of Sarrazin's rebellion flows into a unique oral narrative style, lyrical and colloquial, that catches in dialogic exchange the special argot of women in prison.

Christiane Rochefort (b. 1917) described another kind of imprisonment in *Les Petits Enfants du siècle* (1961). Girls growing up on a high-rise estate, dreaming escape through romantic love (and marriage, and a flat in a better high-rise), are trapped in the machinery that reproduces the workforce. Fantasy novels like *Une rose pour Morrison* (1966), *Encore heureux qu'on va vers l'été* (1975), dreamed more successful flights from the oppression of the patriarchal family, with the help of the alternative communities of contemporary pop and drug culture. Less often discussed are Rochefort's incursions into female nightmare. From her first novel, *Le Repos du guerrier* (1958), to *La Porte au fond* (1988), a narrative of child abuse, Rochefort has explored formative moments of female sexual experience. Both texts ask explicitly: when initiation into womanhood is circumscribed by sadistic and exploitative sexual discourses, generating a context in which women learn to construct themselves as passive victims, how can a woman begin to formulate desires and dreams of her own? Fascinated by female characters whose tongues are bound by complicity and guilt, Rochefort offers illuminating studies in the breaking of silence.

In other writers, the dream of freedom took form within the hard realities of the world of work. Claire Etcherelli (b. 1934), in her novel *Élise ou la vraie vie* (1967), evoked the experience of the young women from the provinces who came to Paris in the fifties to earn a living in the expanding car industry, on the factory floor. Élise wakes up from the state of political unawareness that was the traditional lot of small-town working-class women, confined to domesticity, and suddenly finds her life is the meeting point of racial tensions sparked by the Algerian crisis and tensions between unions and management exacerbated by technological change and the vicissitudes of the post-war international market. In Etcherelli's socialist contextualisations, Élise learns to give up her dependencies on family, brother, and Algerian lover, and makes her own way into the working community. In contrast, the bitter voices of Victoria Thérame's *Hosto-Blues* (1974), of nurses working in a non-unionised private hospital, narrate a near-hopeless struggle to retain shreds of dignity and humanity for themselves and the patients in their care. A language as vivid and argot-laden as Sarrazin's gives a glimpse into a world formerly hidden from history, of squalor, overwork and humiliation. What women can do for themselves, these voices say, depends on the possibilities society offers. Belonging to a marginalised gender and a marginalised class is doubly disabling.

In *La Part des choses* (1972) and in *Ainsi soit-elle* (1975), Benoîte Groult (b. 1920) gave an angry analysis of women's placing in contemporary society. The opening section of the second book, a shorter, more sharply ironic version of *Le Deuxième Sexe*, denounced the marginalisation of women in everyday life and the attempts of men throughout history to push enterprising femininity back into the doll's house. Echoing also that first feminist historian, Christine de Pisan, Groult collected up instances of men's contempt for women, denouncing the hypocrisy of a chivalrous 'respect' that marooned upper-class women on a pedestal while refusing to help the sex as a whole into equality. She noted the ideological pressures on women in twentieth-century consumer society, where advertisements and magazines offer irresistibly seductive (mis)representations of women and their roles. The social construction of female sexuality was thrown into sharp relief with a detailed description of the repressive use of clitoridectomy and infibulation in Muslim countries. Groult juxtaposed to this Western countries' methods for keeping control of the means of reproduction: restricted access to abortion and contraception.

As women's horizons widened, writers tracked the changing shape of traditional relationships. A number of autobiographies and autobiographical fictions have identified the nuclear family as a major source of women's oppression. Marie Cardinal (b. 1929), who first found fame with *La Clé sur la porte* (1972), explored in her autobiography, *Les Mots pour le dire* (1975), the relationship of husband and wife and 'the cultural myth of the happy-ever-after marriage', one of the many means by which men set limits to women's creativity.[6] *La Place* (1983), Annie Ernaux's farewell to her dead father, tried to come to terms with a father–daughter relationship strained by the daughter's transition from one class to another, up the ladder of educational opportunity. Ernaux reported a problem of communication between generations, observing in loving and painful detail differences of language, styles, tastes and manners. She offered a portrait of a daughter inescapably framed by the gaze of a father both eager for her success and afraid of her achievements.

Une femme (1988), exploring Ernaux's relationship to her mother, describes how a shackling version of motherhood handed down for generations, passing on knowledge and skills which have evolved to cope with a situation determined by working-class and petty-bourgeois poverty, must be rejected by the daughter, though she pays it loving tribute in her writing. Ernaux identifies the resentment as well as the affection daughters feel for mothers, and places the resentment's origins in the mother's policing of her daughter's sexuality. The memory of the mother's admonitory phrase 's'il t'arrive un malheur!' ['If something goes wrong'] brings flooding back the daughter's teenage demoralisations: 'fugitive-ment, je confonds la femme qui a le plus marqué ma vie avec ces mères africaines serrant les bras de leur petite fille derrière son dos, pendant que la matrone exciseuse coupe le clitoris' ['for a moment, I identify the woman who has most marked my life with those African mothers who hold their little girl's arms behind her back, while the wise woman bends to circumcise the clitoris']. A similar love–hate relationship was presented in Marie Cardinal's autobiography, only capable of resolution, as in Ernaux, by the death of the mother and the daughter's liberation into a language of her own making. The novel trilogy by Marie Redonnet (b. 1948), *Splendid Hotel* (1986), *Forever Valley* and *Rose Mélie Rose* (both 1987), alle-gorises the repetitive circling that is the traditional mode of women's lives, daughters forever fixed in imitation of the previous generation's patterns.

Very few of the new women writers have been willing to concede any value to the traditional definition of women as primarily wives and mothers. One exception has been Annie Leclerc, whose lyrical prose text *Parole de femme* (1974), frantically hyped by the media, used a form of feminist rhetoric to reject demands for women to take their place in the public sphere. Rather than play men's career games, women should seek to give new value to the domestic space which is traditionally their own: housework, reproduction, child-care. The determining limits of Leclerc's rhetoric show up sharply in *Origines* (1988), her autobiography, which enthusiastically embraces the patriarchal authorities which she identifies at the threshold of all her most important experiences, offering a nostalgic hymn to the secure closures of childhood.

Exploring the mother-figure, overloaded with symbolic value in contemporary society, has been a preoccupation in contemporary French feminist thought. Julia Kristeva focused her attention on the icon of the Virgin Mary and its relevance to women's situation in present-day Western culture. The cult of the Virgin, Kristeva argued, cannot help to improve relations between women (especially the competitive hatred between mothers and daughters), or to establish a new bond of equality between men and women which would not need to use children as mediator.[7] In *Pouvoirs de l'horreur: essai sur l'abjection* (1980), she explored a different mother-fantasy. The fear of women that from time to time becomes a cultural fetish (and is anachronistic in an age of psychological understanding) has much to do, in her view, with the fear of the archaic mother. The thrill felt in the face of horror, the perception of the unknown as monstrous difference, is the recollection of the moment of psychological separation from the Mother, the child's first perception of its own unique identity. Such a perception is terrifying because along with the first joyful recognition that one exists must come the simultaneous knowledge of *non-existence*; hence the cultural and psychological identification of the Mother-figure as both source of life and gateway to death.

Luce Irigaray (b. 1930), author of *Speculum de l'autre femme* (1974), a critique of Plato, Freud and Lacan for which she was expelled from Lacan's *École freudienne*, and *Ce sexe qui n'en est pas un* (1977), essays on feminine sexuality and writing, has focused on the problems and possibilities of the mother–daughter bond in *Et l'une ne bouge pas sans l'autre* (1979) and *Parler n'est jamais neutre* (1985), and attempted to conceive of different forms of the relationship in which mother and daughter can, as she puts it, 'remain alive' together.[8]

With Kristeva and Irigaray, we enter the area of the second kind of contemporary women's writing and thinking, less easy of access than the kind that links itself with relatively conventional realist modes, but at least as important. The difficulties it poses for new readers are in part the same as are posed by the avant-garde male writers and thinkers (the poets, the philosophers and the psychoanalysts) on whose techniques and insights it builds. But they have also an original source, in the desire to find forms of intellectual production which are distinctively feminine – new images, but more important, new perspectives, positions and new syntax, which together can constitute a voice which, in familiar patriarchal culture, has never before been heard. This writing has tried to understand in theory, and model in practice, how the oppression of women's bodies in history is intimately related to women's alienation in language, where they speak as a dependent sex, not subjects in their own right but simply objects of masculine constructions.

The ideological urgencies that drive this need to make a different voice are forcefully evoked in Chantal Chawaf's prose fiction *Rédemption* (1989). Chawaf starts from the assumption of a deadly antagonism between male and female in their stance to life and creativity, which is focused in their different relationships to language. Masculine culture seeks to control the world with the rationalist intellect; it kills. Feminine culture wants only to know the living world, through imagination and the senses; women create. On this basis, her novel stages the bloody drama that lies behind the words men have for women. A Canadian 'vampire', who cut his mistress to pieces, comes to Paris, where he picks up another girl, Olga, in the Parc Monceau and eventually kills her too. The vampire specialises in paper sculpture. He cuts up books into individual words, stabs the paper words (his mother-tongue – 'langue maternelle' – says the text) with little knives and spreads them out in this room, a dissection on display. Olga is a scenario writer, specialising in love scenes. Her art (like Chawaf's) lies in the invention of a new, synthetic kind of discourse. She is trying to invent a poetics of the body that will get beyond the limits of conventional language, to give a heightened perception of what carnal experience really is: 'la symphonie rouge vif du corps vivant' ['the bright red symphony of the living body']. With the immediacy and the complexity of music, her intensely physical writing, with its vivid colours, sharp anatomical images, and its rolling but controlled syntactical flood reproduces the movement of life: 'le flux des corps, un texte éruptif, rouge vif, écorché' ['the flux of bodies, an explosive, bright red, flayed text']. The future, it would seem, will be Olga's. Her art invents a living model, while her lover, who cannot know without destroying, produces a dead analysis. In the last instance, though, women's language will always be drawn back to the vampire of masculine discourse, and this, enraged by its own impotence, will always tear the would-be creative female subject apart.[9]

In the exploration of discursive differences between masculine and feminine, two bodies of work stand apart: those of Julia Kristeva and Hélène Cixous, who, in their different ways, have introduced fresh perspectives into thinking about women. Neither speaks to a mass audience. Both suffer from the sheer impenetrability of style that is inseparable from contemporary French theory, particularly in the work of Derrida and Lacan, which has most influenced their own. Both may often seem to be building a card-house of conjecture and assertion, that only makes sense within the academic assumptions and traditions on which they draw. Their work has nevertheless left distinctive marks on the ways in which other women – and men – now write and think. Their books do not reach a mass audience, but their ideas do, not least through the academic circles in which they move, which have filtered them into the mainstream.

Julia Kristeva (b. 1941) has opened up new ways for women and men to grasp their place in history and society with the double key of linguistics and psychoanalysis.[10] The title of her ground-breaking study of modern French poetry, *La Révolution du langage poétique* (1974), is illuminating in itself. Against the conventional assumption that language is or should be a conservative force, the cement of a given social order, she presents a seductive alternative account of the capacity of language to be a force for revolutionary change.

In this text, which draws on and develops the work of Jacques Lacan, Kristeva presents language as standing at the end of the process that forms the individual subject.[11] This process (the signifying process, 'procès de signifiance') is said by her to have two modes: the 'semiotic' and the 'symbolic'. A child experiences the semiotic mode in the pre-Œdipal stage: that is, while it is aware of no distinction between itself and the mother's body and before it has recognised the existence of the Father and the taboos and limits he imposes. In the semiotic mode, the instinctual drives in the child are organised and patterned by structures mediated by the mother. The child unconsciously acquires a deep intuition of its 'place' in the world, through the way in which the mother responds to its demands to eat, sleep, defecate, laying down basic rhythms and basic assumptions about how the world resists or complies with its needs and desires. In the next mode, the symbolic, entered through the Œdipal parent, the placing process is effected by the explicit laws and rules of a culture. But in the semiotic mode, the child's energies are arranged according to unspoken and unquestioned assumptions, attributed by Kristeva to natural or socio-historical constraints, such as the biological difference between the sexes or family structure. The child slips into its relationships with things and its family, and later with language, according to the patterns laid down here.

The child becomes self-conscious – recognises that it has a

separate existence from its mother's body – at the moment of its entry into the symbolic. It becomes aware at that point of conventional laws and rules, carried by language, that carve the world up in particular ways. With that awareness, it becomes able to produce meaning; that is, it expresses itself in the way that others do, in the dominant discourse. In the semiotic mode, the mother communicates a basic sense of an ordering process to the child. The Law of the Father overlays that base, repressing the primitive rhythms communicated through the mother, instating its own more abstract patterns, and its own hierarchies. Only in a few places, Kristeva proposes, do those repressed, primitive rhythms persist. One is in poetry, or at least a particular kind of poetry: the modernist forms of Rimbaud and Mallarmé, originators of the avant-garde rebellion against the syntax of rationalist prose. Semiotic patterning, according to Kristeva, works on the same associative basis as do poetic creation and dream logic: that is, to use Freud's terms, by slippage or condensation, which produce respectively metonomy and metaphor, the building-blocks of figurative speech. For Kristeva, the power of poetry resides in those moments when its syntax reconstitutes the rhythms of the semiotic mode, remaking contact with the mother-tongue.

Kristeva's theory of the semiotic is important for a number of reasons. In the first place, she is emphasising that language is not just an abstraction. It is rooted in historical and biological experience. Thinking about the relation of the human subject to the rhythms of language is not just an academic exercise. Language rhythms relate crucially to the way subjects position themselves in the world. In the second place, she has found a point where successful attempts to make a new language – both what is said and how we say it – might be made. If the roots of language are in the unspoken, in the child's direct relation to the body of its mother (and its indirect relation to the family and society in which that body is situated), then for a different language to come into being, it is the formative context of family and social relationships that has to be changed. Thirdly, understanding the order of linguistic priorities the theory establishes helps with the critical understanding of what the key technical focuses of avant-garde women's writing must be: not just the images, though new feminine images, as we shall see, are important, but primarily the syntax that links the images together – the rhythms of an utterance, which can destabilise and transform dominant discourse.

Des Chinoises (1974), the product of Kristeva's visit to China in the spring of that year, pursued a connected theme, though it foregrounded the liberation of women rather than the remaking of language, and politics rather than psychoanalysis. In Western Christian culture, Kristeva argued, with its Judaic base, woman is downgraded and represents body as against spirit; the Law of the Spirit is masculine. Woman is required to deny her body, deemed incapable of sexual pleasure, and held in regard only in so far as she accepts a mother-function, in the reproduction of the community. In China, in contrast, the mother has a central role and is perceived as an individual, not simply a reproductive function. Her sexuality has equal status to that of men. Kristeva attributes the difference to different linguistic structures (Chinese language is tonal and ideogrammatic, so closer to the semiotic), to the existence of a matrilineal tradition in Chinese society, and to Maoist policies, which have aligned feminist and collectivist interests. The naivety of Kristeva's analysis of Mao and Maoist China hardly needs pointing out. What is important in this text is her use of China as a Utopian space to evoke a vision of a different place for women, in terms of alternative constructions of language and politics.

Hélène Cixous (b. 1937), founder (1974) and director of the influential Centre d'Études Féminines at the University of Paris VIII (Vincennes), investigates connected issues from the perspective of creative writer, rather than academic or philosopher.[12] Cixous is the primary inventor and exponent of a mode of writing, *écriture féminine*, which presents itself as embodying feminine difference. In *La Jeune Née* (1975), written with Catherine Clément, and *La Venue à l'écriture* (1977), written with Madeleine Gagnon and Annie Leclerc, she set out its distinguishing features. *Écriture féminine* speaks of life, in all its pleasure and variety, compared with masculine writing, which is single-minded and single-voiced, utilitarian and limited – the language of death. It is open to experience, including the experience of others, whereas masculine writing tries to master and dominate other experience with its own. It represents an open, receptive, plural subject, as opposed to the domineering masculine 'I'. It breaks barriers and mixes genres. In place of masculine, ratio-nalist prose it sets lyrical, exuberant poetry, that spills through puns, wordplay and laughter into a multiplicity of meanings. All true poetry is 'feminine writing'; here, Cixous joins Kristeva in praising the revolutionary poetic language of Joyce, Kleist, Genet and Shakespeare, whom she takes as her models.

Cixous's writing has been criticised by Anglo-American and French women for its idealism. Her work does not recognise and oppose the real biological and economic constraints with which most women are burdened. It has been argued that the sense of liberation her texts can generate is no more than a language-effect, which does not engage with contemporary realities. The debate in *La Jeune Née* with Catherine Clément (former diplomat, journalist, philosopher) formulates the problems clearly. Even so, her writing stands as an important gesture towards a different way of being for women.

In her early novels, essays and theatre, Cixous wrote as a daughter seeking to understand what father and mother have made of her, and to break with it. *Dedans* (1969), awarded the Prix Médicis, evoked the primary Œdipal scene by which the subject is engendered: a sequence of identification with and splitting from mother and father, in turn, which initiates the child-subject into social intercourse and language and, simultaneously, kills it – the female subject finds herself imprisoned in a system, pre-formed in a patriarchal mould.

Prénoms de personne (1974) also attacked the single, closed self produced by patriarchal culture. In its place, Cixous proposed her own account of the feminine sense of self, expressed in the punning double-sense of the French pronoun 'personne', which means both 'person' and 'nobody': 'Vacillation de la subjectivité, entre personne et toutes ses individualités possibles' ['Subjectivity swithers, between 'no-one' and a whole host of possible identities']. How we see ourselves depends on how we see our sexual selves, how we define our desire. Freud asked, 'What do women want?' and gave the wrong answer (a penis) because he associated desire and castration. Desire for Cixous is not a sense of something missing, a lack, or absence that has to be satisfied with a specific object. Defining desire in this way, she argued, is the foundation of patriarchal order. It turns desire and especially sexual desire into a means of control, because satisfaction becomes something that can be accorded or withheld by whoever possesses the desired object. Cixous speaks instead of feminine desire as *refusing* ends and objects. Open-ended, outside time, it reaches out to nameless, indefinable possibilities.

Souffles (1975) explored the collusion between the mother and the patriarchy, that traps the daughter in the masculine order of desire. Violent, passionate language, built around the symbolic confrontation of Samson and Delilah, evoked the masochistic pleasure that a woman learns to find in her own destruction. The text rejected this traditional mother and demanded a new kind, which the daughter/writer must invent for herself. The private drama staged in *Souffles* has its public counterpart in *Révolutions pour plus d'un Faust*, published in the same year. This is a maelstrom of a text, whirling through the catastrophes of men's imperialist history, all attributed to diabolical madness. Newcomers to history cannot be or do anything outside the Devil's terms, cannot escape his single, defining vision. The book asks key questions: how to break out of the vicious circle, cease to collude in the reproduction of death and destruction? How to cross from the Book of History, the single authoritative text, to a polyphonic concept of histories, where the stories can be many, and all different?

In the first part of *Angst* (1977), Cixous was still re-enacting the same Oedipal struggle with mother and father/lover. But the second part found the beginnings of hope in a relationship of another kind with Antoinette Fouque, leader of the feminist group Psych et Po. And *Illa* (1980), reiterating the desire for a mother who will help lost daughters back to life like Demeter looking for kidnapped Persephone, found her in the Brazilian writer Clarice Lispector (first celebrated in *Vivre l'orange*, 1979). Cixous thereafter began the task of mothering herself, creating in her texts a feminine voice able to throw off the chains of the Father's language.

With ou l'art de l'innocence (1981) was a dialogue between C-Cordelia (Lear's daughter), the daughter invented by men, who, says Cixous is a creature of fiction ('un être de fiction'), and the still-to-be-written Aura, a creature of writing ('un être d'écriture'). The writing in this text programmatically challenges rationalist prose, multiplying meanings with puns, making new meaning with neologisms, mixing together abstract and concrete (Cixous speaks of hearing words or smelling their scent, picking them up like a child picks up a shell or starfish), introducing breathless punctuation, fragmented syntax, a plethora of verbs, conscious repetition, deliberate contradictions. This superabundance of language, evoking all the repressed superfluity of life, models freedom. It is language that lives in a rich culture, but is not bound fast to it. Cixous offers 'une culture dé-livrée' ['culture un-bound']. *Le Livre de Prométhéa* (1983) again dramatised the heroic attempt to remake familiar rhetoric and metaphors and to reach out for the immediacy, clarity and limitless energy which should characterise the creative fire of feminine creation.

Since the 1970s, as debates on the politics of language and gender have developed in extent and depth, lesbian writing has attracted increasing attention. The beginning of the twentieth century had seen, in the trail of the Decadence, a fashion for lesbian themes which allowed the publication of some fairly minor work: for example, the poetry of Renée Vivien (pseudonym of Pauline Tarn, 1877–1909) or the prose of the actress Liane de Pougy. Their more important contemporary Sidonie-Gabrielle Colette (1873–1954) was better known to the reading public for her luminous novels of childhood, her cats and her sensuous landscapes than for her explorations of the terrain of female homosexuality. *Le Pur et l'impur* (published in 1932, under the title *Ces plaisirs*), which drew together the lesbian themes scattered through Colette's texts of 1900–32, was practically ignored on publication. The novels of Violette Leduc (1907–72), *L'Asphyxie* (1940) and *L'Affamée* (1948), *Ravages* (1955), *Thérèse et Isabelle* (1966), had to wait for recognition until 1964, when her autobiography *La Bâtarde* appeared, with a preface by Leduc's patron, Simone de Beauvoir. The women's movement post-'68 provided the conditions in which the muted, isolated voices could group, gather strength and express themselves, often with a loud and bitter anger reflecting the long time of their silencing.[13]

Of the new lesbian writers, the most successful and, linguistically, the most innovative has been the prose fiction writer Monique Wittig (b. 1935). *L'Opoponax* (1964) explored the processes by which gendered subjectivity is formed in childhood, in the matrix of individual and group relationships, family and friends, home and school, within the varied and complex force-fields generated by spoken and written language. *Les Guérillères* (1969) imagined a Utopian female collectivity, in which the remaking of traditional discourse was the basis for new gender, class and generation relations. *Le Corps lesbien* (1973), celebrating the lesbian erotic, combined urgently sensual sentence rhythms and a powerfully direct vocabulary with erudite and witty games with the rhetorics and discourses of masculine sexuality. *Virgile Non* (1985) combined a satirical attack on the exploitations of women by men with another Utopian vision of lesbian society. This reworking of Dante's *Divine Comedy* begins with grotesquely comic images from the hell of female sexuality constructed by masculine desire (chained processions of wives and mothers, loaded with children, whores bound up in leather and fishnet, teetering on high heels) and ends in a parody of the Beatific Vision, a garden of earthly delights on the horizon of San Francisco, filled with the making of music and the making of soup, and guarded by angels on motorbikes.

Wittig's work underlines the extent to which, for contemporary feminism, language is the key to change. *Brouillon pour un dictionnaire des amantes* (with Sande Zeig, 1976) is a project to start the world over again with a revision of vocabulary, expropriating the naming function that God the Father originally reserved for Adam. In this collection of the words that matter, according to feminine priorities, everything is different: the key figures of myth and legend (Artemis, Athena), the principal agents of history (Boadicea), the central instruments of sexual pleasure (the clitoris). Time itself is divided up differently: the past is ousted by the future, leisure and celebration replace burdensome work. From the natural world, only non-utilitarian elements are selected: in place of such as wheat, coal, horse, the text lists the purely decorative iris, jade, kangaroo. The key emotions identified are release, and violence. Words are described as shifting and variable, tools that need to be 'reactivated' (see entry 'Word') before they can be put to feminist use. Feminists need to know why some words have been privileged over others, and which words are too dangerous for continuing use (see entry 'Dictionary').

As important as changing vocabulary is the restructuring of syntax. Wittig's work has emphasised the problem of the subject pronoun. In her essay 'The Mark of Gender' (1985), she described the aim of her writing as 'to destroy the categories of sex in politics and in philosophy, to destroy gender in language (at least to modify its use)' and explained that once 'the dimension of the person' in language is changed, around which everything else is organised, everything must shift.[14] Changing the concept of the subject involves the restructuring of language. The same process of changing the subject must be undertaken in philosophy, politics and economics, 'because as women are marked in language by gender, they are marked in society by sex'. For this reason, 'personal pronouns are, if I may say so, the subject matter of each one of my books'. In *L'Opoponax*, which models the linguistic and social processes by which sexually undifferentiated childhood is constructed into femininity, Catherine, the central female figure, is figured for most of the text as part of an ungendered group, in the collective 'on'. Wittig explains that 'with this pronoun, that is

neither gendered nor numbered, I could locate the characters outside of the social division by sexes and annul it for the duration of
the book'. In *Les Guérillères*, Wittig replaces the generic third person
plural 'ils' by 'elles', which she designates as a new universal pronoun; under the aegis of 'elles', a new political order is inaugurated
which aims to abolish all divisive distinctions, including those of
gender. *Le Corps lesbien* invents a split pronoun, 'j/e', to represent
the split subjectivity of women, who must inevitably come to
selfhood through the language of the masculine symbolic. The 'j/e'
of this text works her way through the possessive, sadistic fantasies
of inherited sexual culture to a relationship that merges possessive-
ness into the pleasure of the collectivity. The closing line of *Le Corps
lesbien*, a declaration of personal desire, is also a political statement:
'J/e te cherche m/a rayonnante à travers l'assemblée' ['I seek you,
my shining one, through the assembly'].

II WRITING THE INTERFACE: *FRANCOPHONIE*

A francophone is, literally, a (native) speaker of French, and *Francophonie* (a term invented in 1880) designates the collectivity of
French speakers, scattered across the globe. Concentrations of
francophones outside France are highest in Black Africa and the
Maghreb, then Quebec, the Caribbean, Belgium and Switzerland,
the Middle East and Indo-China. Since the early 1960s, the term has
been used especially to cover countries which have their own
indigenous language but where French is the official language,
dominant among cultural elites (Senegal, for example), and countries where, though not an official language, French is still widely
spoken and used for trade and cultural exchanges (the Maghreb,
Egypt).[15]

From the 1960s onwards, francophone writing slowly began to
attract attention. Since the 1980s it has commanded an unprecedented level of European academic interest, recently given a fresh
twist by the rise of women's studies. A considerable number of
texts published in recent years, by men as well as women, indicate
that a major factor in the changes they chart is the awareness of
women's exploitation and of women's role in challenging exploitation of both sexes. Critical perspectives from women's studies
have also been influential in determining the approaches taken to
texts.

The best criticism has been that which has been conscious of the need to avoid plotting Western preoccupations onto non-Western situations. The American critic Gayatri Chakravorty Spivak, who has turned the theoretical spotlight on Third World women's studies, emphasised in an interview of 1986 that First World critics must approach Third World material with informed alertness to the differences between their own position and those they propose to analyse:

> From [your] position, then, I say you will of course not speak in the same way about the Third World material, but if you make it your task not only to learn what is going on there through language, through specific programmes of study, but also at the same time through a *historical* critique of your position as the investigating individual, then you will see that you have earned the right to criticize, and you will be heard.[16]

Quebec

When the Third World begins to spell out the marginalisation it has experienced at the hands of Western interests, others' experience of marginalisation appears in a different light. For a long time, it was Canadian francophone writing that represented the most prominent alternative to the writing of mainland France.[17] Quebec's struggle for separate existence from the other states of English-speaking Canada was linked to its attempt to write itself a separate history of its origins in the French tongue of its original colonisers. That struggle reached its peak in the mid-1960s, with the terrorist tactics of the Front de Libération du Québec. Once the Parti Québécois came to power on 15 November 1976 and marked its ascendancy by the declaration of French as the official language of the province of Quebec, what began to become clear was not what divides the culture of Quebec from the rest of the West, be it English-speaking or French-speaking, but what puts it on the same side of the far bigger cultural divide between North and South. French-Canadian culture, built through resistance, is now set firm on a path of consolidation. Its main problems are those it shares with the larger nations of the West: how to keep an edge of local difference while taking a full share of the benefits of Euro-American market culture.

Francophone writing in Quebec inscribes all the difficulties and contradictions of double identity. Overlooked by far more powerful neighbours, near and far (Britain and France, the United States and the rest of English-speaking Canada), Quebec had to struggle painfully for its existence against their dominance. But that kind of dominance is radically different from the experience of slavery which fell to the Third World. From an early date (the Quebec Act, 1774), the British occupiers allowed the French settlers to speak their own language, fearful of possible alliances with the growing power of the United States. From the 1830s to the present, the cultural movements of European France, Romanticism to postmodernism, have provided a scaffolding within which Quebec writers have been able to design their own space. From the 1890s, there have been translations of French-Canadian texts for the English-Canadian market, made by translators eager to promote cross-cultural understanding.[18] From the 1950s, government subsidy and the workings of the Western market have encouraged creative writing (and radio, television and film) in Quebec. Quebec writers are largely middle-class and university-educated, often university-teaching, with easy access to the media. The first *Dictionnaire des œuvres littéraires du Québec* was published in 1978 with a major subsidy from the Quebec Ministry of Cultural Affairs.

From the late 1970s, the writer's problem has been less one of getting published than of taking an equitable share of what is now a highly profitable industry. The Union des Écrivains Québécois, founded 21 March 1977, as a body with both trade union and cultural interests, works with the Ministry of Cultural Affairs and the Conseil des Arts du Canada to secure writers' interests as well as to mark the cultural presence of Quebec. The novelist Jacques Godbout (b. 1933), writing the preface for the Government-subsidised first edition of the *Petit Dictionnaire des écrivains* (1979), foregrounded equally aesthetics and the question of reward, arguing that when literature becomes an object of trade, writers should have their share of the profit, alongside all those others for whom books represent a living. And he listed publishers, printers, lay-out artists, typographers, binders, distributors, lorry-drivers, packers, secretaries, telephonists, postmen, booksellers, clerks, door-to-door salesmen, teachers, journalists on book pages and book programmes and the whole cultural bureaucracy, all competing with writers for their place in the sun.

Despite the seductions of the market, Québécois writing, especially since the sixties, is committed to developing a language that can represent the living community as a place of distinctive cultural and political energies. The problem is double: how to preserve the strengths of the 'wilderness tradition' while stripping out its negative aspects (the oppressive limits of the poor, inward-turned agrarian Catholic community) and how to imagine a future without the homogenising effects of Americanisation.

The first novel of Gabrielle Roy (1909–83), *Bonheur d'occasion* (Prix Fémina, 1945), set in a poor quarter of Montreal, indicted the misery of the new urban underclass while showing the danger of compensatory fantasies of a lost rural paradise. *La Petite Poule d'eau* (1950), in contrast, overplayed the slow charms of nostalgia-ridden landscape. The short stories of *La Route d'Altamont* (1966) marked a better way forward, exploring ways of establishing diverse and changing relationships with the past, in which respect and affection for what has been do not block the path of change. The little girl growing up in this text experiences very different relationships with her grandparents' and her parents' generation. The woman she becomes chooses her own way to reach the high places, finding a perspective that includes both the horizons of her childhood and routes out to fresh experience.

The poems brought together by Anne Hébert (b. 1916) in *Le Tombeau des rois* (1953; reissued and expanded as *Poèmes*, 1960) were personal and political negotiations with the patriarchal language of cultural tradition, viewed as a death-cult to be transcended. Hébert's novel *Les Fous de Bassan* (Prix Fémina, 1982) was not sanguine about the chances of success. The text confronted the repressive silence of collusion destroying a small inward-looking community at the sea's edge where two adolescent girls have vanished. It undertook the loosening of tongues, with a structure that allowed key actors to confess their own stories in turn, in distinctive voices ranging from the Biblical rhetoric of the tyrant preacher to the village idiot's babble. The past is finally shown plain, together with the truth about the crime. But chillingly, knowing the truth makes no difference. This society that has connived at the cruellest excesses of patriarchal power is linked to the web of tyranny that envelops the whole of Western culture. The girls' murderer goes free; 'civilisation' needs him, to fight in Vietnam.

Puncturing the myths of family and community has been the object of the satirical novels of Marie-Claude Blais (b. 1939). *Une saison dans la vie d'Emmanuel* (1965) followed the grim destiny of a peasant family, a swarming mass of louse-bitten children in the charge of a tyrannical grandmother, their lives dominated by a self-interested and oppressive Catholic Church. Ambition, heroism, desire, creativity, flicker and are crushed. A potential Rimbaud dies of consumption. An ironically-named Héloïse, tormented by repressed adolescent sexuality, turns into a perverted mystic, is thrown out of the haven of her convent and ends up in a brothel. The iconic Mother of Catholic tradition, guardian of the Family, is rewritten as grotesque parody: when grandmother dies, it is on the prostitute's earnings that the family survives.

City life has little better to offer. Jacques Godbout's comic novel *Salut Galarneau!* (1967) evoked the quiet desperation of the average man of Montreal, the Hamburger King, scraping a living within the limiting options of a world that looks for its models to the United States. The child of the 1950s, the King acknowledges, has few choices: be rich, get educated, kick the bucket, or write a book. The city plays of Michel Tremblay (b. 1942) were angrier visions of a culture devastated by its religious inheritance and locked into unresolvable antagonisms of class. *Les Belles Sœurs* (1968) offered a brilliantly-choreographed satire of the hostilities and resentments that spark in a community of working-class women when one of them wins a lottery, a clinical anatomy of the terrors that beset poor women (unwanted pregnancy, prostitution), and an indictment of the tacky materialism of their ambitions, hardly relieved by spots of human feeling.

L'Impromptu d'Outrement (1980) set in dramatic opposition the voices of four sisters in a divided middle-class family, the symbol of divided contemporary society. One, neurotically insistent on the 'correctness' of vocabulary and accent, maintains the standards of elitist bourgeois culture; another, who has broken the mould and embraced the workaday business world, cultivates a popular accent and dialect (the 'joual' of Montreal, which Tremblay and other writers such as Jacques Ferron, Jacques Renaud, Jacques Godbout and Victor-Lévy Beaulieu made in the 1960s and 1970s into an emblem of linguistic resistance; Marie-Claude Blais parodied its pretentions in *Un joualonais, sa joualonie*, 1973). The play ends with an off-stage burst of machine-gun fire, silencing an attempt by the sister-voices to recollect and reproduce an old childhood harmony.

The angry hopelessness of the fragmented, colonised subject of urban Quebec reappears in poetry as much as in prose in, for example, the poems of Gaston Miron (b. 1928) collected in *L'Homme rapaillé* (1970) and *Courtepointes* (1975). The sense of futility that bedevils the contemporary Québécois writer is captured in *Don Quichotte de la démanche* (1974), by Victor-Lévy Beaulieu (b. 1945). In this frenetic, self-reflexive and self-consciously postmodernist novel, the author–hero aspires to write a contemporary epic of that great city, Montreal, and that great nation, Quebec, but can only manage a parody. He invokes in despairing succession Dante, Cervantes, Joyce, and ends up drawing the analogy between Quebec and Joyce's Ireland: a culture still-born, or at best on its last legs, like its writers, only kept alive by artifice and the self-conscious cultivation of shock.

Outside Quebec, the Acadian novelist and dramatist Antonine Maillet (b. 1929) represents a more severely marginalised cultural and linguistic tradition. The stoical, wryly perceptive monologues of *La Sagouine* (1971), an old cleaning woman and former prostitute, written in a literary version of the language of poor Acadians, strike an original note. The novel *Pélagie-la-Charrette*, winner of the 1979 Prix Goncourt, tells a bigger story, that of the founding history of Acadia. This burlesque epic of the scattering and return of French families evicted from Nova Scotia by the British in 1755 foregrounds the history of white Canada, acknowledges the reshaping of the French cultural traditions by the force of English and American interventions, but puts in the foreground, with deceptively deprecating humour, the determination of Acadians to give their own account of themselves. In the crowded wagon driven by Pélagie, a uniquely exuberant incarnation of the Canadian matriarch, the voices jolting back home speak in Acadian rhythms and clichés, tell Acadian folktales and sing Acadian songs. But Maillet's account of her people's history is written not from a narrower but from a far larger perspective than that of many contemporary writers, one which is sensitive to all exclusions: class, gender, language and also race. The indigenous inhabitants of North America (Indian and Inuit) and people of African origin have a place in her story, sometimes travelling with the cart and sometimes helping it along. Black and Indian have no community of language, the text comments, French or otherwise, but they share a deeper community of oppression. Maillet's quiet pointers to these repressed but crucial elements in the dynamic of Canadian history foreshadowed a slow-growing but significant pressure for the reformulation of the dilemmas of the multicultural inheritance, which could provide the energies of the old wilderness with entirely new frontiers.

Sub-Saharan Africa, the Maghreb and the Caribbean

Writing in French in sub-Saharan Africa (the French- or Belgian-colonised territories of West or Equatorial Africa), the Maghreb and the Caribbean is marked, to different degrees, by the experience of slavery.[19] The first French merchants entered what is now Senegal in the sixteenth century, beginning the slave trade that broke up the great native Empires of Africa. The much-trumpeted liberation of the slaves by the Revolution (1794) was short-lived, reversed by Danton in 1802. Slavery was officially abolished in French territory in 1848 by a decree of the Second Republic but the decree was not properly implemented until the early twentieth century. The colonial intrusion, beginning with Algeria in the middle of the nineteenth century, was extended to sub-Saharan Africa from the 1880s onwards, in that ethos of harsh expansionism satirised by Octave Mirbeau in his novel *Le Jardin des supplices* (1899). The decolonisation process was complete by 1962, with the end of the Algerian War. The political relations of the various regions to France are now variously structured. The DOM-TOM (Départements et Territoires d'Outre-Mer) of the 1990s, still administered by France, include the Caribbean dependencies (Guadeloupe, Martinique, Guyana and La Réunion), which have the status of *départements*. Most of the sub-Saharan territories have been independent since the 1960s. In North Africa, Tunisia, Morocco and Algeria are nation-states.

For French sub-Saharan Africa, the moment of Independence which marks the beginning of a new cultural identity started with the Republic of Guinea, in October 1958, and reached most other areas by Summer 1960.[20] Significant regional and national differences began to appear in literature in the following decade. The creative writing which had emerged before then, in the 1920s and 1930s, was a product of the centralised primary and secondary system of education instituted in 1903. From 1927 onwards, the syllabus was the same as in metropolitan France, and all teaching was conducted in French. The brightest students competed for scholarships to institutions of higher education in France.

These were also the years of a European vogue for the culture of the whole of the African continent, which marked a considerable advance on the Eurocentred sentimental exotica of the preceding century produced by such writers as Pierre Loti (1850–1923).[21] The ethnologist Maurice Delafosse, writing 1912–27, was a pioneer of the scientific approach that presumes the right of a society to be heard on its own terms (*Haut-Sénégal–Niger*, 1912). In 1919, the poet Blaise Cendrars published his *Anthologie nègre*, a collection of transcriptions of oral folktales. As the century progressed, the work of other ethnologists and anthropologists such as Michel Leiris and Claude Lévi-Strauss strengthened the cultural bridge and sharpened the political sensitivities it carried. From André Gide's travels to North Africa in 1893–6 had come the liberating confrontation with his own sensuality that produced *Paludes* (1895) and *Les Nourritures terrestres* (1897). In Gide's *Voyage au Congo* (1927), a lengthy stay in Central Africa produced a different orientation: a forceful indictment of the colonial regime.

This perspective was reinforced by the arrival in Paris in the 1920s of the emergent American black consciousness expressed in the culture and politics of the Harlem Renaissance, eager both to rediscover its African roots and to establish its claim for civil rights in the country of its transplanting. In the early 1930s, that vogue encouraged and overshadowed the *Négritude* movement developing on the Left Bank through the efforts of French-speaking Caribbean and African writers, come to Paris for a university education.

Négritude first caught public attention through the single-number review *Légitime Défense*, banned by the French authorities, which was founded in 1932 by the Martinique poet Étienne Lero, a Marxist and Surrealist who looked for inspiration to the Black American revolutionary poets Langston Hughes and Claude McKay. This was succeeded by *L'Étudiant noir*, founded by the Martinique poet Aimé Césaire (b. 1913), the Senegalese Léopold Sédar Senghor (b. 1906) and the Guyanese Léon-Gontran Damas (1912–78), which celebrated the existence of a black cultural tradition different from the European and equal in quality. Robert Desnos wrote a preface for Damas's first volume of poems, *Pigments* (1937), which was banned in 1939. Césaire's militant *Cahier d'un retour au pays natal*, written in 1935 and published in Paris in 1939, had little impact until its author was taken up by André Breton in 1943. Breton secured its republication in volume form in 1947, with a preface by himself. Senghor too, a graver man of the radical establishment, who became first President of the Republic of Senegal, had to wait until after the war for his first published volume, *Chants d'ombre* (1945), which contained his great lyrical vision of Black Africa, 'Femme noire'. His reputation was secured in 1948 by his *Anthologie de la nouvelle poésie nègre et malgache de langue française*, with the introductory essay by Jean-Paul Sartre ('Orphée noir', rpt. *Situations*, vol. III).

The cultural centre of francophone Black African writing began to shift in the 1950s. The founding of the Universities of Dakar (1957) and Abidjan (1963) was a major step towards a new indigenous literature. Education was still conducted in French, but the Dakar Conference of 1963 produced a requirement for francophone African writers to appear on the mainstream syllabus. The 1960s saw the first break with the old themes of colonisation and *Négritude* and the attempt to return to the oral tradition and the interests of ordinary people. Publication was – and remains – a major problem, because of the cost of printing and the absence of a significant internal market. With a literacy rate of 20 per cent and a book costing 5–10 per cent of a worker's monthly wage, writers were driven to European publishing houses such as Seghers. Since 1971, the situation has been improved by the founding of the Nouvelles Éditions Africaines, whose funding comes 52 per cent from African government and the remainder from a mixture of African and European publishing houses: Présence Africaine, first established in 1949, Hachette, Nathan, Armand Colin, Le Seuil.[22]

The central challenge has been to find ways of marrying the written high culture learned from the colonisers with the popular oral tradition. Here a key link has been the folktale. The most important collections were made by Birago Diop (1906–89), whose *Les Contes d'Amadou Koumba* (1947) brought together the French Classical literary tradition and the Islamic inheritance, and Bernard Dadié (b. 1916) (*Légendes africaines*, 1953). Most recently, the folktale has provided a stimulus for experiments in contemporary drama, a genre which had developed a distinctively African content in its subject matter, epic accounts of legendary or historical exploits, or contemporary political satire, but less so in its form.

In the interview with Renée Larrier in 1990, published in the academic journal *Contemporary French Civilization*, the Togolais national theatre director Sénouvo Agbota Zinsou described the increasing numbers of places available for theatre in Togo: the three-thousand-seater Central Hall of the People's Assembly, community centres in nearly all towns, theatres belonging to religious orders, cultural centres in embassies, and the big stadiums. He noted that theatre was flourishing, both in its popular form as improvisation and religious drama, in Togolais, and in the form of plays in French such as his own, including song and dance, and built on the myths and symbols of the oral traditions (*La Tortue qui chante, Les Aventures de Yévi au pays des monstres*). Zinsou described himself as writing in French without any complexes because French was the language he learned at school, and his aim was to communicate on the international as well as the national scene. The spectacular element of his work made it accessible to non-French-speaking compatriots.

Better known internationally, however, is the work of the novelists. The European realist and naturalist tradition has been the preferred form for writers concerned to set out a political analysis of the oppressive nature of black–white relationships. *Batouala* (Prix Goncourt, 1921), by the Caribbean-born administrator René Maran (1887–1960), the first novel in French by a writer of African descent, charted the awakening of a villager to the abuses of the colonial system. Thirty years later, Ousmane Sembène (b. 1923) was confronted with the same exploitation in different historical circumstances. *Le Docker noir* (1956), set in Marseilles, explored the situation of the immigrant worker in the post-war boom (see also Bernard Dadié, *Un nègre à Paris*, 1959). Sembène provided his white readers with an unexpected twist. Diaw Falla, working on the Marseilles docks to feed himself and his family back in Africa, is the unacknowledged author of a prize-winning novel, passed off as her own by his white patron, a woman, of whose murder he stands accused. Sembène's *Les Bouts de bois de Dieu* (1960) presented the 1947 Dakar–Niger railway workers' strike and the changes it brought about not only in black–white relationships but within the black community, accelerating the revision of power relationships between old and young, and men and women, already under way with the advent of spreading literacy and machine-based work processes. *Le Dernier de l'Empire* (1981) confronted post-colonial corruption and personal power struggles among the new establishment. Film-maker as well as novelist, Sembène has developed an auto-referential dimension to his work, quoting and referring to himself and his own productions as part of the process of building a modern Senegalese culture out of indigenous resources. The best of the post-Independence novels is probably the ironic *Les Soleils des Indépendances* (1968) by Ahmadou Kourouma (b. 1927), a sympathetic but unsentimental analysis of feudal and socialist mindsets before and after Independence. In this grotesque comedy set between two funeral celebrations for dispossessed tribal princes, hierarchies are changed but corruptions and exploitations remain.

Writing from Algeria has engaged in a very different kind of dialogue with France, setting much more of the metropolitan agenda.[23] The power balance was tipped by a powerful alliance between left-wing intellectuals and political activists in the late 1950s and early 1960s. Frantz Fanon (1925–61), who was born in Martinique and studied medicine and psychiatry in France, published his first book, *Peau noire, masques blancs*, in 1952. Fanon's experiences in an Algerian hospital during the uprising generated the fiery *L'An V de la révolution algérienne* (1959) and *Les Damnés de la terre* (1961). The latter, a sharp analysis of the antagonism between Western and non-Western values, which charts the pitfalls of self-seeking nationalist as opposed to revolutionary consciousness, is centred on an uncompromising statement of the aims and function of revolutionary violence, the only means, said Fanon, for the masses to change their condition. A chapter on national culture (1959) traces the development of national culture in a colonised country and the relationship between the foreign-educated intellectual and the people, the move from collusion to liberation and the building of the new nation. Fanon defines national literature as a literature of combat; the 'native intellectual' finds his voice in the prisons. Sartre's Preface brought the debate back home, requiring European intellectuals to recognise the need for their own 'decolonisation' and to abdicate the rhetorics of Western humanist culture which had been, he said, alibis for European aggressions.

Writing from the white French mainland on the subject of Algeria is one story. Writing in Algeria has a different trajectory, in which the war with France is part of the long march of resistance to colonisation and the struggle to establish a separate political and cultural identity. From an early point in the twentieth century, various attempts were made by writers of European descent to establish an Algerian literary identity distinct from that of metropolitan France, but they generally failed to include in it the indigenous majority. Albert Camus's novel *L'Étranger* (1942), set in Algeria, did not explicitly address the particular problems of the territory. It raised general questions of the construction of subjectivity, presenting in Meursault, on trial for murder, the type of 'ordinary' unselfconscious man who is interpellated into self-consciousness (and, particularly, consciousness of himself as a political subject) by the apparatus of law. What the text did set up however, which was of particular relevance to Algeria, was a model of the hierarchy of subjects established by the discourses of institutional power in the colonial situation. Meursault is defined as the object of the rule of French law. The Arab he murders is not even an object; he is merely the instrument that makes it possible for Meursault and his judges to enter into the relationship that confirms their separate identities.

Very different explorations of indigenous experience began to emerge in the early 1950s. *Le Fils du pauvre* (1950), a novel by Mouloud Feraoun (1913–62), took the form of an autobiographical manuscript purportedly written in 1939 by a village schoolmaster. It traced the struggles of a peasant family against poverty and debt and their attempts to educate their son for the opportunities offered by the colonial system. Full weight was given to the representation of a culture independent of the coloniser, rooted in the extended family and in Islam. *Algérie*, the trilogy by Mohammed Dib (b. 1920) (*La Grande Maison*, 1952; *L'Incendie*, 1954; *Le Métier à tisser*, 1957), also focused on the specific traditions and values of life in the Algerian countryside. The war of liberation which began in November 1954 produced new versions of the struggle of indigenous consciousness towards self-definition, such as Feraoun's *Journal, 1955–62* and Dib's *Qui se souvient de la mer*, both published in 1962, the year in which independence was proclaimed, or the novels by Mouloud Mammeri (1917–89), *L'Opium et le bâton* (1965), and Assia Djebar (b. 1936), *Les Enfants du nouveau monde* (1962), *Les Alouettes naïves* (1967). Its implications, still working themselves out in Algerian politics, have nevertheless given place, since the early 1970s, to an emphasis on social satire, gender issues and international liberation. The work of Kateb Yacine (1929–89) spans the whole period of development, both in his novels (*Nedjma*, 1956) and his drama, first developed in Paris in collaboration with Jean-Michel Serreau in the 1950s. The trilogy of plays known as *Le Cercle des représailles* (published in 1959: *Le Cadavre encercleé, La Poudre d'intelligence, Les Ancêtres redoublent de férocité*) works out issues related to the war in a process of militant mythologising. *L'Homme aux sandales de caoutchouc* (1971) is a globally ranging celebration of anti-colonial struggle, focused on Vietnam. *Mohammed prends ta valise*, written in Algerian Arabic, toured migrant workers' hostels in France in early 1972.

The failure of the Revolution to keep its promises, especially to women, has been the subject of a growing body of writing produced by Algerian women in the 1970s and 1980s (including for example Aïcha Lemsine (b. 1942), *Ciel de porphyre*, 1978; Assia

Djebar, *Femmes d'Alger dans leur appartement*, 1980). The central place given to Islam in the new nation has led to the writing into civil law of the Islamic presumption of women's inferiority. Women's minority status was enshrined in the Family Code in June 1984. As in the now-abrogated laws of the West, women who are not dependent on their fathers are subject to the authority of a husband whom, by and large, they will not have chosen for themselves. It is harder for women to divorce their husbands than for husbands to divorce their wives. Since the youth uprising of October 1988, which reflected widespread popular discontent with the State and foregrounded demands for rights of organisation and free speech, women's pressure groups have proliferated. In response, Islamic women's groups have also begun to organise, not to call for equality but to approve the dispensations of the Family Code and call for more 'protection' for women, mothers and children (7 December 1989). Western influence is blamed for women's calls for equal rights.[24] There has been no welcome in Algeria itself for the drama of Fatima Gallaire (b. 1944), awarded the Prix Arletty in 1990, which explores the efforts by post-Revolutionary women to free themselves from the hierarchies of the traditional family, patriarchal in origin but, as Gallaire perceives, mediated by a colluding matriarchy. *Princesses, ou Ah! vous êtes venus . . . là où il y a quelques tombes* was staged in New York in 1988 and at the Théâtre Nanterre-Amandiers in Paris in 1991. *Les Co-épouses* appeared at the Théâtre du Lierre, Paris, in 1991.[25]

For Algerian women in particular, the French language is proving to be the site of a painful liberation. It represents for them the French school, the liberating power of secular education and release from everything symbolised by the veil. But it also represents alienation from the cultural forms of pre-school childhood. Assia Djebar's *L'Amour, la fantasia* (1985), a novel cross-cutting of autobiography and historical fiction, confronts French and Arabic written accounts of episodes in the history of Algeria from the French invasion in 1830, and weaves into them Djebar's own contemporary experience. French calls the Arab woman into autonomous existence, in a secular modern world, but it does so at the cost of another part of herself:

Tenter l'autobiographie par les seuls mots français, c'est, sous le lent scalpel de l'autopsie à vif, montrer plus que sa peau. Sa chair se désquame, semble-t-il, en lambeaux du parler de l'enfance qui ne s'écrit plus. Les blessures s'ouvrent, les veines pleurent, coule le sang de soi et des autres, qui n'a jamais séché.

[When you try to write autobiography solely in French, the slow scalpel of a living autopsy reveals more than just the skin. It's as though your flesh flakes off, shreds of that childhood language that can no longer be written. Wounds open and veins weep and there flows your own blood along with that of others, that has never dried.][26]

Writing from the French West Indies, with tighter political links to France, and also geographically and politically close to the United States, inscribes a degree of dependency which makes it harder to establish a separate identity. Maryse Condé (b. 1937) wrote in *Le Roman antillais* (1977), a text which makes frequent reference to the cultural and political theses of Frantz Fanon, of the problems of writers whose speech is split: who know that work in French will not be read locally by ordinary people, Creole-speakers, but will be restricted to a small intellectual elite. Caribbean writing in French is forced to address a Parisian audience constructed within other historical conditions and driven by radically different collective ambitions.

Initially, as Condé pointed out in *La Poésie antillaise* (1977), it was within poetry that a new sensibility began to be formulated, against the languid inward-looking creativity dismissed by Suzanne Césaire in the review *Tropiques* (founded 1941) as a lullaby literature of hammocks and hibiscus. In the first instance, the lyrical violence of the *Négritude* movement, and the work of Aimé Césaire and Damas, influenced such poets as Georges Desportes and Guy Tirolien. Later, the focus of personal anguish and political militancy became specifically Caribbean nationalism. *Antillanité*, invented and theorised by Édouard Glissant (b. 1928), emphasises the plural inheritance of the modern Caribbean community and looks to create a new future on the basis of a past better understood. With the exception of the first black Caribbean novel, *Questions de couleur: blanches et noirs* (Oruno-Lara, 1923), a fierce dialogue against racism which, Condé points out, anticipated Fanon by forty years, prose fiction has been slow to match the rebellious vitality of the poetry and its ability to create forms and symbols for the new politicised collective consciousness. The novels of the Martiniquais Joseph Zobel developed a style linked to popular language to address a central Caribbean theme, the cultivation of the land, in the sharp political perspective of the debate over land ownership. In *La Lézarde* (Prix Renaudot, 1958), Édouard Glissant's poetic prose worked a magical transformation on the changing river landscape, from its rural source, through sorry towns and down to the port, foregrounding the individual and social energies that inhabit it and constituting a dream version of a present filled with the possibilities of a revolutionary future. But it is chiefly since the 1970s that the novel has come into its own, especially with the emergence of women writers who have taken a distinctive grasp of their own and their country's history.

The collaboration of Simone Schwarz-Bart (b. 1938), a native of Guadeloupe, and her husband André, of Polish origin, which began in 1967 with *Un plat de porc aux bananes vertes*, a novel about a woman from Martinique dying in obscure poverty in Paris, produced a double-handed account of the exchanges of black and white in the colonial history of Guadeloupe.[27] André Schwarz-Bart's novel *La Mulâtresse Solitude* (1972) was a realist narrative of the fate of the enslaved blacks who were brought from Africa to Guadeloupe between 1760 and 1802. In the figure of Solitude, it explored the twilight existence of the mulatta woman, whose skin colour makes her marginal to both races (a frequent theme of Caribbean writing, as it is of many Afro-American texts). It presented a lyrical dream of black freedom, its highpoint the heroic and futile stand of the former slaves against the Republican soldiers on the heights of Matouba, in May 1802, and evoked the disempowering sense of non-being experienced by blacks caught in the web of white oppression.

In *Pluie et vent sur Télumée Miracle* (1972), Simone Schwarz-Bart completed the chronicle. Her version is written from inside, through subjects who speak within the textures of an everyday where the lyrical and the real – the magical and mysterious and the practicalities of survival – are indistinguishable, and in a language and tone that negotiate their own space between West Indian Creole and standard French. The text casts into dramatic metaphors the scarring effect of a history that has been internalised by its victims, and points to two agencies which, together, might end their disempowerment. Within the black community, by tradition, the onus falls on the women to bind the wounds of the community and to preserve its values. A subversive, subterranean chain of support connects the women, who uphold the dignity of family, village, and black culture, encircled by the white oppressors. But between the black community and the world outside must also stand mediators, outsiders from within. These are the writers who will speak honestly of the imposed limitations as well as the resistant strengths of the Caribbean inheritance.

A harder-edged version of the same theme is offered by another Guadeloupian, Maryse Condé herself, author of best-selling novels and short stories (*Ségou 1: Les Murailles de terre*, 1984; *Ségou 2: La Terre en miettes*, 1985; *Moi, Tituba, sorcière . . . Noire de Salem*, 1986; *Les Derniers Rois mages*, 1992).[28] Her writing faces up to the problems of inventing a new space that can hold both the seas and forests of the island and the towers of the mainland metropolis, Paris or New York, and take hold of the energies within them — make them all, in the rhetoric of the island inheritance, places to conjure with. Condé too recuperates the empowering events and symbolic figures of black Caribbean history and folklore, while confronting the collusions and betrayals of black by black which she shows seconding exploitation by whites. But hers is a harsher vision, that dispenses with the mediating lyrical perspective that tries to soothe the pain of an inheritance of deprivation, and has no time for rural nostalgia. *Heremakhonon* (1976) is a denunciation of any cult of Black African roots that can disregard the corruption and internal oppressions of post-Revolutionary black states.

* * *

Dividing her time between France, West Africa and the United States, Condé stands emblematically on the borders of a new kind of writing in French, one which will be at least as significant as any seen so far. In the dialogues now engaging between the texts and writers of the francophone world and metropolitan France, for all the antagonisms, corruptions and suspicion generated on and between both sides, there is still enough of past value and future potential to convey the hope that the human capacity to renew language, subjects and history is not yet exhausted.

Far more is at issue here than the mere games played by time with space of which Beckett's Watt spoke, recalled in the Introduction with which the present Guide began. For Frantz Fanon, Condé's political mentor, writing in *Les Damnés de la terre* to organise culture for action, the European game was concluded and something different must be found. For its own sake, for Europe, and for humanity, declared the prophetic voice, look now to the Third World for a fresh start.

Beyond the moment of Fanon's text, in the very different circumstances of the late twentieth century, the task takes on a different kind of urgency. The subject of the future hangs in the balance as models of oppression, familiar forms in all cultures, seek to draw it back into the same old stories. Best, perhaps, for the last word of this account to go to Assia Djebar who, in the concluding pages of *L'Amour, la fantasia*, spoke of her determination to find a unifying form: one that will bring the resistant subjects of her own country into the same dance as the resistant, as well as the oppressor, Europeans with whom its history is shared. On the common ground of writing, in French, Djebar takes her place alongside Pauline Rolland, one of the radicals of 1848 deported to Algeria after the coup d'état of 1852, and identifies the words and the images to engender a future liberation:

J'ai rencontré cette femme sur le terrain de son écriture: dans la glaise du glossaire français, elle et moi, nous voici aujourd'hui enlacées. Je relis ces lettres parties d'Algérie; une phrase me parvient, calligraphie d'amour, enroulant la vie de Pauline:

'En Kabylie, écrit Pauline, en juillet 1852, j'ai vu la femme bête de somme et l'odalisque de harem d'un riche. J'ai dormi près des premières sur la terre nue, et près des secondes dans l'or et la soie . . .'

Mots de tendresse d'une femme, en gésine de l'avenir: ils irradient là sous mes yeux et enfin me libèrent.

[I met this woman on the ground of her writing: now she and I embrace in the clay of French words. I read again those letters written from Algeria; one sentence reaches me, a calligraph of love, rolling up Pauline's life:

'In Kabylia', Pauline writes, 'in July 1852, I saw women who were beasts of burden, or odalisques in a rich man's harem. I slept by the first on the bare ground, and slept by the others in their gold and silk . . .'

Words of love from a woman, pregnant with the future: they radiate before my eyes and make me free at last.]

Notes

Notes to the Introduction

1. Samuel Beckett, *Watt* (Paris: Olympia Press, 1953).
2. For a survey of recent critical theory on who reads and what is reading, see Andrew Bennett (ed.), *Readers and Reading* (London and New York: Longman, 1995).
3. *En attendant Godot* (Paris: Éditions de Minuit, 1952); first performance in Paris, under the direction of Roger Blin, 1953.
4. Gayatri Chakravorty Spivak, 'Practical Politics of the Open End', *The Post-Colonial Critic: Interviews, Strategies, Dialogues* (New York and London: Routledge, 1990), p. 103. For a general account of the academic debate on the canon in the Anglo-Saxon world, see the essays in *Critical Inquiry*, vol. X (September 1983), which analyse the ideology of canon-formation in the English and American contexts to show how the canon emerges through specific institutions and practices with a well-defined class base. The dominant line is that which was established by Frank Kermode in 1979 ('Institutional Control of Interpretation', *Salmagundi*, vol. 43, Winter 1979, pp. 72–86). Kermode argued that canons are strategic constraints by which societies maintain their own interests. This is because the canon allows control over the texts a culture takes seriously and over the methods of interpretation that establish the meaning of 'serious'.
5. Pierre Bourdieu, *Ce que parler veut dire: l'économie des échanges linguistiques* (Paris: Fayard, 1982). See also J.-P. Sartre, *Qu'est-ce que la littérature? (Situations II)* (Paris: Gallimard, 1948); Roland Barthes, *Le Degré zéro de l'écriture* (Paris: Seuil, 1957); Renée Balibar, *Les Français fictifs. Le Rapport des styles littéraires au français national* (Paris: Hachette, 1974); and the overview by Jacques Dubois, *L'Institution de la littérature: introduction à une sociologie* (Brussels: Éditions LABOR, 1978).
6. See Pierre Bourdieu, *Homo Academicus* (1984), for some thought-provoking comments on how the processes of maintaining a canonical syllabus in French universities (writing guides, as opposed to conducting original research) can be seen as helping universities to remain instruments of cultural reproduction rather than places of subversion.
7. For accounts of the history of the book and of publishing in France see Antoine Compagnon and John Lough, *Writer and Public in France* (Oxford: Clarendon Press, 1978). Henri-Jean Martin has published with Roger Chartier and J.-P. Vivet an *Histoire de l'édition française*, 4 vols (Paris: Promodis, 1982–6) and is currently producing another multi-volume work on the same theme with Roger Chartier (*Histoire de l'édition française*, Paris: Fayard, 1989–present).
8. Régis Debray, *Le Pouvoir intellectuel en France* (Paris: Éditions Ramsay, 1979); trans. David Macey (London: Verso, 1981), with a useful Introduction by Francis Mulhern which gives the parallel discussion in the English context.

9. *Lire*, no. 86 (October 1982), pp. 23–32; reported in Jacques Breton, *Le Livre français contemporain*, 2 vols (Paris: Éditions SOLIN, Malakoff, 1988).

10. Lawrence Venuti (ed.), *Rethinking Translation: Discourse, Subjectivity, Ideology* (London and New York: Routledge, 1992), p. 9. The book includes useful references to major essays on translation by such writers as Walter Benjamin, Jacques Derrida and Paul de Man. For an extended account of one particular moment when the translation process made a significant intervention in history, see the studies and primary texts in Doris Y. Kadish and Françoise Massardier-Kenney (eds), *Translating Slavery: Gender and Race in Women's Writing, 1783–1823* (Kent, Ohio and London: Kent University State Press, 1994).

11. *The Politics of Tradition: Placing Women in French Literature*, Yale French Studies, No. 75 (Autumn 1988). Re-edited as Joan DeJean and Nancy K. Miller (eds), *Displacements: Women, Tradition, Literatures in French* (Baltimore and London: Johns Hopkins University Press, 1991).

12. Criticism in this area has been transformed by the work of Paul Zumthor (b. 1915); see for example his *Essai de poétique médiévale* (Paris: Éditions du Seuil, 1972); and *Langue, texte, énigme* (Paris: Éditions du Seuil, 1975). For useful general introductions covering all genres in the period, see D. Boutet and A. Strubel, *La Littérature française du moyen âge* (Paris: Presses Universitaires de France, 1978); Jean-Charles Payen, *La Littérature française*, Vol. I: *Le Moyen Âge* (Paris: Artaud, 1984); Lynette Muir, *Literature and Society in Medieval France* (London: Macmillan, 1985).

Notes to Chapter 1

1. Roger Price, *A Concise History of France* (Cambridge: Cambridge University Press, 1993), cites the sociologist Theda Skocpol's definition of the State as 'a set of administrative, policing and military organisations headed, and more or less well coordinated, by an executive authority' (p. 2) and offers a useful introductory perspective on power relations within a State.

2. See for historical and cultural background: Franco Simone, *Il rinascimento francese* (Turin: Società Editrice Internazionale, 1961), trans. H. Gaston Hall, *The French Renaissance* (London: Macmillan, 1969); Fernand Braudel, *Civilisation matérielle et capitalisme, XVe–XVIIIe siècle*, vol. I (Paris: Armand Colin, 1967); Pierre Vilar, *Oro y Moneda en la Historia (1450–1920)* (Barcelona: Ediciones Ariel, 1969), trans. Judith White, *A History of Gold and Money* (London: New Left Books, 1976); Robert Mandrou, *Des humanistes aux hommes de science: XVIe et XVIIe siècles* (Paris: Éditions du Seuil, 1973); Perry Anderson, *Lineages of the Absolutist State* (London: New Left Books, 1974); R. J. Knecht, *Renaissance Warrior and Patron: The Reign of Francis I*, rev. edn (Cambridge: Cambridge University Press, 1994); Natalie Zemon Davis, *Society and Culture in Early Modern France* (Cambridge: Polity Press, 1987). Single-volume histories: A. J. Krailsheimer, *The Continental Renaissance (1500–1600)*

(Harmondsworth: Penguin, 1971); I. D. McFarlane. *A Literary History of France. Vol. II: Renaissance France 1470–1589* (London: E. Benn, 1974).

3. See Frances A. Yates, *The French Academies of the Sixteenth Century* (London: The Warburg Institute, 1947); Anthony Levi (ed.), *Humanism in France in the late Middle Ages and the Early Renaissance* (Manchester: Manchester University Press, 1970).

4. See Elizabeth L. Eisenstein, *The Printing Revolution in Early Modern Europe* (Cambridge: Cambridge University Press, new edn 1993); also L. Febvre and H. J. Martin, *L'Apparition du livre* (Paris: Albin Michel, 1958), trans. David Gerard, *The Coming of the Book: The Impact of Printing 1450–1800* (London: New Left Books, 1976).

5. Mikhail Bakhtin, *Rabelais and his World*, trans. Hélène Iswolsky (Cambridge, Mass. and London: M.I.T. Press, 1968), pp. 470–1 (first published Moscow, 1965). See, on Rabelais, M. A. Screech, *The Rabelaisian Marriage: Aspects of Rabelais's Religion, Ethics and Comic Philosophy* (London: Arnold, 1958); A. J. Krailsheimer, *Rabelais* (Bruges: de Brouwer, 1967); Lucien Febvre, *Le Problème de l'incroyance au XVIe siècle: la religion de Rabelais* (2nd edn; Paris: Albin Michel, 1968); Dorothy Gabe Coleman, *Rabelais: A Critical Study in Prose Fiction* (Cambridge: Cambridge University Press, 1971); M. A. Screech, *Rabelais* (London: Duckworth, 1979); Terence Cave, *The Cornucopian Text: Problems of Writing in the French Renaissance* (Oxford: Clarendon Press, 1979); Carol Clark, *The Vulgar Rabelais* (Glasgow: Pressgang, 1983).

6. See, on the Pléiade, Henri Chamard, *Histoire de la Pléiade*, 4 vols (Paris: Didier, 1939–40); Grahame Castor, *Pléiade Poetics: A Study in Sixteenth-Century Thought and Terminology* (Cambridge: Cambridge University Press, 1964). On du Bellay, see Dorothy Gabe Coleman, *The Chaste Muse, a Study of Joachim du Bellay's Poetry* (Leiden: Brill, 1980).

7. See Isidore Silver, *Ronsard and the Hellenic Renaissance in France. I: Ronsard and the Greek Epic* (St Louis: Washington University, 1961); *Ronsard and the Hellenic Renaissance in France. II; Ronsard and the Grecian Lyre, Part 1* (Geneva: Droz, 1981); E. Armstrong, *Ronsard and the Age of Gold* (Cambridge: Cambridge University Press, 1968); Terence Cave (ed.), *Ronsard the Poet* (London: Methuen, 1973); Margaret M. McGowan, *Ideal Forms in the Age of Ronsard* (Berkeley, Los Angeles and London: University of California Press, 1985).

8. See, on Marot, C. A. Mayer, *Clément Marot* (Paris: Nizet, 1972). For sixteenth-century poetry see Henri Weber, *La Création poétique au XVIe siècle en France de Maurice Scève à Agrippa d'Aubigné* (Paris: Nizet, 1956).

9. On the influence of Ficino, see Yates, *The French Academies*, and A. H. T. Levi, 'Rabelais and Ficino', in James A. Coleman and Christine Scollen-Jimack (eds), *Rabelais in Glasgow* (Glasgow: Coleman and Scollen-Jimack, 1984), pp. 71–85.

10. See I. D. McFarlane (ed.), *The 'Délie' of Maurice Scève* (Cambridge: Cambridge University Press, 1966); Dorothy Gabe Coleman, *Maurice Scève, Poet of Love: Tradition and Originality* (Cambridge: Cambridge University Press, 1975).

11. See Dorothy O'Connor, *Louise Labé, sa vie et son œuvre* (Paris: Presses Françaises, 1926); Keith Cameron, *Louise Labé – Renaissance Poet and*

Feminist (New York and Oxford: Berg Women's Series, 1990). On women writers in Renaissance Europe see Katharina M. Wilson (ed.), *Women Writers of the Renaissance and Reformation* (Athens and London: University of Georgia Press, 1987); Natalie Zemon Davis and Arlette Farge (eds), *Histoire des femmes en occident*, vol. 3: *XVIe–XVIIIe siècles* (Paris: Plon, 1991).

12. See Pierre Jourda, *Marguerite d'Angoulême, Duchesse d'Alençon, Reine de Navarre, 1492–1549*, 2 vols (Paris: Champion, 1930); Jules Gelernt, *World of Many Loves. The 'Heptaméron' of Marguerite de Navarre* (Chapel Hill: University of North Carolina Press, 1966); Lucien Febvre, *Autour de l'Heptaméron: amour sacré, amour profane* (Paris: Gallimard, 1971).

13. Febvre, *Autour de l'Heptaméron*, gives a rich account of the war of ideas within the Reform. See also Mandrou, *Des humanistes aux hommes de science*.

14. On sixteenth-century drama see Timothy J. Reiss, *Toward Dramatic Illusion: Theatrical Technique and Meaning from Hardy to 'Horace'* (New Haven: Yale University Press, 1971); Geoffrey Brereton, *French Tragic Drama in the Sixteenth and Seventeenth Centuries* (London: Methuen, 1973); Donald Stone Jr, *French Humanist Tragedy: A Reassessment* (Manchester: Manchester University Press, 1974).

15. See Richard L. Regosin, *The Poetry of Inspiration. Agrippa d'Aubigné's 'Les Tragiques'* (Chapel Hill: University of North Carolina Press, 1970).

16. See Donald Frame, *Montaigne, a Biography* (London: Hamish Hamilton, 1965); *Montaigne's 'Essais': A Study* (Englewood Cliffs, New Jersey: Prentice-Hall, 1969); R. A. Sayce, *The Essays of Montaigne: A Critical Exploration* (London: Weidenfeld and Nicolson, 1972).

Notes to Chapter 2

1. Boris Porshnev, 'Popular Uprisings in France before the Fronde' (Moscow, 1948), rpt. in P. J. Coveney (ed. and intro.), *France in Crisis (1620–75)* (London: Macmillan, 1977). For historical background see also Richard Bonney, *L'Absolutisme* (Paris: Presses Universitaires de France, 1989).

2. H.-J. Martin, *Livre, pouvoirs et société à Paris au XVIIe siècle (1598–1701)*, 2 vols (Geneva: Librairie Droz, 1962).

3. On preciosity see Georges Mongrédien (ed.), *Les Précieux et les précieuses* (Paris: Mercure de France, 1939); René Bray, *Préciosité et les précieux, de Thibaut de Champagne à Jean Giraudoux* (Paris: Albin Michel, 1948); Roger Lathuillière, *La Préciosité* (Geneva: Droz, 1966).

4. See, on seventeenth-century theatre, Henry Carrington Lancaster, *A Study of French Dramatic Literature in the Seventeenth Century*, 9 vols (Baltimore: Johns Hopkins Press, 1929–42); John Lough, *Paris Theatre Audiences in the Seventeenth and Eighteenth Centuries* (Oxford: Oxford University Press, 1957); Georges Mongrédien, *La Vie quotidienne des comédiens au temps de Molière* (Paris: Hachette, 1966); Henry Phillips, *The Theatre and its Critics in Seventeenth-Century France* (Oxford: Oxford University Press, 1980).

5. For an account of developments in seventeenth- and eighteenth-century poetry, see Odette de Mourgues, *Metaphysical, Baroque and Précieux Poetry* (Oxford: Clarendon Press, 1953); Imbrie Buffum, *Studies in the Baroque from Montaigne to Rotrou* (New Haven: Yale University Press, 1957); Robert Sabatier, *Histoire de la poésie française*, vol. II: *XVIIe siécle*, vol. III: *XVIIIe siècle* (Paris: Albin Michel, 1975).

6. The best traditional account of the theories of French classicism is René Bray, *La Formation de la doctrine classique en France* (Lausanne: Payot, 1931). For discussion of its terms see Pierre Magnard, *Nature et Histoire dans l'apologétique de Pascal* (Paris: Les Belles Lettres, 1975). The problematics of the term 'classicism' are set out in David Lee Rubin (ed.), *Continuum*, I and II (New York: AMS Press, 1990). See also C. J. Gossip, *Introduction to French Classical Tragedy* (London: Macmillan, 1981).

7. See Octave Nadal, *Le Sentiment de l'amour dans l'œuvre de Pierre Corneille* (Paris: Gallimard, 1948); Serge Doubrovsky, *Corneille et la dialectique du héros* (Paris: Gallimard, 1963); Jacques Scherer, *Le Théâtre de Corneille* (Paris: Nizet, 1984); Anne Ubersfeld, *Le Théâtre et la cité, de Corneille à Kantor* (Brussels: Association Internationale de la Sémiologie du Spectacle, 1991); David Clarke, *Pierre Corneille: Poetics and Political Drama under Louis XIII* (Cambridge: Cambridge University Press, 1992).

8. See Lucien Goldmann, *Racine* (Paris: L'Arche Éditeur, 1956); Peter France, *Racine's Rhetoric* (Oxford: Clarendon Press, 1965); Odette de Mourgues, *Racine, or The Triumph of Relevance* (Cambridge: Cambridge University Press, 1967); Alfred Bonzon, *La Nouvelle Critique et Racine* (Paris: Nizet, 1970); David Maskell, *Racine: A Theatrical Reading* (Oxford: Clarendon Press, 1991); Mitchell Greenberg, *Subjectivity and Subjugation in Seventeenth-Century Drama and Prose: The Family Romance of French Classicism* (Cambridge: Cambridge University Press, 1992); Michael Hawcroft, *Word as Action: Racine, Rhetoric and Theatrical Language* (Oxford: Clarendon Press, 1992); Richard Parish, *Racine: The Limits of Tragedy* (Paris/Seattle/Tubingen: Biblio 17, Papers on Seventeenth-Century French Literature, 1993).

9. See, on comedy, Geoffrey Brereton, *French Comic Drama from the Sixteenth to the Eighteenth Century* (London: Methuen, 1977). See, on Molière, Lionel Gossman, *Men and Masks: A Study of Molière* (Baltimore: Johns Hopkins Press, 1963); J. Guicharnaud, *Molière, une aventure théâtrale* (Paris: Gallimard, 1963); Charles Mazouer, *Molière et ses comédies-ballets* (Paris: Klincksieck, 1993).

10. See, on the links of maxim and novel, Geoffrey Bennington, *Sententiousness and the Novel: Laying Down the Law in Eighteenth-Century Fiction* (Cambridge: Cambridge University Press, 1985).

11. See Wendy Gibson, *Women in Seventeenth-Century France* (London: Macmillan, 1989). For an account of women's contribution to developing the genre of the novel see Joan DeJean, *Tender Geographies: Women and the Origins of the Novel in France* (New York and Oxford: Columbia University Press, 1991).

12. See, on the moralists, A. J. Krailsheimer, *Studies in Self-Interest from Descartes to La Bruyère* (Oxford: Clarendon Press, 1962); Maurice

Magendie, *La Politesse mondaine et les théories de l'honnêteté en France de 1600–1660* (Paris, 1963).

13. See Frederick Copleston, *A History of Philosophy*, vol. 4: *Descartes to Leibniz* (London: Burns & Oates, 1958); Peter France, *Rhetoric and Truth in France from Descartes to Diderot* (Oxford: Clarendon Press, 1972); Jean-François Revel, *Descartes inutile et incertain* (Paris: Stock, 1976).

14. See Jean Mesnard, *Pascal, l'homme et l'œuvre* (Paris: Hatier, 1951); Lucien Goldmann, *Le Dieu caché: étude sur la vision tragique dans les 'Pensées' de Pascal et dans le théâtre de Racine* (Paris: Gallimard, 1955); J. H. Broome, *Pascal* (London: Edward Arnold, 1965); Patricia Topliss, *The Rhetoric of Pascal* (Leicester: Leicester University Press, 1966); Nicholas Hammond, *Playing with Truth: Language and the Human Condition in Pascal's 'Pensées'* (Oxford: Clarendon Press, 1994).

15. See Odette de Mourgues, *Two French Moralists: La Rochefoucauld, La Bruyère* (Cambridge: Cambridge University Press, 1978); Jean Lafond, *La Rochefoucauld, augustinisme et littérature* (Paris: Éditions Klincksieck, 2nd rev edn, 1980); Vivien Thweatt, *La Rochefoucauld and the Seventeenth-century Concept of the Self* (Geneva: Droz, 1980).

16. See Marcel Gutwirth, *Un merveilleux sans éclat: La Fontaine et la poésie exilée* (Geneva: Droz, 1987).

17. See de Mourgues, *Two French Moralists*; Michael S. Koppisch, *The Dissolution of Character: Changing Perspectives in La Bruyère's 'Caractères'* (Lexington: French Forum, 1981).

18. See Nancy K. Miller, 'Plots and Plausibilities in Women's Fiction', in *Subject to Change: Reading Feminist Writing* (New York: Columbia University Press, 1988); also Barbara Worshivky, *'La Princesse de Clèves', the Tension of Elegance* (The Hague: Mouton, 1973).

Notes to Chapter 3

1. For intertextuality see Judith Still and Michael Worton, *Textuality and Sexuality: Reading Theories and Practices* (Manchester: Manchester University Press, 1993), especially the Introduction.

2. Theodor Adorno and Max Horkheimer, *Dialektik der Aufklärung* (New York: Social Studies Association, 1944), trans. John Cumming, *Dialectic of Enlightenment* (London: Verso Editions, 1979); Jean-François Lyotard, *La Condition postmoderne, rapport sur le savoir* (Paris: Éditions de Minuit, 1979); Jürgen Habermas, *Der philosophische Diskurs der Moderne: Zwölf Vorlesungen* (Frankfurt-am-Main: Suhrkamp Verlag, 1985), trans. Frederick Lawrence, *The Philosophical Discourse of Modernity* (Oxford: Polity Press, 1987). For a discussion of the relationship of Foucault and Habermas to the Enlightenment see Lois McNay, *Foucault and Feminism: Power, Gender and the Self* (Cambridge: Polity Press, 1992).

3. For overviews of Enlightenment thought see Ernst Cassirer, *Die Philosophie der Aufklärung* (Tübingen: Mohr, 1932), trans. Fritz C. A. Koelln and James P. Pettegrove, *The Philosophy of the Enlightenment* (Princeton: Princeton University Press, 1951); Paul Hazard, *La Crise de la conscience européenne* (Paris: Boivin, 1935); *La Pensée européenne au XVIIIe siècle: de Montesquieu à Lessing* (Paris: Boivin, 1946); Jacques Roger, *Les Sciences de*

la vie dans la pensée française du XVIIIe siècle (Paris: Armand Colin, 1963); Peter Gay, *The Enlightenment: An Interpretation*, 2 vols (London: Wildwood House, 1967, 1973).

4. On Voltaire see Theodore Besterman, *Voltaire* (Harlow: Longman, 1969); René Pomeau, *La Religion de Voltaire* (Paris: Nizet, rev. edn, 1969); Ira O. Wade, *The Intellectual Development of Voltaire* (Princeton, New Jersey: Princeton University Press, 1969).

5. See Ira O. Wade, *The Clandestine Organization and Diffusion of Philosophic Ideas in France from 1700 to 1750* (Princeton: Princeton University Press, and London: Oxford University Press, 1938); Robert Darnton, *The Literary Underground of the Old Régime* (Cambridge, Mass.: Harvard University Press, 1982), *Édition et sédition: l'univers de la littérature clandestine au XVIIIe siècle* (Paris: Gallimard, 1991).

6. See Robert Shackleton, *Montesquieu, a Critical Biography* (Oxford: Oxford University Press, 1961); Jean Starobinski, *Montesquieu par lui-même* (Paris: Éditions du Seuil, 1963).

7. See Arthur M. Wilson, *Diderot* (New York: Oxford University Press, 1972); Peter France, *Diderot* (Oxford: Oxford University Press, 1983).

8. Galvano Della Volpe, *Rousseau e Marx e altri saggi di critica meterialistica* (Rome: Editori Riuniti, 1956), trans. John Fraser, *Rousseau and Marx* (London: Lawrence and Wishart, 1978). See also C. E. Vaughan, *The Political Writings of Rousseau* (Cambridge: Cambridge University Press, 1915); Ronald Grimsley, *Rousseau and the Religious Quest* (Oxford: Clarendon Press, 1968); Robert Derathé, *Jean-Jacques Rousseau et la science politique de son temps* (Paris: J. Vrin, 2nd edn 1970); Jean Starobinski, *Jean-Jacques Rousseau: la transparence et l'obstacle* (Paris: Gallimard, 1971); Maurice Cranston, *Jean-Jacques: The Early Life and Work of Jean-Jacques Rousseau* (London: Allen Lane, 1983), and *The Noble Savage: Jean-Jacques Rousseau 1754–62* (Chicago: University of Chicago Press, 1991).

9. See Jean Ehrard, *L'Idée de nature en France dans la première moitié du XVIIIe siècle* (Geneva: Slatkine, 1981).

10. See C. B. Macpherson, *The Political Theory of Possessive Individualism: Hobbes to Locke* (Oxford: Clarendon Press, 1962).

11. See Hans-Jürgen Lüsebrink and Manfred Tietz (eds), *Lectures de Raynal. 'L'Histoire des deux Indes' en Europe et en Amérique au XVIIIe siècle* (Oxford: The Voltaire Foundation, 1991).

12. For a short account of the development of economic theory in the period, see the chapter ' "Moeurs", "Lois" and Economics', in Ira O. Wade, *The Structure and Form of the French Enlightenment*, vol. I (Princeton, N.J.: Princeton University Press, 1977), esp. pp. 465–515.

13. See Robert Darnton, *The Business of Enlightenment: A Publishing History of the Encyclopédie 1755–1800* (Cambridge, Mass.: The Belknap Press of Harvard University Press, 1979); 'Philosophers Trim the Tree of Knowledge: The Epistemological Strategy of the *Encyclopédie*', in *The Great Cat Massacre* (USA: Basic Books, and Great Britain: Allen Lane, 1984; rpt. Harmondsworth: Penguin, 1985). See also John Lough, *The 'Encyclopédie'* (Harlow: Longman, 1971).

14. See, on theatre, Henri Lagrave, *Le Théâtre et le public à Paris de 1715–1750* (Paris: Klincksieck, 1972); Martine de Rougement, *La Vie*

théâtrale en France au XVIIIe siècle (Paris and Geneva: Champion/ Slatkine, 1988); Pierre Larthomas, *Le Théâtre en France au XVIIIe siècle*, 2nd edn (Paris: Presses Universitaires de France, 1989). On Marivaux see Henri Coulet and Michel Gilot, *Marivaux, un humanisme expérimental* (Paris: Larousse, 1973); on Beaumarchais, René Pomeau, *Beaumarchais, ou la bizarre destinée* (Paris: Presses Universitaires de France, 1987).

15. John Lough, *Writer and Public in France* (Oxford: Clarendon Press, 1978).

16. See Angus Martin (ed. and intro.), *Anthologie du conte en France 1750–99: philosophes et cœurs sensibles* (Paris: UGE, 1981).

17. Robert Darnton, 'Readers Respond to Rousseau: The Fabrication of Romantic Sensitivity', in *The Great Cat Massacre* (USA: Basic Books, and Great Britain: Allen Lane, 1984; rpt. Harmondsworth: Penguin, 1985).

18. See Georges May, *Le Dilemme du roman au XVIIIe siècle* (New Haven: Yale University Press/Paris: Presses Universitaires de France, 1963). See, for the development of the French novel, Henri Coulet, *Le Roman jusqu'à la Révolution*, 2 vols (Paris: Armand Colin, 1967–8). See also Peter Brooks, *The Novel of Worldliness: Crébillon, Marivaux, Laclos, Stendhal* (Princeton, New Jersey: Princeton University Press, 1969); Vivienne Mylne, *The Eighteenth-Century French Novel: Techniques of Illusion* (Cambridge: Cambridge University Press, 2nd edn, 1981). On individual authors see Jean Sgard, *Prévost romancier* (Paris: Librairie José Corti, 1989); A. and Y. Delmas, *À la recherche des 'Liaisons dangereuses'* (Paris: Mercure de France, 1964); Laurent Versini, *Laclos et la tradition: essai sur les sources et la technique des 'Liaisons dangereuses'* (Paris: Klincksieck, 1968).

19. William Ray, *Story and History: Narrative Authority and Social Identity in the Eighteenth-Century French and English Novel* (Cambridge, Mass. and Oxford: Basil Blackwell, 1990), p. 9.

20. See, on the situation of women in the eighteenth century, Samia I. Spencer (ed.), *French Women and the Age of Enlightenment* (Bloomington and Indianapolis: Indiana University Press, 1984); Jennifer Birkett, ' "A Mere Matter of Business": Marriage, Divorce and the French Revolution', in Elizabeth M. Craik (ed.), *Marriage and Property* (Aberdeen: Aberdeen University Press, 1984); Dorinda Outram, *The Body and the French Revolution: Sex, Class and Political Culture* (New Haven and London: Yale University Press, 1989); Lynn Hunt (ed.), *Eroticism and the Body Politic* (Baltimore: Johns Hopkins University Press, 1991). See, on women writers, Joan Hinde Stewart, *Gynographs: French Novels by Women of the Late Eighteenth Century* (Lincoln and London: University of Nebraska Press, 1993).

21. On the French–English connection see F. C. Green, *Minuet: A Critical Survey of French and English Literary Ideas in the Eighteenth Century* (London: Dent, 1935); H. W. Streeter, *The Eighteenth-Century English Novel in French Translation: A Bibliographical Study* (New York: Publications of the Institute of French Studies, 1936).

22. Béatrice Didier, *Écrire la Révolution: 1789–99* (Paris: Presses Universitaires de France, 1989). On the 'domestication' of the French Revolution, see Jack Hayward, *After the French Revolution: Six Critics of*

Democracy and Nationalism (Hemel Hempstead: Harvester Wheatsheaf, 1992), which includes studies of Joseph de Maistre, Saint-Simon, Constant, Tocqueville, Proudhon and Blanqui.

23. See, on the press and publishing, Robert Darnton and Daniel Roche (eds), *Revolution in Print: The Press in France 1775–1800* (Berkeley and Los Angeles: University of California Press, 1989); Lough, *Writer and Public in France*; Jeremy D. Popkin, *Revolutionary News: The Press in France (1789–99)* (Durham, USA: Duke University Press, 1990).

24. See, on the orators, Didier, *Écrire la Révolution*; essays by Philippe Roger, Peter France and Eric Walter in John Renwick (ed.), *Language and Rhetoric of the Revolution* (Edinburgh: Edinburgh University Press, 1990).

25. See Graham Rodmell, *French Drama of the Revolutionary Years* (London and New York: Routledge, 1990).

26. See Adorno and Horkheimer, *Dialektik der Aufklärung*; Roland Barthes, *Sade, Fourier, Loyola* (Paris: Éditions du Seuil, 1971); Gilbert Lély, *Vie du marquis de Sade* (Paris: Mercure de France, rev. edn, 1989); Lucienne Frappier-Mazur, *Sade et l'écriture de l'orgie* (Paris: Nathan, 1991). See also the prefatory essays by various scholars in D.-A.-F. de Sade, *Œuvres complètes*, vol. I, ed. Michel Delon (Paris: Gallimard, 1990).

27. See Emmanuel Le Roy Ladurie, 'Du social au mental: une analyse ethnographique', in *Histoire de la France rurale*, eds Georges Duby and Armand Wallon, vol. 2 (Paris: Seuil, 1975); Mark Poster, *The Utopian Thought of Restif de la Bretonne* (New York: New York University Press, 1971); Pierre Testud, *Restif de la Bretonne et la création littéraire* (Geneva and Paris: Librairie Droz, 1977).

28. Published in Élisabeth Badinter (ed.), *Condorcet, Prudhomme, Goyomar . . . Paroles d'hommes (1790–93)* (Paris: POL éditeur, 1989), pp. 174–5. On women in the Revolution see Paule-Marie Duhet (ed.), *Cahiers de doléances des femmes et autres textes* (Paris: des femmes, 1981); *Les Femmes dans la Révolution française* (Paris: EDHIS, 1982); Élisabeth Badinter (ed.), *A. L. Thomas, Diderot, Madame d'Épinay . . . Qu'est-ce qu'une femme?* (Paris: POL éditeur, 1989); Élisabeth Roudinesco, *Madness and Revolution: The Lives and Legends of Théroigne de Méricourt* (Paris: Éditions du Seuil, 1989); Olwen H. Hufton, *Women and the Limits of Citizenship in the French Revolution* (Toronto: University of Toronto Press, 1992).

29. See Gabriel de Broglie, *Madame de Genlis* (Paris: Librairie Académique Perrin, 1985).

30. See Simone Balayé, *Madame de Staël: lumières et liberté* (Paris: Éditions Klincksieck, 1979); Marie-Claire Vallois, *Fictions féminines: Mme de Staël et les voix de la Sibylle* (Saratoga, USA: ANMA Libri, 1987); Madelyn Gutwirth, Avriel Goldberger, and Karyna Szmurlo (eds), *Germaine de Staël: Crossing the Borders* (New Brunswick, New Jersey: Rutgers University Press, 1991); Simone Balayé, *Madame de Staël – écrire, lutter, vivre* (Geneva: Droz, 1994).

Notes to Chapter 4

1. V. Hugo, *William Shakespeare, in Œuvres complètes*, ed. Jean Massin, 18 vols (Paris: Le Club Français du Livre, 1967–9), vol. XII, pp. 306–7. The

title of Part II, 'The Bourgeois Century', is taken from Roger Magraw, *France 1815–1914: The Bourgeois Century* (London: Fontana Paperbacks, 1983).

2. See Hayden White, *Metahistory: The Historical Imagination in Nineteenth-Century Europe* (Baltimore and London: Johns Hopkins University Press, 1973); Stephen Bann, *The Clothing of Clio: A Study of the Representation of History in Nineteenth-Century Britain and France* (Cambridge: Cambridge University Press, 1984); Ceri Crossley, *French Historians and Romanticism* (London and New York: Routledge, 1993).

3. Alfred de Vigny, *Le Journal d'un poète* in *Œuvres complètes*, ed. F. Baldensperger, 2 vols (Paris: Gallimard, Bibliothèque de la Pléiade, 1960), vol. II; Stendhal, *Œuvres complètes*, ed. Victor del Litto, 50 vols (Geneva: Cercle du Bibliophile, 1970), vol. XXVII.

4. See D. G. Charlton (ed.), *The French Romantics*, 2 vols (Cambridge: Cambridge University Press, 1984), vol. I, p. 187.

5. See Henri-Jean Martin and Roger Chartier (eds), *Histoire de l'édition française*, 4 vols (Paris: Promodis, 1982–6), vol. II; James Smith Allen, *Popular French Romanticism: Authors, Readers and Books in the Nineteenth Century* (Syracuse: Syracuse University Press, 1981) and *In the Public Eye. A History of Reading in Modern France* (Princeton: Princeton University Press, 1991).

6. See François Furet and Jacques Ozouf, *Lire et écrire: l'alphabétisation des Français de Calvin à Jules Ferry*, 2 vols (Paris: Éditions de Minuit, 1977).

7. See Françoise Parent-Lardeur, *Les Cabinets de lecture. La lecture publique à Paris sous la Restauration* (Paris: Payot, 1982).

8. See Michael Moriarty, 'Structures of Cultural Production in Nineteenth-Century France', in Peter Collier and Robert Lethbridge (eds), *Artistic Relations. Literature and the Visual Arts in Nineteenth-Century France* (New Haven and London: Yale University Press, 1994), pp. 15–29 (p. 22).

9. See Lise Queffélec, *Le Roman-feuilleton français au XIXe siècle* (Paris: Presses Universitaires de France, 1989).

10. See F. W. J. Hemmings, *The King of Romance: A Portrait of Alexandre Dumas* (London: Hamish Hamilton, 1979).

11. See Jean-Louis Bory, *Eugène Sue: le roi du roman populaire* (Paris: Hachette, 1962); *Europe*, vol. LX, pp. 643–4 (November–December 1982); Umberto Eco, *The Role of the Reader. Explorations in the Semiotics of Texts* (Bloomington and London: Indiana University Press, 1979), pp. 125–43.

12. See Walter Benjamin, *Charles Baudelaire: A Lyric Poet in the Era of High Capitalism* (London: New Left Books, 1973); and *Paris, capitale du XIXe siècle* (Paris: Éditions du Cerf, 1989); Susan Buck-Morss, *The Dialectics of Seeing: Walter Benjamin and the Arcades Project* (Cambridge, Mass. and London: MIT Press, 1989); Christopher Prendergast, *Paris and the Nineteenth Century* (Oxford: Blackwell, 1992); T. J. Clark, *The Painting of Modern Life. Paris in the Art of Manet and his Followers* (London: Thames and Hudson, 1985); Roger Bellet (ed.), *Paris au XIXe siècle. Aspects d'un mythe littéraire* (Lyons: Presses Universitaires de Lyon, 1984).

13. See Louis Chevalier, *La Formation de la population parisienne au XIXe siècle* (Paris: Plon, 1950) and *Classes laborieuses et classes dangereuses à*

Paris, pendant la première moitié du XIXe siècle (Paris: Plon, 1958); Jeanne Gaillard, *Paris, la ville 1852–1870* (Paris: Champion, 1977).

14. On Romanticism, see Charlton (ed.), *The French Romantics*. This work also contains full bibliographical information on every aspect of the Romantic movement. For an excellent short introduction published since Charlton's work, see Stephen Bann, 'Romanticism in France', in Roy Porter and Mikulaš Teich, *Romanticism in National Context* (Cambridge: Cambridge University Press, 1988), pp. 240–59.

15. See Simone Balayé, *Madame de Staël: lumières et liberté* (Paris: Klincksieck, 1979); Ghislain de Diesbach, *Madame de Staël* (Paris: Perrin, 1983).

16. See Pierre Barbéris, *À la recherche d'une écriture: Chateaubriand* (Paris: Mame, 1974); Pierre Clarac, *À la recherche de Chateaubriand* (Paris: Nizet, 1975); Jean-Marie Roulin, *Chateaubriand, l'exil et la gloire* (Paris: Champion, 1994). On *René* see Pierre Barbéris, *'René' de Chateaubriand: un nouveau roman* (Paris: Larousse, 1973).

17. See David Hillery, *Lamartine: The 'Méditations Poétiques'* (Durham: University of Durham, 1993).

18. See Suzanne Bernard, *Le Poème en prose de Baudelaire jusqu'à nos jours* (Paris: Nizet, 1959); Henri Corbat, *Hantise et imagination chez Aloysius Bertrand* (Paris: José Corti, 1975).

19. See Pierre-Georges Castex, *Le Conte fantastique en France de Nodier à Maupassant* (Paris: José Corti, 1951).

20. See A. Richard Oliver, *Charles Nodier: Pilot of Romanticism* (Syracuse: Syracuse University Press, 1964); Hilda Nelson, *Charles Nodier* (New York: Twayne, 1972); Frank Paul Bowman, *Mérimée: Heroism, Pessimism, and Irony* (Berkeley and Los Angeles: University of California Press, 1961); A. W. Raitt, *Prosper Mérimée* (London: Eyre and Spottiswoode, 1970); Maxwell A. Smith, *Prosper Mérimée* (New York: Twayne, 1972); Peter Cogman, *Mérimée: 'Colomba' and 'Carmen'* (London: Grant and Cutler, 1992).

21. See Tzvetan Todorov, *Introduction à la littérature fantastique* (Paris: Éditions du Seuil, 1970). For an attack on this approach to the fantastic text, see the important preface by Michel Crouzet to his edition of Théophile Gautier, *L'Œuvre fantastique. I: Nouvelles; II: Romans*, 2 vols (Paris: Bordas (Classiques Garnier), 1992).

22. See David Scott, *Pictorialist Poetics: Poetry and the Visual Arts in Nineteenth-Century France* (Cambridge: Cambridge University Press, 1988).

23. See Richard Wrigley, *The Origins of French Art Criticism from the Ancien Régime to the Restoration* (Oxford: Clarendon Press, 1993); M. R. Orwicz (ed.), *Art Criticism and its Institutions in Nineteenth-Century France* (Manchester: Manchester University Press, 1994).

24. See Dennis Porter, *Haunted Journeys. Desire and Transgression in European Travel Writing* (Princeton: Princeton University Press, 1991); Alain Borer et al., *Pour une littérature voyageuse* (Paris: Éditions Complexe, 1992).

25. Magraw, *France 1815–1914*, p. 31.

26. See the chapters by D. G. Charlton (pp. 33–75) and Frank Paul Bowman (pp. 76–112) in Charlton (ed.), *The French Romantics*, vol. I.

27. See W. D. Howarth, *Sublime and Grotesque: A Study of French Romantic Drama* (London: Harrap, 1975); Barry V. Daniels (ed.), *Revolution in the Theatre: French Romantic Theories of Drama* (Westport, Connecticut and London: Greenwood Press, 1983); Annie Ubersfeld, *Le Roi et le bouffon. Étude sur le théâtre de Hugo de 1830 à 1839* (Paris: José Corti, 1974); Jean Gaudon, *Victor Hugo et le théâtre* (Paris: Éditions Suger, 1985); Charles Affron, *A Stage for Poets: Studies in the Theatre of Hugo and Musset* (Princeton: Princeton University Press, 1971); Eric L. Gans, *Musset et le drame tragique* (Paris: José Corti, 1974); Bernard Masson, *Musset et le théâtre intérieur* (Paris: Armand Colin, 1974); David Sices, *Theatre of Solitude. The Drama of Alfred de Musset* (New Hampshire: University Press of New England, 1974); Ceri Crossley, *Musset: 'Lorenzaccio'* (London: Grant and Cutler, 1983); Robin Buss, *Vigny: 'Chatterton'* (London: Grant and Cutler, 1984).

28. See Malcolm Cook, *Fictional France: Social Reality in the French Novel, 1775–1800* (Providence and Oxford: Berg, 1993).

29. On Constant, see John Cruickshank, *Benjamin Constant* (New York: Twayne, 1974); Dennis Wood, *Benjamin Constant. A Biography* (London and New York: Routledge: 1993). On *Adolphe*, see Alison Fairlie, *Imagination and Language. Collected Essays on Constant, Baudelaire, Nerval and Flaubert*, ed. Malcolm Bowie (Cambridge: Cambridge University Press, 1981); Dennis Wood, *Constant: 'Adolphe'* (Cambridge: Cambridge University Press, 1987).

30. See Louis Maigron, *Le Roman historique à l'époque romantique* (Paris: Champion, 1912); Georg Lukács, *The Historical Novel* (London: Merlin Press, 1962); 'Le Roman historique', *Revue d'histoire littéraire de la France*, 75, 2–3 (March–June 1975), pp. 195–444; H. E. Shaw, *The Forms of Historical Fiction* (Ithaca: Cornell University Press, 1983).

31. See James Doolittle, *Alfred de Vigny* (New York: Twayne, 1967); Pierre Flottes, *Vigny et sa fortune littéraire* (Bordeaux: Ducros, 1970); Jacques-Philippe Saint-Gérand, *Alfred de Vigny: vivre, écrire* (Nancy: Presses Universitaires de Nancy, 1994).

32. See Richard B. Grant, *The Perilous Quest. Image, Myth and Prophecy in the Narratives of Victor Hugo* (Durham, N.C.: Duke University Press, 1968); Victor Brombert, *Victor Hugo and the Visionary Novel* (Cambridge, Mass.: Harvard University Press, 1984); Kathryn M. Grossman, *The Early Novels of Victor Hugo* (Geneva: Droz, 1986); Rachel Killick, *Hugo: 'Notre-Dame de Paris'* (Glasgow: University of Glasgow, 1994).

33. See Georg G. Iggers, *The Cult of Authority: The Political Philosophy of the Saint-Simonians* (The Hague: Nijhoff, 1970); Jean-René Derre (ed.), *Regards sur le saint-simonisme et les saint-simoniens* (Lyons: Presses Universitaires de Lyon, 1986); Neil McWilliam, *Dreams of Happiness: Social Art and the French Left, 1830–1850* (Princeton: Princeton University Press, 1993).

34. See Erich Auerbach, *Mimesis. The Representation of Reality in Western Literature* (Princeton: Princeton University Press, 1953); Herbert J. Hunt, *Balzac's Comédie Humaine* (London: Athlone Press, 1959); Harry Levin, *The Gates of Horn. A Study of Five French Realists* (New York: Oxford University Press, 1966); Pierre Barbéris, *Balzac: une mythologie réaliste*

(Paris: Larousse, 1971); George Lukács, *Studies in European Realism* (London: Merlin Press, 1972); Christopher Prendergast, *The Order of Mimesis. Balzac, Stendhal, Nerval, Flaubert* (Cambridge: Cambridge University Press, 1986); Victor Brombert, *The Hidden Reader. Stendhal, Balzac, Hugo, Baudelaire, Flaubert* (Cambridge, Mass. and London: Harvard University Press, 1988); Graham Robb, *Balzac. A Biography* (London: Picador, 1994).

35. See Anthony R. Pugh, *Balzac's Recurring Characters* (London: Duckworth, 1975); David Bellos, *Balzac: 'Old Goriot'* (Cambridge: Cambridge University Press, 1987).

36. See F. W. J. Hemmings, *Stendhal. A Study of his Novels* (Oxford: Clarendon Press, 1964); Michel Crouzet, *Stendhal et le langage* (Paris: Gallimard, 1981) and *Stendhal et l'italianité* (Paris: José Corti, 1982); Michel Guérin, *La Politique de Stendhal* (Paris: Presses Universitaires de France, 1982); Ann Jefferson, *Reading Realism in Stendhal* (Cambridge: Cambridge University Press, 1988); Prendergast, *The Order of Mimesis*, pp. 119–47.

37. See Victor Brombert, *The Romantic Prison* (Princeton: Princeton University Press, 1978); C. W. Thompson, *Le Jeu de l'ordre et de la liberté dans 'La Chartreuse de Parme'* (Aran: Éditions du Grand Chêne, 1982); Alison Finch, *Stendhal: 'La Chartreuse de Parme'* (London: Edward Arnold, 1984).

38. See Richard B. Grant, *Théophile Gautier* (Boston: Twayne, 1975); Joseph Savalle, *Travestis, métamorphoses, dédoublements: essai sur l'œuvre romanesque de Théophile Gautier* (Paris: Minard, 1981).

39. See Curtis Cate, *George Sand: A Biography* (London: Hamish Hamilton, 1975); Francine Mallet, *George Sand* (Paris: Grasset, 1976); Nancy K. Miller, 'Idealism in the Novel: Recanonizing Sand', in Joan DeJean and Nancy K. Miller (eds), *Displacements: Women, Tradition, Literatures in French* (Baltimore and London: Johns Hopkins University Press, 1991).

40. See Claire Goldberg Moses, *French Feminism in the 19th Century* (Albany: SUNY Press, 1984).

41. See Sandra Dijkstra, *Flora Tristan: Feminism in the Age of George Sand* (London: Pluto Press, 1992).

42. See Margaret Gilman, *The Idea of Poetry in France from Houdar de la Motte to Baudelaire* (Cambridge, Mass.: Harvard University Press, 1958); Sylvain Menant, *La Chute d'Icare. La Crise de la poésie française* (Geneva and Paris: Droz, 1981); *Lectures de la poésie du XVIIIe siècle, Œuvres et critiques* (1982) vol. VII, p. 1; Keith Aspley and Peter France (eds), *Poetry in France: Metamorphoses of a Muse* (Edinburgh: Edinburgh University Press, 1992); Christopher Prendergast (ed.), *Nineteenth-century French Poetry. Introduction to Close Reading* (Cambridge: Cambridge University Press, 1990).

43. See Édouard Guitton, *Jacques Delille et le poème de la nature en France de 1750 à 1820* (Paris: Klincksieck, 1974); Will Munsters, *La Poétique du pittoresque en France de 1700 à 1830* (Geneva and Paris: Droz, 1991).

44. See Francis Scarfe, *André Chénier: His Life and Work, 1762–1794* (Oxford: Clarendon Press, 1965); Richard A. Smernoff, *André Chénier* (Boston: Twayne, 1977).

45. See Barbara Johnson, 'Gender and Poetry: Charles Baudelaire and Marceline Desbordes-Valmore', in Joan DeJean and Nancy K. Miller, *Displacements: Women, Traditions, Literatures in French*, pp. 163–81; Michael Danahy, 'Marceline Desbordes-Valmore and the Engendered Canon', *Yale French Studies*, 75 (1988), pp. 129–47; Laurence M. Porter, 'Poetess or Strong Poet? Gender Stereotypes and the Elegies of Marceline Desbordes-Valmore', *French Forum*, 18, 2 (May 1993), pp. 94–185.
46. See Hillery, *Lamartine: The 'Méditations Poétiques'*, p. 2.
47. See François Germain, *L'Imagination d'Alfred de Vigny* (Paris: José Corti, 1961).
48. See Pierre Albouy, *La Création mythologique chez Victor Hugo* (Paris: José Corti, 1963); Alfred Glauser, *La Poétique de Hugo* (Paris: Nizet, 1978).
49. See A. G. Lehmann, *Sainte-Beuve. A Portrait of the Critic* (Oxford: Clarendon Press, 1962); Norman H. Barlow, *Sainte-Beuve to Baudelaire. A Poetic Legacy* (Durham, N.C.: Duke University Press, 1964); José Cabanis, *Pour Sainte-Beuve* (Paris: Gallimard, 1987).
50. See Pamela M. Pilbeam, *The 1830 Revolution in France* (London: Macmillan, 1991).
51. See Alain Pessin, *Le Mythe du peuple et la société française au XIXe siècle* (Paris: Presses Universitaires de France, 1992).
52. See Lawrence Watson, 'Rimbaud and Auguste Barbier', *French Studies Bulletin*, 23 (Summer 1987), pp. 12–14.
53. See Lloyd Bishop, *The Poetry of Alfred de Musset: Styles and Genres* (New York: Peter Lang, 1987).
54. See P. E. Tennant, *Théophile Gautier* (London: Athlone Press, 1975); Constance Gosselin Schick, *Seductive Resistance: The Poetry of Théophile Gautier* (Amsterdam and Atlanta: Rodopi, 1994).

Notes to Chapter 5

1. See Roger Magraw, *France 1815–1914: The Bourgeois Century* (London: Fontana, 1983), pp. 89–155; Theodor Zeldin, *France 1848–1945*, 5 vols (Oxford: Oxford University Press, 1979–81); Jean Tulard (ed.), *Dictionnaire du Second Empire* (Paris: Fayard, 1995).
2. See David H. Pinkney, *Napoleon III and the Re-Building of Paris* (Princeton: Princeton University Press, 1958); Anthony Sutcliffe, *The Autumn of Central Paris: The Defeat of Town Planning* (London: Edward Arnold, 1970) and *Paris: An Architectural History* (New Haven and London: Yale University Press, 1993); Jeanne Gaillard, *Paris, la ville 1852–1870* (Paris: Champion, 1977); Maurice Agulhon, *La Ville de l'âge industriel: le cycle haussmannien* in Georges Duby (ed.), *Histoire de la France urbaine*, 5 vols (Paris: Éditions du Seuil, 1983), vol. IV.
3. See H. W. Paul, *From Knowledge to Power: The Rise of the Science Empire in France* (Cambridge: Cambridge University Press, 1985).
4. See D. G. Charlton, *Positivist Thought in France (1852–1870)* (Oxford: Clarendon Press, 1959) and *Secular Religions in France (1815–1870)* (London: Oxford University Press, 1963); Jean-Thomas Nordmann, *Taine et la critique scientifique* (Paris: Presses Universitaires de France, 1992); Brian Rigby (ed.), *French Literature, Thought and Culture in the Nineteenth*

Century: A Material World: Essays in Honour of D. G. Charlton (London: Macmillan, 1993).

5. See Laura Kreyder, *L'Enfance des Saints et des autres: essai sur la comtesse de Ségur* (Paris: Nizet, 1987); Marie-Christine Vinson, *L'Éducation des petites filles chez la comtesse de Ségur* (Lyons: Presses Universitaires de Lyon, 1987); Claudine Beaussant, *La Comtesse de Ségur, ou l'enfance de l'art* (Paris: Laffont, 1988).

6. See Simone Vierne, *Jules Verne* (Paris: Balland, 1986); Jean Bessière, *Modernités de Jules Verne* (Paris: Presses Universitaires de France, 1988); Arthur B. Evans, *Jules Verne Rediscovered: Didacticism and the Scientific Novel* (Westport: Greenwood Press, 1988); William Butcher, *Verne's Journey to the Centre of the Self. Space and Time in the 'Voyages Extraordinaires'* (London: Macmillan, 1990).

7. See Roger Bellet, *Presse et journalisme sous le Second Empire* (Paris: Armand Colin, 1967); Henri-Jean Martin and Roger Chartier (eds), *Histoire de l'édition française*, 4 vols (Paris: Promodis, 1982–6).

8. See Roger Bellet, *L'Aventure dans la littérature populaire au XIXe siècle* (Lyons: Presses Universitaires de Lyon, 1985); A. H. Deverres, 'Paul Féval and the Novel', in Cedric E. Pickford (ed.), *Mélanges de littérature française moderne offertes à Garnet Rees* (Paris: Minard, 1980), pp. 131–44.

9. See Jonathan Culler, *Flaubert. The Uses of Uncertainty* (London: Elek, 1974); Raymonde Debray-Genette, *Flaubert à l'œuvre* (Paris: Flammarion, 1980); P. M. Wetherill (ed.), *Flaubert: la dimension du texte* (Manchester: Manchester University Press, 1982), and *Flaubert, la femme, la ville* (Paris: Presses Universitaires de France, 1983); Diana Knight, *Flaubert's Characters* (Cambridge: Cambridge University Press, 1985); Stirling Haig, *Flaubert and the Gift of Speech* (Cambridge: Cambridge University Press, 1986); Christopher Prendergast, *The Order of Mimesis: Balzac, Stendhal, Nerval, Flaubert* (Cambridge: Cambridge University Press, 1986), pp. 180–211.

10. See Stephen Ullman, *Style in the French Novel* (Oxford: Basil Blackwell, 1964), pp. 94–120; Tony Tanner, *Adultery in the Novel* (Baltimore: Johns Hopkins University Press, 1979); Stephen Heath, *Flaubert: 'Madame Bovary'* (Cambridge: Cambridge University Press, 1992).

11. See Maurice Agulhon et al., *Histoire et langage dans 'L'Éducation sentimentale' de Flaubert* (Paris: C.D.U./SEDES, 1981); essays by Tim Unwin (pp. 13–25) and P. M. Wetherill (pp. 27–38) in Keith Cameron and James Kearns (eds), *Le Champ littéraire: 1860–1900. Études offertes à Michael Pakenham* (Amsterdam and Atlanta: Rodopi, 1996); Christopher Prendergast, *Paris and the Nineteenth Century* (Oxford: Blackwell, 1992), pp. 29–30, 111–25.

12. See Anne Ubersfeld and Guy Rosa (eds), *Lire 'Les Misérables'* (Paris: José Corti, 1985); Victor Brombert, *Victor Hugo and the Visionary Novel* (Cambridge, Mass.: Harvard University Press, 1984), pp. 86–139.

13. See Robert Ricatte, *La Création romanesque chez les Goncourt (1851–1870)* (Paris: Armand Colin, 1953).

14. See Ruth Moser, *L'Impressionnisme français. Peinture, littérature, musique* (Paris and Geneva: Droz, 1952); Enzo Caramaschi, *Réalisme et impressionnisme dans l'œuvre des frères Goncourt* (Pisa: Libreria Galiardica, 1971); Ullmann, *Style in the French Novel*, pp. 121–45.

15. See Colette Becker, *Les Apprentissages de Zola: du poète romantique au romancier naturaliste* (Paris: Presses Universitaires de France, 1993); Frederick Brown, *Zola, A Life* (London: Macmillan, 1996). On *Thérèse Raquin*, see Claude Schumacher, *Zola: 'Thérèse Raquin'* (Glasgow: University of Glasgow, 1992); Russell Cousins, *Zola: 'Thérèse Raquin'* (London: Grant and Cutler, 1992).

16. See Jean Gaudon, *Le Temps de la contemplation* (Paris: Flammarion, 1969); Susanne Nash, *'Les Contemplations'* of Victor Hugo: An Allegory of the Creative Process (Princeton: Princeton University Press, 1976); Peter Cogman, *Hugo: 'Les Contemplations'* (London: Grant and Cutler, 1984); Alfred Glauser, *La Poétique de Hugo* (Paris: Nizet, 1978).

17. See Richard D. Burton, *Baudelaire and the Second Republic* (Oxford: Clarendon Press, 1991).

18. See Barbara Johnson, *Défiguration du langage poétique* (Paris: Flammarion, 1971); Leo Bersani, *Baudelaire and Freud* (Berkeley, Los Angeles and London: University of California Press, 1977); Graham Chesters, *Baudelaire and the Poetics of Craft* (Cambridge: Cambridge University Press, 1988); F. W. Leakey, *Baudelaire: Collected Essays*, ed. Eva Jacobs (Cambridge: Cambridge University Press, 1990); Graham Robb, *La Poésie de Baudelaire et la poésie française 1838–1852* (Paris: Aubier, 1993).

19. See Richard D. Burton, *Baudelaire in 1859* (Cambridge: Cambridge University Press, 1988).

20. See David H. T. Scott, *Sonnet Theory and Practice in Nineteenth-Century France: Sonnets on the Sonnet* (Hull: University of Hull Publications, 1977).

21. See Barbara Wright and David H. T. Scott, *Baudelaire: 'La Fanfarlo' and 'Le Spleen de Paris'* (London: Grant and Cutler, 1984); Prendergast, *Paris and the Nineteenth Century*, pp. 126–63; essays by Sonya Stephens (pp. 39–47), Steve Murphy (pp. 49–61) and J. A. Hiddleston (pp. 65–70) in Cameron and Kearns (eds), *Le Champ littéraire: 1860–1900*.

22. *See* Jean-Pierre Richard, Poésie et profondeur (Paris: Éditions du Seuil, 1955); Ross Chambers, *G. de Nerval et la poétique du voyage* (Paris: José Corti, 1969); Prendergast, *The Order of Mimesis*, pp. 148–79.

23. See Lawrence Watson and Rosemary Lloyd (eds), *Patterns of Evolution in Nineteenth-Century French Poetry* (Deddington: The Tallents Press, 1991).

24. See Edgard Pich, *Leconte de Lisle et sa création poétique* (Lyons: Université de Lyon II, 1975).

25. See Alvin Harms, *Théodore de Banville* (Boston: Twayne, 1983); *Théodore de Banville en son temps, Bulletin d'Études Parnassiennes et Symbolistes*, 9–10 (Spring–Autumn, 1992).

26. See Alvin Harms, *José-Maria de Heredia* (Boston: Twayne, 1975); Walter Ince, *Heredia* (London: Athlone Press, 1979).

27. See *Watteau 1684–1721* (Paris: Éditions de la Réunion des Musées Nationaux, 1984).

28. See Georges Zayed, *La Formation littéraire de Verlaine* (Geneva: Droz, 1956); Claude Cuénot, *Le Style de Paul Verlaine* (Paris: C.D.U., 1962); Susan Taylor-Horrex, *Verlaine: 'Fêtes galantes' and 'Romances sans paroles'* (London: Grant and Cutler, 1988).

Notes to Chapter 6

1. See Paul Lidsky, *Les Écrivains contre la Commune* (Paris: Maspéro, 1970); Pierre Masson, *Le Disciple et l'Insurgé: roman et politique à la Belle Époque* (Lyons: Presses Universitaires de Lyon, 1987).

2. Zola, *Les Rougon-Macquart*, ed. Armand Lanoux and Henri Mitterand, 5 vols (Paris: Gallimard, Bibliothèque de la Pléiade, 1966–70), vol. I, p. 4. See René-Pierre Colin, *Zola, renégats et alliés. La République naturaliste* (Lyons: Presses Universitaires de Lyon, 1988); Robert Lethbridge and Terry Keefe (eds), *Zola and the Craft of Fiction* (Leicester: Leicester University Press, 1990).

3. See David Baguley, *Naturalist Fiction. The Entropic Vision* (Cambridge: Cambridge University Press, 1990); Brian Nelson (ed.), *Naturalism in the European Novel. New Critical Perspectives* (New York and Oxford: Berg, 1992).

4. See Charles Castella, *Structures romanesques et vision sociale chez Maupassant* (Lausanne: L'Âge d'Homme, 1972); Michael G. Lerner, *Maupassant* (London: Allen and Unwin, 1975); Mariane Bury, *Maupassant* (Paris: Nathan, 1991); Christopher Lloyd and Robert Lethbridge (eds), *Maupassant conteur et romancier* (Durham: University of Durham, 1994).

5. See Guy Rosa, ' "Quatrevingt-treize" ou la critique du roman historique', *Revue d'Histoire Littéraire de la France*, 75 (March–June 1975), pp. 329–43; Sandy Petrey, *History in the Text: 'Quatrevingt-treize' and the French Revolution* (Amsterdam: John Benjamins, 1980); Victor Brombert, *Victor Hugo and the Visionary Novel* (Cambridge, Mass.: Harvard University Press, 1984), pp. 205–29.

6. See *Colloque Jules Vallès* (Lyons: Presses Universitaires de Lyon, 1975); Roger Bellet, *Jules Vallès. Journalisme et révolution*, 2 vols (Tusson: Du Lérot, 1987–9); Walter Redfern, *Feet First: Jules Vallès* (Glasgow: Glasgow University Press, 1992).

7. See Walter Redfern, *Georges Darien: Robbery and Private Enterprise* (Amsterdam: Rodopi, 1985).

8. See Marie-Claire Bancquart, *Anatole France, un sceptique passionné* (Paris: Calmann-Lévy, 1984); and *Anatole France* (Paris: Éditions Julliard, 1994).

9. See Jean Beauvard et al., *La Petite Musique de Verlaine: 'Romances sans paroles', 'Sagesse'* (Paris: C.D.U./SEDES, 1982).

10. See Robert Greer Cohn, *The Poetry of Rimbaud* (Princeton: Princeton University Press, 1973); C. A. Hackett, *Rimbaud, A Critical Introduction* (Cambridge: Cambridge University Press, 1981); Antoine Fongaro, *Sur Rimbaud, Lire 'Illuminations'* (Toulouse: Les Cahiers de Littératures, 1985) and *Segments métriques dans la prose d' 'Illuminations'* (Toulouse: Les Cahiers de Littératures, 1993); André Guyaux, *Poétique du fragment. Essai sur les 'Illuminations' de Rimbaud* (Geneva: À la Baconnière, 1985); Kirstin Ross, *The Emergence of Social Space: Rimbaud and the Paris Commune* (London: Macmillan, 1988); Steve Murphy, *Le Premier Rimbaud ou l'apprentissage de la subversion* (Paris and Lyons: Éditions du CNRS/ Presses Universitaires, 1990) and *Rimbaud et la ménagerie impériale* (Paris and Lyons: Éditions du CNRS/Presses Universitaires, 1991); G. M. Macklin, *A Study of Theatrical Vision in Arthur Rimbaud's 'Illuminations'*

(Lewiston, New York, Queenston, Ontario and Lampeter: Mellen Press, 1993).

11. See François Caradec, *Isidore Ducasse, Comte de Lautréamont* (Paris: La Table Ronde, 1970); Jean Decottignies, *Préludes à Maldoror: vers une poétique de la rupture en France, 1820–1870* (Paris: Armand Colin, 1973); Robert Pickering, *Lautréamont/Ducasse: thématique et écriture* (Paris: Minard, 1988).

12. See Michel Dansel, *Tristan Corbière: thématique de l'inspiration* (Lausanne: l'Âge d'Homme, 1985); Élisabeth Aragon and Claude Bonnin, *'Les Amours jaunes'* (Toulouse: Presses Universitaires du Mirail, 1992).

13. See *Littératures* (special issue on Cros), 22 (Spring 1990).

14. See Noel Richard, *À l'Aube du symbolisme* (Paris: Nizet, 1961); Philip Stephan, *Paul Verlaine and the Decadence* (Manchester: Manchester University Press, 1974).

15. See Jean-Pierre Richard, *L'Univers imaginaire de Mallarmé* (Paris: Éditions du Seuil, 1961); Malcolm Bowie, *Mallarmé and the Art of Being Difficult* (Cambridge: Cambridge University Press, 1978); Leo Bersani, *The Death of Stéphane Mallarmé* (Cambridge: Cambridge University Press, 1982); Bertrand Marchal, *Lecture de Mallarmé* (Paris: José Corti, 1985) and *La Religion de Mallarmé* (Paris: José Corti, 1988); Peter Dayan, *Mallarmé's 'Divine Transposition': Real and Apparent Sources of Literary Value* (Oxford: Clarendon Press, 1986); Penny Florence, *Mallarmé, Manet and Redon: Visual and Aural Signs and the Generation of Meaning* (Cambridge: Cambridge University Press, 1986); Gordon Millan, *Throw of the Dice. The Life of Stéphane Mallarmé* (London: Secker and Warburg, 1994); Michael Temple, *The Name of the Poet: Onomastics and Anonymity in the Works of Stéphane Mallarmé* (Exeter: Exeter University Press, 1995).

16. See James Kearns, *Symbolist Landscapes: The Place of Painting in the Poetry and Criticism of Mallarmé and his Circle* (London: Modern Humanities Research Association, 1989), pp. 87–122.

17. See Richard Griffiths, *The Reactionary Revolution: The Catholic Revival in French Literature, 1870–1914* (London: Constable, 1966); Antoine Prost, *Histoire de l'enseignement en France (1800–1967)* (Paris: Armand Colin, 1968).

18. Théodule Ribot's *La Philosophie de Schopenhauer* (1874) and the French translation of Hartmann's *Philosophie des Unbewussten [Philosophie de l'inconscient]* (1877) were very influential. See Lilian R. Furst, *Counterparts: The Dynamics of Franco-German Literary Relationships 1770–1895* (London: Methuen, 1977).

19. See Frederick Burwick and Paul Douglass, *Crisis in Modernism: Bergson and the Vitalist Controversy* (Cambridge: Cambridge University Press, 1992); Mark Antliff, *Inventing Bergson: Cultural Politics and the Parisian Avant-Garde* (Princeton: Princeton University Press, 1993).

20. See Jean Pierrot, *L'Imaginaire décadent* (Paris: Presses Universitaires de France, 1977); Jennifer Birkett, *The Sins of the Fathers: Decadence in France, 1870–1914* (London: Quartet Books, 1986); Mikuláš Teich and Roy Porter (eds), *Fin de siècle and its Legacy* (Cambridge: Cambridge University Press, 1990).

21. See Georges Zayed, *Huysmans peintre de son époque* (Paris: Nizet, 1973); André Guyaux, Christian Heck, Robert Kopp, *Huysmans: une esthétique de la décadence* (Geneva and Paris: Slatkine, 1987); Pierre Bernier et al., *Joris-Karl Huysmans: 'À rebours'* (Paris: C.D.U./SEDES, 1990); Christopher Lloyd, *Joris-Karl Huysmans and the Fin-de-siècle Novel* (Edinburgh: Edinburgh University Press, 1990).

22. See B. G. Rogers, *The Novels and Stories of Barbey d'Aurevilly* (Geneva: Droz, 1967); Ph. Berthier et al., *Barbey d'Aurevilly: 'L'Ensorcelé' et 'Les Diaboliques'* (Paris: C.D.U./SEDES, 1988).

23. See Philippe Jullian, *Jean Lorrain ou le Satyricon 1900* (Paris: Fayard, 1974); Birkett, *The Sins of the Fathers*, pp. 191–224.

24. See M. Schwarz, *Octave Mirbeau: vie et œuvre* (The Hague and Paris: Mouton, 1966); Reg Carr, *Anarchism in France: The Case of Octave Mirbeau* (Manchester: Manchester University Press, 1977); Pierre Michel and Georges Cesbron, *Octave Mirbeau* (Angers: Presses Universitaires d'Angers, 1992).

25. See H. P. Clive, *Pierre Louÿs (1870–1925): A Biography* (Oxford: Clarendon Press, 1978); Gordon Millan, *Pierre Louÿs ou le culte de l'amitié* (Aix-en-Provence: Pandora Editions, 1979).

26. See Birkett, *The Sins of the Fathers*, pp. 131–58.

27. See Anna Balakian (ed.), *The Symbolist Movement in the Literature of the European Languages* (Budapest: Akadémiai Kiadó, 1982); Robert L. Delevoy, *Le Symbolisme* (Geneva: Skira, 1982).

28. Raymond Furness, *Wagner and Literature* (Manchester: Manchester University Press, 1982), p. 6.

29. See Clive Scott, *Vers Libre* (Oxford: Clarendon Press, 1990).

30. See J. C. Ireson, *L'Œuvre poétique de Gustave Kahn* (Paris: Nizet, 1962).

31. See Jean-Louis Debauve, *Laforgue en son temps* (Neufchâtel: À la Baconnière, 1972); David Arkell, *Looking for Laforgue* (Manchester: Carcanet, 1979); J. A. Hiddleston, *Laforgue aujourd'hui* (Paris: José Corti, 1988); Michele Hannoosh, *Parody and Decadence: Laforgue's 'Moralités légendaires'* (Columbus: Ohio State University Press, 1989).

32. See Karl D. Uitti, *The Concept of Self in the Symbolist Novel* (The Hague and Paris: Mouton, 1961).

33. See Claude de Grève, *Georges Rodenbach* (Brussels: Labor, 1988).

34. See Kathleen M. McGilligan, *Édouard Dujardin: 'Les Lauriers sont coupés' and the Interior Monologue* (Hull: University of Hull, 1977).

35. See the edition of the poem by Mitsou Ronat (Paris: Change errant/d'atelier, 1980); Gardner Davies, *Vers une explication rationnelle du 'Coup de dés'* (Paris: José Corti, 1953); Bowie, *Mallarmé and the Art of Being Difficult*, pp. 91–145; David Scott, *Pictorialist Poetics: Poetry and the Visual Arts in Nineteenth-Century France* (Cambridge: Cambridge University Press, 1988), pp. 138–69; Penny Florence, *Mallarmé, Manet and Redon. Visual and Aural Signs and the Generation of Meaning* (Cambridge: Cambridge University Press, 1986), pp. 84–126.

36. See Régis Debray, *Le Pouvoir intellectuel en France* (Paris: Ramsay, 1979); Geraldi Leroy (ed.), *Les Écrivains et l'Affaire Dreyfus* (Orleans: Presses Universitaires d'Orléans, 1983); Pascal Ory and Jean-François Sirinelli, *Les Intellectuels en France, de l'Affaire Dreyfus à nos jours* (Paris: Armand

Colin, 1986); Jeremy Jennings (ed.), *Intellectuals in Twentieth-Century France: Mandarins and Samurais* (London: Macmillan, 1993).

37. See Anne-Marie Thiesse, *Le Roman du quotidien: lecteurs et lectures populaires à la Belle Époque* (Paris: Le Chemin Vert, 1984).

38. See Michel Raimond, *La Crise du roman* (Paris: José Corti, 1967); Antoine Compagnon, *La Troisième République des lettres de Flaubert à Proust* (Paris: Éditions du Seuil, 1983).

39. See Philip Ouston, *The Imagination of Maurice Barrès* (Toronto: University of Toronto Press, 1974); C. Stewart Doty, *From Cultural Rebellion to Counter-revolution: The Politics of Maurice Barrès* (Athens, Ohio: Ohio University Press, 1976); André Guyaux, Joseph Jurt and Robert Kopp (eds), *Barrès: une tradition dans la modernité* (Paris: Champion, 1991).

40. See Karl D. Uitti, *La Passion littéraire de Remy de Gourmont* (New Jersey and Paris: University of Princeton and Presses Universitaires de France, 1962); Richard Sieburth, *Instigations: Ezra Pound and Remy de Gourmont* (Cambridge, Mass.: Harvard University Press; 1978).

41. See Marie Maclean, *Le Jeu suprême. Structure et thèmes dans 'Le Grand Meaulnes'* (Paris: José Corti, 1973); Robert Gibson, *The Land Without a Name: Alain-Fournier and his World* (London: Elek, 1975) and *Alain-Fournier: 'Le Grand Meaulnes'* (London: Grant and Cutler, 1986); Claude Herzfeld, *'Le Grand Meaulnes'* (Paris: Nizet, 1983).

42. See Robert Sabatier, *La Poésie du XXe siècle*, 3 vols (Paris: Albin Michel, 1982–8), vol. I; Peter-Eckhard Knabe and René Trousson (eds), *Émile Verhaeren: poète, dramaturge, critique* (Brussels, Éditions de l'Université de Bruxelles, 1984).

43. See Alexandre Maurocordato, *L'Ode de Paul Claudel*, 2 vols (Paris: Lettres Modernes, 1978); Henri Guillemin, *Charles Péguy* (Paris: Éditions du Seuil, 1981).

Notes to Chapter 7

1. Roland Barthes, *Leçon inaugurale de la chaire de sémiologie littéraire du Collège de France* (Paris: Éditions du Seuil, 1978), p. 23, trans. Richard Howard, in Susan Sontag (ed.), *Barthes: Selected Writings* (Oxford: Fontana Paperbacks, 1983), p. 466.

2. See Régis Debray, *Le Pouvoir intellectuel en France* (Paris: Éditions Ramsay, 1979); John Lough, *Writer and Public in France* (Oxford: Clarendon Press, 1978); John Ardagh, *France Today* (Harmondsworth: Penguin Books, 1987).

3. See Emily Apter, *Feminizing the Fetish: Psychoanalysis and Narrative Obsession in Turn-of-the-Century France* (Ithaca, N.Y. and London: Cornell University Press, 1991). On the general history of psychoanalysis in France and the particular history of the Lacanian School see Élisabeth Roudinesco, *La Bataille de cent ans: histoire de la psychanalyse en France*, vol. I: *1885–1939* (Paris: Ramsay, 1982); vol. II: *1925–85* (Paris: Éditions du Seuil, 1986); vol. II, trans. Jeffrey Mehlman, *Jacques Lacan & Co. A History of Psychoanalysis in France, 1925–85* (London: Free Association Books, 1990). On Lacan see David Macey, *Lacan in Contexts* (London and New York: Verso, 1988); Malcolm Bowie, *Lacan* (Cambridge, Mass.

and London: Harvard University Press, 1991). For psychoanalytical terms see Jean Laplanche and J.-B. Pontalis, *Vocabulaire de la psychanalyse* (Paris: Presses Universitaires de France, 1967). For the applications of psychoanalysis in literary criticism see Elizabeth Wright, *Psychoanalytic Criticism. Theory in Practice* (London and New York: Methuen, 1984); Maud Ellmann (ed. and intro.), *Psychoanalytic Literary Criticism* (London and New York: Longman, 1994).

4. On Kojève see Roudinesco, *La Bataille de cent ans*, and Shadia B. Druty, *Alexandre Kojève: The Roots of Postmodern Politics* (New York: St Martin's Press, 1994). See also Michael Kelly, *Hegel in France* (Birmingham: Birmingham School of Modern Languages, 1992). For an overview of the development of twentieth-century French philosophy see Vincent Descombes, *Le Même et l'Autre. Quarante-cinq ans de philosophie française (1933–1978)* (Paris: Éditions de Minuit, 1979), trans. L. Scott-Fox and J. M. Harding, *Modern French Philosophy* (Cambridge; Cambridge University Press, 1980).

5. On existentialism see Hazel E. Barnes, *Humanistic Existentialism: The Literature of Possibility* (Lincoln: University of Nebraska Press, 1959); Mark Poster, *Existential Marxism in Postwar France, from Sartre to Althusser* (Princeton, New Jersey: Princeton University Press, 1977); Andrew Dobson, *Jean-Paul Sartre and the Politics of Reason: A Theory of History* (Cambridge: Cambridge University Press, 1993).

6. On structuralism see Terence Hawkes, *Structuralism and Semiotics* (London: Methuen, 1977); Raman Selden and Peter Widdowson, *A Reader's Guide to Contemporary Literary Theory* (Hemel Hempstead: Harvester Wheatsheaf, 1993).

7. See the selections from Febvre's work collected in Peter Burke (ed.), *A New Kind of History from the Writings of Febvre*, trans. K. Folca (London: Routledge & Kegan Paul, 1973).

8. See Luc Ferry and Alain Renaut, *La Pensée 68: essai sur l'anti-humanisme contemporain* (Paris: Éditions Gallimard, 1988).

9. See David Couzens Hoy (ed.), *Foucault: A Critical Reader* (Oxford: Basil Blackwell), 1986; David Macey, *The Lives of Michel Foucault* (London: Hutchinson, 1993).

10. See Francis Mulhearn (ed. and intro.), *Contemporary Marxist Literary Criticism* (London and New York: Longman, 1992). On ideology see Terry Eagleton (ed. and intro.), *Ideology* (London and New York: Longman, 1994).

11. See Raman Selden, *The Theory of Criticism* (London: Longman, 1988); and Selden and Widdowson, *A Reader's Guide to Contemporary Literary Theory*, for a lucid introduction to Derrida's writing; Christopher Norris, *Deconstruction: Theory and Practice* (London: Methuen, 1982).

12. A version of postmodernism as a contestatory force is argued by Linda Hutcheon in *A Poetics of Postmodernism: History, Theory, Fiction* (New York and London: Routledge, 1988) and *The Politics of Postmodernism* (New York and London: Routledge, 1989). See, on creative writers and critical debates, Edmund J. Smyth (ed.), *Postmodernism and Contemporary Fiction* (London: B. T. Batsford, 1991). See, on Lyotard, Geoffrey Bennington, *Lyotard. Writing the Event* (Manchester: Manchester

University Press, 1988); Andrew Benjamin (ed.), *The Lyotard Reader* (Oxford: Blackwell, 1989).

13. See Mark Poster (ed. and intro.), *Jean Baudrillard: Selected Writings* (Cambridge: Polity Press, 1988).

14. Ronald Bogue, *Deleuze and Guattari* (London: Routledge, 1989).

Notes to Chapter 8

1. This was only fully realised in the 1950s with the publication of his unfinished novel *Jean Santeuil* and his critical work *Contre Sainte-Beuve*. For full details see the 4-volume Pléiade edition of *À la recherche du temps perdu*, ed. Jean-Yves Tadié (Paris: Gallimard, 1987–9).

2. He translated *The Bible of Amiens* (1904) and *Sesame and Lilies* (1906). His collected *Pastiches et mélanges* were published in 1919.

3. See Jean-Yves Tadié, *Proust et le roman* (Paris: Presses Universitaires de France, 1971); Jean-Pierre Richard, *Proust et le monde sensible* (Paris: Éditions du Seuil, 1974); Maya Slater, *Humour in the Works of Proust* (Oxford: Oxford University Press, 1979); J. M. Cocking, *Proust* (Cambridge: Cambridge University Press, 1982); Leighton Hodson (ed.), *Marcel Proust. The Critical Heritage* (London and New York: Routledge, 1989); Julia Kristeva, *Le Temps sensible. Proust et l'expérience littéraire* (Paris: Gallimard, 1994); Michael Sprinkler, *History and Ideology in Proust: 'A la recherche du temps perdu' and the Third French Republic* (Cambridge: Cambridge University Press, 1994).

4. See William W. Holdheim, *Theory and Practice of the Novel. A Study on André Gide* (Geneva: Droz, 1968); David H. Walker, *André Gide* (London: Macmillan, 1990).

5. See Paul Valéry, *Œuvres*, ed. Jean Hytier, 2 vols (Paris: Gallimard, Bibliothèque de la Pléiade, 1960), vol. I, pp. 988–1014.

6. See Maurice Rieuneau, *Guerre et révolution dans le roman français 1919–1939* (Paris: Klincksieck, 1974); Frank Field, *Three French Writers and the Great War* (Cambridge: Cambridge University Press, 1975); Holger Klein (ed.), *The First World War in Fiction* (London: Macmillan, 1976); John Cruickshank, *Variations on Catastrophe: Some French Responses to the Great War* (Oxford: Clarendon Press, 1982); Jean Relinger, *Henri Barbusse: écrivain combattant* (Paris: Presses Universitaires de France, 1994).

7. See John Flower, *Literature and the Left in France* (London: Methuen, 1985).

8. See E. Tonnet-Lacroix, *Après-guerre et sensibilités littéraires (1919–1924)* (Paris: Publications de la Sorbonne, 1991).

9. On Giraudoux and the poetic novel see 'L'Âge du roman poétique (1920–1930)', in Michel Raimond, *La Crise du roman* (Paris: José Corti, 1967), pp. 224–43. On Ramuz see David G. Bevan, *The Art and Poetry of Charles-Ferdinand Ramuz* (New York: Oleander Press, 1977). On Giono see Pierre Citron, *Giono, 1895–1970* (Paris: Éditions du Seuil, 1990).

10. See Calogero Giardina, *L'Imaginaire dans les romans de Raymond Radiguet* (Paris: Didier, 1991).

11. See Nicholas Hewitt, *The Golden Age of Louis-Ferdinand Céline* (Leaming-

ton Spa, Hamburg, New York: Berg, 1987); Ian Noble, *Language and Narration in Céline's Writings* (London: Macmillan, 1987).

12. See Robert Soucy, *Fascist Intellectual: Drieu la Rochelle* (Berkeley and Los Angeles: University of California Press, 1979); Marie Balvet, *Itinéraire d'un intellectuel vers le fascisme: Drieu la Rochelle* (Paris: Presses Universitaires de France, 1984); Rima Drell Reck, *Drieu la Rochelle and the Picture Gallery Novel: French Modernism in the Inter-War Years* (Baton Rouge: Louisiana State University Press, 1990).

13. See Camus's preface to the two-volume Pléiade edition of Martin du Gard's complete works (Paris: Gallimard, 1955), vol. I, pp. ix–xxxi.

14. See Olivier Rony, *Jules Romains ou l'appel au monde* (Paris: Laffont, 1992).

15. See Alan Rose, *Surrealism and Communism. The Early Years* (New York: Peter Lang, 1991).

16. See Roger Cardinal, *Breton: 'Nadja'* (London: Grant and Cutler, 1986).

17. See Jacqueline Lévi-Valensi, *Aragon romancier* (Paris: SEDES, 1989).

18. See W. D. Redfern, *Paul Nizan: Committed Literature in a Conspiratorial World* (Princeton: Princeton University Press, 1972); Bernard Alluin and Jacques Deguy (eds), *Paul Nizan écrivain* (Lille: Presses Universitaires de Lille, 1988); Michael Scriven, *Paul Nizan: Communist Novelist* (London: Macmillan, 1988).

19. See P. M. Cryle, *The Thematics of Commitment* (Princeton: Princeton University Press, 1985), ch. VI, pp. 218–41.

20. See Susan R. Suleiman, *Authoritarian Fictions. The Ideological Novel as a Literary Genre* (New York: Columbia University Press, 1983).

21. See J. E. Flower, *Writers and Politics in Modern France* (London: Hodder and Stoughton, 1977); Mary Jean Green, *Fiction in the Historical Present: French Writers and the Thirties* (Hanover and London: University Press of New England, 1986); Alice Yager Kaplan, *Reproductions of Banality: Fascism, Literature and French Intellectual Life* (Minneapolis: University of Minnesota Press, 1986); Geraldi Leroy and Anne Roche, *Les Écrivains et le Front Populaire* (Paris: Presses de la Fondation Nationale des Sciences Politiques, 1986); Nicholas Hewitt, *'Les Maladies du Siècle': The Image of Malaise in French Fiction and Thought in the Inter-War Years* (Hull: Hull University Press, 1988).

22. See Cecil Jenkins, *André Malraux* (Boston: Twayne, 1972); Thomas Jefferson Kline, *André Malraux and the Metamorphosis of Death* (New York and London: Columbia University Press, 1973); Robert S. Thornberry, *André Malraux et l'Espagne* (Geneva: Droz, 1977); Barrie Cadwallader, *Crisis of the European Mind: A Study of André Malraux and Drieu la Rochelle* (Cardiff: University of Wales Press, 1981); David G. Bevan (ed.), *Via Malraux: Essays by Walter Langlois* (Wolfville: The Malraux Society, 1986); Geoffrey T. Harris, *André Malraux: A Re-evaluation* (London: Macmillan, 1995).

23. See Malcolm Scott, *Mauriac: The Politics of a Novelist* (Edinburgh: Scottish Academic Press, 1980) and *The Struggle for the Soul of the French Novel: French Catholic and Realist Novelists 1850–1970* (London: Macmillan, 1989); John E. Flower and Bernard C. Swift (eds), *François Mauriac: Visions and Reappraisals* (Oxford, New York, Munich: Berg, 1989); *François Mauriac et les romanciers de l'inquiétude de 1914 à 1945* (Paris: Grasset, 1991).

24. See Gerda Blumenthal, *The Poetic Imagination of Georges Bernanos* (Baltimore: Johns Hopkins University Press, 1965); J. E. Flower, *Bernanos: 'Journal d'un curé de campagne'* (London: Edward Arnold, 1970); Colin W. Nettlebeck, *Les Personnages de Bernanos romancier* (Paris: Minard, 1970).

25. See Paul Reed, *Sartre: 'La Nausée'* (London: Grant and Cutler, 1987); Jean Deguy, *'La Nausée' de Jean-Paul Sartre* (Paris: Gallimard (Foliothèque 28), 1992).

26. See Anthony Cheal Pugh (ed.), *France 1940: Literary and Historical Reaction to Defeat* (Durham: University of Durham, 1991).

27. See Frederick J. Harris, *Encounters with Darkness: French and German Writers on World War II* (Oxford: Oxford University Press, 1983); Margaret Atack, *Literature and the French Resistance: Cultural Politics and Narrative Forms, 1940–1950* (Manchester: Manchester University Press, 1989). On the liberation see *French Cultural Studies*, V, 15 (October 1994), pp. 219–300 (special issue on 'Culture and the Liberation'); H. R. Kedward and Nancy Wood (eds), *The Liberation of France: Image and Event* (New York and Oxford: Berg, 1995).

28. See Jacques Debû-Bridel, *Les Éditions de Minuit. Historique et Bibliographie* (Paris: Éditions de Minuit, 1954).

29. See William Kidd, *Vercors: 'Le Silence de la mer' et autres récits* (Glasgow: University of Glasgow, 1991); James W. Brown and Lawrence D. Stokes (eds), *'The Silence of the Sea'/'Le Silence de la mer': A Novel of French Resistance during the Second World War by 'Vercors'* (New York and Oxford: Berg, 1992).

30. See S. Beynon John, *Saint-Exupéry: 'Vol de nuit' and 'Terre des hommes'* (London: Grant and Cutler, 1990).

31. See J. E. Flower, *Roger Vailland: The Man and His Masks* (London: Hodder and Stoughton, 1975).

32. See Christina Howells, *Sartre's Theory of Literature* (London: Modern Humanities Research Association, 1979); Mark Poster, *Existential Marxism in Post-War France* (Princeton: Princeton University Press, 1975); Rhiannon Goldthorpe, *Sartre: Literature and Theory* (Cambridge: Cambridge University Press, 1984); Charles G. Hill, *Jean-Paul Sartre: Freedom and Commitment* (New York: Peter Lang, 1992); Christina Howells (ed.), *The Cambridge Companion to Sartre* (Cambridge: Cambridge University Press, 1992); Andrew Dobson, *Jean-Paul Sartre and the Politics of Reason: A Theory of History* (Cambridge: Cambridge University Press, 1993).

33. See John Cruickshank, *Albert Camus and the Literature of Revolt* (Oxford: Oxford University Press, 1959); Bruce Pratt, *L'Évangile selon Albert Camus* (Paris: José Corti, 1980); Susan Tarrow, *Exile from the Kingdom: A Political Re-reading of Albert Camus* (University of Alabama Press, 1985); Philip Thody, *Albert Camus* (London: Macmillan, 1989); J. C. Isaac, *Arendt, Camus and Modern Rebellion* (New Haven and London: Yale University Press, 1992); J. McBride, *Albert Camus: Philosopher and Littérateur* (New York: St Martin's Press, 1992); Jean Guérin, *Albert Camus: portrait de l'artiste en citoyen* (Paris: F. Bourin, 1993); Ray Davison (ed.), *L'Étranger* (London: Methuen, 1988); Adèle King (ed.), *Camus's 'L'Étranger': Fifty Years On* (London: Macmillan, 1992); E. J. Hughes, *Camus: 'Le Premier homme', 'La Peste'* (Glasgow: University of Glasgow French and German Publications, 1995).

34. See J. E. Flower, *Pierre Courtade: The Making of a Party Scribe* (New York and Oxford: Berg, 1995).

35. See Nicholas Hewitt, *Literature and the Right in Post-War France: The Story of the 'Hussards'* (New York and Oxford: Berg, 1996); Christopher Lloyd, *Aymé: 'Uranus'/'La Tête des autres'* (Glasgow: University of Glasgow French and German Publications, 1992).

36. See Deirdre Bair, *Samuel Beckett: A Biography* (London: Vintage, 1990); Leslie Hill, *Beckett's Fiction: In Different Words* (Cambridge: Cambridge University Press, 1990); David Watson, *Paradox and Desire in Samuel Beckett's Fiction* (London: Macmillan, 1991).

37. On the *nouveau roman*, see the important collections of essays by Alain Robbe-Grillet, *Pour un nouveau roman* (Paris: Gallimard (Coll. Idées), 1963); Nathalie Sarraute, *L'Ère du soupçon* (Paris: Gallimard (Coll. Idées), 1964); Michel Butor, *Répertoire*, 5 vols (Paris: Éditions de Minuit, 1960–75). See also Jean Ricardou, *Problèmes du nouveau roman* (Paris: Éditions du Seuil, 1967) and *Le Nouveau Roman* (Paris: Éditions du Seuil, 1973); *Nouveau Roman: hier, aujourd'hui*, 2 vols (Paris: UGE (Colloque de Cérisy), 1972); Stephen Heath, *The Nouveau Roman* (London: Elek, 1972); Ann Jefferson, *The Nouveau Roman and the Poetics of Fiction* (Cambridge: Cambridge University Press, 1980); Celia Britton, *The Nouveau Roman: Fiction, Theory, Politics* (London: Macmillan, 1992).

38. See John Fletcher, *Alain Robbe-Grillet* (London: Methuen, 1983); Raylene L. Ramsay, *Robbe-Grillet and Modernity: Science, Sexuality, and Subversion* (Gainsville, Tallahassee, Tampa: University Press of Florida, 1992).

39. See Elf Jongeneel, *Michel Butor et le pacte romanesque* (Paris: José Corti, 1988); Jean Duffy, *Butor: 'La Modification'* (London: Grant and Cutler, 1990).

40. See Valerie Minogue, *Nathalie Sarraute and the War of the Words* (Edinburgh: Edinburgh University Press, 1981); Sheila M. Bell, *Nathalie Sarraute and the Feminist Reader* (London and Toronto: Associated University Press, 1993).

41. See Marcelle Marini, *Territoires du féminin: avec Marguerite Duras* (Paris: Éditions de Minuit, 1977); Micheline Tison-Braun, *Marguerite Duras* (Amsterdam: Rodopi, 1985); Sharon Willis, *Marguerite Duras: Writing on the Body* (Illinois: University of Illinois Press, 1987); Leslie Hill, *Apocalyptic Desires* (London: Routledge 1993); David Coward, 'Marguerite Duras', in Michael Tilby (ed.), *Beyond the Nouveau Roman* (London and New York: Berg, 1990), pp. 39–63. On *Moderato cantabile* see David Coward, *Duras: 'Moderato cantabile'* (London: Grant and Cutler, 1981).

42. See Renate Günther, *Duras: 'Le Ravissement de Lol V. Stein' and 'L'Amant'* (London: Grant and Cutler, 1993).

43. See *Claude Simon: analyse, théorie* (Paris: UGE (Colloque de Cérisy), 1975); Celia Britton (ed.), *Claude Simon* (London and New York: Longman, 1993); Mary Orr, *Claude Simon: The Intertextual Dimension* (Glasgow: University of Glasgow French and German Publications, 1993); Alastair Duncan, *Claude Simon: Adventures in Words* (Manchester: Manchester University Press, 1994).

44. See Anthony Cheal Pugh, *Simon: 'Histoire'* (London: Grant and Cutler, 1982).

45. See Robert M. Henkels, *Robert Pinget: The Novel as Quest* (Alabama: University of Alabama Press, 1979).

46. On Ollier see the *Review of Contemporary Fiction*, 8 (Summer 1988).

47. See Susan Hayward and Ginette Vincendeau (eds), *French Film: Texts and Contexts* (London: Routledge, 1990); Jill Forbes, *The Cinema in France: After the New Wave* (London: British Film Institute/Macmillan, 1992).

48. See Jacques Bens (ed.), *Oulipo, 1960–1980* (Paris: Christian Bourgeois, 1981); Warren F. Motte (ed.), *Oulipo: A Primer of Potential Literature* (Lincoln: University of Nebraska Press, 1986). See also Claude Simonnet, *Queneau déchiffré* (Paris: Julliard, 1962); C. Sanders, *Raymond Queneau* (Amsterdam and Atlanta: Rodopi, 1994). On *Zazie dans le métro* see Walter Redfern, *Queneau: 'Zazie dans le métro'* (London: Grant and Cutler, 1980); Michel Bigot, *'Zazie dans le métro' de Raymond Queneau* (Paris: Gallimard (Foliothèque, 34), 1994).

49. See D. Bellos, 'Literary Quotations in Perec's *La Vie mode d'emploi*', *French Studies*, LXI, 2 (April 1987), pp. 180–94 (p. 186). See also Warren F. Motte, *The Poetics of Experiment: A Study of the Work of Georges Perec* (Lexington, Kentucky: French Forum, 1984); Claude Burgelin, *Georges Perec* (Paris: Éditions du Seuil, 1988); David Bellos, *Georges Perec: A Life in Words* (London: Harvill Press, 1995).

50. See Serge Koster, *Tournier* (Paris: Veyrier, 1985); Arlette Bouloumié, *Michel Tournier: le roman mythologique* (Paris: José Corti, 1988); Colin Davis, *Michel Tournier: Philosophy and Fiction* (Oxford: Clarendon Press, 1988); David Gascoigne, *Michel Tournier* (New York and Oxford: Berg, 1996).

51. See Germaine Brée, *Le Monde fabuleux de J. M. G. Le Clézio* (Amsterdam: Rodopi, 1990); Jean Ominus, *Pour lire Le Clézio* (Paris: Presses Universitaires de France, 1994).

52. See David Gascoigne, 'Patrick Grainville', in Tilby (ed.), *Beyond the Nouveau Roman*, pp. 229–55.

53. See Roland Barthes, *Sollers écrivain* (Paris: Éditions du Seuil, 1979); Leslie Hill, 'Philippe Sollers and *Tel Quel*', in Tilby (ed.), *Beyond the Nouveau Roman*, pp. 100–22; Edmund J. Smyth (ed.), *Postmodernism and Contemporary Fiction* (London: Batsford, 1991); Malcolm Pollard, *The Novels of Philippe Sollers: Narrative and the Visual* (Amsterdam and Atlanta: Rodopi, 1994).

54. See Colin W. Nettlebeck, 'Getting the Story Right: Narratives of World War II in Post-1968 France', *Journal of European Studies* 15 (1985), pp. 77–116; Alan Morris, *Collaboration and Resistance Reviewed: Writers and the 'Mode Rétro' in Post-Gaullist France* (New York and Oxford: Berg, 1992).

55. See Colin W. Nettlebeck and Penelope Ann Hueston, *Patrick Modiano: pièce d'identité* (Paris: Minard, 1986); Alan Morris, *Patrick Modiano* (New York and Oxford: Berg, 1996).

56. See Patrick Combes, *La littérature et le mouvement de Mai* (Paris: Éditions de Minuit, 1984); Keith Reader, *The May 1968 Events in France: Reproductions and Interpretations* (London: Macmillan, 1993).

57. See Jean-Claude Lebrun and Claude Prévost, *Nouveaux Territoires*

romanesques (Paris: Messidor Éditions Sociales, 1990); Colin W. Nettlebeck, 'The "Post-Literary" Novel: Echenoz, Pennac and Company', *French Cultural Studies*, V, 14 (June 1994), pp. 113–38.

58. See Christopher Robinson, *Scandal in the Ink: Male and Female Homosexuality in Twentieth-Century French Literature* (London: Cassell, 1995).

59. See Stephen Heath, 'Night Books', in David Hollier (ed.), *A New History of French Literature* (Cambridge, Mass. and London: Harvard University Press, 1989), pp. 1054–60; and Nettlebeck, 'The "Post-Literary" Novel', pp. 117–18.

60. See Peter Broome and Graham Chesters, *An Anthology of Modern French Poetry, 1850–1950* (Cambridge: Cambridge University Press, 1976) and *The Appreciation of Modern French Poetry, 1850–1950* (Cambridge: Cambridge University Press, 1976).

61. See Anne Hyde Greet, *Apollinaire et le livre du peintre* (Paris: Minard, 1977); Margareth Wijk, *Guillaume Apollinaire et l'Esprit Nouveau* (Lund: W.K. Geerup, 1982): Antoine Fongaro, *Apollinaire poète: exégèses et discussions 1957–1987* (Toulouse: Presses Universitaires du Mirail-Toulouse, 1988).

62. See Claude Debon, *Guillaume Apollinaire après 'Alcools'. I: 'Calligrammes', le poète et la guerre* (Paris: Minard, 1981); Willard Bohn, *Apollinaire, Visual Poetry, and Art Criticism* (Lewisberg: Bucknell University Press: London and Toronto: Associated University Presses, 1993).

63. See Monique Chefdor, *Blaise Cendrars* (Boston: Twayne, 1980).

62. Pierre Reverdy, *En vrac* (Monaco: Éditions du Rocher, 1956), p. 139. See Clive Scott, *Reading the Rhythm: The Poetics of French Verse, 1910–1930* (Oxford: Clarendon Press, 1993).

65. See René Plantier, *L'Univers poétique de Max Jacob* (Paris: Klincksieck 1963); Gerald Kamber, *Max Jacob and the Poetics of Cubism* (Baltimore and London: The Johns Hopkins Press, 1971).

66. See Mary Ann Caws, *La Main de Pierre Reverdy* (Geneva: Droz, 1979); Michel Collot, *Horizon de Reverdy* (Paris: Publications de l'École Normale Supérieure, 1981); Andrew Rothwell, *Textual Spaces: The Poetry of Pierre Reverdy* (Amsterdam: Rodopi, 1989); 'Pierre Reverdy 1889–1989', *Nottingham French Studies*, 28, 2 (Autumn 1989).

67. See Christine M. Crow, *Paul Valéry: Consciousness and Nature* (Cambridge: Cambridge University Press, 1972), and *Paul Valéry and the Poetry of Voice* (Cambridge: Cambridge University Press, 1982); Brian Stimpson, *Paul Valéry and Music* (Cambridge: Cambridge University Press, 1984).

68. See Sarane Alexandrian, *Le Surréalisme et le rêve* (Paris: Gallimard, 1974); J. H. Matthews, *The Imagery of Surrealism* (Syracuse: Syracuse University Press, 1977); Marcel Jean, *Autobiographie du surréalisme* (Paris: Éditions du Seuil, 1978); Robert Stuart Short, *Dada and Surrealism* (London: Octopus Books, 1980); Keith Aspley, *André Breton the Poet* (Glasgow: University of Glasgow French and German Publications, 1989); Mark Polizotti, *Revolution of the Mind: The Life of André Breton* (London: Bloomsbury, 1995).

69. Lautréamont, *Les Chants de Maldoror*, in *Lautréamont: Germain Nouveau*,

Œuvres complètes, ed. Pierre-Olivier Walzer (Paris: Gallimard, Bibliothèque de la Pléiade, 1970), p. 225.

70. See Jean Yves Debreuille, *Éluard ou le pouvoir du mot* (Paris: Nizet, 1977); Jean-Charles Gateau, *Paul Éluard et la peinture surréaliste* (Geneva: Droz, 1982); and *Paul Éluard, le frère voyant* (Paris: Laffont, 1988); Clive Scott (ed.), *Anthologie Éluard* (London: Methuen Educational, 1983).

71. On Péret, see Jean-Michel Goutier, *Bejamin Péret* (Paris: Veyrier, 1982). On Char, see Jean-Claude Mathieu, *La Poésie de René Char, ou Le Sel de la Splendeur,* vol. I: *Traversée du surréalisme;* vol. II: *Poésie et résistance* (Paris: José Corti, 1984–5); Michael Bishop, *René Char, les dernières années* (Amsterdam: Rodopi, 1990); Eric Marty, *René Char* (Paris: Éditions du Seuil, 1990).

72. See Roger Little, *Saint-John Perse* (London: Athlone Press, 1973); Marie-Laure Ryan, *Rituel et poésie: une lecture de Saint-John Perse* (Berne: Peter Lang, 1977); Mireille Sacotte, *Saint-John Perse* (Paris: Pierre Belfond, 1991).

73. See J. A. Hiddleston, *L'Univers de Jules Supervielle* (Paris: José Corti, 1965); Robert Vivier, *Lire Supervielle* (Paris: José Corti, 1971); Paul Villaneix, *Le Hors-venu, ou le personnage poétique de Supervielle* (Paris: Klincksieck, 1972); Yves-Alain Favre, *Supervielle: la Rêverie et le chant dans 'Gravitations'* (Paris: Nizet, 1981).

74. See Malcolm Bowie, *Henri Michaux: A Study of his Literary Works* (Oxford: Clarendon Press, 1973); Jean-Pierre Martin, *Henri Michaux: Écritures de soi. Expatriations* (Paris: José Corti, 1994).

75. See Ian Higgins (ed.), *Le Parti pris des choses* (London: Athlone Press, 1979) and *Francis Ponge* (London: Athlone Press, 1979); Jean Pierrot, *Francis Ponge* (Paris: José Corti, 1993).

76. See Pierre Seghers (ed.), *La Résistance et ses poètes,* 2 vols (Paris: Marabout, 1978); Jean Gaucheron, *La Poésie, la Résistance* (Paris: Les Éditeurs français réunis, 1979); Ian Higgins (ed.), *Anthology of Second World War French Poetry* (London: Methuen, 1982).

77. Higgins, *Anthology of Second World War French Poetry,* p. 27.

78. Ibid., pp. 19–24.

79. See Maxwell Adereth, *Aragon: The Resistance Poems* (London: Grant and Cutler, 1985).

80. On Emmanuel, see Alain Bosquet, *Pierre Emmanuel* (Paris: Seghers, 1959). On the importance of Pierre Jean Jouve for Emmanuel, see Margaret M. Callander, *The Poetry of Pierre Jean Jouve* (Manchester: Manchester University Press, 1965).

81. See Ian Higgins, 'Jean Tardieu's Oradour', *French Studies,* XLVIII, 4 (October 1994), pp. 425–38.

82. See the Higgins anthology of Second World War French poetry for examples of all of the types of reference discussed here.

83. See Claude Marie Beaujeu, *L'Alexandrin dans le 'Crève-cœur' d'Aragon* (Paris: Presses de l'Université de Paris-Sorbonne, 1993); Adareth, *Aragon: The Resistance Poems,* pp. 53–70; and Higgins, *Anthology of Second World War French Poetry,* pp. 31–44.

84. On post-war French poetry, see C. A. Hackett, *New French Poetry. An Anthology* (Oxford: Basil Blackwell, 1973); Michael Bishop, *The Contem-*

porary Poetry of France: Eight Studies (Amsterdam: Rodopi, 1985); Michel Baude and Jeannine Baude (eds), *Poésie et spiritualité en France depuis 1950* (Paris: Klincksieck, 1988); Marie-Claire Bancquart, *Poésie 1945–1960, les mots, la voix* (Paris: Presses de l'Université de Paris-Sorbonne, 1989); Richard Stamelman, *Lost Beyond Telling: Representations of Death and Absence in Modern French Poetry* (Ithaca and London: Cornell University Press, 1990); Martin Sorrell (ed. and trans.), *Modern French Poetry: A Bilingual Anthology* (London: Forest Books, 1992). On Bonnefoy, see John T. Naughton, *The Poetics of Yves Bonnefoy* (Chicago and London: University of Chicago Press, 1984); Daniel Leuwers, *Yves Bonnefoy* (Amsterdam: Rodopi, 1988).

85. See Marie-Claire Dumas (ed.), *La Poésie de Philippe Jaccottet* (Paris: Honoré Champion, 1986).

86. On Deguy, see Michael Bishop, *Michel Deguy* (Amsterdam: Rodopi, 1988); Jean Moussaron and Jacques Derrida, *La Poésie comme avenir. Essai sur l'œuvre de M. Deguy* (Grenoble: Syllabe, 1992). On Dupin, see Maryann De Julio, *Rhetorical Landscapes: The Poetry and Art Criticism of Jacques Dupin* (Lexington, Kentucky: French Forum, 1992); E. Loze, *Approaches de Jacques Dupin* (Amsterdam: Rodopi, 1993). On Guillevic, see Gavin Bowd, *Guillevic, sauvage de la modernité* (Glasgow: Glasgow University French and German Publications, 1993); Michael Brophy, *Eugène Guillevic* (Amsterdam: Rodopi, 1993). On recent women's poetry, see Martin Sorrell (ed. and trans.), *Elles. A Bilingual Anthology of Modern French Poetry by Women* (Exeter: Exeter University Press, 1995).

87. For a history of the development of film in France, see Susan Hayward, *French National Cinema* (London and New York: Routledge, 1993).

88. Two invaluable sources for this section have been David Bradby, *Modern French Drama 1940–1990* (Cambridge: Cambridge University Press, rev. edn 1991), with its thorough accounts of the material practices of contemporary French theatre and the work of key directors and details of the staging of individual plays; and David Bradby and David Williams, *Directors' Theatre* (London: Macmillan, 1988). See also Geneviève Serreau, *Histoire du 'nouveau théâtre'* (Paris: Éditions Gallimard, 1966); John Fletcher (ed.), *Forces in Modern French Drama* (London: University of London Press, 1972); Bettina L. Knapp, *French Theatre, 1918–39* (London: Macmillan, 1985); Jean Duvigneaud and Jean Lagoutte, *Le Théâtre contemporain: culture et contre-culture* (Paris: Librairie Larousse, 1974); Henri Béhar, *Le Théâtre dada et surréaliste* (Paris: Éditions Gallimard, 1979).

89. Keir Elam, *The Semiotics of Theatre and Drama* (London and New York: Methuen, 1980).

90. A difficult but rewarding consideration of issues appears in Jacques Derrida's essay on Antonin Artaud, 'La Parole Soufflée', *Tel quel*, no. 20 (Winter 1965), coll. in Jacques Derrida, *Writing and Differance*, trans. Alan Bass (London: Routledge and Kegan Paul, 1978).

91. See Jean-Louis Barrault, *Réflexions sur le théâtre* (Paris: Jacques Vautrain, 1949), *passim*, for Barrault's collaboration with Claudel. See, on Claudel, Jacques Madaule, *Le Drame de Paul Claudel* (Paris: Desclée de Brouwer, 1947); Michel Lioure, *L'Esthétique dramatique de Paul Claudel* (Paris:

Armand Colin, 1971). For background see Richard Griffiths, *The Reactionary Revolution: The Catholic Revival in French Literature* (London: Constable, 1966).

92. See Roger Shattuck, *The Banquet Years: Origins of the Avant-Garde in France, 1885 to World War I* (New York: Vintage Books, 1968); Michel Arrivé, *Les Langages de Jarry* (Paris: Klincksieck, 1972); Henri Béhar, *Jarry dramaturge* (Paris: Nizet, 1980).

93. 'Trois conférences prononcées à l'université de Mexico. I: Surréalisme et révolution' (26 February 1936), coll. in Antonin Artaud, *Messages révolutionnaires* (Paris: Éditions Gallimard, 1971). Other pieces by Artaud referred to are collected in *Le Théâtre et son double* (1938).

94. See Sartre's theoretical writings, coll. in Jean-Paul Sartre, *Un théâtre de situations*, ed. Michel Contat and Michel Rybalka (Paris: Gallimard, 1973); also Robert Lorris, *Sartre dramaturge* (Paris: Nizet, 1975). See Camus's theoretical writings, coll. in Albert Camus, *Théâtre, récits, nouvelles*, ed. Roger Quilliot (Paris: Gallimard, 1962); also Ilona Coombs, *Camus, homme de théâtre* (Paris: Nizet, 1968); Edward Freeman, *The Theatre of Albert Camus: A Critical Study* (London: Methuen, 1971).

95. Georges Bataille, 'Notes: La question coloniale. D'un caractère sacré des criminels (Genet)', *Critique* no. 35 (April 1949), pp. 365–71 and 371–3; rpt. in *Œuvres complètes XI: Articles I (1944–49)* (Paris: Éditions Gallimard, 1988), p. 469. See, on Genet, Richard N. Coe, *The Vision of Jean Genet* (London: Peter Owen, 1968); Richard C. Webb (ed.), *File on Genet* (London: Methuen Drama, 1992); Edmond White, *Genet* (London: Chatto and Windus, 1993).

96. 'Jean Genet talks to Hubert Fichte', tr. Patrick McCarthy, *The New Review*, IV, 37 (April 1977), pp. 9–21; first published in German, *Die Zeit* (20 February 1976), p. 17.

97. See Dominique Nores (ed.), *Les Critiques de notre temps et Beckett* (Paris: Garnier Frères, 1971); James Knowlson and John Pilling, *Frescoes of the Skull, the Later Prose and Drama of Samuel Beckett* (London: John Calder, 1979); Ruby Cohn, *Just Play: Beckett's Theater* (Princeton: Princeton University Press, 1980); James Acheson and Kateryna Arthur (eds), *Beckett's Later Fiction and Drama* (New York: St Martin's Press, 1987); Jonathan Kalb, *Beckett in Performance* (Cambridge: Cambridge University Press, 1989); Christopher Ricks, *Beckett's Dying Words* (Oxford: Clarendon Press, 1993); James Knowlson, *Damned to Fame: The Life of Samuel Beckett* (London: Bloomsbury, and New York: Simon and Shuster, 1996).

98. See, on Ionesco, Richard N. Coe, *Ionesco: a Study of his Plays* (London: Methuen, rev. edn 1971); Emmanuel C. Jacquart, *Le Théâtre de dérision: Beckett, Ionesco, Adamov* (Paris: Gallimard, 1974).

99. See Philippe Madral, *Le Théâtre hors les murs* (Paris: Éditions du Seuil, 1969); Judith Graves Miller, *Theater and Revolution in France since 1968* (Lexington: French Forum, 1977).

100. See Bradby and Williams, *Directors' Theatre*; and Ruby Cohn, 'Ariane Mnouchkine: Playwright of a Collective', in Enoch Brater (ed.), *Feminine Focus: The New Women Playwrights* (New York and Oxford: Oxford University Press, 1989), pp. 53–63.

101. See essays in Brater (ed.), *Feminine Focus*, especially Sue-Ellen Case, 'From Split Subject to Split Britches'; Elin Diamond, 'Benmussa's Adaptations: Unauthorized Texts from Elsewhere'; Jeannette Laillou Savona, 'In Search of a Feminist Theater: *Portrait of Dora*'; and Sharon A. Willis, 'Staging Sexual Difference: Reading, Recitation and Repetition in Duras's *Malady of Death*'. Also see Celita Lamar, *Our Voices, Ourselves: Women Writing for the French Theatre* (New York: Peter Lang, 1991).

102. On Cixous, see also Morag Schiach, 'Staging History', Chapter 4 in *Hélène Cixous: A Politics of Writing* (London and New York: Routledge, 1991); Jennifer Birkett, 'The Limits of Language: The Theatre of Hélène Cixous', in John Dunkley and Bill Kirton (eds), *Voices in the Air: French Dramatists and the Resource of Language* (Glasgow: University of Glasgow French and German Publications, 1992).

103. A good introduction to Vinaver and Koltès is the anthology in English, David Bradby and Claude Schumacher (eds), *New French Plays* (London: Methuen Drama, 1989). On Vinaver, see Anne Ubersfeld, *Vinaver dramaturge* (Paris: Librairie théâtrale, 1989).

Notes to Chapter 9

1. Julia Kristeva, 'Le Temps des femmes', in *33/34 Cahiers de recherche de sciences des textes et documents*, No. 5 (Winter 1979), pp. 5–19.

2. See, for historical and cultural context, Claire Duchen, *Feminism in France from May '68 to Mitterrand* (London: Routledge & Kegan Paul, 1986); Claire Laubier (ed.), *The Condition of Women in France: 1945 to the Present* (London and New York: Routledge, 1990); Évelyne Sullerot, *La Presse féminine* (Paris: Armand Colin, 1963); Samra-Martine Bonvoisin and Michele Maignien, *La Presse féminine* (Paris: Armand Colin, 1986). On feminist criticism see Elissa D. Gelfand and Virginia Thorndike Hughes, *French Feminist Criticism: Women, Language and Literature: An Annotated Bibliography* (New York and London: Garland, 1985); Gayle Greene and Coppélia Kahn (eds), *Making a Difference: Feminist Literary Criticism* (London: Methuen, 1985); Toril Moi, *Sexual/Textual Politics: Feminist Literary Theory* (London: Methuen, 1985); Judith Newton and Deborah Rosenfelt (eds), *Feminist Criticism and Social Change: Sex, Class and Race in Literature and Culture* (London: Methuen, 1985); Mary Engleton (ed.), *Feminist Literary Criticism* (London: Longman 1991). For anthologies see Elaine Marks and Isabelle de Coutivron, *New French Feminisms: An Anthology* (Brighton: Harvester, 1981); Toril Moi (ed.), *French Feminist Thought: A Reader* (Oxford: Basil Blackwell, 1987).

3. See Josyane Savigneau, *Marguerite Yourcenar: l'invention d'une vie* (Paris: Gallimard, 1990).

4. See Mary Evans, *Simone de Beauvoir: A Feminist Mandarin* (London: Tavistock, 1985); Claude Francis et Fernande Gontier, *Simone de Beauvoir* (Paris: Librairie Académique Perrin, 1985); Elizabeth Fallaize, *The Novels of Simone de Beauvoir* (London: Routledge, 1988); Toril Moi, *Simone de Beauvoir: The Making of an Intellectual Woman* (Oxford: Blackwell, 1994).

5. See Adèle King, *French Women Novelists: Defining a Female Style* (London: Macmillan, 1989); Margaret Atack and Phil Powrie (eds), *Contemporary French Fiction by Women: Feminist Perspectives* (Manchester and New York: Manchester University Press, 1990). The discussion that follows focuses on women's prose writing. For women's drama, see the general section on twentieth-century theatre in Chapter 8. Women's poetry has been of relatively less importance, and has certainly received less public and critical attention than that of English and American women poets. There is no room to redress that imbalance here, but see the new reader compiled and translated by Martin Sorrell, *Elles: A Bilingual Anthology of Modern French Poetry by Women* (Exeter: University of Exeter Press, 1995).

6. Lucile Cairns, *Marie Cardinal: Motherhood and Creativity* (Glasgow: University of Glasgow French and German Publications, 1992).

7. 'Héréthique de l'amour', in *Tel Quel*, 74 (Winter 1977), pp. 30–9; rpt. as 'Stabat Mater' in *Histoires d'amour* (Paris: Denoël, 1983).

8. See Diana J. Fuss, *Essentially Speaking* (London: Routledge, 1990); Margaret Whitford, *Luce Irigaray: Philosophy in the Feminine* (London: Routledge, 1991).

9. See also Chawaf, 'La Chair linguistique', *Les Nouvelles Littéraires*, 26 May 1976.

10. See, on Kristeva, Toril Moi (intro. and ed.), *The Kristeva Reader* (Oxford: Basil Blackwell, 1986); John Lechte, *Julia Kristeva* (London: Routledge, 1990).

11. Jacques Lacan's psychoanalytical theorisation of the formation of the human subject and its simultaneous entry into language and gendered self-awareness has been crucial for the development of feminist theory. Toril Moi has offered one of the clearest explanations of how Lacan conceptualises child development as a movement between two orders, the Imaginary and the Symbolic: 'The Imaginary corresponds to the pre-Oedipal period when the child believes itself to be a part of the mother, and perceives no separation between itself and the world. . . . The Oedipal crisis represents the entry into the Symbolic Order. This entry is also linked to the acquisition of language. In the Oedipal crisis the father splits up the dyadic unity between mother and child and for-bids the child further access to the mother and the mother's body. . . . [F]rom now on the desire for the mother or the imaginary unity with her must be repressed. This first repression is what Lacan calls the pri-mary repression and it is this primary repression that opens up the unconscious. . . . When the child learns to say "I am" and distinguish this from a "you are" or "he is", this is equivalent to admitting it has taken up its allotted place in the Symbolic Order. . . . To enter into the Symbolic Order means to accept the phallus as the representation of the Law of the Father. All human culture and all life in society is domi-nated by the Symbolic Order. . . .' (Toril Moi, *Sexual/Textual Politics*, pp. 99–100). Lacan argued that women have no autonomy as subjects in the masculine Symbolic; feminist thinking on language pursues the consequences of this. See also Jane Gallop, *Feminism and Psychoanalysis: The Daughter's Seduction* (London: Macmillan, 1982); Elizabeth Grosz,

Jacques Lacan: A Feminist Introduction (London: Routledge, 1990). On Freud and feminism see Juliet Mitchell, *Psychoanalysis and Feminism* (London: Allen Lane, 1974).

12. See, on Cixous, Susan Sellers (ed.), *Writing Differences: Readings from the Seminar of Hélène Cixous* (Milton Keynes: Open University Press, 1988); Morag Schiach, *Hélène Cixous: A Politics of Writing* (London and New York: Routledge, 1991).

13. See George Stambolian and Elaine Marks, *Homosexualities and French Literature* (Ithaca and London: Cornell University Press, 1979); Lilian Faderman, *Surpassing the Love of Men: Romantic Friendship and Love between Women from the Renaissance to the Present* (New York: William Morrow, 1981); Shari Benstock, *Women of the Left Bank: Paris 1900–1940* (Austin: University of Texas Press, 1986). On Colette, see Diana Holmes, *Colette* (London: Macmillan, 1991); on Leduc, see Alex Hughes, *Violette Leduc: Mothers, Lovers and Language* (London: Modern Humanities Research Association, 1994); see also essays on Colette, Leduc, Wittig, by Diana Holmes, Alex Hughes and Jennifer Birkett in Alex Hughes and Kate Ince (eds), *French Erotic Fiction: Women's Desiring Writing* (Oxford and Washington, DC: Berg, 1996).

14. First published in *Feminist Issues*, 5 (2) (Fall 1985); revised for Nancy K. Miller (ed.), *The Poetics of Gender* (New York: Columbia University Press, 1986), pp. 63–73. Other essays by Wittig on her own writing are collected in *The Straight Mind and Other Essays* (Hemel Hempstead: Harvester Wheatsheaf, 1992). For a useful account of the politics of gender, which makes frequent reference to Wittig, see Judith Butler, *Gender Trouble: Feminism and the Subversion of Identity* (London: Routledge, 1990).

15. See Jean-Jacques Luthi, Auguste Viatte and Gaston Zananiri, *Dictionnaire général de la francophonie* (Paris: Letouzey et Ané, 1986); Michel Tétu, *La Francophonie: histoire, problématique et perspectives* (Paris: Hachette, 1988). I am indebted to Alec Hargreaves for his advice on this section.

16. Gayatri Chakravorty Spivak, 'Questions of Multiculturalism', in *The Post-Colonial Critic: Interviews, Strategies, Dialogues*, ed. Sarah Harasym (London: Routledge, 1990), p. 62. See also Gayatri Chakravorty Spivak, *In Other Worlds: Essays in Cultural Politics* (London: Methuen, 1987), especially 'French Feminism in an International Frame' (1981) and 'Foreword to Mahasweta Devi, *Draupadi*' (1981). For general theorisations of the relations of centre and periphery see Edward W. Said, *Orientalism* (London: Routledge & Kegan Paul, 1978); *Post/Colonial Conditions: Exiles, Migrations and Nomadisms*, Yale French Studies, No. 82, vol. I (New Haven and London: Yale University Press, 1993).

17. See W. H. New, *A History of Canadian Literature* (London: Macmillan, 1989); Maurice Lemire (ed.), *Dictionnaire des œuvres littéraires du Québec*, 2nd edn (Montreal: FIDES, 1980–7); Réginald Hamel, John Hare and Paul Wyczinski, *Dictionnaire des auteurs de la langue française en Amérique du Nord* (Montreal: Éditions Fides, 1989).

18. Sherry Simon, 'The Language of Cultural Difference', in Lawrence Venuti (ed.), *Rethinking Translation: Discourse, Subjectivity, Ideology* (London and New York: Routledge, 1992).

19. See Alain Rouch and Gérard Claveuil (eds), *Littératures nationales d'écriture française: Afrique noire/Caraïbes/Océan Indien. Histoire littéraire et anthologie* (Paris: Boréas, 1986).
20. See Dorothy S. Blair, *African Literature in French* (Cambridge: Cambridge University Press, 1976). A useful, wide-ranging collection of essays on individual authors is Mildred Mortimer, *Journeys through the French African Novel* (Portsmouth, New Hampshire, and London: Heinemann Educational Books and James Currey, 1990).
21. See Alec G. Hargreaves, *The Colonial Experience in French Fiction* (London: Macmillan, 1981).
22. See Manon Brunet, 'Présence Africaine dans l'institution littéraire africaine contemporaine'. *Contemporary French Civilization*, VIV, 2 (Summer/Fall 1990), pp. 275–91.
23. Because of space restrictions, attention here has been limited to Algerian writing. See, for the wider account, Jean Déjeux, *Dictionnaire des auteurs maghrébins de langue française* (Paris: Karthala, 1984), *La Littérature maghrébine d'expression française* (Paris: Presses Universitaires de France, 1992) and *Maghreb: Littératures de langue française* (Paris: Arcantère Éditions, 1993). Mention should nevertheless be made here of the Tunisian novelist and essayist Albert Memmi (b. 1920) and the Moroccan novelists Driss Chraïbi, Abdelkébir Khatibi and especially Tahar Ben Jelloun (Prix Goncourt, *La Nuit sacré*, 1987). In France, *beur* culture (that of second-generation children of Maghrebian origin, born in France) has established its own contestatory space, with its own writing; see Alec G. Hargreaves, *Voices from the North African Immigrant Community in France: Immigration and Identity in Beur Fiction* (New York and Oxford: Berg, 1991); and Michel Laronde, *Autour du roman beur: Immigration et identité* (Paris: L'Harmattan, 1993).
24. Association pour l'Égalité devant la Loi entre les femmes et les hommes – Algérie, 'Les Luttes de femmes en Algérie', *Nouvelles Questions Féministes*, nos 16–17–18 (Paris, 1991), pp. 17–28.
25. See Denise Brahimi, 'Fatima Gallaire, une Algérienne et le théâtre', in *Bulletin of Francophone Africa*, vol. 4, no. 7 (London, Spring 1995).
26. Cit. Denise Brahimi, *Appareillages* (Paris: Éditions Deuxtemps Tierce, 1991), who gives an important account of gender positions within bilingual writing. See, on Assia Djebar, Jean Déjeux, *Assia Djebar, romancière algérienne et cinéaste arabe* (Sherbrooke: Naaman, 1984). See, on women's writing in the Maghreb, Winifred Woodhill, *Transfigurations of the Maghreb: Feminism, Decolonization and Literatures* (Minneapolis: University of Minnesota Press, 1993). For an overview and trans-national anthology of Arab women's writing, see Margot Badran and Miriam Cooke (eds), *Opening the Gates: A Century of Arab Feminist Writing* (London: Virago, 1990).
27. On Simone Schwarz-Bart, see Leah D. Hewitt, *Autobiographical Tightropes* (Lincoln: University of Nebraska Press, 1990).
28. On Maryse Condé, see ibid.

Bibliography

The Notes give sources and suggestions for further reading on particular authors or themes. The aim has not been to be comprehensive but rather to direct students to stimulating, up-to-date and readable texts, which often have their own bibliographies. The following are useful works of general reference.

General reference guides: A. H. T. Levi, *Guide to French Literature*, 2 vols (Chicago and London, Detroit and London: St James Press, 1992, 1994), and Peter France (ed.), *The New Oxford Companion to Literature in French* (Oxford: Clarendon Press, 1995), are both organised alphabetically. Denis Hollier (ed.), *A New History of French Literature* (Cambridge, Mass. and London: Harvard University Press, 1989), gives a chronological survey of French literature in its cultural context in the form of extended specialist essays on particular events and themes, linked to particular dates. Of the multi-volume studies available, the most useful is the 9-volume *Littérature Française*, ed. Claude Pichois (Paris: Éditions Arthaud, 1974–84).

For *general historical background*, see Colin Jones, *The Cambridge Illustrated History of France* (Cambridge: Cambridge University Press, 1994); Roger Price, *An Economic History of Modern France (1730–1914)* (London: Macmillan, 1981) and *A Concise History of France* (Cambridge: Cambridge University Press, 1993).

On some *specific themes*, see Frederick Copleton, *A History of Philosophy*, 7 vols (rpt. London: Search Press, 1976); Roger Magraw, *A History of the French Working Class*, 2 vols (Oxford and Cambridge, Mass.: Blackwell, 1992); Georges Duby and Michelle Perrot (eds), *Histoire des femmes en Occident*, 5 vols (Paris: Plon, 1991–2); Rosemary O'Day, *The Family and Family Relationships (1500–1900): England, France and the United States* (London: Macmillan, 1994). See also Fernand Braudel's stimulating overview, *L'Identité de la France*, 3 vols (Paris: Arthaud-Flammarion, 1986).

For a comprehensive bibliography of *women writers*, see Claire Buck (ed.), *Bloomsbury Guide to Women's Literature* (London: Bloomsbury Publishing, 1992). A more selective range of names, with fuller information, appears in Eva Martin Sarton and Dorothy

Wynne Zimmerman (eds), *French Women Writers: A Bio-Bibliographical Source Book* (New York, Westport, Connecticut and London: Greenwood Press, 1991).

Index

(*Note*: Bibliographical references appear in italics. Dates are not given for critics.)

ST. JOHN FISHER COLLEGE LIBRARY

0 1220 0051635 3

PQ 305 .B524 1997
Birkett, Jennifer.
A guide to French literature

ABC 0672